GOVERNORS STATE UNIVERSITY LIBRARY

S0-BYN-325

3 1611 00255 4878

# LOS ANGELES

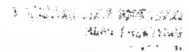

# LOS ANGELES

## GLOBALIZATION, URBANIZATION AND SOCIAL STRUGGLES

Roger Keil

JOHN WILEY & SONS

Chichester • New York • Weinheim • Brisbane • Singapore • Toronto

GOVERNORS STATE UNIVERSITY
UNIVERSITY PARK

Copyright © 1998 by John Wiley & Sons Ltd, Baffins Lane, Chichester, West Sussex
PO19 1UD, England

National 01243 779777  International (+44) 1243 779777

HT384.L77 K45 1998

Keil, Roger, 1957–

Los Angeles,
  globalization,

service enquiries): cs-books@wiley.co.uk

vw.wiley.co.uk or http://www.wiley.com

Copyright, Designs and Patents Act, 1988, to be
author of this work.

may be reproduced, stored in a retrieval system,
, electronic, mechanical, photocopying, recording,
of the Copyright, Designs and Patents Act 1988 or
under the terms of a licence issued by the Copyright Licensing Agency, 90 Tottenham Court Road,
London W1P 9HE, UK, without the permission in writing of John Wiley & Sons Ltd., Baffins Lane,
Chichester, West Sussex PO19 1UD, UK.

OTHER WILEY EDITORIAL OFFICES

John Wiley & Sons, Inc., 605 Third Avenue, New York, NY 10158-0012, USA

WILEY-VCH Verlag GmbH, Pappelallee 3, D-69469 Weinheim, Germany

Jacaranda Wiley Ltd, 33 Park Road, Milton, Queensland 4064, Australia

John Wiley & Sons (Asia) Pte Ltd, 2 Clementi Loop #02-01, Jin Xing Distripark, Singapore 129809

John Wiley & Sons (Canada) Ltd, 22 Worcester Road, Rexdale, Ontario M9W 1L1, Canada

LIBRARY OF CONGRESS CATALOGING-IN-PUBLICATION DATA

Keil, Roger, 1957–
    Los Angeles : globalization, urbanization, and social struggles /
Roger Keil.
        p.  cm. — (World cities series)
    Includes bibliographical references and index.
    ISBN 0-471-95778-X (cloth). — ISBN 0-471-98352-7 (pbk.)
    1. Urbanization—California—Los Angeles.  2. Sociology, Urban—
California—Los Angeles.  3. International economic relations—
Social aspects.  I. Title.  II. Series.
HT384.L77K45  1998
307.76'09794'94—dc21                                              98–20621
                                                                       CIP

BRITISH LIBRARY CATALOGUING IN PUBLICATION DATA

A catalogue record for this book is available from the British Library

ISBN 0-471-95778 X (hardback)
ISBN 0-471-98352 7 (paperback)

Typeset in 9/12pt Caslon 224 from author's disks by Mayhew Typesetting, Rhayader, Powys
Printed and bound in Great Britain by Bookcraft (Bath) Ltd, Midsomer Norton
This book is printed on acid-free paper responsibly manufactured from sustainable forestry,  for which at
least two trees are planted for each one used for paper production.

For

Ute Lehrer,

who took me back to Los Angeles

# Contents

*viii*

# PREFACE

You can check out any time you like,
But you can never leave.

The Eagles, *Hotel California* (1976)

David Harvey argues that there is a dialectical relationship between 'urbanization' as a 'process' and the 'city' as a 'thing'. He goes on to explain that

> understanding urbanization is integral to understanding political–economic, social, and cultural processes and problems. But this is true only if we consider urbanization as a process (or more accurately, a multiplicity of processes) producing a distinctive mix of spatialized permanences in relation to each other. The idea that a thing called a city has causal powers in relation to social life is untenable. Yet the material embeddedness of spatial structures created in the course of urbanization are in persistent tension with the fluidity of social processes, such as capital accumulation and social reproduction (Harvey, 1996: 419).

This dialectic captures some of the fluid sociospatial processes that have made Los Angeles into a point of reference – a thing as it were – in our collective mind at the end of the millennium. There is a place, however intangible and evasive, which we choose to call Los Angeles or Southern California. Some have rated the importance of this place high enough to think of it as *The City* plain and simple (Scott and Soja, 1996). Out of the 'multiplicity of processes' that have constituted (and deconstructed) Los Angeles during this century, I have, in this book, particularly focussed on urban politics, movements and agency. It has been my intention to demonstrate that, during the formative periods of Fordist and after-Fordist (or globalized) urbanization in Los Angeles, local social collectives of all kinds have influenced the way in which these formative periods have congealed into generalized models of development. The formative period I concentrate on here is that of *world city formation* (Friedmann, 1995), a time that roughly spans the 20 years during which Tom Bradley was the mayor of the city of Los Angeles, still the core urban jurisdiction in an urbanized region of close to 15 million people. Urbanization today is an entirely globalized social process. It produces places that are equally globalized: Los Angeles is a material node of the global economic, social, cultural and ecological system. Yet globalized urbanization does not just come to pass like a 'natural' process but occurs through and against social struggles. These struggles are a major focus of this book.

This work is not explicitly theoretical. It is narrative, essayistic and argumentative; theoretical discussions are implicit reference points. Yet, it will perhaps help the reader to know that besides world city theory, there are three other major discourses I have found helpful in understanding the urbanization process in Los Angeles. First, there is what has been commonly referred to as the French Regulation School. In the context of this school I have been mostly interested in those approaches that have dealt with local and regional modes of regulation and particularly with urban and local politics (Mayer, 1994). Second, related to but not entirely congruent with this approach, has been the – mostly American – literature on urban regimes and growth machines (Logan and Molotch, 1987; Logan and Swanstrom, 1990; Stone and Sanders, 1987; Lauria, 1997). This body of work has been instrumental in bringing clarity to urban political processes in the capitalist city. Third, I have been strongly guided by an understanding of the urban as expressed in the work of Henri Lefebvre (1991, 1996) and David Harvey (1982, 1985a, b, 1989a, b, 1996). I have gleaned from this tradition especially the notion that it is through the production of space that capitalism has reproduced itself through the past decades. There could be no better place than Los Angeles to illustrate this. But the book was meant to be about Los Angeles and not about theory. I have discussed the above theoretical pillars in more detail elsewhere (Keil, 1993).

Los Angeles cannot be subject to encyclopedic treatment. The account that follows is selective. It was written with a specific goal: to show the significance of local politics, movements and agency in the current restructuring process of Southern California. It was not meant to be a comprehensive travel guide to the galaxies that make up that urban region. Nor could it. Among the past works that have come close to defining Los Angeles for all of us (and the generations before us) there has been, to my knowledge, only one that achieved a near universal treatment of the urban region. I am referring to Anton Wagner's *Los Angeles: Werden, Leben und Gestalt der Zweimillionenstadt in Südkalifornien* (1935).[1] Wagner literally *walked* through each neighborhood of the city at a time when Los Angeles had already suffered its first automobile gridlock downtown. The data collected and the photographs taken during his stay in Los Angeles make Wagner's the only universal study we have of the city; and the only one we will ever have.[2]

The other significant books that have captured Los Angeles at various moments in this century are, next to Kevin Starr's series of California histories, Carey McWilliams' *Southern California: An Island on the Land* (1979, orig. 1946); Robert Fogelson's *The Fragmented Metropolis: Los Angeles, 1850–1930* (1967); Reyner Banham's *Los Angeles: The Architecture of Four Ecologies* (1971); and above all Mike Davis' *City of Quartz* (1990).[3] Any one of these monographs make the enterprise of adding another narrative a daunting affair.

I have made difficult choices in presenting my material. The reader will not find, in this book, much about Orange County, Disneyland, exurbia, the carceral city or postmodern culture. There is an excellent body of literature which has said much about these and other subjects and to which I felt I did not want to add. There is little on transportation, infrastructure, housing, population and urban history. There is no single chapter on African American, Latino and Asian Los Angeles. Such gaps are regrettable, yet unavoidable. If this project were to be started again, I would try to fill them.

Much of this writing goes back to a pattern of research laid down during my dissertation field work. I published some of the material presented here in an earlier version as *Weltstadt – Stadt der Welt: Internationalisierung und lokale Politik in Los Angeles* with Westfälisches Dampfboot in Münster (Keil, 1993). I am grateful to the publisher for granting me permission to use that book as a base for the work I am presenting here. Fragments of the material in this book have been presented in English language publications by me before. I have referenced these passages where I thought it appropriate.

I first came to Los Angeles to stay in the summer of 1986. In the years to follow, I lived there several times for many months at a time and have returned regularly since I moved to Toronto in 1991. Like Anton Wagner, I crisscrossed the city, took photographs, conducted more than 70 formal interviews,[4] had countless informal conversations and took hundreds of pages of notes on my travels. Unlike Wagner, I used the car. Notes from participant observation in dozens of public meetings, and hundreds of documents, as well as scholarly and popular texts, form the core of the research material.

The longer I lived in and revisited Los Angeles, the more I became convinced that the analysis of the urban process is itself a political intervention. The reflexion of urbanization cannot do without participation. The book before you emerged through critique and discussion, participation and observation. It has its roots in the fascination which Los Angeles has had on me. It is about the significance of agency; it is about making structures.

# INTRODUCTION: SPACING SOUTHERN CALIFORNIA

> If we are a nation of extremes, Los Angeles is an extreme among us. . . . What Los
> Angeles is to excess, all cities are to some extent.
>
> Sara Comstock, 1928

Los Angeles sits like a car-seat cover, carefully strapped across the elevations of
the Santa Monica and San Gabriel Mountains, tugged in at the coastline and open
towards the north and east where the deserts begin. Underneath the cover, the big
story of California history is played out in suprahuman intensity and temporality.
It is a story of plate tectonics and earthquakes. Compression and strike–slip
motion set the slow but unhaltable pace for the constant reshaping of Southern
Californian landscapes.

> The Los Angeles Basin alone has been squeezed about a centimetre a year for two
> million two hundred thousand years. The sites of Laguna Beach and Pasadena are
> fourteen miles closer together than they were 2.2 million years ago. This happened an
> earthquake at a time. For example, the Whittier Narrows earthquake of 1987 lessened
> the breadth of the Santa Monica Mountains and raised the ridgeline (McPhee, 1994:
> 266).

Undead at all times, the seat under the cover is good for many a surprise eruption
and certain shifts that measure times in eternities. Yet, many features of today's
Southern Californian landscape are witnesses of a more tangible and recent
change. The dramatic shift of the mouth of the Los Angeles River from where the
International Airport is today and to its current Long Beach location in 1825 after
catastrophic flooding in the San Gabriel Mountains, is among them. Nothing under
and above the seatcover of built and natural environments in Southern California
is stable, nothing but change itself.[1]

No wonder, the place has been puzzling observers for all time. Edward Soja
asked in his *Postmodern Geographies*:

> What is this place? Even knowing where to focus, to find a starting point, is not easy,
> for, perhaps more than any other place, Los Angeles is everywhere. It is global in the
> fullest sense of the word. . . . [T]he seers of Los Angeles have become countless, even
> more so as the progressive globalization of its urban political economy flows along
> similar channels, making Los Angeles perhaps the epitomizing world-city, un ville
> devenue monde (Soja, 1989: 222–223).

In this book, I will invert Soja's take on Los Angeles and rather observe how *le
monde devenu ville*, how the world became a city. Since the beginning of the
1980s, many 'seers' of Los Angeles proposed that a new type of urbanism
paradigmatically emerged in Los Angeles: the post-Fordist world city. Unlike in any

other place, the elements of an entirely globalized period of urbanization came together in Southern California. While some had earlier described the allegedly *singular* character of Fordist urban form in Los Angeles as the new *general* type (e.g. Warner, 1972), the traditional role of Los Angeles both in urban theory and in the popular imagination was to be the 'other'. Los Angelization was considered mostly unique and predominantly undesirable. The exceptionalist narrative tended to fantastic caricature, quick dismissal and superficiality. It is now common, of course, to call Los Angeles 'the first American city' (Weinstein, 1996) and to observe, as Garreau does in his popular *Edge City* that 'every single American city that *is* growing is growing in the fashion of Los Angeles' (Garreau, 1991: 3). Scott and Soja (1986) likened Los Angeles to 'the paradigmatic industrial metropolis of the modern world' – just as important for the emergence of urban form as was previously Manchester, Paris or Chicago. They posited that research on Los Angeles in the 1980s would yield important insights into the current historical geography of capitalism overall. Ten years later, in the introduction to a volume of essays on Los Angeles programmatically called *The City: Los Angeles and Urban Theory at the End of the Twentieth Century* (Scott and Soja, 1996), the same authors sound more cautious in assessing what Los Angeles signifies at the turn of the millennium:

> It is still an open question, . . ., whether to view Los Angeles as an exceptional case, a persistently peculiar and unreproducible type of a city, or as an exemplary, if not paradigmatic, illustration of the essential and generalizable features of late-twentieth-century urbanization. Similarly, the historical geography of Los Angeles invites continuing debate between those who see in it the achievement of a sort of urban utopia and the American Dream and those who see little more than the dystopian nightmares of a 'Hell Town' grown to gargantuan proportions (Soja and Scott, 1996: 1–2).

Two general kinds of rhetoric can be distinguished, then. One is a kind of *hyperbolic exceptionalism*. In this case, Los Angeles has been treated as the big exception in the history of urbanism (Banham, 1971). The other tradition puts Los Angeles into a context of *paradigmatic normalcy*. In this case, Los Angeles has been assumed to be the future model for all cities (Warner, 1972). Both – ultimately heuristic – traditions find their corresponding cases in the actual local production of myths and visions; they also oscillate between emphasizing the uniqueness of 'LA's the place' and conjuring up normalcy – as in the technological idiom of the general plan, the so-called *Silverbook*, of 1972. 'Hyperbolic exceptionalism' has set the city apart from others not just in time, but also in space. That is, Los Angeles has been perceived as a city very much different not just from those of the previous century but from everything that has preceded it in the history of urbanism (Banham, 1971; Warner, 1972). Ironically, though, it can be argued that much of this rhetoric had its origin in the city's headstart into the normalcy of late capitalist urbanization. Los Angeles, then, can be understood as the archetypal twentieth-century form. This trendsetting character has been embellished and amplified, moreover, by the odd fact that Los Angeles has been on the cutting edge of not one but two periods of the urbanization of capital in this century: the full cycle of post-World War II urbanization, and the emergent roller coaster of post-

Fordist spatial formation processes. Yet we should not confuse the specific shape of post-Fordist urbanism that is emerging in Southern California with our theoretical propositions; the historical geography of Los Angeles in the current era has only limited clues to offer for the theoretical understanding of time and space in post-Fordism. By treating Los Angeles as merely a heuristic prop for the project of the critique of current urbanization one creates neither a valid narrative of Los Angeles nor a generally viable theory.[2] There does not seem to be an end to attempts to give special treatment to Los Angeles as a place of all places. A recent issue of the British journal *City* (1996: 2) returns to the myth that Los Angeles has represented for the most part of the last generation: 'But it can still be asked: What is L.A.? A favored answer is another interpretation of the slogan "It All Comes Together in L.A.", to the effect that it is *the* Post-Modern City, and thereby an image of the future for all of us.' Or is it?

Any analysis claiming an extreme position in this debate would be foolish at best and misleading at worst. While it is safe to say that in Los Angeles a new type of urbanism has emerged (or even maybe new types in the plural), the lessons that can be drawn from this insight are only transferable on a very high level of abstraction and not in concrete terms. It will be necessary to avoid the mistake often made in previous decades when the hegemonic model of urbanist analysis tended to turn every city on earth into a conceptual 'Chicago'. In contrast to the Fordist period of urbanization, which was characterized by a certain equalization of urban form and structure, the current period of urbanization does not seem to allow for a paradigmatic case due to its wild differentiation of regional regimes of accumulation. In fact, the determining characteristic of this period is typological variation in a generalized global context. A 'Chicago' type model would not be useful. Los Angeles, therefore, can best be described as a 'limited paradigm' reflecting the abstract but not the concrete form of the post-Fordist world city.

## SCALING LOS ANGELES

It is always important to explain where one comes from when talking about Los Angeles. The city has no end, no middle and no limits. Any attempt to find a fixed point from which to look at the urban region must fail in the final instance just as miserably as the attempts at fly-by or drive-by hyperbole (Soja, 1989; Baudrillard, 1987). Much writing on Los Angeles has an automatic starting point at LAX, the giant airport by the Pacific Ocean where pundits and philosophers of the *fin de siècle* tend to land before immersing themselves into Lalaland. If not from afar, most ink spent on Los Angeles originates in the city's Westside. Whereas Europeans and New Yorkers have still the upper hand in claiming Los Angeles as the ultimate exotic wonder of the world, Westsiders have put many local spins on a local historical geography from their class and often gender-specific (meaning white and male) points of view.

In the heart of the map of meaning of Los Angeles is the actual city by that name, the core metropolis of the urban area, a city of about 3.5 million. Founded on what is today the Los Angeles River in 1781 as *El Pueblo de Nuestra Senora la Reina de*

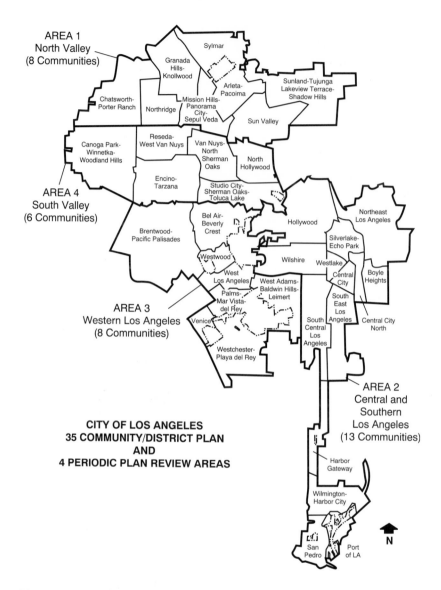

**Figure 0.1** *City of Los Angeles (Courtesy City of Los Angeles, Planning Department)*

*Los Angeles sobre el rio de la Porciúnculá*, Los Angeles has developed through annexations into an odd shape with a central body in the coastal basin, connected with the port by a shoestring, and with a huge extension in the northwest, into the San Fernando Valley (Figure 0.1). The size of just the city of Los Angeles compared to other North American cities is enormous. A map generated by the city's planning department graphically depicts the extension of Los Angeles encompassing the combined land areas of St Louis, Milwaukee, Cleveland, Minneapolis, Boston, San Francisco, Pittsburgh and Manhattan (Figure 0.2).

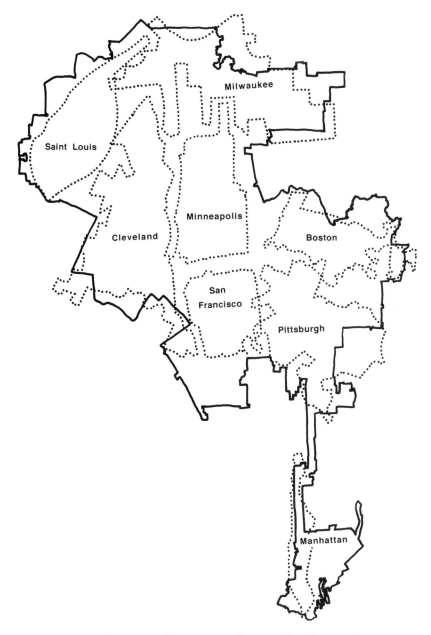

**Figure 0.2** *How big is L.A.? (Source: City of Los Angeles, Planning Department; Graphics Ute Lehrer)*

At the next scale, there is Los Angeles County (Figure 0.3) which is congruent with the Long Angeles–Long Beach Standard Metropolitan Statistical Area. Los Angeles County has 8.86 million inhabitants and includes 88 autonomous cities. Los Angeles County is still the most important and most populous of the five counties that make up the region, being home to 61% of its population (see Table

**Figure 0.3** *Los Angeles County (courtesy of Los Angeles County Department of Regional Planning)*

0.1).[3] Counties are important governance units responsible for protection, health and public assistance (Dear, 1996b: 68) and they constitute important political territories and boundaries for identities. As Los Angeles has grown into a megacity, Los Angeles County has become somewhat of a central city for an urbanized region of 14.5 million.

A political boundary-setting exercise of a different kind is performed by the regional planning and policy coordination agency, the Southern California Association of Governments (SCAG) (Figure 0.4). It encompasses six counties (Los Angeles, Orange, Riverside, San Bernardino, Ventura and Imperial). One hundred and sixty-three cities are part of this association's jurisdiction. It overlaps to a large degree with an economic definition of the Los Angeles area which became popular during the 1980s, the so-called sixty mile circle, first introduced by Security Pacific National Bank (Figure 0.5)[4] as the basis for their financial operations, encompasses a land area of 7700 square miles, at least 132 local jurisdictions and parts of five counties (Security Pacific, 1984, 1987). In the mid-

**Table 0.1** *Population growth in the five-county region of Los Angeles (000s)*

| Census year | Los Angeles | (*) | Orange | San Bernadino | Riverside | Ventura | Five-county region |
|---|---|---|---|---|---|---|---|
| 1900 | 170 | (68) | 20 | 28 | 18 | 14 | 250 |
| 1910 | 504 | (78) | 34 | 57 | 35 | 18 | 648 |
| 1920 | 936 | (81) | 61 | 73 | 50 | 28 | 1 150 |
| 1930 | 2 209 | (85) | 119 | 134 | 81 | 55 | 2 597 |
| 1940 | 2 786 | (86) | 131 | 161 | 106 | 70 | 3 253 |
| 1950 | 4 152 | (84) | 216 | 282 | 170 | 115 | 4 934 |
| 1960 | 6 011 | (78) | 709 | 501 | 303 | 199 | 7 724 |
| 1970 | 7 042 | (71) | 1 421 | 682 | 457 | 378 | 9 981 |
| 1980 | 7 478 | (65) | 1 932 | 893 | 664 | 530 | 11 496 |
| 1990 | 8 863 | (61) | 2 411 | 1 418 | 1 170 | 669 | 14 531 |

(*) = Los Angeles County as percentage of total regional population.

Source: Soja and Scott (1996: 3).

1980s, the 12 million inhabitants of this area achieved a gross regional product of almost $250 billion (Soja, 1989: 224).

Lastly, in this brief overview, another take on the boundaries of Southern California is provided by a growing literature on the ecological region of Los Angeles. The notions of airsheds, watersheds and ecological footprints or carrying capacity are beginning to reverberate (ever so faintly) on the policy level. As the *Atlas of Southern California* found recently: 'Southern California is making halting progress toward living within the carrying capacity of its air shed and river basins. Regulatory strategies, technological innovations and increasingly informed behavior by residents have contributed to this progress' (Dear, 1996b: 66). These efforts are concretely expressed, as will be shown in more detail in Chapters 3 and 11, in air pollution policies and planning along the Los Angeles River. The airshed is the governance area of the South Coast Air Quality Management District (SCAQMD) which covers the nondesert areas of Los Angeles, Orange, Riverside and San Bernardino counties (Figure 0.6). The SCAQMD – in cooperation with SCAG – develops air quality management plans in irregular sequence (the most recent ones were 1989, 1991, 1994 and 1997). These plans have jurisdiction (sanctioned by the federal Environmental Protection Agency and by the California Air Resources Board) for the improvement of air quality in the district. Yet, they are more than that: Since the 1980s, they have constituted a major discursive plane on which territorial decisions in the region have been made. Equally, the plans to renaturalize the Los Angeles River or to strengthen this river's flood control capacities have had considerable impact on planning and land-use policies in the region. They codetermine the boundaries of human settlement in this volatile ecological region (Keil and Desfor, 1996; Figure 0.7). With growing concerns and constraints regarding the limits to regional growth in Southern California, ecosystemic – more than political or economic – boundary-setting has gained significance in policy discussions. An ecosystemic view of sorts has entered the historical–geographic narrative of Los Angeles as part of an ecological moderniza-tion strategy for the region.

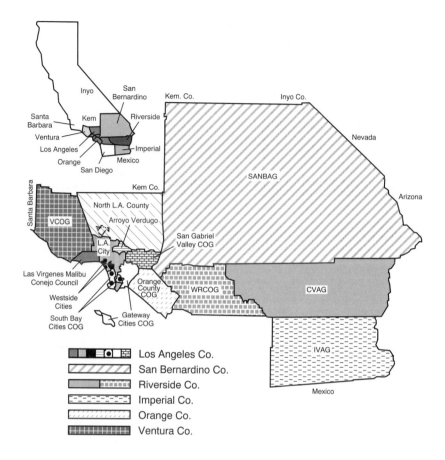

**SCAG is made up of 6 counties which are divided into 34 subregions**

*Figure 0.4* *The SCAG region (Courtesy of Southern California Association of Governments)*

## CONTESTED SPATIALITIES

Soja took the Security Pacific Bank's definition of the urban area – the 60-mile-circle – one stop further and argued that the city was, indeed, embedded between 'security' and 'pacific'; in between the peripheral military bases encircling the city like a bastion and the eastern seacoast of the Pacific Basin lies an urban region that is home to more and more pronounced oppositions, contradictions and disparities than any other place in the world (Soja, 1989: 224). Defining the city in the perimeter of the 60-mile circle has constituted a problem for Soja and others, though. As Derek Gregory has pointed out, the parodic Chicago School adaption of Soja's view from the top of City Hall into the nonconcentric circles of Los Angeles leaves us longing for some life on the street:

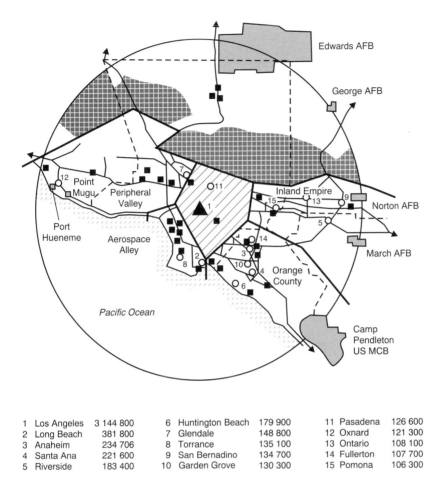

| 1 | Los Angeles | 3 144 800 | 6 | Huntington Beach | 179 900 | 11 | Pasadena | 126 600 |
|---|---|---|---|---|---|---|---|---|
| 2 | Long Beach | 381 800 | 7 | Glendale | 148 800 | 12 | Oxnard | 121 300 |
| 3 | Anaheim | 234 706 | 8 | Torrance | 135 100 | 13 | Ontario | 108 100 |
| 4 | Santa Ana | 221 600 | 9 | San Bernadino | 134 700 | 14 | Fullerton | 107 700 |
| 5 | Riverside | 183 400 | 10 | Garden Grove | 130 300 | 15 | Pomona | 106 300 |

*Figure 0.5* Security and Pacific (Source: Soja, 1989: 226; courtesy of the author)

> [Soja's] experimental geography – 'taking Los Angeles apart' – derives much of its power from an arresting re-presentation of a series of commonplace models of the city (most obviously those developed by the Chicago School) in a radically new and aggressively contrary vocabulary. . . . His parodic intimations of the world of Burgess and Hoyt function as a telling critique of the theoretical mainstream but largely fail to evoke the lifeworlds of mainstreet (Gregory, 1994: 295).

The fact that mainstreet does not appear implies a loss of 'the multiple voices of those who *live* in Los Angeles – other than Soja himself – and who presumably learn different things from it' (Gregory, 1994: 301). Gregory, from here, turns our attention to Mike Davis' illumination of 'the social struggles that are part of the production and consumption of these metropolitan social spaces' (Gregory, 1994: 303). The noirish realism cherished by Gregory and Davis has been challenged by Rosalyn Deutsche who has pointed out that even the spaces these authors inhabit in Los Angeles are male and exclusive spaces sparsely used by women; and that this male discourse largely eclipses the spheres of 'domestic violence, ambiguous

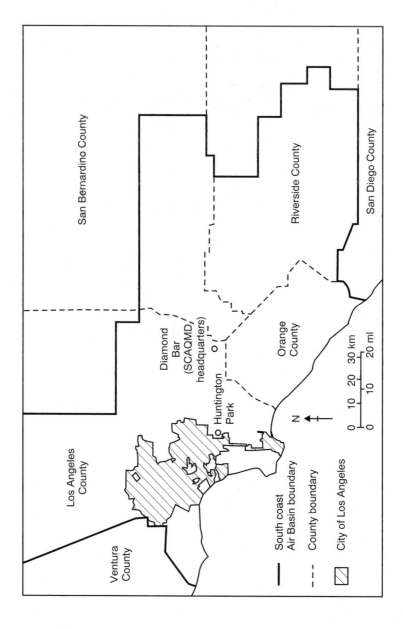

**Figure 0.6** *Air Quality Management District (Gene Desfor and Roger Keil copyright; Graphics by Geography Department, York University)*

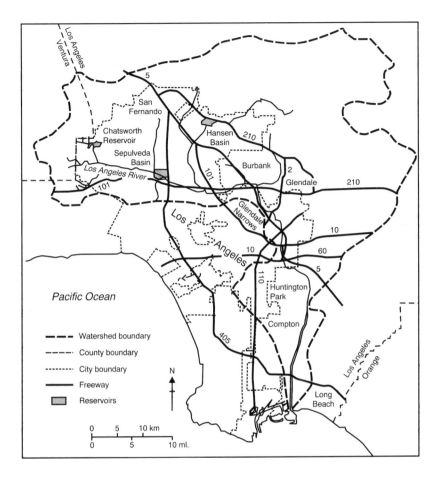

**Figure 0.7** *Los Angeles River watershed (Gene Desfor and Roger Keil copyright; Graphics by Geography Department, York University)*

family identities' and 'psychic geography' of urban dwellers. In drawing a connection between the authors of critical urban studies on Los Angeles and *auteurs noirs* of a previous period, Deutsche critiques both for their 'appeal to independent grounds of meaning, protecting the authority of a single reference point, [which] cleanses sexuality and difference from urban discourse and from its picture of the city' (Deutsche, 1996: 253). This leaves us still largely on 'masculine terrain'.

And what about the 'psychic geography'? What do we know about the everyday in Los Angeles without reference to the inscriptions of not just sexism but also racism into the life of communities and individuals? The Rodney King episode, for example, presents both an unusual event of extraordinary violence and an everyday threat to the bodies of people of color in Los Angeles. It both incorporates and is a spot on the landscape of racist violence of Los Angeles and a site on the psychic geography not just of the city's African Americans:

***Plate 0.1*** *March 3rd, 1991 (from George Holliday video, courtesy of CNN)*

> Rather than imagine racial power being produced in the soft space of ideological 'superstructure', the world saw it exercised at another point of production – at the material 'base' where the nightstick met the skull. And unlike 1980s and 1990s racial controversies over affirmative action, ethnocentrism, and multiculturalism, the King beating bore the familiar markings of the 1950s and 1960s – rather than being encased carefully in definitions of merit and neutrality, old-time white supremacy was boldly and crudely inscribed on the body of King. You don't need any fancy theory to figure out what went on between the L.A. police and Rodney King. That's true. But the Rodney King events are also particularly illuminating for an approach that focuses on the ideological, because part of what was revealed in the Rodney King saga was the need for an account of how racial power continues to work, blatantly in the King case, decades after it has been outlawed as a matter of formal decree, cultural convention, and elite preference (Crenshaw and Peller, 1993: 57).

In Deutsche's critique of the seers of Los Angeles we get a glimpse that the street of a city cannot substitute for the everyday. Though some have focussed in on the public street space (Ruddick, 1996) and privatized residential communities (Flusty, 1994) as places where the quotidian is constructed, they have largely overlooked aspects of struggle and conflict in their role of defining the everyday. The preoccupation with Los Angeles as a private city, a built environment of personal atomization, has prevented us from recognizing the city's quotidian reality as a politically constituted event, as an instance of the political itself. We are used to read social conflict like Black–Korean tensions through the landscape of the marketplace and residential segregation, through the icons of liquor stores and minimalls. Little do we know about the civic interactions, class struggles, democratic deliberations that shape the relationships of these groups into a universe of quotidian galaxies. Everyday Los Angeles, first and foremost, is a result, terrain and origin of political and social struggles. I will continue to return to these struggles throughout this book. Everyday Los Angeles is the fleeting reality which exists momentarily and constantly in the multiple communities of the multi(sub)-cultural city: layered realities of material practices, expectations, dreams, plans, art, music, use of territory, etc. While the street serves as the classical stage for the everyday, there is more to this dimension than the occupation with sidewalks, asphalt and chance encounters. Driving through Los Angeles still has the best handle on the diversity of the city's everyday but one is bound to miss the aspects of everyday Los Angeles which are not readily obvious by glancing at them from a car window.

Los Angeles presents a confusing mix of the predictability of the Fordist urban form and the unpredictability of the post-Fordist world city. On the one hand, there is the fascination with the equalization of the middle class consumer life style based on single-family home owner occupancy and automobility. On the other hand is a surreal polarization of rich and poor often meters apart in the urban fabric. In fact, the unprecedented fragmentation of urbanity is based on the equalization of spatiality in the bungalow landscape of the post-World War II period. Just like the ephemeral postmodern facades of Melrose Avenue have latched onto streetscapes of an earlier time, the multicultures of Los Angeles have inscribed themselves into the lawn-, yard-, and home-cultures of the American Dream.

Much of this dream was built on the promise of individual freedom expressed in two essentially connected artifacts: the security of the single family home and the mobility of the private car. One rested on the availability of space and cheap credit and the other on the construction and maintenance of roads and freeways (see Chapter 4). As the urban region filled up with people and cars, the private spaces of freedom mutated into carceral, gated communities and more and more people found their mobility confined by homelessness and poverty (Davis, 1994a; Flusty, 1994). To many, Los Angeles deteriorated from a place characterized by the dialectic of generalized well-being and individual self-fulfillment to a site of despair, brutalization, balkanization and Hobbesian individualization.

## THEMING HISTORICAL GEOGRAPHY

Without denying the structured segmentation of Los Angeles, it is an arbitrary choice where one starts any trip through the region. Ultimately, one will turn up with similar observations whatever route one takes. The simultaneity and diachronicity of the city's everyday are open to probe from any angle. One could take a traditional historical venture point and risk to be always too early or too late and always mispositioned. Is the *pueblo* in the center of Los Angeles, celebrated in its tourist guise at Olvera Street, a good place to unravel the area's historico-geographical narrative (Parson, 1991)? Or perhaps the Mission in San Juan Capistrano, in southern Orange County: to follow the trail of the missionaries both in its historical trajectory through the periods of Spanish, Mexican, Anglo and global Los Angeles and in its geographical itinerary, first from the south to the north, later in all directions, carving out pathways of development from the foot trails, to the ranching roads, orchard alleyways, railroads to the freeways and flight routes of today (DeMarco, 1988; Meyer, 1981)? It would be a start but soon after one would lose track of one's own mission and purpose in the maze of trajectories and itineraries which have crisscrossed the area through all times.

Perhaps because of the stark reality of constant instability, Los Angeles presents itself in a mood of denial. It exists despite itself and is successful marketing its impossibility. This is nowhere as obvious as in its theme parked landmarks of everyday simulacra through which it presents itself to the world. Connected in an imaginary V-shape which shadows the region like a Stealth bomber, Disneyland in Anaheim, Universal Studios in North Hollywood and the Getty Center in Brentwood mark the extent to which entrepreneurs and entertainers have gained control over the representation of urban life as spectacle. All three sites allow visitors to be in Los Angeles without ever seeing the city. The more visitors there will be at Disneyland, Universal Studios and the Getty Center, the more will miss out on the 'real' Los Angeles. Visiting these sites is not like visiting the Guggenheim in New York or the Louvre in Paris (not even like visiting Eurodisney), sites deeply imbricated with the fabric of a city which give them meaning beyond themselves. The Los Angeles experience is willfully shut out from the tourist gaze and more so, from the tourist step.

Theme parks are the replacement realities for material life-worlds elsewhere in the city and in the world. The Getty Center, for example, presents a collection of artifacts assembled from past ruling classes predominantly from the Western world. In a city inhabited by millions of marginalized people, the reproduced splendor of the global and historic elites mocks those who are less fortunate, legitimizes the desires of the local wealthy and satisfies the wants of an international tourist clientele. Disneyland and Universal Studios operate on a different logic. They draw the masses to a more populist feat. With an estimated attendance of 14.25 million visitors to Disneyland in Anaheim, 5.4 million to Universal Studios in Universal City, 3.65 million visitors to Knott's Berry Farm in Buena Park and 3.4 million visitors to Six Flags Magic Mountain in Valencia, Southern California represents the largest concentration of theme parks anywhere in the world but Florida (*Amusement Business Magazine*, 1997). The imprint, particularly, of Disney on the historical geography of Southern California is overwhelming. Engrained in the Anaheim bungalowscape since the 1950s, the traditional all-American theme park is currently undergoing a major extension. On the parking lot of the home of Bambi and Mickey Mouse, in early 1998, construction has begun for the $1.4 billion California Adventure Park, scheduled to be opened in 2001. This newest addition to 'Theme City, CA' will include a park re-creating California in symbolic represen-tations, a shopping and entertainment mall, a 750-room hotel and a 3500-seat theater. California, in 1998 still a state in the American Union with plenty of human and natural ecologies, will be re-created in 'three lands – Hollywood, Paradise Beach and Golden State'. The effect of such image engineering will be that '[t]ourists will no longer actually have to visit Yosemite, Huntington Beach or Death Valley – Disney will package it up for them' (Fisher, 1998b: 8). Meanwhile, down the street, at the Baseball Stadium which Disney leases from the city of Anaheim to house the entertainment corporation's Anaheim Angels, a major rejuvenation was finished in 1998 to provide baseball fans with an entirely simulated water-fall landscape replete with fabricated rocks, choreographed lighting as well as pyrotechnic and musical effects (Fisher, 1998a). Theming California is also at the heart of this Disney project: 'We're recreating the California coastline. We'll have cascading waterfalls and six geysers that throw water in the air,' confirmed stadium manager Kevin Uhlich on the eve of the official opening on April 1, 1998 (quoted in Fisher, 1998a: 1). While Disney occupies more and more land and more and more imaginary space in the construction of the region's historical geography, anything else disappears into an almost prehistorical mist of unreality. If Disney is what we ended up with, there is little indication that anyone could retrace a reasonable and defensible historico-geographical narrative to the Mission of San Juan Capistrano. Once Death Valley exists behind an entrance way at which Mickey Mouse sells tickets, there is little hope that anyone can still piece together a plausible story of Southern California. Let's leave the 'real-and-imagined' (Soja, 1996) spaces of Orange County for the moment. Many realities both articulated with and hidden by 'Theme City, CA' are still in need of explanation and interpretation.

## TOPOGRAPHICAL REVOLUTIONS

From the carpet of human settlement which stretches across the Southland, a number of vertical elevations protrude into the smoggy sky. While throughout this horizontal city, palm trees still tend to both crown and limit heights of residential settlement, central business districts and edge cities are now dotting the region anywhere from Tustin and Irvine in the southeast to Warner Center in the northwestern San Fernando Valley, from Long Beach in the south to Glendale in the north, and from Santa Monica in the west to Pasadena and the Inland Empire in the east. Central and well-attached to other centers such as Century City and Westwood through the elevated seam of Wilshire Boulevard, downtown Los Angeles is still the number one business and commercial center in the carpet's fabric. In addition to these economic points of high density and symbolized power as well as real estate value, Los Angeles, once a city of single-family homes, has grown up and out in areas where stodgy condominium and rental properties dominate the built environment. In Westwood and West Hollywood, in the Westlake area, in large parts of west Los Angeles and Santa Monica and in many regions along the coast, in Brentwood, Pacific Palisades and everywhere in the San Fernando Valley, high residential densities have started to bulge from the flat surface of the planes and hillsides of Southern California.

Elsewhere, the urban region, once a flowering desert chaparral, later a citrus factory and cattle ranch, industrialized heavily, densely and profusely. Particularly close to the oil fields where refineries and secondary petro-industries sprung up as well as along the Alameda corridor from Long Beach to the San Gabriel Valley where industrial suburbs exploded into America's largest branch plant economy, the built environment of Southern California belied its reputation of smalltownish middle America. As the bungalows were eaten up by dingbat apartment buildings, neighborhoods like Van Nuys, South Gate, Pico Rivera or Torrance grew in the shadow of large, Fordist industrial facilities. As the industries disappeared from these communities since the mid-1970s, closely knit working-class communities withered away and made room for both a new wave of immigration and new development.

Both comes together in the Alameda corridor. Here, Los Angeles had been mostly two things, industrial and Anglo, since both settlers from other parts of the United States and industry began to arrive in the 1920s. Built in what Fulton (1997: 66) called a 'sun and moon pattern' of industrial and residential communities on Los Angeles' Eastside, the so-called 'hub cities' (see Chapter 10) remained stable Fordist suburbs until deindustrialization hit in the 1970s. The Alameda corridor, once the heavy industrial spine of a major internal rustbelt, underwent large-scale demographic and economic restructuring. What used to be one of the whitest areas in all of Los Angeles became an immigrant stronghold with a large percentage of the population predominantly from Mexico and Central America. In fact, the concentration of Hispanic populations in the southeast and east of Los Angeles is so high that east Los Angeles, Maywood, Walnut Park, Huntington Park, Commerce and Cudahy are among the 10 least diverse communities in the entire region (only matched by the lily-white beach communities of Orange County, Allen and Turner, 1997: 243, Table 9.2).

At the same time, Los Angeles's rekindled dreams of leadership in the Pacific Century have made the Alameda corridor the site of a high-speed railway linking the port of Los Angeles–Long Beach to the downtown. This project (to be completed in 2001) is functionally and symbolically tied in with two more megaprojects which are set to propel Los Angeles into premier position among Pacific Rim competitors in global trade: the retrofitting of the port of Los Angeles and the expansion of Los Angeles International Airport. All three projects, which have been met with heavy opposition from local communities, environmental and social justice groups, signify a continuously widening rift between the urban region's growth machine goals and the interests of locally dependent businesses and citizens. Critics have voiced concerns that the major infrastructure expansions will divert economic activity away from local economic circuits, will destroy engrained supplier–customer relationships, will create jobs elsewhere and will leave neighbors bearing the brunt of the projects' environmental costs. Nowhere else in the region are the differences as pronounced between economically and socially vulnerable and dependent communities on the one hand and the megalomaniacal aspirations of a globally oriented local growth machine on the other (Newton, 1997). As communities in the eastern hub cities are becoming more demographically globalized, poorer and more economically stressed, the reliance on globally minded megaprojects as a growth strategy appears as a bitter medicine. It also calls into question the stilted attempts, after the uprising of 1992, of Rebuild LA and of its foster child LA PROSPER to create a hegemonic variant of community economic development in the exact same areas that might be sucked dry from suprastructural developments such as the Alameda corridor, the port retrofit and the expansion of LAX (Rebuild LA, 1997).

The changes along the Alameda Corridor point to a wider phenomenon of social and demographic change. If it was not for the major differences in scale and size, by 1940, demographic representations of Los Angeles looked much like those of other American cities for much of the second half of this century: a large white 'donut' surrounded a small 'hole' of communities of color. In 1990, this continued to hold only partly. There were still mostly concentrations of poverty in the inner city (a difficult concept at any rate in Los Angeles); there were also concentrations

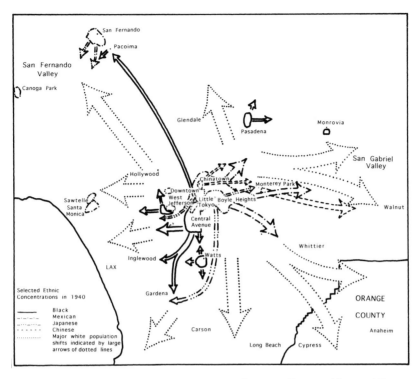

**Figure 0.8** *Major shifts in ethnic populations after 1940 (Source: Allen and Turner, 1997: 51; graphics: Ute Lehrer)*

of the black population in the southwestern-central area and of people of Mexican origin in southeast-central Los Angeles while whites were most concentrated in the outer suburbs of the region. Yet, there were also new trends. African Americans now have their highest concentrations in a large area between the San Diego and Long Beach freeways; persons of Mexican origin are to be found predominantly in the old urban core, between the Santa Ana Freeway and the Foothill Freeway and increasingly in the old black neighborhoods of Watts, Compton and along Central Avenue. They also have large concentrations in Wilmington, San Pedro, San Fernando, Santa Ana and parts of the Inland Empire. The development which has most exploded common perceptions of urban ecology, though, has been the large concentrations of East Asian, particularly Chinese persons in Monterey Park, Alhambra, San Marino and the eastern San Gabriel Valley. These 'digressions' from the expected, standard American urban mold is indicative of an intense redefinition of social, economic and cultural boundaries for which there has been no precedent (see Figure 0.8).

## PLANNING MOBILITY

One would assume that planning ought to play a major role in this process of redefinition. Yet, as the institutions of state intervention such as the community redevelopment agencies, planning departments, special purpose governments and the like have lost credibility with their foes both on the neoliberal right and the neopopulist left, there is little in the way of planning that would address these issues that straddle city and county boundaries across the region. While the South Coast Air Quality Management Board and the SCAG have introduced certain new governance mechanisms for the technical and infrastructural regulation of land, air and people in the region (Keil, 1998), little has been achieved in the way of planning and democratic regulation of human and natural communities in the Southland. Where there has been planning, much damage has been done. A case in point is the disaster the region has experienced in its attempt to redesign its transit and traffic patterns. With the freeways filled to capacity and no major projects planned for the 'plains of id' and 'autopia' (Banham, 1971), Los Angeles voters decided in 1980 that tax monies be raised to build an extensive rail-based transit system. Voters had earmarked $130 billion over 30 years for a grid of rapid transit and subway lines across the region. The Blue Line from Los Angeles to Long Beach opened on July 14, 1990 and parts of the Green Line (from Hawthorne to Norwalk) and the Red Line (from Union Station downtown along Wilshire Boulevard) had followed suit. The extension of the Red Line through Hollywood into the San Fernando Valley and the Blue Line link to Pasadena have been delayed (see Figure 0.9).

On January 14, 1998, the dream of a rail-based transportation future for Los Angeles came to at least a temporary, yet many think to a permanent, end. The directors of the Metropolitan Transit Authority (MTA) suspended for at least six months all work on its Eastside, Mid-City and Pasadena rail lines, projects for which the authority had already spent $300 million. This sum, however, is a mere tip of an iceberg of public funds which have already been sunk into the prestigious projects (Simon, 1998). In the mid-1990s, rail transit in Los Angeles constituted a seriously overpriced, out-of-control burden on the taxpayers of the urban region. Particularly compared to its most viable alternative, the bus system, rail was underused, oversubsidized, and overpoliced[5] to an alarming degree (Table 0.2).[6]

Opponents to the mega rail plans are scattered across the political landscape. On the one hand are the free marketeers who claim that Los Angeles will be more decentralized, private and sprawled in the future and does not need public rail transit of the kind proposed by the MTA. Among the most vocal proponents of this view are a group of University of Southern California professors who paint a picture of a Southern Californian future which is less dense, high tech, more wealthy and more dispersed. Rail would not make much sense in this scenario and these critics propose a more flexible, van-based and privatized transportation system to deal with both diversity and dispersion in Southern California (Moore II, Richardson, and Gordon, 1997; Gordon and Richardson, 1996). These proponents of an ever-expanding and renewable Los Angelization of Los Angeles share with their leftist counterparts a disdain for rail and a concern for the region's bus system which, while used daily by 350 000 people, has suffered deterioration for which critics blame the MTA's one-sided obsession with rail. On the other end of the political spectrum, progressive activists of the Labor/Community Strategy Center (L/CSC) founded a Bus Riders' Union (BRU) in 1994 and have continuously

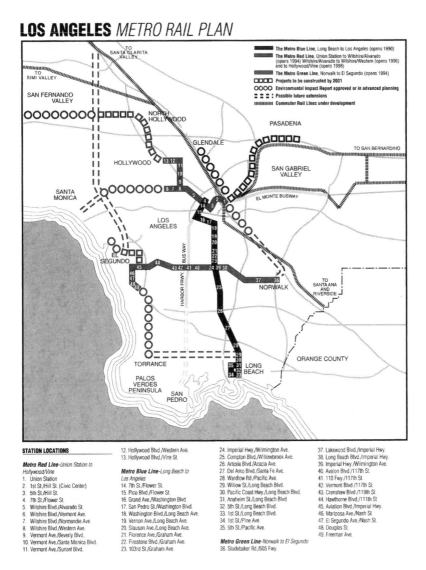

## LOS ANGELES *METRO RAIL PLAN*

**Figure 0.9** *Los Angeles Metro Rail Plan (courtesy of the Metropolitan Transportation Authority)*

won court and political battles against the MTA over bus fees, spending priorities and civil rights. While cooperating with the neoliberal opponents of rail transit on occasion, it has been the priority of the BRU to further the cause of poor and working people who are the core paying patrons of the transportation authority (L/CSC, 1996). Whatever the outcome of the debates on the future of rail in Los Angeles, public transit remains a critical public planning problem in a city where the majority of trips are taken daily by cars which continue to foul up the air of the basin and the valleys. Accessibility to the region's labor markets, residential areas and public and environmental amenities is less than equitably distributed. Sprawl

**Table 0.2**  *A graphic comparison of the bus and rail systems*

|  | Bus system | Rail system |
| --- | --- | --- |
| Daily ridership | 350 000 | 26 000 |
| Racial composition | 81% people of color/19% white | 50% people of color/50% white |
| Core rider economic status | 'Profoundly poor' | Middle class |
| Load factors | Most overcrowded in US | Running half empty |
| Dependability | Late/often passes you by | On time |
| Quality | Dirty to filthy | Clean and new |
| Age of capital | Oldest bus fleet in US | New and modern |
| Amenities | None, seat is optional | Computer racks/four seats for every three passengers |
| Subsidy per passenger | $0.33 to $1.17 | $5 to $25 |
| Security subsidy per passenger | $0.03 | $1.17 |
| Riders fare as percent of cost of service (or 'fare box recovery ratio') | 30–35% | 7–9% |
| Fare increases | 170% over 10 years | 23% over 5 years |
| Percent of MTA discretionary funds for total ridership | 30% for 94% of riders | 70% for 6% of riders |

Source: L/CSC (1996: 5) courtesy of L/CSC.

and gridlock have melded into a complex policy problem unparalleled in any other North American city. But the fight over rail and buses also shows that the political and social landscape of Los Angeles has matured into a lively public arena where social movement and activist groups have demonstrated continuous presence in the face of utter adversity. Public planning, while under pressure in the neoliberal atmosphere of the 1990s, has found unforeseen backers and attackers in the countless interventions by 'the oppressed as policy makers' (Labor/Community Strategy Center, 1996: 1) and the 'insurgent practices' of 'a thousand tiny empowerments' (Sandercock, 1998).

## PRIVATE PUBLICS

One of the major inhibitions to regional planning has historically been the sharp division in political jurisdiction in the countless cities, counties and special districts of which the Southern Californian carpet consists. Home rule was a 'sacred principle' in twentieth-century America and particularly in California, where the state allowed local communities to incorporate at their discretion beginning in 1879. This defied Dillon's Rule, an earlier superior court decision which characterized local governments as creatures of the state. Los Angeles, like other cities, established a home rule charter. Los Angeles County, also granted home rule in 1913, governed the patchwork of 'unincorporated areas' that lay interspersed between the few cities able to incorporate due to a strong enough tax

## Los Angeles County

Unincorporated areas

*Figure 0.10* *Unincorporated and incorporated areas, Los Angeles County (Courtesy of Los Angeles County Department of Regional Planning)*

base. This all changed in 1954 when the small city of Lakewood in the South Bay demonstrated through a service delivery plan with the county that a hybrid of home rule and contracted services from the county was feasible. Dozens of cities followed the 'Lakewood Plan' and incorporated since the 1950s (see Chapter 10; Lemon, 1996: 208). Today, this 'balkanization' of power in Southern California has become the basis for, and has become subject to, globalization. Scaling and spacing Southern California now entails different markers than those set by the ranchers, local real estate entrepreneurs, progressive reformers and federal policymakers in the past. Local jurisdictions have now become the contested playground of globally imbricated interests of landed property, diasporadic bourgeoisies and uprooted working classes (see Figure 0.10).

In addition to the multitude of scalar jurisdictions and competing public policy arenas, political space in Southern California has become increasingly privatized. As Steven Flusty has shown,

> traditional public spaces are increasingly supplanted by such privately produced (although often publicly subsidized) 'privately owned and administered spaces for public aggregation' as shopping malls, corporate plazas and electronic mass media. In these new, post-public spaces, access is predicated upon real or apparent ability to pay. People, goods, actions and ideas narrowly perceived as inimical to the owner's sensibilities and maximized profit are unaccommodated or removed by private security as quickly as they are manifested. In such spaces, exclusivity is an inevitable by-product of the high levels of control necessary to insure that irregularity, unpredictability and inefficiency do not interfere with the orderly flow of commerce (Flusty, 1994: 13).

As a result of this process, formerly public political spaces and jurisdictions are now reinvented as private milieux and 'spatial justice' is eroded. Universal City's artificial urban mainstreet 'Citywalk' is an excellent example of how urbanity is being privatized, yet chief among those newly privatized political arenas are the relatively affluent residential communities 'sealed behind a crusty perimeter, fenced off or built within walls sometimes reinforced by a stealthy periphery of densely landscaped berms', which Flusty calls 'luxury laagers' (Flusty, 1994: 22). While snob appeal had created separated residential spaces in Los Angeles at least since the 1950s, the emergence of more and more luxury laagers over the last decade is a general trend to build spaces deliberately cut off not just from the social and cultural spatiality of the rest of Los Angeles but also from its political space. As some of the older wealthy neighborhoods in Los Angeles have been retrofitted to comply with the new standards of security hysteria which accompany the trend of privatization, the main thrust of laager-building has been in the newer residential suburbs in Orange County and the desert valleys. These newly gated communities often combine a manufactured natural environment replete with lakes and instant palm forests and golf courses with a manufactured village life which is based on the fundamental agreement of the residents that what is urban about a city should be left in front of the gates (Figure 0.11).

## REBUILDING THIRDSPACE

This book's argument, sketched in so few lines in these opening paragraphs, will always be expressly local and detailed yet always aware of the fissures created by the globalization of communities and economies experienced in Los Angeles. Once again, let me return to the Los Angeles universe of Ed Soja whose implicit rejoinder to Gregory's and Deutsche's critique, presented at the beginning of this chapter, ventures into the 'trialectics' of an all-rounded perspective. Rather than admitting to incompleteness of his earlier male parochialism view, he breaks through to the other side of the all-encompassing simultaneity of perspective:

> Understanding the city must involve both views, the micro and the macro, with neither inherently privileged, but only with the accompanying recognition that no city – indeed no lived space – is ever completely knowable no matter what

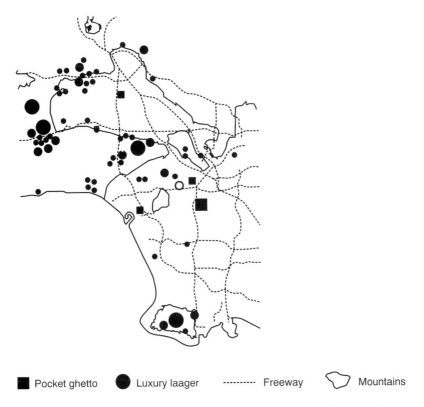

■ Pocket ghetto     ● Luxury laager     ---------- Freeway     ⬠ Mountains

**Figure 0.11** *Los Angeles area interdictory residential complexes (Source: Flusty, 1994: 24; courtesy of author)*

perspective we take, just as no one's life is ever completely knowable no matter how artful or rigorous the biographer. The appropriate response to the micro vs. macro choice is thus an assertive and creative rejection of the either/or for the more open-ended both/and also . . . (Soja, 1996: 310).

Invoking Lefebvre, Soja correctly delegitimizes 'legibility' of the city as an illusion, a too simple attempt to understand the variable dialects of the urban, the social and the everyday. He particularly singles out *visual* legibility as 'treacherous' because it creates the false impression as if we could read complex realities off the surfaces of urban appearances (Soja, 1996: 312).

Yet it appears that Soja himself escapes into a generalized abstracted view which, in delegitimizing the visual readability of the everyday in the city, also devalues the practices of urbanites who reform and revolutionize the urban constantly. The totality of complex urbanity, in Soja's world, is a rat cage of codependency in which actors have lost direction and control over their actions. Visualized through the spiralling image of Soja's *Thirdspace* graphics, this rat cage reality exists in a relationship of critical tension to the post-rebellion quest for pacified neoliberalism as expressed in the symbolism of the urban fixer-squad Rebuild LA. But Soja's imagery also shares with the semiotics of the latter a trinitarian desire for unity, inclusiveness and stability (Figure 0.12).

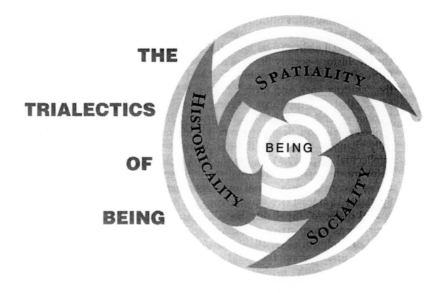

**Figure 0.12** *Rebuilding Thirdspace (Source: Soja, 1996: 71 (courtesy of the author) and Rebuild L.A., 1997: 1)*

In the chapters to follow I have attempted to travel a different road. While accepting the demand for complexity implied in Soja's appeal to trialectics and thirdspatiality and rejecting the simplicity of community pacification expressed through the symbolic politics of Rebuild LA, I situate the new structured coherence of Los Angeles in a world characterized by social struggle, political conflict and liberatory politics. This is the space where the abstract and concrete rights to the city are conjoined, a space between the political and civil spheres of society. It is an intensely political space (Kofman and Lebas, 1996: 41; Kirby, 1993). The simultaneity of congealed past local struggles and of the realities of a constantly revolving, globalized urban world is the topic of this book. In this context, Henri Lefebvre has reminded us that while 'global processes (economic, social, political, cultural) have formed urban space and shaped the city', it is by

> enabling groups to insert themselves, to take charge of them, to *appropriate* them; and this by inventing, by sculpting space (to use a metaphor), by giving themselves rhythms. Such groups have also been innovative in how to live, to have a family, to raise and educate children, to leave a greater or lesser place to women, to use and transmit wealth. These transformations of everyday life modified urban reality, not without having from it their motivations. The city was at one and the same time the place and the milieu, the theatre and the stake of these complex interactions (Lefebvre, 1996: 104–105).

I see Los Angeles as a site of utopian dreams and real politics, of reel and real images, of global and local struggles that make a city. In the core of this effort is always human agency because as Marx once said, theory and social critique have to be tested *ad hominem* to be relevant. This is a book about spaces inhabited by the people of Los Angeles.

# PART I

IMAGES AND NARRATIVES

# CHAPTER 1

# REEL IMAGES AND REAL POLITICS

## REEL IMAGES: LOS ANGELES IN THE MOVIES

Throughout the 1980s and 1990s, the Hollywood movie industry has made Los Angeles the scene of celluloid speculations on our urban future. Clearly, the film with the biggest influence on the way we have come to view not just Los Angeles but the contemporary metropolis in general was Ridley Scott's magisterial *Blade Runner*, which eternalized a brief stretch of Broadway in downtown Los Angeles as the ultimate image of the decayed, internationalized second city into which, we were told, urban America is going to be turned. The film stretches the boundaries of our imaginations in many ways. It questions the concept of one universal urban reality which has characterized modernist views of cities. It presents instead a patchwork of barely connected realities forming a layered city structured by fault lines along which social earthquakes threaten to happen any minute; this patchwork makes it seem unlikely that 'the urban' will ever be a common, unified experience shared by the majority of the city's population(s). *Blade Runner* toys with our sense of humanity and, ultimately, agency: the lines between humans and cyborg replicants are blurred. We lose our sense of how the social is manufactured and who exactly has control over it. Society is losing its center and social actors are reconfiguring their identities.

While *Blade Runner* examines the internal world of the internationalized city for which Los Angeles became a graphic prototype, the movie *Die Hard* from 1988 throws some light on the relationships between the local and the global. The scene of the film is *Fox Plaza*, a postmodern office tower in Century City. The motion picture's main characters include employees of a Japanese multinational corporation, a gang of mostly European terrorists, good and bad cops of the Los Angeles Police Department and of the FBI, as well as a New York detective on vacation. The setting is heavily symbolic. The terrorists take the office workers hostage in order to get access to their company's bonds which are stored in the building's vault. These assets are the accumulated profits derived from the multinational's operations, large-scale building projects, in the Third World. The attack by the 'European Union' of terrorists on 'Japan' takes place in America; it is a true simulacrum of the current phase of globalized urbanization. Capital seems to have become deterritorialized, denationalized and footloose.

In this depiction, innocent local places are threatened by external processes over which they have no control. The globalization of urban centers leads to a new landscape of power which reflects the need of global capital to create a built environment and infrastructure that will serve its needs. In the shadow worlds of office parks and intelligent buildings, international airports and edge cities, as well as palaces of high culture and other venues of postmodern spectacle, an isolated globalized environment takes shape, one which has little connection to the ins and

**Plate 1.1**  *Broadway, Los Angeles (Roger Keil)*

**Plate 1.2**  *Fox Plaza, Century City (Roger Keil)*

outs of daily life in the city. A new type of city emerges – the world city – of which Los Angeles is a prime example.

A more recent series of movies has attempted a different depiction of Los Angeles. From the quirkiness of *LA Stories* to the romanticism of *Grand Canyon* and the stark realism of *Boyz in the Hood*, the reel world has finally turned into the real world. What you see is what you get. Reborn, in a more palatable form, is the celebrated cynical and hardboiled spirit of *noirish* Los Angeles of decades past. But now, the asocialness of the private eye has become a common phenomenon. The new Los Angeles cinema is family entertainment, and it is mind-numbing and demobilizing. The most spectacular example of this new style is Robert Altman's brilliant *Short Cuts* of 1993, in which a set of despicable characters endlessly and aimlessly roam the cultural nothingness and wasteland of a contemporary Los Angeles: it is a world without meaning; a world without political options.

Enter *Pulp Fiction*, Quentin Tarantino's controversial bad guy flick from 1994 which takes to an extreme what *Short Cuts* began. The social – now in an underworld setting – has ceased entirely to be of importance. But in contrast to the way in which the characters in Altman's *Short Cuts* unknowingly weave their physical and moral realities into a social fabric which retains redeemable and ethical qualities, *Pulp Fiction* appears as a trip from one remote out-of-control space station to the next. Equally, *Pulp Fiction*, like any good postmodern tale, shatters our sense of time and history through a counterclimactical sequence of its episodes. Both spatial coherence and temporal progress are denied as access points for crafting a reality in which thinking and acting individuals can gain control over their lives. Criminal ethics or no ethics at all have replaced the pathological world of *Blade Runner* and *Short Cuts*. As the social disappears and the city becomes an empty shell of arbitrarily linked space stations and prison cells, the political equally fades as a space in which social change can happen.

At least one movie stands out from this recent crop of depoliticized sagas: *Falling Down* with Michael Douglas and Robert Duvall (1993). The film offers a recipe for action, but it is not of the kind we should hope for. It is the vigilante story of an aerospace worker who has recently been fired. He takes his wrath out on the entire city. Anybody who is different – and everybody in Los Angeles is – becomes a victim in the name of normalcy. While the film stops short of advocating open fascist violence, Michael Douglas's character – whose car's vanity plate reads 'D-Fense' – declares war on the fabric of the world city. It is the America of *Die Hard* finally gone sour. Are these movies any indication of where Los Angeles is headed today? Has the city become devoid of the political? Are the few remaining options of the kind that *Falling Down* seems to suggest? These questions will occupy us through much of this book.

## REALITY CHECK: WORLD CITY FORMATION

While motion pictures give us more or less appropriate images of urban restructuring in the current period, they hardly explain this process. Let us go from the reel to the real, then. The work of the so-called 'LA School'[1] has provided us with a wealth of information on these new polarities and fragmentations. In fact, the LA

*6*
—

situation has been both the model for Friedmann's (1986, 1995) work on world cities and the basis for much of the discussion on paradigmatic shifts in urbanization worldwide during the 1980s and 1990s. Six main lines can be discerned in the discourse.[2]

The first such narrative is grounded in a tradition of *political economy*. In a series of articles on Los Angeles and in his magisterial *City of Quartz* (1990) the author who has most fruitfully constructed this particular narrative over the past few years is Mike Davis. In his writings, Davis has outlined the broad development of the space-specific regimes of accumulation and modes of regulation in Los Angeles since the city as we know it emerged during the real estate frenzy of the beginning of the twentieth century. The hicktown with the bloodiest labor relations in the nation became the first postindustrial city despite its preindustrial guise. Davis' work has developed into the political conscience of 'the other LA' struggling not to be drowned in the dominant project of the postmodern world class city. This analysis of ruling-class formation and power structures in the Southland especially have helped to define urbanization in Los Angeles-since-Fordism as a highly contested process shaped by class struggles in space.

The second narrative is predominantly *economist*. Mostly identified with the systematic studies of Allen Scott (1988b, 1993a), it differs from the tradition of political economy in that it stresses the economic geography of place rather than its political underpinnings. It argues that the current restructuring of Southern California can be explained as a set of changes in the region's space economy (production, labor markets and reproduction). Theoretically, the new economic geography (on which the economist narrative of Los Angeles rests) explicitly rejects the static nature of classical economist narratives: 'We add the modifier "political" to economics, "historical" to sociology, and so bring growth and change to the forefront' (Storper and Walker, 1989: 3). In spite of the emphasis on political and historical dimensions to the city, however, economic *space* remains the central category in this view. The new economic geography – via the concept of social regulation – has embarked on the analysis of the social factors that presently generate an altered economic environment. While taking into account – on the level of theory – a minimum of historical and political perspectives on the restructuring of the 'industrial districts' of Southern California in an era of 'flexibilization', the economist narrative has rarely entered the fields of political and historical praxis. The Los Angeles area, in this view, is one of the new urban agglomerations of capitalism. Decidedly, the social and political aspects of geographies are secondary, both in reality and in our understanding of urbanization, to the modern metropolis' 'primary function as a focus of production and work projected through a regime of agglomeration economies and polarization effects' (Scott, 1988b: 217). Unfortunately, despite the pronounced intention of the economist narrative not to underrate noneconomic factors, the social, the political and the historical are mere embellishments to space and economy (Storper and Scott, 1989).

Whereas the first narrative introduced a diachronic view and the second entertains a mostly synchronic notion, the third narrative does away with many of our traditional ideas of space and time altogether. Authors like Michael Dear and Edward Soja have deconstructed Los Angeles into a fragmented pattern of places and temporalities in a way that suggests the existence of a total(itarian) syn-chronicity. This synchronicity is presented as the future of 'the city' incarnated in Los Angeles. The third narrative has grown out of the analysis of geographies, space and planning in the postmodern city. In contrast to the tradition of political economy and the economist approaches described above, it is a cultural concept of the city in the classical sense. In addition, it constitutes the most visible break with the traditional materialist rhetoric of urbanization by exploding both the class foundations of the social production of the city and the customary privilege of history over geography in materialist urban theory (Dear, 1986, 1996a; Soja, 1989, 1996). This work has recently been rekindled through a series of major publications which have further dwelled on Los Angeles as the ultimate locale of postmodern urbanism (Scott and Soja, 1996; Soja, 1996).

A fourth narrative bases its analysis mostly on recent advances in cultural studies. One book in particular stands out in this literature: the attempt to come to terms with the aftermath of the Rodney King beating of 1991 and of the urban uprising of 1992 in a collection of excellent essays edited by Robert Gooding-Williams (1993). In addition and in contrast to many scholarly studies and muckraking journalistic pieces on both Rodney King and the Los Angeles uprising, Robert Gooding-Williams' edited volume does not expect the reader to take statistics about poverty and police brutality as explanations for these events. This would be equally misleading as to attack the Rodney King trial for misreading 'the facts' as presented by the video evidence (as if there were facts just lying around to be picked up). This belief in the power of allegedly neutral facts would be, in Robert Gooding-Williams' words, succumbing 'again to the positivist fantasy that there are brute facts that speak for themselves' (1993: 167). This 'positivist fantasy' is challenged – more than anything else – in this powerful collection of essays. It explores the dialectics of domination through physical force and refined ideological strategies and between the factual and the discursive multifaceted explanation of both the Rodney King beating and the uprising that followed the scandalous Simi Valley acquittals. The book is testimony to both the largely increased sophistication in the social sciences in questions of racialization, class and gender, *and* the return of the social and of a discourse of solidarity beyond the political tribalism which has characterized much of the postmodern debate.

A fifth narrative attempts to look at Los Angeles in the light of historic and recent ecological change (Davis, 1994a, 1995b, 1996; Keil and Desfor, 1996; McPhee, 1989; FitzSimmons and Gottlieb, 1996). Much of this narrative is the subject matter of the third chapter and need not be elaborated now.

A sixth narrative is the 'world city hypothesis' which has used Los Angeles as a case in point (Friedmann, 1986, 1995; Friedmann and Wolff, 1982; Keil, 1993). Since this literature provides the backbone for the empirical study presented in this book, a slightly more extensive discussion will follow below.

Taken together, the six narratives presented here have created an image of the urban region that appears as the paradigmatic growth pole of both the Fordist and the post-Fordist regimes. Los Angeles is depicted as the place where the transition from a Fordist mass productive/consumptive mode to more flexible forms of production/consumption has been happening in model fashion. The main venues of the post-Fordist economy – services, high technology and crafts production –

8

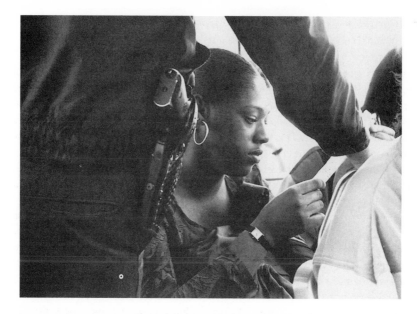

*Plate 1.3* *Los Angeles County Sheriff controlling ticket of Blue Line patron; South Los Angeles, April 1992 (Roger Keil)*

are well represented in the changing economy of Los Angeles. Culturally, demographically and institutionally, the region appears like an image in a kaleidoscope.

Implicitly, all of the above narratives make statements about the role of politics in the restructuring process. Yet, with a few notable exceptions – and particularly the work of Mike Davis – none of these approaches has been able to synthesize the conceptual antagonisms of periodization and spatialization on the one hand and the place-specific and the microstructural on the other. Politics as the transmitter belt of global restructuring has not been a prime concern of this literature. I will now suggest an alternative approach.

## INTERNATIONALIZATION AND GLOBALIZATION

World city theory originated at a time when the common parlance in academic and popular discourses mostly concerned itself with internationalization rather than globalization. While present in the English language since the 1960s, the latter term was only popularized during the last decade of the twentieth century. Mostly through the work of cultural theorists, we have begun to understand that 'the international' is different from 'the global':

> Any theory of the international, or global, would need to recognise both the totally different presuppositions, as well as conceptualizations resulting from them, of both these terms: at their simplest, the whole historical problematic of the formation of nation-states, the proliferation of the nineteenth and especially twentieth century of the idea of the nation, nationalism and national cultures . . . and the distinctive,

historical, and unequal, conditions in which the notion of the '*international*' was constructed (King, 1991b: 4).

The international was constructed alongside the emergence of the nation-state; the global is congruent with the creation of the trans- or a-national. The global view has been supported by changes in the representation of the world as whole, the astronaut view of the globe, the growing predominance of concepts like 'mother earth' or gaia, all of which are just abstractions which do not make much sense as King reminds us without 'taking especial notice of the economic, political, cultural and nation-state elements in the development of the world order and the "global dimensions" possibly focusing on the cultural, spatial, technological, material and representational dimensions of the construction of globality' (King, 1991b: 5). In contrast to the divine view of the astronauts, our view is always situated in a mundane fashion: in a world which is increasingly compressed and whose most imminent units, nationally constituted societies, are more and more subjected to multiculturalism and polyethnicity, 'the conditions of and for the identification of individual and collective selves and of individual and collective others are becoming ever more complex' (Robertson, 1991: 71–72; Keil and Kipfer, 1994).

When I refer to internationalization in this book, I predominantly mean the way in which economies were transformed worldwide in the 1970s and 1980s when foreign direct investment increased in most nation-states and when the Fordist regime of accumulation which had rested on some degree of national integrity under the umbrella of the pax americana came unhinged due to the internationalization of national economies. This phase also laid the ground for the emergence of global command centers, the world or global cities.

Beginning in the 1980s, though, a new process started which I prefer to refer to as 'globalization'. This process explodes the notion that the world economy can still be viewed mostly as the sum of the relationship between national economies. Globalization rather suggests that other spatial scales of economic organization, both sub- and supralocal, are gaining in significance *vis-à-vis* the nation state. Elsewhere, Stefan Kipfer and I have critiqued the ideological uses of the term 'globalization' by either the proponents or opponents of such a process (Keil and Kipfer, 1994; Kipfer and Keil, 1995). We have suggested instead to treat globalization as a series of material and discursive processes through which it, globalization, is crystallized and articulated. These processes are complexes of social relationships and political conflicts. Globalization, in this view, is not a natural process (as it appears in much of neoliberal discourse and is often mirrored in the view of its opponents).

## WORLD CITY FORMATION

It is useful to look at Los Angeles as one of about 30 world cities that span the globe as the skeleton of the New World Order of global capitalism (Knox and Taylor, 1995) (see Figure 1.1). Such world cities are places where this newly globalized economic world has a tangible concrete reality. Global flows of capital

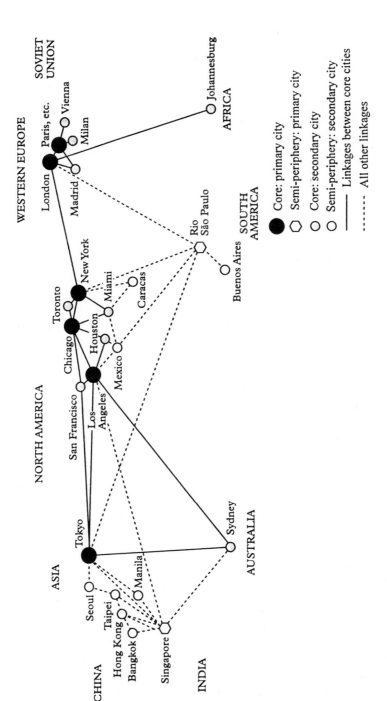

**Figure 1.1** *World city hierarchy (Source: Friedmann, 1986; courtesy of the author)*

and labor move through world cities, and are controlled from there. This gives civil society and local politics in such places a specific role: they are not just *products* but also *producers* of these seats of seemingly universal global power.

In a previous period of world city literature, this specific kind of cities was mostly identified with the seats of national and international economic and political power. Rather than being seen as specific products of a new global urbanization dynamics, these metropolises were considered hubs of national economies with some connection to international trade or politics (Hall, 1966). With the onset of the age of the multinational corporation, however, the view of world cities changed significantly. Cohen found a series of global cities in the early 1980s and linked their emergence directly to changes inside corporations and to the spread of productive services. Global cities, in this view, were both the nodal points of the new international division of labor (NIDL) and of multinational corporations which were seen at the heart of that NIDL (Cohen, 1981).

This perspective, however, was still fairly limited to a concept of world cities whose *function* seemed to be clear but whose actual *formation* had not even been thought about. This changed with John Friedmann and Goetz Wolff's seminal conceptual article 'World City Formation: An Agenda of Research and Action', which was published in 1982. While recognizing that the world city was somehow linked to the emergence of a new global accumulation regime (later to be called 'global formation' by Chase-Dunn, 1989), the authors started to look at the social and political processes that actually produced the world city locally.

> Being essential to both transnational capital and national political interests, world cities may become bargaining powers in the ensuing struggles. They are therefore also major arenas for political conflict. How these conflicts are resolved will shape the future of the world economy. Because many diverging interests are involved, it is a multifacetted struggle (1982: 312).

Despite this recognition of the relevance of the local struggles in world city formation, Friedmann and Wolff's analysis did not really extend to the study of these conflicts on the urban level. And little has been written since to develop this point.

World cities are mostly located in the center or the semiperiphery of the world economy. While these urban centers have a number of visible and functional similarities, they differ among each other and they are differentiated internally corresponding to their function in the international division of labor. World cities are commonly treated as creatures of anonymous global capital forces. They are believed to be 'the control centers of the global economy' (Friedmann and Wolff, 1982: 21). The need for nodal points to coordinate global economic activity contributes to the emergence of world cities and these cities also have to be understood as production sites for specific services and goods needed to keep the global economy afloat (Sassen, 1991). The attention of most world city researchers is still on the role these control centers play in the organization of the global economy or, as Friedmann puts it, on how they 'articulate larger regional, national, and international economies' (1995: 22). Yet, without the intricate local economies

of place and space one finds in world cities, economies that consist of manufacturing, services, real estate, political and social organizations etc., there would
not be a global economy. Rather than being mere creatures of some undefined
'global economy', world cities come alive as production centers in their own right
which both feed off and feed into what Friedmann has called the 'space of global
accumulation' (Friedmann, 1995; Sassen, 1991, 1994). Little in these discussions,
however, speaks to the political process proper that structures and restructures the
economic nodality of world cities. We will return to this shortly.

In contrast to the pathology and delinquency of the movie versions of Los
Angeles, the emerging analytical view represented in some of the world city
literature maintains the relevancy of local social and political realities. 'Global
capital' is ubiquitous with its products and symbols. But it achieves this state of
ever-presence only through a dialectical process; it relies on the increased fragmentation of urban societies for its acceptance into every nook and cranny of the
world. While globalization appears as a force destructive of local life-worlds, it
does, in fact, come to fruition in a world of increasingly less universal points of
reference. As a case in point, societies and communities in today's large cities have
become more diverse, culturally differentiated and politically expressive of such
differentiations. In fact, one could argue that cities have become places where the
social and functional middle has disappeared. Instead, they have developed into
both the (globalized) centers of the world economy, and the internationalized
'other' of the devalued sectors (where women, people of color and immigrants have
a majority). Both find 'the strategic terrain for their operations' in global cities
(Sassen, 1994: 124). Globalization threatens the fabric of concrete places in the
abstract space of globalization. Yet, without at least some functionality of the local,
it seems, globalization cannot unleash its destructive force. Without the intricate
local economies of place and space one finds in world cities – economies that
consist of manufacturing, services, real estate, political and social organizations
etc. – there would not be a global economy (Sassen, 1991, 1994).

World city theory is concerned with the governance of complexity (Keil,
forthcoming). One way to capture the complex sociospatiality of the world city in
perhaps oversimplified, yet strikingly appropriate terms, is to differentiate between
the 'citadel' and the 'ghetto' of the world city. These metaphors express the
correlated and dialectical structure of polarization present in those cities whose
splendor and luxury rest on a new kind of poverty and misery. In fact, the
contraposition of citadel and ghetto is both a spatial and a functional relationship:
rich and poor define each other. The metaphors aptly describe the contradictions
of the internal structure of some of the world cities which fall apart into internationally oriented centers of economic power, entrenched in the glass and steel
ziggurats of the new downtowns on the one hand, and into the miserable housing
areas and production sites of the increasingly internationalized proletariat on the
other. The metaphors of 'citadel' and 'ghetto' seem to be an ideal starting point for
the analysis of politics in the world city in general and of Los Angeles in particular
(Friedmann, 1986, 1995; Friedmann and Wolff, 1982).

Yet, the emergence of a new global–local arrangement should not be viewed in
metaphors of confrontation between static poles but rather as a process of mutual
definition and as a result of material relationships of power. Not only do traditional

communities take up the fight against intrusive global capital, but these communities are restructured in the process, *concurrently changing their political and social reality*. Sociospatial restructuring in the world city builds the foundation for new political orientations; the local politics of global capitalism experiences a qualitative redefinition. In other words: the uprooted class fragments and territorial communities of the world city battle the 'footloose world economy' (in its concrete fragments – a hardly unified global capital and its local political and social allies); they strike compromises, win political victories and suffer defeats (Castells, 1983).

Urbanization is one of the material dimensions of globalization and world city formation is one dimension of this general process of globalized urbanization. Two related processes characterize major urban centers today: the globalization of the urban region and the fragmentation of urban civil society and polity. Urban politics is the forum where the nexus of the global and the local is produced. While rarely beneficial to local communities, the regulation of these relationships through local politics, I will argue, is the reality in which world cities take shape. Local regulation of the global has to be seen as the strategic area of urban politics in world cities. In seeing world city formation both as a locally contingent and as a globally induced process, I suggest four main aspects:

1. Globalization is a relationship fraught with contradictions that play themselves out in the local political sphere.
2. The global city or world city is an important place where globalization takes shape.
3. The articulation of local places within the global economy is centrally dependent on local political struggles.
4. Given the specific function of any world city in the global urban hierarchy, local politics will take on place-specific forms. They reflect both this external relationship of place to space and the internal contradictions of place.

## LOCAL POLITICS

World cities generate specific local politics. Particularly important for the definition of the political sphere of the world city seem to be at least eight political arenas. By arenas I do not intend to mean policy fields in the classical departmental sense of cabinet politics but open discursive fields of relevant issues whose borders are not clearly delineated.[3]

The first arena important for the definition of the political sphere of the world city has to do with the internationalization of the local economy. Often, growth strategies pursued by the local elites are immediately linked to global markets, foreign investment, economic megastructures etc. Local social movement groups at times are aware of operating in such an internationalized environment which expands the boundaries of local politics both conceptually and geographically. In Los Angeles, the internationalization of the local economy has been part of the growth doctrine of the city and county for more than two decades. It was personified in Mayor Bradley's Project World City and carried out through the

*14*
—

redevelopment process and other means. The internationally oriented growth of the urban economy is the most prominent feature of Richard Riordan's political program. Chapters 6–8 deal with the internationalization of urban economic space in Los Angeles.

The second arena or centrally important theme of world city politics is immigration. Global cities' role as international traffic hubs (like airports) and magnets for employment places them in a border situation. Local immigration policies and state practices in dealing with immigration are often different from those of other cities in the same country. And national or regional policy regarding immigration is frequently written using a particular world city as an example or as a threat to the rest of the immigrant country. Los Angeles continues to be a major magnet for immigration, the epitomized border town towards the Third World. In any case, the question of citizenship is going to be decisive in world city politics. It is becoming apparent that the umbrella of national citizenship and naturalization does not suffice to cover the multiple layers of citizenship that characterize life in the world city. As long as citizenship has a ring of national belonging and privilege and not urban and community rights, and as long as citizenship is claimed by the right as a birth right (as it happened to a degree in the debate around Proposition 187), progressive local politics in world cities cannot easily claim the term. Chapter 7 deals with immigrant Los Angeles (see Figure 1.2).

The third arena, partly as a consequence of immigration, is the increased significance of cultural politics and political action linked to various identities. Without a constant negotiation of boundaries, the diverse world city communities that live in close proximity to one another would not be sustainable even for a short time. Any case study of the Los Angeles rebellion will attest to this (Gooding-Williams, 1993). A central concern of this political arena is racism.[4] This arena is addressed in various chapters, but especially in 7, 11 and 12.

The fourth arena is the tendency for cultural politics to gravitate around issues that dichotomize the urban polity into an internationalist camp – backed by the local bourgeoisie championing spectacle and 'world class culture' – versus community culture – as a true *world* culture of immigrant communities that are defending both their new neighborhood identities and their cosmopolitan origins. With cultural politics of the mercenary kind (Davis and Keil, 1992) and acropolis planning (Berelowitz, 1990) in a slump, high culture is in somewhat of a state of distress and elites are in disarray, Los Angeles has recently experienced a reprieve from the rapid pace of the 1980s culture of spectacle, the new Getty Center notwithstanding. Chapters 2, 3, 5, 8 and 9 enter this territory of cultural polarization in the globalized city.

The fifth arena of world city politics is the constant need to strike new territorial compromises between the local and the global, between spaces used as modules of the global economy and places used predominantly for the reproduction of local community. Often these functions overlap and compete in one spatial unit. This is the core of politics in many Los Angeles communities from suburban Chinatown Monterey Park and urban Koreatown to old industrial and Latino Huntington Park, from multiracial Carson in the South Bay, to the Vietnamese communities of Orange County. In each of these communities, immigrant business cultures support and compete with residential communities for space and

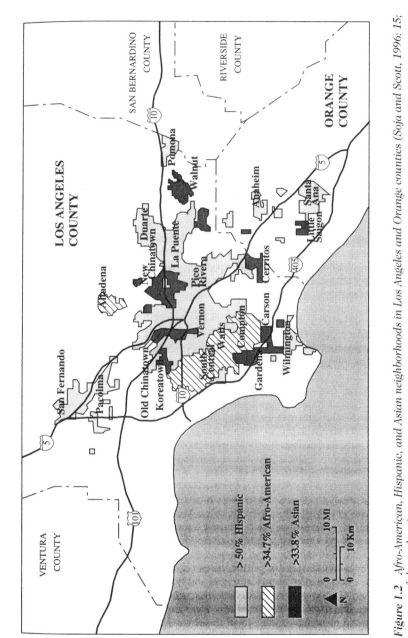

**Figure 1.2** *Afro-American, Hispanic, and Asian neighborhoods in Los Angeles and Orange counties (Soja and Scott, 1996: 15; courtesy of the authors)*

meaning. The traditional competition between exchange value and use value type uses of the city, of course, continues unabatedly. Chapters 6–10 deal with issues of global and local imbrications.

A sixth arena or field of concern are the new types of class struggle generated in the emerging low-wage service and manufacturing sectors that undermine the social compromise of the Fordist era and are part of the establishment of a more flexible and deregulated work environment. An excellent example is the attempt of the Los Angeles Manufacturing Action Project (LAMAP) to organize the low-wage, mostly immigrant manufacturing workers in Los Angeles County (LAMAP, 1995). Chapter 11 provides a narrative of new class struggles in Southern California.

A seventh area of concern in the politics of the world city is social welfare. While social problems are expected to increase during the process of world city formation, the local state seems less and less willing and capable to deal with the rising demands for transfer payments and welfare costs. Despite obvious failures of neoliberal policies since Reagan and Thatcher, the dismantling of the post-World War II welfare state continues apace with workfare, and the privatization of public services in the arsenal of every government locally or internationally. Consequently, questions of social services and collective consumption are likely to be present on any social justice agenda in world cities. The fiscal crises of local government have led to severe cutbacks and threats of cutbacks in social services. In the 1980s, a huge shadow state of social service provision which increasingly was set up to service an internationalized clientele began to partly replace traditional local state functions in welfare provision. Chapters 7, 9 and 11 provide a discussion of collective consumption type conflicts in the global city.

The eighth area which, in some ways, can be seen as the all-encompassing one in which the entire future of the urban region is to be decided and where all social and political conflicts ultimately come together, is the struggle for the sustainability of world cities. The sustainability of world cities depends on the integration of the seven aforementioned political arenas into a new mode of regulation which encompasses societal relationships with nature. Paradoxically, only in this world of near-complete internationalized urbanization, is such a step conceivable. Ecologically sustainable and livable urban environments now can, in fact, only be achieved if we create urban civil societies that live up to the demands of globalization. That is, the societal relationships with nature shaped in today's cities will have to encompass global populations, globalized everyday practices, and internationally diversified gender relations as well as images and uses of nature. A world city environment, then, has to be construed as an array of urban ecologies: 'environments' in the plural. An environmental master plan will be increasingly difficult to imagine in such a context. Politics and policies as well as research agendas for the new urban environments constituted by world city formation need to replace the abstract and generalized concept of 'sustainability' by multiple sustainabilities of active local communities. Networking between these sustainabilities locally and supraregionally remains a main challenge. Since 'environmental racism' is a structural element of a world city's social fabric, the struggle against this type of social injustice has a central role in achieving world city sustainability. An analysis of environmental issues in the process of world city formation in Los Angeles is presented in Chapters 2, 3 and 11.

The challenge of sustainability presents itself mostly as one of urban politics. Sustainability in world cities refers to a specific urban ecology which emerges from a world city's relationship to the global economy and to other world cities. Yet, the discourse on ecology and the construction of the relationships of the human and the natural environments reflect these cities' formation as world cities. Hence, I suggest that world city environmental politics has to be both 'global and local', that it should address the issue of restructuring, and that it needs to locate itself in a context structured by the demands of a pluralized 'postmodern' political realm of multiple contradictions based on class, gender, 'race', ethnicity and sexual identities (Keil, 1995). I would add that in light of the eight arenas identified above, it is perhaps this last one in which most political battles of the coming years will take place. I would argue that it is in the field of environmental justice that local politics finds its currently most comprehensive and challenging testing ground (Pulido, 1994, 1996a,b).[5]

With these arenas or fields of concern as orientation, I will argue in this book that urban politics is an important factor in world city formation and that progressive politics has an important part to play in the local political arena. In the next chapter, I explore some of the utopias that have accompanied and codefined the historical geography of Los Angeles and provided the discursive context of real politics.

# CHAPTER 2

# 'WANNABE-UTOPIAS'

The phrase 'world class city', which came into vogue in the push toward the 1984 Olympic Games, is sound-bite shorthand for cosmopolitanism – a rather more intimidating term. And cosmopolitan is indeed what Los Angeles is in the feverish throes of becoming (Knight, 1990: 7).

Los Angeles looks back upon a rich history of utopian projects which have been realized to varying degrees as programs of urban development and sociospatial design. As historian Kevin Starr wrote in the epilogue of the final report of the LA 2000 Committee, 'Los Angeles envisioned itself, then externalized that vision through sheer force of will, springing from a platonic conception of itself, the Great Gatsby of American cities' (Starr, 1988). Many of these visions never had a chance to be implemented. They remained fragmented 'wannabe-utopias', which sprang directly from the interests of specific segments of the ruling classes of Los Angeles without ever gaining influence over the entire urban society. The class relationships and political structures, the cultural and economic restrictions of Southern California, defied their implementation. When tied to the material urbanization process, such utopias would guide the movement of capital in space. This often was based on a pervasive mythology of Los Angeles as a place different from all other places. Where these mythologies were used to buttress planning and urban development, they tended to appear as unconcealed moments in class struggle with racist overtones.

Sculpted by the dreams and profit interests of the real estate sector, the railway barons and the oil companies, the city has always entertained big plans for a big future. Boosterism was the way of life of the white master race that turned ranchos and orange groves into suburban subdivisions. Their visionary products were the 'wonderful, wild areas of California with silver, golden, diamond, paradisal, rivieral, miramaral, venetian names', which were already admired by German reporter Egon Erwin Kisch in the 1920s (Kisch, 1948). The producers of the myth often were not the developers and landowners themselves but urban intellectuals who designed Southern California in utopian and dystopian images. In most cases, the activities of these intellectuals were directly linked to the growth sectors of the local economy: real estate, agriculture, film, aerospace and more recently high culture and finance. These sectors gave the work of artists and intellectuals an economic base and defined their discursive framework (Davis and Keil, 1992).

In 1969, for example, when the products of Fordist military production from the Los Angeles region found ample use on the battlefields of Indochina, and when local universities were in upheaval, a Los Angeles magazine declared the Middle Ages in Los Angeles to be over: 'The intellectuals, now that we have reached a plateau of fairly widespread economic well-being, are beginning to emerge from their ivory towers and the community is beginning to recognize that

***Plate 2.1*** *Mural West Los Angeles (Roger Keil)*

***Plate 2.2*** *New development, Pearblossom Highway (Roger Keil)*

what it desperately needs is *ideas*.' The public role of the 'new class' of the
intellectual 'technostructure' was tied into their changing function in the local
economy: 'Whereas we once subsisted primarily by selling oranges, real estate, oil
and movies to the world, what Los Angeles sells now is brainpower. . . . Systems,
ideas and life styles' (*Los Angeles*, 1969: 27). Ultimately, intellectuals were
considered capable of holding the balance of power in Los Angeles: 'If their
energy and intelligence can be harnessed they stand an excellent chance of
giving the city that rebirth of hope which it so badly requires' (*Los Angeles*,
1969: 52).

In hindsight, it is clear that the intellectuals and artists of the 1970s, 1980s and
1990s contributed much to the project of the world city. As 'mercenaries' for
international capital which built a citadel for itself in downtown Los Angeles they
overfulfilled all expectations (Davis and Keil, 1992). This role was confirmed and
celebrated in the work of the LA 2000 Committee where intellectuals were given a
key function in the creation of the regional coherence of multicultural society. As
the committee's president confirmed, this involvement was considered part of the
'development of a new intellectual tradition of Southern California'. The annual
report of the committee stated:

> For two centuries, Los Angeles has been a magnet drawing to it individuals seeking
> sunshine, fame or fortune. The efforts and energies of these pioneers, entrepreneurs,
> artists and intellectuals created a great city. Today, individuals, citizens of Los
> Angeles, look ahead to the year 2000, aware that our collective actions will shape the
> evolution of our city (LA 2000, 1988: 2).

This confusion of the producers of myth with the builders of the city is a pervasive
ideological figure at a place where the view of the urban masses who built the city
was mostly obstructed. Planned as a pure, white city, Los Angeles at all times
struggled with the conceptual integration of its 'swarthy and checkered history'
(Krieger, 1986). Purity, sunshine, health, and the culture of the good life have been
the metaphors in which the discursive and bloody battles of the region's dominant
classes have historically been waged; such metaphors eclipse the impure, deva-
stated, sick, antihuman and violent real history. What we are looking at, then, is a
tradition of pervasive arcadian mythology: the planning of an Aryan paradise
failing to account for its ruthless but impossible historical implementation (Davis
and Keil, 1992). The production of urban images implied the programmatic
exclusion of people of color and of the working classes from the imaginary reality,
from the riches and from the power of the urban region.[1] This model of exclusion
also helped define the notion of a world class city whose deproletarianized and
whitewashed image stood in clear contrast to the social and economic reality of
world city formation. On the one hand, in Kevin Starr's sense, Los Angeles was
self-conceived and a product of its homegrown mythologies. On the other hand,
the urban region also became a favorite object of external mythologies which
complemented and completed internal lore. In most cases, the city was depicted in
extremes that changed with intellectual fashions and economic cycles (Rosenstiel,
1989).

***Plate 2.3*** *Disneyland, 'it's a small world' (Roger Keil)*

## A METROPOLITAN VILLAGE

The metropolitan character of Los Angeles always had to be reaffirmed in order to counter the myth of the 'enormous village' which was plausible to visitors and inhabitants of the city as an epistemological tool but hardly lent itself as a slogan for urban development. When the Pacific Southwest Academy in Los Angeles published the preliminary studies for a general plan for Los Angeles in the beginning of the 1940s, Clarence Dykstra addressed exactly this problem in his introduction: 'Los Angeles is one of the great cities of the world. In fact, it is more than a city; it is a metropolis' (Dykstra, 1941: 3). In calling Los Angeles one of the great cities of the world, the city is assigned the 'normal' urbanity. In the same volume, however, Richard Neutra, architect and builder of modernist Los Angeles, provides evidence for the parallel rhetoric of exceptionalism. Neutra reports that the participants of the Congrès Internationaux d'Architecture Moderne (CIAM) in Brussels in 1930 produced depictions of dozens of cities at the same scale:

> The scale and symbols were found well-suited for practically all world-cities except Los Angeles. For this metropolis the chosen scale produced a monstrously oversized chart. The numerous sectional mounts necessary to compose the Los Angeles map filled huge walls of the exhibition hall, practically monopolizing the space. The required symbolic indications, such as the location of workers' quarters, garden districts, cottage suburbs, multi-storey apartments, slum and blighted areas, and business zones, quite easily noted on European and east American city maps, were shown to be almost ridiculously inapplicable when charting Los Angeles. A map produced according to this established set of rules became a huge and strange jungle of misunderstandings, not possible of interpretation even by connoisseurs and experts (Neutra, 1941: 189).

The concern of the local elites about the acceptance of the urban character of Los Angeles is mostly reflected in their continuous attempts to replace 'provincialism' with 'cosmopolitanism'. Attempts of this sort, particularly in the cultural area, can be observed historically up until the current project to constitute the world class city: 'Today, the city is straddled between the worldliness and its numbing inverse, the deep-seated provincialism, that long ago made it the Official National Joke in matters cultural' (Knight, 1990).[2]

In the definition of the urban in Los Angeles we find the elements of later visions and utopias. Problems are identified as consequences of the same growth processes that engendered metropolitanization and exceptionalism in the first place: 'For there are disadvantages as well as advantages in continuing growth, in the development of outlying areas and in the rapid increase of functions, overlapping organizations, and interrelated problems. Los Angeles cannot now, in its moments of pride, overlook the responsibilities which stem from the presence of millions within its circle of influence' (Dykstra, 1941: 3).

Between the longing for urbanity and the discounting of growth, Los Angeles has been caught in a vicious cycle in which the identification of development goals always leads back to the same dilemmas; growth creates problems which it cannot solve by itself. The only option open to the growth process is to project strategies of solutions into the future, that is, to continue propelling growth itself (Prigge, 1988: 210). Growth remains the centerpiece of urban discourse in Los Angeles although what we once knew as the Los Angeles growth machine collapsed during the 1980s and 1990s (Fulton, 1997). Historically, the discussion about growth has always taken place in the mirror of the struggle of different fragments of the ruling classes in Southern California for centralization or decentralization.[3]

## SHARING THE DREAM: PLACE MAKING IN THE WORLD CLASS CITY

One centralized vision was provided by the LA 2000 Committee during the 1980s. In 1985, Tom Bradley, the mayor of Los Angeles, appointed 84 citizens under the chair of Bank of America's chief executive, James P. Miscoll and the presidency of Jane Pisano to draft a strategic plan intent on articulating a vision for Los Angeles and to build popular consensus around it. Eventually, up to 150 people served on the respective committees. Work plan and procedure of the committee reflected the new international confidence of Los Angeles: supposedly, the plan was to uncover the indigenous needs of a population in a process which was increasingly experienced as having been determined by exogenous global forces: 'The result will be a future which the people of Los Angeles want and shape rather than a future determined by external forces which we chose to ignore' (LA 2000, 1986: 1). Not surprisingly, the bulk of the committee's members were far from being representative of the needs of the general populace. The lack of critical potential when it came to analyzing the present precluded LA 2000's capacity to make sense of the future.

When the committee's final report was published in 1988, the future of Los Angeles appeared dissected into five neatly organized sections: livable communities, environmental quality, individual fulfillment, enriching diversity and 'a crossroads city'. Each section was equipped with a 'hardware' (law and justice, infrastructure,

**Plate 2.4** *At the time when LA 2000 was active, the city's homeless populated a dusty campground in the east of the downtown (Roger Keil)*

literacy, 'art as a bridge', and economic development respectively) and a 'software' (growth management, environmental management, education for a twenty-first century, social services and international strategies) (LA 2000, 1988). In sum, this was the *projection* of a regulated and efficient environment, in which every aspect of urban life is organized into small, controllable units, whose purpose is to serve the whole. In other words, the plan lays out the requested social and economic division of labor of capitalism's twenty-first-century model city in the Southland.

The LA 2000 Committee and its brainchild, the Downtown Strategic Plan, wanted to build regional unity under the hegemony of the increasingly inter-nationalized downtown bourgeoisie, a project already partly realized in the vertical and horizontal growth of the central city as expressed in the Opening Vision Statement of the Downtown Strategic Plan Advisory Committee in 1989:

> Fifteen years ago the SILVER BOOK articulated a vision for the future of downtown Los Angeles. Much of that vision has been realized. It is now time for that vision to evolve, just as our community continues to evolve. We thus offer the following initial statement of our vision of downtown Los Angeles. Upon completion our study perios (sic), a final vision statement will mature, complete with specific goals, objectives, and recommendations for implementations. We believe the opportunity is at hand for Los Angeles to more fully become a classic world city, full of life, diversity and

excitement – with identity and character growing from its history, its history and culture. It is clear to us, even at the outset of our work, that bold plans need to be offered and implemented to complete our urban center (Downtown Strategic Plan Committee, 'Opening Vision Statement', September 28, 1989).

Meanwhile, other 'place entrepreneurs'[4] were creating a unified utopian vision for a future Los Angeles that would consist of 'urban village' cores. The boosters of downtown indulged in a utopia that looked like the cleaned up kid-brother of the *Blade Runner* scenario – a dense urban concrete megaworld with high-tech transit and 'intelligent' buildings inhabited by a new breed of office worker urbanites. In contrast, the '25-Downtown-Solution' for the regional future was made up of images of a simpler, 'kinder and gentler', preurban past (Leinberger, 1988; Leinberger and Lockwood, 1986).

The urban-village concept 'represented a quest for old-fashioned social order' in an urban reality whose features already seem beyond explicability and grasp. Although the 'urban village' concept suggested less urban density, it in fact tended to multiply urbanization manifold. Thus, while proponents of the concept praised the technical and financial – sometimes also political – benefits and efficiencies of a decentralized city, critics pointed out that, 'in part, the purpose behind the densely populated urban village is for developers to make maximum use of a shrinking supply of land' (Clifford, 1989: A, 1). Whereas the developers and entre-preneurs who continue to boost the polycentric outer-city model fall in line with the neo-Jeffersonian ideals and myths of decentralized democracy put forward by the middle-class slow-growth movement in Southern California, they in fact advocate nothing short of an even distribution of profits for the area's real estate industry. The proposed development of urban village cores would be a collective regional exercise in planning from the top down. Utopia would become an institutional enterprise: 'Government, developers and business must formulate a more satisfying vision of what the newly created as well as the existing urban village cores should be' (Leinberger, 1989: V, 5). By comparison, then, both the centralized and the decentralized 'wannabe'-utopias have long and competing traditions in the Southland. However, the LA 2000's solution resembled the more unitarian discourse of the modern utopia, simultaneously imperialist both in the region and the world, corporatist and comprehensive as a social project. The decentralized 'solution' operated on a discursive plane which can be characterized as postmodern: it hails the vernacular, is pluralistic, entrepreneurial and, in its rhetoric, an affair of private business. Both aspects, however, continue to coexist as two potential plans for action. In the post-uprising image of a rebuilt Los Angeles, the need for a reconciliation of the competing centralized/decentralized visions became all apparent (Rebuild LA, 1997).

The visions which accompanied the Fordist period of urbanization in Los Angeles were predominantly contained in the borders of the national economy and the regional geography. International references did not yet belong to the set of relevant rhetorics that dominated the discourse in Los Angeles. Even the long term plan – called *Silverbook* because of its silver color jacket cover – which a citizen committee submitted to Mayor Yorty in 1972 only spoke of regional center functions for the downtown and national major central functions for the region. This occurred even though the *Silverbook* worked out the visionary and planning

**Plate 2.5** *Downtown skyline at night (Roger Keil)*

guidelines which should be used to erect the world city citadel in Los Angeles (Committee for Central City Planning, 1972).

The integration of internationalization into the local rhetoric happened slowly but steadily thereafter. The overwhelming ideological tradition of the 'pure white' city, however, prevented a simple paradigm shift. Only towards the end of the 1970s were there indications of an internationalization of the vision of urban development in Los Angeles. At first, internationalization was recognized as a problem which was expected to emerge from future growth processes. The Agenda '77 Committee – which, under the chair of UCLA planner Harvey Perloff, submitted a work program to Mayor Bradley in 1977 – identified the international character of the city as a mixed blessing that lay beyond local control:

> One problem which is national in scope, but particularly severe in local impact – that of undocumented aliens – we frankly found largely beyond us. Trends suggest that in the not-too-distant future, say over the next two decades, Los Angeles will be mainly a Latin city. Obviously, this will impact both the nature of the City's problems and the realistic measures that will be needed to meet such problems (Agenda '77 Committee, 1977: 2).

This rhetoric acknowledges the incipient internationalization of Los Angeles but it also views it as external to urbanization in Los Angeles: internationalization as a supraurban problem.

Only in the newer visions and projects does internationalization, finally, appear as a positive element of the rhetoric. Since the beginning of the 1980s – particularly since the 1984 Olympics, which denoted Los Angeles, without doubt, globally as '*the* place' – the hegemonic rhetoric has begun to address the unique/

***Plate 2.6*** *Toytown, Skid Row (Roger Keil)*

paradigmatic character of an internationalized Los Angeles directly as a trademark of Southern California and a fertile matrix of future development.

In recent years, urbanist phantasies have increasingly been connected to and contextualized in discourses on nature and environment (Keil and Graham, 1998). Two major fields in which conflicting notions of environmentalism have served as narrative and discursive planes for the development of larger regional designs in Los Angeles are the fight against air pollution and discussions around flood control and land-use policies at the Los Angeles River. Planning and policy documents regarding these two cases, as well as statements by members of the policy community, express conflicting notions of control, management and environmental regulation that define the specific relationship of urban ecology, the economy, the local state and local civil society. The documents include consecutive versions of the South Coast Air Quality Management District's (SCAQMD) Air Quality Management Plans (1989, 1991, 1994, 1997), the LACDA agreement (1995) and the draft Los Angeles River Master Plan (Los Angeles County Department of Public Works, 1995).[5]

There is, of course, no unity among urban elites, particularly when there are competing hegemonic projects, as is the case in Los Angeles. The documents in question are also negotiating platforms on which struggles around the meaning of urban environments and on the role of civil society in regulating these can be waged (see Bloch and Keil, 1991). The very idea of hegemony implies that elite positions intersect with popular interests in various socio-spatial domains and can only be kept apart analytically. In practice, ideologies and actions mix in the policy process in an unpredictable way. Mass homeownership, fiscal conservatism, and racism have been typical features of popular ideologies while different segments of the ruling classes of Los Angeles have been in notorious disagreement on the future of the region for decades.

*Plate 2.7* *Watts, organic garden (Roger Keil)*

*Plate 2.8* *Ecological modernization, Los Angeles (Roger Keil)*

Sectoral competition plays into spatial and class competition in the urban environment of Los Angeles, where political incorporation has meant rigid socio-spatial segregation. Issues such as air pollution in an entire airshed and land use policies for an entire watershed will lead to conflict among various elite groups representing the subspaces and partial economic interests of these areas. Ecological modernization (Hajer, 1995) has been a contentious proposition in Southern California.

## CONCLUSION

The utopian answer is both global and secular: in an age when the 'end of history' has been announced, local government agencies have taken on projects of meta-historical proportions. The pathos of these utopias is their stubborn insistence on unified regional regulatory powers at a time when the movement of capital in space perversely fragments the city. In reality, they are rather mere 'wannabe'-utopias, hegemonic, discursive projects that serve as the syndicated basis for political negotiation in the years to come. In concluding the narratives presented in this chapter, I would like to suggest three areas in which Los Angeles is currently remaking itself. In each of these areas, I argue, political conflict has defined the scope and reach of the wannabe-utopias discussed above.

One narrative is hegemonic but not entirely without merit for the attempt to create a better urban society in Los Angeles. It is the attempt, of government and private sector institutions, to create new forms of governance that will redefine the political space that is Los Angeles. Prominent examples include the intended regulation of air pollution through the SCAQMD which encompasses the nondesert areas of four southern Californian counties and 13 million people; and the growing political influence of the voluntary intercity governing agency Southern California Association of Government (SCAG), which includes 188 cities in six counties. Other hegemonic projects to pull the region together ideologically on a somewhat smaller scale have been the Rebuild LA effort since the 1992 riots, and the continuing redevelopment of the downtown which has recently come to be supported by a high-price, commuter (rather than community) oriented, rail-based transportation policy including subways, light rail and regional trains radially converging in the downtown of Los Angeles. These institutions and projects, their policies and regulations as well as their planning and political practice, attempt to implant a new sense of Los Angeles as a city, as a unified political space. In the absence of a unified elite strategy, this process which is driven by the traditional and emergent power centers of Los Angeles nevertheless leaves cracks and niches where counterhegemonic forces can make their mark.

The second, alternative, tendency to establish a larger political community in the city is represented by social movement groups and other initiatives coming out of civil society. Among such initiatives are the campaigns of the Labor/Community Strategy Center (L/CSC) which has consistently challenged the hegemonic spatial narrative of the Los Angeles area. When, in the early 1980s, General Motors wanted to close its last production site in Southern California, the Van Nuys plant in north Los Angeles, auto workers and community activists fought the multinational's conception of space as abstract, global economic space in which decisions in a Detroit corporate boardroom could unidirectionally affect communities in Los Angeles. Proposing instead a radical concept of 'regional planning from below', the Coalition to Keep GM Van Nuys Open fought the plant closing successfully for almost a decade, positing that the workers and the community had a right to a commitment by General Motors to maintain production in the area. From the shop floor, this coalition moved into the larger community in the late 1980s, and the L/CSC was born. This organization has been monitoring and contesting the lopsided, business-oriented and undemocratic air pollution control measures put forward by the SCAQMD since 1989. The center has become one of the first voices in the US of the emergent movement against environmental racism and for environmental justice. In 1994, the center's watchdog organization was instrumental in organizing a Bus Riders Union (BRU). The campaign led to a temporary restraining order against the Metropolitan Transit Authority's attempts to raise fares and to eliminate most discount passes. Large-scale mobilization of both movement activists and community people as well as broad recognition in the political debate also characterized the L/CSC's campaigns to develop a Rebuild LA from the Bottom-up strategy after the rebellion in 1992; to intervene in the debate on California's Proposition 187 in 1994 which aimed at barring undocumented immigrants from certain government services like schools or medical care(see Chapter 11).

Finally, there is another strategy to reappropriate the political through the reorganization of space: 'progressive cities'. While the fragmentation of the political territory in Southern California into dozens of small incorporated cities has historically been an instrument of class and racial segregation, it has, in the recent past, also created the possibilities for smaller communities to establish progressive municipal administrations. In Santa Monica, a coalition of middle-class radicals and renters have been able to sustain a progressive regime since 1979. A strict rent control law, managed urban growth and – for a while – an exemplary homeless policy have been the most consistent 'progressive' features of this seaside community which has also experienced large-scale gentrification and economic expansion. West Hollywood, a city which was only incorporated in 1984, brought together a majority tenant population and a strong lesbian and gay community to form a municipality which can still be considered pathbreaking in questions of social policy, human rights and rent control. While these west-side communities are fairly well-off in socioeconomic terms, poorer communities on the east side have also been experimenting with new municipal strategies to revive their deindustrialized economic base, to discuss sustainable development and to build links with other progressive municipal initiatives around Southern California (see Chapter 10).

# CHAPTER 3
# SPACE, NATURE AND CIVIL SOCIETY

In the beginning man (*sic*, R.K.) created the city and its environs. It was a place of beauty and possessed of great natural charm. The earth brought forth green things, the sky sparkled and so did the waters of the ocean. Other men heard about the mecca – and they, too, sought it out.

The newcomers arrived singly but many came in waves brought on by wars, economic pestilence, and the emergence of the city as a major center of technology in man's time. Although it was built upon sand, mixed with oil, the city learned how to tap its greatest need: water. Soon it flourished and so did many – although not all – of those who dwelt there. The people of the city produced celluloid products called movies and citrus and complex instruments which could conquer inner and outer space (but they could not help the people where they lived). In time, they produced even their own way-of-life and there came forth barbecues and swimming pools, colorful costumes and ceramic artifacts. The city's inhabitants toiled hard but they also paid homage to a great god whose name was fun and this made the land more valuable. All of the products of that place were marketed by the people from the city and its environs (by that time, many believed the latter to be the former). As a result, still more men heard of this fabulous Eden and they, too, moved there.

Soon the city became both wide and long; a low dense land of concrete, wood and stucco, looped together by great cement serpents. These connected its parts but they could not join its people. And when it was very late, the inhabitants looked out toward where the horizon used to be. They saw it had changed and a mist went up. . .
(Preamble of the Summary Report of the Los Angeles Goals Council, November 1969).

There is something haunting in this poetic history of modern human settlement in Los Angeles. External nature and humanity are seen in a fateful embrace: a paradisal lure leads to increased urbanization which in turn destroys both, 'nature' in its natural form and 'society' in its civil form. Ecologies and people are disjointed from themselves and from each other. Both are constantly re-created in their negativity: pollution and social crisis.

Contemplating the relationship between nature and civil society in Los Angeles poses a problem from the start, for most people would assume that nature and civil society are two concepts which do not have a useful referent in the Southern California metropolis.[1] When we hear about Los Angeles, 'social' never comes without qualifiers like 'problems', 'unrest', 'pathology'. Nature is seen as non-existent, manufactured or dangerous. After all, Los Angeles is the ultimate site of disaster, earthquake, floods, droughts and fire. To many Europeans and eastern Americans who look at the landscapes of Southern California, there is little to appreciate in the city's natural beauty. To these observers, a natural desert (considered 'worthless' in their eyes) is covered by a manufactured cultural desert of facades and falsities (i.e. Hollywood). Many exiles and expatriates (important since they have written extensively about Los Angeles) have been as cynical in their judgement as reporter Egon Erwin Kisch: 'Everybody knows that Hollywood is a paradise, a fairy garden, a land of magic. We would like to add, however, that no garden-city on the entire globe is situated on a more cheerless, dreadful, infertile

32

***Plate 3.1*** *'Matterhorn', Disneyland (Roger Keil)*

place than Hollywood. It was a wasteland, before the film industry located here because of the strength of the sunlight and the lack of rain, and it has remained a wasteland since.'[2] Both nature and civil society are not ready-made categories in Los Angeles and need to be reconstructed as objects of our analysis before we can relate them to one another. This reconstruction is based on the awareness, of course, that nature does not have to be 'natural' in the pastoral or pristine sense; and civil society does not have to be civil.

## CIVIL SOCIETY

Los Angeles has existed in the popular American (and global) imaginary as the anti-city, a place where the urban as a form of historiogeographical human achievement does not exist. While New York has been cast as LA's oppositional urban model, and, in fact, the ultimate human living space, the *oikoumene*, Arthur Krim has shown how Los Angeles figured in the national imagination as terra *incognita*, the unknown, suburban territory (Krim, 1992: 121). No density, no street life, no soul, no places to linger, no salons, and hardly any sidewalk cafes! Ergo, where there is no public, there can be no civil society. Automobiles have eaten urban society and low density has destroyed what was left of urban community. There is no reason why the following passage from Jane Jacobs' *Death and Life* (first published in 1961) could not also be found in a contemporary depiction of Los Angeles:

> Los Angeles is an extreme example of a metropolis with little public life, depending mainly instead on contacts of a more private social nature. . . . Such a metropolis lacks means for bringing together necessary ideas, necessary enthusiasms, necessary money. Los Angeles is embarked on a strange experiment: trying to run not just projects, not just gray areas, but a whole metropolis, by dint of 'togetherness' or nothing. I think this is an inevitable outcome for great cities whose people lack city public life in ordinary living and working (Jacobs, 1993 [1961]: 95–96).[3]

What is missing in Jacobs' portrait of Los Angeles – which rests on assumptions about certain links between city form and social organization – is urban civil society. We could have left the task of refuting Jacobs' vilification of Los Angeles to the unfaltering authority of Reyner Banham's resurrection of Southern California in his *Los Angeles: The Architecture of Four Ecologies* (1971) – still one of the most incisively insightful books on Los Angeles more than a quarter century after its first publication – had it not been for the persistence until today of the common perception of Los Angeles as an unlivable city.[4]

The creeping unease that characterizes urban society in Joan Didion's *White Album* (1979) erupted into full-fledged misery and mass discomfort in the two decades after The Doors and Charles Manson. In particular, the 1980s have added insult to injury in the reality and the construction of Los Angeles as a bad and uncivilized place. This depiction has taken two forms. One was gradual and evolutionary, one was explosive and catastrophic: on the one hand, Los Angeles entered its formative years as a 'world city', which authors of the 'LA School' have widely analyzed as a comprehensive process of urban restructuring. Illustrated by the powerful imagery of the *Blade Runner* scenario, the narrative of internationalization and economic change has turned Los Angeles, with its sweatshops, mean streets and social contradictions, into a 'Dickensian hell' of a new *fin de siècle*. Notions of Los Angeles as the capital of the Pacific Rim and of the twenty-first century as well as a Third World city in the First World have become the matter of folklore and scholarly writing alike. The decade ended with a paradoxical event. Mike Davis, perhaps LA's greatest critic/promoter since Carey McWilliams, hurled his *City of Quartz* (1990) into the public domain and – unintentionally I am sure – gave people around the world (many of whom had never been in Los Angeles) a sophisticated excuse to enshrine their misgivings about the place in a legitimate discourse of LA-bashing.[5]

The other way in which Los Angeles entered the global public imaginary as a bad place was the sequence of events following the Rodney King beating, particularly the 1992 rebellion. Violence, racism and unruliness became the hallmarks of a civilization gone awry, a kind of perpetual Beirut or Sarajevo, a city beyond salvage and redemption. In the context of this chapter, it is necessary to add that, as time progressed, the social upheaval of 1992 has been less and less contextualized in terms of the restructuring processes described above and more in terms of the series of 'natural' catastrophes (fire, floods and earthquakes) that hit the region in the early 1990s. Bring on the locusts!

34
—

***Plate 3.2*** *Makeshift shelter after 1987 earthquake (Roger Keil)*

How does this image of Los Angeles need to be corrected? Certainly, Los Angeles is an unusually violent place full of social and economic contradictions, injustice and conflict. But the existence of a civil society is impossible to deny. Traditional ideas of urban civility and urbanity (of the Jane Jacobs kind) never sufficed for understanding Los Angeles. Moreover, our modernist concept of how people of various social classes, 'races', ethnicities, gender etc. live together in a city do not do the Southern California metropolis justice. Los Angeles remains opaque to the explanatory powers of both the specific bourgeois urbanity of the modernist period and to its critics. The former rested on the separation of an insular bourgeois civility from the dangerous classes segregated into working-class suburbs or inner-city slums. The urban masses of the modernist city only gained access to the elitist temple of modernity (read civil society) at the elite's arbitrary will. They were excluded as a rule. The critics of the bourgeois view of urbanity have not done much better themselves. The rationality of the progressive critique of the bourgeois city often was a mere negative image of what the dominant classes of the region called urban life. Carey McWilliams and Mike Davis with their brilliant analyses notwithstanding, generations of immigrant and domestic left-wing intellectuals have failed – perhaps until recently – to develop a powerful counternarrative to the elite visions of Los Angeles. The city has not been well understood, nor have viable political and social alternatives been created.

The failure to capture the contradictory civility of Los Angeles in a politically meaningful way, that is, to understand how the society of Los Angeles regulates itself (or not), has been a contributing factor in creating the quotidian and catastrophic dynamics which have defined Southern California. A brief glance into the history of Los Angeles might bring some clarity here. Since 1781, the City of the Angels had combined the violent reality of a frontier town with the will of its political classes to found a new civilization. The often millenary attempts of white visionaries and missionaries to re-create their eastern or midwestern origins on the Pacific Coast were exclusionary from the start. The native people, who had almost been extinguished under the rule of the missions, became invisible appendices to Yankee rule, as did those who came later: Mexicans, Chinese, African Americans and finally, in more recent years, immigrants from the southern hemisphere. Civility in Los Angeles was a form of white domination: 'This was white power at its most powerful' (Dunne, 1991: 28).

Both restructuring and rebellion have called this 200-year-old structure of domination into question. Particularly after the uprising of 1992, the entire fabric of civility in Los Angeles was in tatters. It remains to be seen what will replace it in the long term. One aspect has already become obvious in the process: the hundreds of thousands of working-class Angelenos, most of them people of color (who are a majority in the city), have begun to claim spaces of alternative civility that represent a major challenge to the anglo, middle-class society Los Angeles was believed to be. Excluded from the benefits of world city formation, these communities have started to build a civil society from below: in churches, labor unions, political organizations, environmental groups, neighborhood associations and other forms, the poor and disenfranchised of Los Angeles have created a network of democratic self-organization. This counterstrategy has been a *popular civility* which questions the racism, the bigotry, the sexism and the class rule that had characterized the model of civil society that persisted for the past two centuries. The result has been an *insurgent civil society* which has been mostly unnoticed in the common descriptions of Los Angeles as a place of ultimate evil (Keil, 1993: 8, 297). Los Angeles, then, refers us back to the critical interpretation we find in the writings of Marx who viewed civil society as a dehumanizing space at worst and as a space of conflict and struggle at best.[6]

## NATURE

> Thus primary nature may persist, albeit in a completely acquired and false way, within 'second nature' – witness urban reality (Lefebvre, 1991: 229).

> No grass grows in Hollywood (Kisch, 1948: 288).

Nature has had a mixed career in Los Angeles. Few observers have sung the praises of Southern California as expressly as Carey McWilliams in the following passage from his famous: *Southern California: An Island on the Land* (1979 [1946]: 4–5). Entering Southern California from the north or the east is a profound experience of the senses and 'even the most obtuse observer, the rankest neophyte, can feel that he has entered a new and distinct province of the state [of California]. . . . The mountains no longer shut off the interior from the sea. The air is softer, the ocean bluer, and the skies have a lazy and radiant warmth. South of Point Conception, a new Pacific Ocean emerges: an ocean in which you can actually bathe and swim, an ocean that sparkles with sunlight, an ocean of many and brilliant colors. Here is

***Plate 3.3*** *Venice Beach, Los Angeles (Roger Keil)*

California del Sur, the Cow Countries, sub-tropical California, the land South of Tehachapi.' Since European colonization of the area, the landscapes of Southern California have henceforth served as canvas on which real estate development and industrialization have inscribed themselves. Originally a mix of agriculture, ranching and resorts, the area became the home of the most extensive industrial ensemble outside of the Ruhr Valley and a virtual symbol of degraded natural environments, built on water imperialism and freeway concrete.

Much has been written about 'the constitutive role of landscape in the emergence of Southern California. A picturesque conjugation of beach, desert, mountain and citrus grove – emblazoned on millions of postcards and orange crate labels – once defined Los Angeles in the imagination of the entire world. Nature, wild or domesticated, provided the essential "use-value" supports for the greatest continuous real-estate boom in history' (Davis, 1994a: 39).[7] The *biological* concept of growth has nowhere been turned as successfully into a *social* category as with regards to LA: 'Growth was the business of Los Angeles', writes John Gregory Dunne in a typical characterization of Los Angeles, 'from the mountains to the desert, from the desert to the sea, as the jingle of a local radio station repeats over and over every day' (Dunne, 1991: 28). Even critical analyses of Los Angeles' urbanization place 'growth' in the center of their narrative as if it was a natural force (for a recent example see Soja and Scott, 1996). In the replacement of fields and orchards by houses and streets, the natural condition of urban settlement became its threatening 'other'. The Los Angeles River is a case in point. Described as a 'beautiful river' by the first Spanish explorers with 'much water easy to take on either bank' (Los Angeles County Department of Public Works, 1995: 104), it later became a threat (floods) and a stand-in for urban and social decay: its 'prime purpose' of being a flood control channel makes the riparian ecology 'rest-nature'; in popular representations (including in the many films that use the river as a race

**Plate 3.4** *Los Angeles, ca. 1870. Oil/canvas detail (James Doolin, artist); An original work of art, owned and commissioned by the Los Angeles Metropolitan Transportation Authority (Photograph: Roger Keil; reproduced by permission of the artist)*

track or in the Red Hot Chili Peppers' song 'Under the Bridge') the river is site and source of criminal and deviant behavior. The domesticization and trivialization of the mediterraneanesque natural conditions in millions of front and backyards proceeded apace. But behind the retaining walls and flood sewers lurked California's bad side: landscape as a monster that lifted its head over and over again to devour humans and beasts in what some have described as virtual nemetic experiences (McPhee, 1989; Davis, 1995a).

Let me entertain a few common depictions of Los Angeles' nature. In an essay on the dialectic of ordinary disaster in Los Angeles, Mike Davis has argued succinctly that representations of the nature of Los Angeles have suffered historically from the misunderstandings which Anglo-American newcomers brought to the region's ecologies. Expecting humid, temperate climes, these new Californians mistook the mediterranean landscapes of the Southland for an arid desert (Davis, 1995a: 224). This misrepresentation had two dimensions. First, they led to a misreading of natural cycles of water and types of vegetation as well as to the possibilities for farming and ranching. Water was seen mostly as a product of technologically based import rather than as a local – limited – resource. Irrigation technology and water engineering became part of a self-fulfilling prophecy of urbanization versus desertification. Water was the commodity of possibility and the human-controlled source of regional growth and development. While the mediterranean landscape continued to fuel the production of myth and real estate, its material ecology was marginalized conceptually and physically. Second, the shallow version of mediterraneanism was an excellent tool for 'selling sunshine, not earthquakes and deluges', which would rather be linked to the 'deep mediterraneity' shaped by droughts, floods, landslides and earthquakes (Davis, 1995a: 225). And Davis continues: 'Nothing so distinguishes Southern California from classical Anglo-American environments as the contrasting roles of extreme events or catastrophes. . . . High-intensity, low frequency events ("disasters") are the ordinary agents of landscape and ecological change' (Davis, 1995a: 227).

The engineered hydraulic society (Sambale, 1994; Gottlieb and FitzSimmons, 1991) of Southern California is always in danger of succumbing to either extraordinary or ordinary disasters. Hardly any 'buffer against temperamental Mediterranean nature' is left (Davis, 1995a: 235). Costs for the quotidian regulation of socioecological crisis – that is, preventing or dealing with the consequences of fires, earthquakes and floods – are already becoming prohibitive (Palm and Hodgson, 1992). The urban region has outgrown its capacity to engineer a natural veneer over a cataclysmic natural base.

Davis's take on the catastrophic landscape of Southern California is one pole of a dialectical relationship in which nature in Los Angeles has been seen as either nonexistent or – as in Davis's argument – of overriding importance as human-made or as a threatening structural condition of human life in the region. In Banham's Los Angeles (1971), this dialectic is obvious. The British architecture historian chooses three ecologies – the beaches, the foothills and the plains – for their natural-topographical qualities in structuring human life in the region. A fourth one, surprisingly, has no immediate natural base: it is Autopia, the freeway system, which 'in its totality is now a single comprehensible place, a coherent state of mind, a complete way of life, the fourth ecology of the Angeleno' (Banham, 1971: 213). As in the opening quote, nature in Los Angeles is both a lost or paved paradise and a hellish death trap. Nature in Los Angeles comes in its most destroyed and its most destructive form.

The first three ecologies in Banham's Los Angeles – hills, plains and beaches – are connected through a system of watersheds: 'The San Gabriel River, the Los Angeles River, and the Big Tujunga (Bigta Hung-ga) are the principal streams that enter the urban plain' (McPhee, 1989: 194). This watershed from the mountain to the sea is the structural topography on which all Los Angeles' societal relationships with nature unfold. It is the 'in-between' of snow-capped peaks and ocean:

> Los Angeles is overmatched on one side by the Pacific Ocean and on the other by very high mountains. With respect to these principal boundaries, Los Angeles is done sprawling. The San Gabriels, in their state of tectonic youth, are rising as rapidly as any range on earth. Their loose inimical slopes flout the tolerance of the angle of repose. Rising straight up out of the megalopolis, they stand ten thousand feet above the nearby sea, and they are not kidding with this city. Shedding, spalling, self-destructing, they are disintegrating at a rate that is also among the fastest in the world. The phalanxed communities of Los Angeles have pushed themselves hard against these mountains, an aggression that requires a deep defense budget to contend with the results (McPhee, 1989: 184).

The mountains are slowly being carried to the sea. Yet, since protective flood control measures have attempted to shield the plains from overrun and debris (e.g. through the establishment of debris basins and concreted channels), little sand arrives at the beaches today. The built environment (the human made fourth ecology in an extension of Banham's Autopia) has broken the chain of events that connect the mountains and the ocean through the floodplains in-between. Los

**Plate 3.5**  *Rest-nature, port of Los Angeles (Roger Keil)*

Angeles overall, not just at its northern borders, as McPhee tells us, is built witness of 'the confrontation of the urban and the wild' (McPhee, 1989: 184).

## REPRESENTATIONS OF NATURE

The result of this confrontation has been the wild urban nature of Los Angeles which has been both backdrop and topic of widespread artistic, scholarly and popular representations. In these representations, we find implicit statements on nature, civil society and the city. Let us – appropriately – begin with motion pictures, the city's most prominent art form.

Michelangelo Antonioni's *Zabriskie Point* is the story of Mark, a student who gets involved in a demonstration on a Southern California university campus. In an ensuing shootout, Mark thinks he will be held for the killing of a policeman, a crime he did not commit, and flees. Stealing a small aircraft, he flies east into the desert. Leaving the city behind, he sees below him a woman in a car. Daria, the woman, is on her way to Arizona to link up with her boss who is a developer of exurban megaprojects. Mark and Daria meet and make love in the desert sand of Death Valley at Zabriskie Point. Attempting to take the plane back to Los Angeles, Mark is killed by the police. When Daria hears of the death of her lover on the radio, she imagines blowing up her boss's luxury bungalow, located in the pristine wilderness of the desert. To the chilling sound of Pink Floyd's 'Careful with that axe, Eugene', we see, from every camera angle possible, the building and its interior – including the refrigerator and the furniture – explode.

Antonioni's intended critique of the consumer society of the 1960s provides us with a forbiddingly dystopian view of Los Angeles. What we see is a city mired in violence and political disruption from which Mark and Daria are trying to escape.

At the same time, however, the subtext of the film has it that the developers, in a frightening version of the fable of the tortoise and the hare, are already planning to export Los Angeles to the most remote of places. We are caught in a vicious circle in which the escape from Los Angeles will always lead us back to the city. Inevitably, the construction of nature as an escape route is being blocked by the recognition that the city now seems to predate the natural environment.

Mark and Daria's journey eastward from Los Angeles connects *absolute natures*,[8] antipodes of our cultural understanding of nature: the water and the land, the ocean and the desert. These transformed 'absolute natures' have become part of the mythology of Los Angeles:

> [A]ccounts of Southern California are besotted with metaphysical generalizations about cars and water. The region's infamous sprawling geometry is universally attributed to the automobile (primus mobile) acting upon an oasis conjured from the desert with cheap, stolen water. In noir versions of the story, freeway and aqueduct are equally envisioned as the symbols of conspiracy and power struggle (Davis, 1994a: 39).

In terms of commonplace (and thoroughly anthropocentric) imagery of natures, *Zabriskie Point* is also a trip from the fertility of the sea to the wasteland of Death Valley whose counterpoint is the hippieish love-in at Zabriskie Point. We realize that natures do not come naturally anymore. Absolute natures (or first natures, as Lefebvre would have it) are being reworked into *social natures* by urbanization. The coast becomes a waterfront, and the desert becomes a hot-spring suburb. The dystopia of *Zabriskie Point* shows that urbanization produces natures as much as it produces cities. One does not exist without the other anymore. Yet, they remain antipodal opposites. One does not *become* the other. Nature is never fully engulfed by the urban, and the urban can never completely conquer the natural environment. Landslides, earthquakes and rising water levels bear witness to the precarious nature of urbanization in environments like Southern California.

## Spatial Practices

Let us go back to the desert around Los Angeles for a second representation. Our tour guide now is British painter David Hockney. When we follow Hockney out of the city into the desert, we do not just leave the urban for the natural; we rediscover the city, its spatiality and ourselves in it. David Hockney created classic pictures of Southern California and of its spatial restructuring during the post-World War II era. *The Splash* and *A Bigger Splash* (Plate 3.6), two of his paintings from the 1960s, show a flat uniformity characteristic of the image of California during this period: endless suburbs, quiet hillsides, the elements of the 'simple but good life' that had been nurtured on the successes of the local defense industry. Life was depicted with generous, yet precisely delineated strokes that did not attempt to hide their emergence from art in the age of mechanical reproduction. Like a poster, Hockney's painting advertised and created a moment in a mass communication and production process, the legitimacy of which had not yet been questioned. It was the Golden Age of Fordism. Thomas Pynchon, the cynical chronicler of the Golden State in the Golden Age, has captured this period:

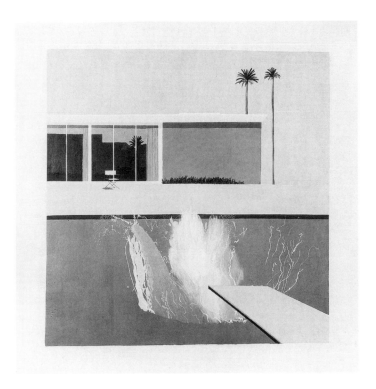

***Plate 3.6*** *David Hockney, A Bigger Splash (1967) Acrylic 96"×96" Reproduced by permission of the artist.*

Zoyd had grown up in the San Joaquin . . . and would eventually return to the same sunny, often he could swear haunted, landscape to get married, one afternoon on a smooth gold green California hillside, with oak in darker patches, a freeway in the distance, dogs and children playing and running, and the sky, for many of the guests, awriggle with patterns of many colors, some indescribable. . . .It may have taken hours or been over in half a minute, there were few if any timepieces among those assembled, and nobody seemed restless, this after all being the Mellow Sixties, a slower-moving time, predigital, not yet so cut into pieces, not even by television. It would be easier to remember the day as a soft-focus shot, the kind to be seen on 'sensitivity' greeting cards in another few years. Everything in nature, every living being on the hillside that day, strange as it sounded later whenever Zoyd tried to tell about it, was gentle, at peace – the visible world was a sunlit sheep farm. War in Vietnam, murder as an instrument of American politics, black neighborhoods torched to ashes and death, all must have been off on some other planet (Pynchon, 1990: 37–38).

Hockney's early paintings are filled with a similar aesthetic:

Hockney's pictures of swimming pools (. . .) are contemporary adaptations of the conventional literary and artistic theme of the Golden Age. The voluptuous and sybaritic bather is a primary symbol of that classical myth of origin, a myth that speaks of a lost, pastoral Arcadia of peace and harmony, which stands in sharp contrast to the convulsively animated world of history. The image functions as a refusal of the impure world of the everyday, and its use finds its implicit meaning in

42

**Plate 3.7** *David Hockney, Pearblossom Hwy., 11–18 April 1986 (2nd version) Photographic collage. Reproduced by permission of the artist.*

the gap between those Edenic origins and the crushing realities of contemporary life. In the profound and assertive social upheavals of the 1960s – the social reorientations in which the artist himself was deeply engaged – Hockney's committed embrace of the world as constituted was met by the countervailing force of a viscerally inflected sense of loss (Knight, 1988b: 38).

Only the restless element of the 'splash' which segments Hockney's picture announces the approaching tremors of the social reorientations of the decade in the center of which there is a feeling of loss.

In contrast, Hockney's later work, particularly his collages of photographs – like *Pearblossom Highway* (Plate 3.7) – shows an image of tremendous disjuncture. The artist has moved out of the apparent security of the suburban backyard – from the realm of enclosed civility, from the built environment – into the seemingly barren emptiness of the desert just beyond the last Southern California edge city on the urban fringe. The depicted landscape is rife with the premonition of impending urbanization, even though there are neither humans nor settlements anywhere in sight. The expectant tension of the 'splash' threatening the peacefulness of the Golden Age has entirely yielded to a depressing insight: the streets and the garbage, and, one can add, the graffiti, the drugs, the decay . . . arrive even before the people get there. Flat and even colors have made room for myriad collaged photographs. The modernist-realist representation of the world is now supplemented by the deconstructive and reconstructive postmodern gaze. Parcels of reality are thrown together to create a fragmented, pluralist space. The collage as a piece of art is also a new spatial image. The ubiquitous urbanity of postsuburbia does not lend itself to simple representation:

The world that remains is plural, fragmented, a collage. . . . Collage started in art. . . . Now the reality is evident for everybody. In Los Angeles, the collage is the form of the new civilization. There is no Culture with a big C, but plural cultures in the same place. Los Angeles is an unlimited, sprawling gigantic collage, a display of fragments: cars, streets, architecture, cultures, races, languages. . . . But each part of the collage has a goal. All these cars crisscrossing the freeways have their destinations. They drive to a specific point – organized movement moving into one direction (Kapuscinski, 1987: 46).

The self-confident single focus perspective of (the man behind) the diver in *A Bigger Splash* has now been supplemented by multiple parallel perspectives of spatial perception – none of which is privileged. While the speed of the automobile symbolizes ways of seeing and moving in the space of modernity, the (seeing) subjects are now emancipated from the one-dimensional meta-perspective of the driver/diver. 'It is simply the driver's choice, while the passenger may gaze else-where: at the litter along the road, for example. Space is wider than possible with any kind of camera' (Hoy, 1988: 64). Simultaneously, as Hockney himself remarks, the attitude of the viewer towards the piece of art is changing:

In Pearblossom Highway, (. . .) you're deeply aware of the flat surface but at the same time you start making a space in your head. And yet the space is not the illusionistic kind where you feel, 'Oh, I could walk into that', only if you tried, you'd kill yourself or you'd hurt yourself anyway; you'd be walking into a brick wall. No, here you don't feel you need to walk into it because you're already in it. (. . .) Take a look at Pearblossom, and then look at a standard photographic rendition of the same scene, and you realize that you're beginning to deal with a more vivid way of depicting space and rendering the experience of space (Hockney, 1988: 96–97).

The continuous oscillation of given and produced, of inherited and projected space could hardly be illustrated in a better way; only the hyperreal aspects of the collage seem to live up to the demands of the multiple gaze of postmodern articulations. Spaces do not stand for themselves, and people do not rule over spaces as if they were mere containers of their actions, territory to be covered by their agency. Spaces of retreat, of quietness and privacy have disappeared. Space and time have become total(itarian) experiences. While the war in Vietnam could still be banned from the California Eden, there is now a 'degree of personal political responsibility that must be accepted for events all over the world' (Berger, quoted in Soja, 1989: 22). In *Pearblossom Highway*, we are in the center of that star of lines, which Berger assumes to be constitutive for our experience of space and time (quoted in Soja, 1989: 22). The expansion of the social experience of space also creates new spheres of agency. While the globe has become the space of reference for human agency, new microworlds, in turn, become more significant. There is a multiplication of points of power and conflict. This is what Stuart Hall has described as 'a generalization of "politics" to spheres which hitherto the left assumed to be apolitical; a politics of the family, of health, of food, of sexuality, of the body . . . and thus a politics which is always positional' (Hall, 1991: 63). The complexity of the production of space accounts for the relevance of agency in its production: 'Space is at once result and cause, product and producer; it is also a *stake*, the locus of projects and actions deployed as part of specific strategies, and hence also the object of *wagers* on the future – wagers which are articulated, if never completely' (Lefebvre, 1991: 142–143).

## REPRESENTATIONAL URBAN SPACES OR: SURFING THE LA RIVER

> On a world scale, space is not just discovered and settled, it is also changed in a way that its 'raw material', i.e., 'nature', is threatened through this *domination*, which is not *appropriation*. The general urbanization is one aspect of this immense expansion (Lefebvre 1975: 114).

> Now that the Los Angeles River is back on the map, what will it become? Can people live with nature without trying to conquer it? Can a city unlock its gates to the wilderness? Is the L.A. River finally just a flood-control project, or is it a real river? Who owns it and who will finally run it? (Coburn 1994: 14; quoted on LA River Tour website).

Let us travel a little farther through the spatial nature of Southern California, which I have invoked already through the representations of space in *Zabriskie Point* and the spatial practices depicted in Hockney's work. Our trip takes us now to the virtual Los Angeles River. A website created at Jefferson High School in Los Angeles allows travellers on the internet to enter the watershed of the Los Angeles River.[9] When asked about the 'real' river, most people in Southern California will be indifferent to, or ignorant of, its existence. Flowing in mostly concreted channels from the headwaters north of the San Fernando and San Gabriel valleys, along Griffith Park and the downtown, then straight to the ocean by Long Beach, the river has historically played a minor role in the imagination of Angelenos. With the exception of rare but regular periods of torrential rainfall, the river's main claim to fame has been its role as the site of many celluloid car chases. Bedded in concrete by the Army Corps of Engineers around the middle of the twentieth century, the Los Angeles River has recently begun to catch the interest of conservationists, artists and urbanists. Faced with another round of flood control engineering of the traditional kind, groups like the Friends of the Los Angeles River (FoLAR) have lobbied for alternative approaches to flood control, a renaturalization of the river, and the integration of the river into the urbanist concept of the Los Angeles region (Browne and Keil, 1996; Keil and Desfor, 1996; Keil, 1998). As a consequence of these efforts, the river has enjoyed more public attention in recent years. It has, however, neither gained visibility as a used urban space and naturalized ecosystem, nor increased its significance in the imagination of space with most Angelenos.

A virtual visit of the Los Angeles River is perfectly characteristic of representational space: 'embodying complex symbolisms, sometimes coded, sometimes not, linked to the clandestine or underground side of social life, as also to art' (Lefebvre, 1991: 33). The trip along the river has basically two dimensions: one corresponds to the topography of the riparian system and takes us in sections from the headwaters to Long Beach; the other is a set of articulations with nature and human society. In this second dimension, we can learn more about plants,

***Plate 3.8*** *The Los Angeles River (Roger Keil)*

animals, birds, microorganisms, water, human impact, art and history pertaining to the Los Angeles River. The virtual trip is, of course, a classic simulacrum, a piece of art, a science project, a political act, a spatial strategy all rolled into one. It is a representational, lived space, simultaneously material and imagined, 'real' and intangible.

The website achieves something as a representational space that has not yet been achieved in the fields of spatial practices and representations of space: it brings together LA's urbanity and ecology in a new space of centrality. Nature is virtually (in the double sense of the word) brought into the city. The symbolic force of the river tour transecting the urban region (and thus creating urban space), is complemented by the compelling presence of wildlife, water and greenery in the heart of the city. The presence of reed, bamboo and crayfish is established – without hierarchical deflection – alongside the presence of central urbanity. This brings to mind an insightful (while not entirely new) observation made by David Harvey: 'We must recognize that the distinction between *environment* as commonly understood and the *built environment* is artificial and that the urban and everything that goes into it is as much a part of the solution as it is a contributing factor to ecological difficulties' (1996: 60). In the end, nature and space come together in urbanity. Destroyed in waves of disurbanization from the plans of Baron Haussmann to the Fordist 'suburban solution', urbanity is creeping back to our cities from the margins. To Lefebvre, the destruction of urbanity was a function of the proletariat being expelled from the urban center in the classic case of the restructuring of nineteenth century Paris (1996: 76). The reclamation of urbanity has since been a constant theme of urban struggles in places as diverse as Paris and Los Angeles.

Linked to the search for urbanity has been the notion of centrality, itself subject to redefinition in the current period: 'The globalization of the city is a fundamental phenomenon. In the future, the city will be polycentric, a multiplicity of centres, diversified but conserving a Centre. There is no urbanity without a centre. I believe in a general urbanization. There will remain vast spaces but deserted, little inhabited' (Lefebvre, 1996: 208). Not accidentally, nature has historically been seen as the matter neither of urbanity nor of centrality. Yet I propose that crossing the ontological divide of space and nature will necessitate the application of the concepts of urbanity and centrality to nature itself – just as producing spatiality has become a matter of occupying the margins. The more *urban* Southern California became, however, the less *civil* it became. In apparent contrast to Henri Lefebvre's understanding of the replacement of first nature by second nature in the process of urbanization, Los Angeles' production of second nature did not benefit the humanist agenda of building a better place for people. The destruction of first nature through human agency ended as a zero-sum game: no nature and no city. 'It was the first metropolis on wheels, defined by the automobile and a tank of gas, expanding in every direction, its distances making it unavailable to the walker in the city and obliterating the idea of a central community' (Dunne, 1991: 28). The destruction of natural ecologies and human community did not find redemption in a new synthesis of urbanization and ecology. No new *oikoumene* emerged. Urbanity and civil society did not become congruent. Instead, external nature and social structure were made disposable in a world fragmented into privatized cultural and economic artifacts of industrial capitalism, and more specifically, of Fordism. Commodification and individualization counteracted 'ecological' societal relationships with nature.

Moreover, the external extinction of nature through the extension of urbanization beyond the desert frontier was accompanied by internalized oblivion on the side of the Angelenos. While most people in Los Angeles continue to enjoy the famous 'outdoor life-style', they have learned to do so in flagrant disregard for nature. Where possible, of course, Angelenos and Angelenas are protecting themselves individually against the dangers of both urban and global ecological crises. One stays out of the sun and out of the ozone and one consumes bottled water and organic food. For those that are – due to social and environmental injustices – not so lucky to escape the 'bad' side of urban nature, those working in the factories and living next to refineries, neither the city nor its nature are benign sites. Los Angeles still revels in the symbolism of palm-tree-lined street, magnificent beaches and snow-capped mountains but its inhabitants pay little attention to the metabolism that keeps their urban region alive: air has become an object of engineering and life-style repairs, the Los Angeles River has no place in the city's inventory of natural places; food, water, energy are entering the region on a linear one-way street without much concern for the natural world's circular metabolism.

## WORLD CITY NATURES

In the environmental problems of the world city lies a key to the structure of institutionalized racism on the one hand and to popular civility on the other (Keil, 1995). In Los Angeles, the lines of conflict of national and international dynamics converge, and carve a segregated pattern of sociospatiality into the local landscape. The discrepancies are stark but invisible to many casual observers. Most visitors

***Plate 3.9*** *Smog and smoking (Roger Keil)*

only see the sunny side, the beaches, Beverly Hills, Disneyland, Universal Studios, the wealth, the palm trees. They do not see homelessness, poverty, environmental degradation, drugs and violence. The homes and workplaces of the hundreds of thousands of low-wage workers, the gardeners, seamstresses, janitors, etc. are not on tourist itineraries. Like most white Angelenos, tourists never set foot into the neighborhoods where the majority of the internationalized low-wage proletariat lives and works. The tourist gaze has no interest in the refineries and oil derricks in the backyards of the barrios, for the polluted sweatshops where printed circuits are fabricated for Southern California's high-tech industries. Outsiders do not experience the work conditions of undocumented Mexican immigrants in the furniture factories from which toxic fumes waft across adjacent school yards.

The white and wealthy minority of Los Angeles has increasingly created an environment for itself in the hills, beachside communities and desert suburbs. From there, the white and wealthy rule the urban region. Many people of color suffer from environmental racism. In the poorest neighborhoods where most non-whites live, everyday life is a threatening affair. Here, toxics are concentrated, children live with lead poisoning, and youth have a reduction of lung capacity otherwise known only in long-term smokers (Mann, 1991). But in the way in which people have tried, in this situation of environmental racism, to give their everyday life dignity and coherence, we find the roots for the civility of neighborhoods and communities.

In Los Angeles, nature as well as civil society have been articulated with specific hegemonic conceptions and projects. For at least the past 100 years, they have been recognized as white middle- and upper-class territory. Environment-alism has been defined, circumscribed and triggered by hegemonic developments in the political economy of space in Southern California. Growth has always been the major factor in this definition, and the meaning of 'environmental' has usually been linked to urbanization and expansion in Los Angeles: oil drilling, the sub-urban waste crisis, rising urban density, freeway extension, garbage incineration have been milestone issues in the framing of environmentalism in the region. This meaning of environmentalism has recently been challenged by subaltern social groups (see Chapter 11). The new form of environmentalism 'goes by a variety of headings: grassroots, popular, livelihood, resistance, environmental justice, and resource struggles' (Pulido, 1996a: 4).

Subaltern environmentalism has taken a specific form in Los Angeles due to the urban region's traditional injustices and inequalities which have placed people of color, women and the working class in a position of structural discrimination and oppression. This structural injustice has found its expression throughout the urban region in rigid patterns of segregation and a correlated geography of pollution and social inequality (Mann, 1991). In Los Angeles, a peculiar mixture of working-class environmentalism, radical ecologism and environmental justice has characterized the movement's reaction to these specific conditions of oppression. Like elsewhere in the United States, the strongest feature of this movement's ideology has been the predominance of notions of environmental racism which can be defined as 'racial minorities' disproportionate exposure to environmental hazards. . . . Racism and the struggle for equality are the entry point for marginalized groups to the discourse of subaltern environmental struggles in the United States' (Pulido, 1996a: 17–19). The predominance of ecological hotspots in minority and low-income communities in Los Angeles has created a new field of struggle where traditional civil rights and social justice concerns can be articulated with (and expressed through) 'green' discourses and struggles.

The second set of conditions of oppression have been constituted by the crisis of the Fordist regime in Los Angeles with its automobile-based, single-family-home urban landscape and its massive, military-industrial complex. In this crisis period, the largely immigrant working class, as well as women and people of color, demanded access to the real and discursive spaces of Los Angeles civil society (and also of political society and the economic sphere). Women (such as the Mothers of East Los Angeles), people of color (like the Concerned Citizens of South Central Los Angeles and La Causa/Communities for a Better Environment), and labor groups (such as the Labor/Community Strategy Center) appeared on the scene as powerful political actors. They have challenged the class/race nexus of civil society and nature in Los Angeles by inserting notions of environmental and social justice, of citizenship, of public health and gender equity into the landscape of both the environmental and civic movements of the city (Pulido, 1996b).

## Environmental Justice and Civic Environmentalism

In contrast to elite concepts designed to keep or extend the status quo (see Chapter 2), popular and insurgent groups in civil society tend to construct their positions on environmental issues as points of departure for larger social and ecological change. While the planning and policy agencies of the local state tend to concentrate on establishing control, subaltern groups tend to focus on liberation for humans and/or nonhuman nature. Whereas the plans regulating air and river in Los Angeles reflect local elites' interest in control and order, which I have characterized as 'policing ecology', popular resistance to elite policies is often an attempt to green and democratize the polis (Keil, 1998). 'Political socialization' as part of a larger democratization process – as opposed to the 'manufacture of consent' – best describes the politics of the subaltern groups.

While radical social justice organizations have increasingly articulated environmental concerns with their agendas of economic democracy and political liberation (civil rights), more moderate popular organizations have been explicitly critical of the traditional control and order approach to regulating nature in Los Angeles. The single most important example in this respect has been the recent demand by mainstream environmental groups to 'liberate' the Los Angeles River from its concrete straightjacket and to renaturalize part of the riparian system and floodplain. Proposals to find alternatives to concreting the river – and reducing a complex urban ecological system to the function of a flood control channel – have been in the forefront of the public debate since the beginning of the 1990s. Rather than extending the deceptive control of humans in the Los Angeles Basin over the powerful natural forces of precipitation, floods and groundwater by adding walls on top of the existing levees in the lower stretches of the river, the alternative proposals rely on ecosystemic diversion and absorption of flood waters, more ecologically friendly construction (fewer sealed surfaces) in the headwaters of Los Angeles' streams, and integration of more diversified means of flood control into the built and natural environment of the urban region (creating a system of basins, parks, wetlands and drainage areas in the entire floodplain). Traditional conservation groups like FoLAR and Tree People have increasingly made connections between their ecological projects and social concerns. They have argued, for example, that greening the river – which has obvious ecosystemic advantages for nonhuman nature and wildlife that need no elaboration – would also have benefits in terms of Los Angeles' urbanist appearance (city on a river), its social welfare (urban parks as a programmatic measure against neighborhood deterioration) and economic health (urban development with rather than against nature).

Los Angeles' environmental justice groups are more radical and tend to challenge – not just use – procedural channels and substantive policies. Alternative environmental management practices are considered insufficient in a situation in which environmental racism and injustice remain unaddressed. Environmental justice groups are more likely to support a popularly oriented, democratically controlled government planning process than one which is based on the rationale of the marketplace. Market-based regulation in conjunction with existing undemocratic state policies is regarded as the worst – and currently most likely – combination of hegemonic environmental policies (see Chapter 11).

## CONCLUSION

The social and natural spaces of Los Angeles explored in this essay – the desert frontier, the postmodern spatiality of Los Angeles' civil society and the virtual river – are places that are, to use Katz's words, 'of a piece' (1995: 166), both social and natural. Urbanity resides in them through our spatial practices, representations of space and representational spaces – all part of our wider politics of urbanity. Los Angeles continues to straddle the margins of nature through its ceaseless urbanization. While McPhee assumed that hedged in between the mountains and the sea, 'Los Angeles is done sprawling' (1989: 184), there is, really, no end to its expansion. The fourth ecology keeps pushing the limits. Let us give Lefebvre the last word, in what sounds like an observation reiterating the representation of space in Hockney's *Pearblossom Highway*: 'There is something stupendous and fascinating [about Los Angeles]. You are and yet are not in the city. You cross a series of mountains and you are still in the city, but you don't know when you are entering it or leaving it' (Lefebvre, 1996: 208).

# PART II

(UN)MAKING FORDISM

# CHAPTER 4

# ARSENAL AND THROW-AWAY-CITY

This is America, home of the free, little pink houses for you and me.
John Mellencamp

Instant throw-away-cities are hardly feasible no matter how hard the folk in Los
Angeles try.
David Harvey

I am convinced we cannot afford the tradition of 'throw away cities'.
Tom Bradley

The redefinition of the urban historical geography and identity in Los Angeles has,
for about a generation, been contextualized in rampant restructuring processes.
The region's industrial base was undermined, and high- and low-end service
industries and low-wage manufacturing sectors experienced enormous growth. I
will explore this further in Parts II and III. Los Angeles, after World War II, was
something like the western 'front city', the American city closest to the 'evil
empire' on the other side of the cold war.[1] From here, the wars in Korea and
Vietnam were provisioned and logistically supported. Here, the American Dream
was built in its most sprawling and appalling form of single-family homes and
freeways. As Castells and Hall (1994: 88) have written:

> Through its media industries Southern California went on to project this image [of
> being a new urban spatial form, R.K.], massively and successfully, to the entire world;
> but behind it, at the core of its real estate and advanced services businesses, the
> defense industry provided the real dynamo of growth.

The period between the Watts riots in 1965 and the rebellion of 1992 saw the United
States being transformed from a Fordist national economy to a post-Fordist
internationalized economy. California – and particularly the Los Angeles area –
signify this shift more than any other part of the United States. By 'Fordist' I mean
the hegemony of an economic and social formation under capitalism which links
mass production (Taylorism and the assembly line) – an intensive, highly productive and efficient regime of accumulation – to generalized mass consumption.
The mode of social regulation which helped keep this system stable and made it
appear normal rested on a 'social contract' of capital and labor that lasted roughly
from the end of World War II to the late 1960s. Under the existence of this 'social
contract' (expressed among other things in the famous postwar accord between
management and labor in the major industries like auto and steel), labor peace, a
high standard of living symbolized by workers' access to a variety of consumer
goods, and an unprecedented level of welfare state performance existed. The
arrangement was buffered and supported by the Keynesian policies of an aggressively interventionist federal government, which fueled industrial production and
private consumption through highway programs, loans and tax cuts for home-

54

***Plate 4.1*** *Watts Towers (Roger Keil)*

owners, military expenditure, etc. The economy was built around two major commodities from which all other consumption needs and production seemed to emanate: the private automobile; and the single-family home (creating the consumerist, suburban family).

The United States during this period was an almost self-sustaining economy; most of the goods consumed were produced domestically. International agreements (most importantly the Bretton Woods monetary pact) and the sheer power of the victorious US military machine secured not only its domination over half of the industrialized (and most of the unindustrialized) world (outside the Soviet empire), but also the hegemony of the 'Fordist model' in much of the West. Los Angeles was the trendsetting center of automobile and suburban culture, a playground of consumerism, dream capital of the world, and arsenal of the pax americana.

The Watts uprising of 1965, more than any other event, signified the beginning of the end of this era of growth, this seamless expansion of the American way of life. The discovery of the blind spots of the post-World War II growth period (which had systematically underemployed and underpaid black and female workers and rested mostly on a white core working class in its high-wage mass-production facilities) came with thunder and lightning, the eruption of the ghettos and the move of the civil rights movement to a more economic agenda (Aglietta, 1979). But it also came with the economic crises of 1967 and 1973. The world and the nation were to look different after that, and between 1974 and the recession of 1982, much of the traditional industrial landscape and much of the social system that regulated it was catapulted out of orbit. Disastrous deindustrialization (mostly in the so-called northeastern 'rustbelt'), the fiscal crisis of cities, plant closures, and the defeat in Vietnam all marked this period. Los Angeles suffered many of these effects, particularly the deindustrialization and elimination of its productive core stretching over 30 miles along the Long Beach Freeway (with mass-production facilities also in other parts of the region).

If in the United States, and in Los Angeles for that matter, we have moved beyond the Fordist period, which path have we taken? For want of a better word, we have entered the *post-Fordist* era. I use this term only to denote a period *after* Fordism, without trying to make any normative statements on where things are going. Yet, differences in the way goods are being produced and consumed now, and the way they were produced and consumed during the previous period, could not be more pronounced. Here is a cursory look at changes that typify this shift to a post-Fordist era:

- The American economy (and its flagship, California) has become industrialized in new regions (e.g. Orange County) and new sectors (e.g. high tech).
- Capital and labor markets as well as real estate and land markets have been thoroughly globalized.
- The Fordist model of production (assembly line and Taylorism) has been selectively replaced by more flexible methods of organizing production. Some of the buzzwords of this change are just-in-time, teamwork, flexibilization, computerization, etc.
- The restructuring of production has often come at the expense of the traditional high-wage workforce; particularly after the crisis of 1982, the so-called 'Reagan revolution' created millions of low-wage, low-security and often part-time jobs, often held by women and minorities.
- In the United States, this shift has been accompanied by a move from a manufacturing-based economy to one which has come to rest increasingly on a boom in the service sector. In contrast to other major industrial economies (Germany, France, Sweden), the predominance of the service sector in the US has come to pass by delinking production from services altogether.
- The post-World War II 'social contract' has, for all practical purposes, been eliminated. This takes several forms which include the abandonment of Keynesian liberal welfare policies; the breach of the labor accord in the major industries; and a departure from the equalizing and standardizing consumption patterns under Fordism in favor of polarization and segmentation of consumption norms.
- The use of space has been reversed and redefined. Both the suburbs and the inner cities are being remade completely. Exurbanization and edge city developments have taken hold.

The period between Watts and the rebellion of 1992 corresponds to the duration, functionality and coherence of the political regime of Tom Bradley. It is useful to think of this period as both a mode of social regulation linked to the expansion and contraction of the local economy (its regime of accumulation) and as a political regime (the Bradley Coalition), creating a purposeful program for the restructuring of Los Angeles. The implementation of this program ('The World Class City') meant both a funneling of global capital into distinct parts of the city (assisted by the redevelopment process and other economic development programs), and the complete makeover of local state and society in order to accommodate this process.

The demographic profile of Los Angeles has changed dramatically during the Bradley era. Consider that in 1970 only 14% of the population in the five-county Los Angeles area were Hispanics while 75% were white; there were 8% African Americans and 3% Asians/others. In 1980, the numbers had changed to 24% Hispanic, 61% white, 9% black and 6% Asian/others. In 1990, it had shifted even more towards a majority non-white urban region with 33% Hispanic, 50% white, 9% Asian and 8% black (Dear, 1996b: 12). What these figures signify is that 25 years ago, Los Angeles was a fairly standard 'black and white' American city. Its sizable (14%) Hispanic population was attributable more to the city's location and history than to economic factors. Large-scale immigration from south of the border had hardly begun; Los Angeles' 'immigrant industries' were still nascent. Previous economic Mexican immigration had largely been reversed.

The 'black and white' appearance of the city prestructured the politics of the Bradley era. While much of Bradley's initial program can be understood as a liberal, civil-rights-influenced attempt to 'rebuild LA', his later program to develop 'world class city' Los Angeles counteracted this initial program in intent and praxis. Whereas the internationalization of the region, of course, cannot be attributed to Bradley's administration entirely, the mayor put policies in place that helped facilitate the process. By doing so, Bradley assisted in changing the city in a way that undermined his own political power base in the city.

The ethnic and social restructuring of Los Angeles has often consisted of redefining, and forming entirely new, communities. Little Tokyo and Bunker Hill were obliterated in their historical forms and replaced by something new; other communities like Monterey Park, America's first suburban Chinatown (Horton, 1995) and Little Tokyo (see Chapter 9) were created as new sociospatial entities in the Los Angeles area. It is necessary to understand that immigration does not just result in increased numbers of certain people in certain areas but the destruction and reconstruction of communities. These communities change a city from within. They have a class structure and a structure of domination of their own.

These processes of 'creative destruction' of communities led to a new landscape of power in Los Angeles. The local state now has to react to a set of demands wholly different from those of a generation ago. While the Bradley administration was fairly successful in 'managing' the redevelopment process in certain parts of the city (for example, by flexibilizing the Community Redevelopment Agency to the needs of specific communities in order to control and conquer these needs), it was fighting an uphill battle in others. For years Koreatown has been demanding to be put onto the political map through a redesignation of council districts. Sand-wiched between the black community to the south, the white community to the west and north and the Latino communities to the east, the Koreans' voice in city politics has been minimal.

The very preconditions on which the Bradley coalition was built do not exist anymore; the political landscape has shifted, new sublocal class structures and new intercommunity relations have sprung up which the existing local state has not been able to integrate. The regulatory system that held together the post-Watts city did not hold up to the pressures put on the city's structure by increased internationalization (Davis, 1987). The period between the uprisings of 1965 and 1992 spans the move from the corporate city, the typical headquarter city of the Fordist period, to the internationalized world city, a module of global capitalism. This transformation implied both a redefinition of Los Angeles' position in the national and international economy and a thorough internal restructuring of the urban region. Through most of the twentieth century, Los Angeles (like other American cities) was a Fordist corporate city. The Urban Renewal process was started in the late 1940s/early 1950s. It quickly shed all resemblance it ever had to a public housing program and became a process by which various sectors of the local bourgeoisie profited from turning inner-city space into a corporate domain. At the same time, major branch plants in auto, rubber and aerospace started blanketing the suburbs from Van Nuys in the north to Torrance and Long Beach in the south and Pico Rivera in the east. Rebecca Morales writes: 'Within four years of the war's end, there were seven automakers in Los Angeles with an annual capacity of approximately 650 000 cars. The Los Angeles car industry in 1950 was making thirteen different models, more than Detroit, and was second to Detroit in the manufacture of automobiles worldwide' (1992: 208). While Los Angeles remains an important location for automobile-related manufacturing and services, no major auto plant has operated in Southern California since the General Motors facility in Van Nuys was closed in 1991.

As the suburbs were industrialized in a large-scale and Fordist manner, the inner city started to fall apart into a corporate citadel, eating into formerly residential (mostly poor) neighborhoods and a decaying ring of industrial and residential spaces. Contrast this postwar pattern with the current industrial urban landscape and the new spatial relations of production and consumption:

> In the United States, Fordism spanned the period from the 1920s to the 1970s. Since then the U.S. economy has become more open to international competition, resulting in smaller market shares and more unstable demand. The increased market uncertainty required that manufacturers shift to more responsive production methods. Greater flexibility in the less predictable market was obtained through advanced manufacturing systems, technology and labor jointly applied to smaller runs of more specialized products. Firms were also reorganized to make rapid market adjustments manageable. Functions that were part of large, integrated firms have, in some instances, been spun off, a process that is called 'vertical disintegration'. With a larger number of smaller production units linked in the manufacture of a car, proximity has increased in importance, resulting in the creation of spatially identifiable industrial districts. Yet other economic activities that are more market-oriented, such as research and design, have broken away from the central headquarters to be closer to the centers of popular taste. . . . In many respects, Los Angeles effectively illustrates the difference between old and new forms of industrialization (Morales, 1992: 205).

That is, Los Angeles, like other urban centers, saw an elimination of its Fordist industrial core and the rise of new industrial, crafts and service sectors. The separation of corporate headquarters from production that had characterized the Fordist city was now taken one step further into the development of a quasi-independent business services sector (computers, software, hardware, xeroxing, advertising, accounting, law firms, etc.) making its home in some of the secondary nodal points of Southern California (like the Wilshire corridor, Century City, but also locations in Santa Monica, in the valleys and in Orange County). The downtown was left mainly to various government functions and the increasingly internationalized and concentrated banking industry. Supported by public and private development schemes, huge amounts of foreign (mostly Canadian, British, Japanese and Chinese) capital came into the downtown but also into the other centers in the 1980s.

In the shadows of the glitzy towers and the cultural acropolis of Bunker Hill (home of the Museum of Contemporary Art and the Disney Music Hall construction site), the garment industry with its 125 000 employees in Los Angeles County in the late 1980s reintroduced sweatshop conditions to the center of the city, conditions thought to have been eliminated (or exported) in the era of Fordist mass production. The city became more segmented and more segregated than ever before. The influx of foreign capital and immigration did not break, but rather, reinforced Los Angeles' track record of having been the most segregated city in North America. This happened largely because both investment and settlement followed paths that had been laid out to them by the logic of local land, labor and housing markets blazing a trail through communities. Large-scale destruction of communities has not been a function of internationalization as such; rather, international investors have piggybacked onto local dynamics of creative destruction.[2]

Since the late 1980s, the low in international real estate markets (linked to the crisis of the Japanese economy), the national recession in the United States, the end of the cold war with its effects on the California defense industries, and finally, the rebellion of 1992 threw the Southern California economic miracle into a crisis of proportions unknown since the Depression of the 1930s. Adding a sense of crisis to the rapid pace of restructuring – which previously had been perceived mostly in terms of a boom economy – created new preconditions for politics in Los Angeles. For the first time since the early 1970s, the entire political sphere had to address issues unrelated to excessive urban growth and had to face problems of widespread decline. Through much of the past 20 years, politics in Los Angeles has gravitated around two oppositional, yet closely related issues: on one hand, the boosterism of the local growth coalition, downtown redevelopment and Mayor Tom Bradley's project to make Los Angeles a 'world class city' (epitomized, among other things, by the Olympics in 1984); on the other hand, growth-control initiatives often championed by 'West Side liberals'. From the point of view of the hegemonic powers – intoxicated with tales of Pacific *grandesse* and never-ending prosperity throughout the 1980s – the politics of decline and restructuring were relegated to marginal status, left to the unemployed manufacturing workers and displaced communities of color who were considered necessary driftwood in the modernization process that would make Los Angeles the capital of the Pacific Rim. Early in the 1990s, stagnation and decline moved briefly to center stage after the booming 1980s and before the economic turnaround in California later in this decade. In 1993, this emergent period of stasis brought in Los Angeles Mayor Richard Riordan and – as Mike Davis (1994c: 495–506) has called it – a Jurassic rebirth of white, conservative Republicanism in a majority nonwhite and Democratic city and the passing, in the fall of 1994, of the anti-immigrant Proposition 187, whose proponents were headquartered in Orange County, southeast of Los Angeles.

## FIRESTORM AND EARTHQUAKE: URBAN HISTORY AS CATASTROPHE THEORY?

The emergence of Fordism in Los Angeles was not just a matter of exogenous factors, even though growth and wealth in Southern California are sometimes credited solely to the explosion of the armament industry during World War II (Hirsch, 1971). 'The Japanese attack of Pearl Harbor (. . .) opened the door for Los Angeles's massive industrial expansion and urbanization' wrote Gottlieb and Wolt (1977: 296) accordingly. The influx of war- and defense-related federal funds into the urban region in the wake of World War II, the cold war, and the wars in Asia, was indeed central moment of the recent urbanization in Los Angeles (cf. Bloch, 1987; Clark, 1983). The well-being of the urban economy has been linked directly with American foreign policy. This relationship has lasted up to this day, and the post-cold war downturn in military spending has severely affected the Los Angeles region. Perhaps more than in other American cities, the American war machine in Los Angeles has been welded together with the system of Fordist mass production and privatized mass consumption, within the 'lifespace' of freeways and single-family homes.

One could add to the catastrophic beginning of Fordism an equally catastrophic ending, in which Fordism would disappear 'naturally' in the rubble of the Big Quake as it was born in the fire of the Japanese bombardment. This scenario – between war and earthquake – would be a mere reflection of events rooted outside of Los Angeles, a city without history, and perhaps a city without future. A narrative like that exaggerates a tendency which characterizes much of the available literature on Los Angeles: Los Angeles as a phoenix rising from the desert sand. Implicitly, what we encounter in these descriptions is the rise and fall of Los Angeles as a *city in Fordism*. This chapter will recount this history.

Instead of describing Los Angeles just as any city of this period, I will present its endogenous patterns of development and local conditions and dynamics as elements of a process through which the Fordist model became rooted. In contrast to the *city in Fordism* I will call this ensemble of local dynamics the *Fordist city*. In this I follow Mike Davis' suggestion to make 'the place-specific mode of subsumption of labor and the organization of class struggles' the object of our research (Davis, n.d.).[3] I posit that the 'national Fordist regime' (cf. Hirsch and Roth, 1986: 46ff.) had known significantly differentiated local versions from the start. The goal of this narrative is to increase our understanding of local modifications of the Fordist formation which is usually seen as in an (inter)national frame of reference. The constitution of Fordism as a national system can only be grasped, I will argue, if one includes the development of places. The structured coherence of Fordist Los Angeles will be considered as a constitutional element of American Fordism rather than only its product.

## LOS ANGELES: CITY IN FORDISM

Americanism, Not Fordism (Strike poster, Los Angeles, 1937).

Los Angeles, the second largest metropolitan region in the USA, is literally the product of the technological age – the era of the automobile, the airplane and the rocket (Crouch and Dinermann, 1963: 3).

Los Angeles indeed appears as the paradigmatic product of the Keynesian–Fordist formation in the United States. The region's growth has been directly related to defense expenditures, to federal housing subsidies, to federal transportation legislation, and to the prime sectors of the national post-World War II economy. Los Angeles was born as a 'monopoly capitalist' city which never experienced the typical dense growth of the 'industrial capitalist' city of the nineteenth century (Soja, Morales and Wolff, 1983). Backed by Veterans' Administration (VA) and Federal Housing Administration (FHA) mortgages, central workers bought suburban homes, which drastically increased demand for consumption goods (Florida and Feldmann, 1988: 189). Suburban life required personal automobile transport, individualized consumer goods (for food preparation, laundry, entertainment) resulting in an expanded job description for household work. The standardization of food and consumption goods streamlined the interior of the single-family homes, and automobile-oriented fast food restaurants and drive-ins of all sorts completed the Fordist suburban setting. Peripheral workers, often segregated by race and ethnicity, were concentrated in the barrios of the Eastside or the ghetto of South Central, occupying an aging and deteriorating housing stock. Freeways – the vital infrastructure of suburban-based automobile transport – disemboweled the inner city. The city was functionally divided into dichotomous spaces. The main contradiction was the bipolarity of inner city and suburb. The separation of labor markets and urban geographies into black and white, urban and suburban was a strategy through which wage differentials and control over workers could be maintained in a system in which the core sector of the working class was located in relatively highly paid, secure and mostly unionized sectors. This core was defined through the peripheral existence of African Americans, immigrants and women.

Postwar suburbanization provided a giant opening through which capital could flow into profitable circuits, including direct investment into suburban industries, into infrastructure and housing, and credit-fueled private consumption. The suburbs served as giant lightning rods for concrete use values through which value flowed and expanded. Even if this 'suburban solution' was not necessarily the only possible path of development, a spatially concentrated form of urbanization would not have accommodated so easily the masses of privatized consumption goods around which the suburbs were built (Walker, 1981: 409).

At the level of the national political regulation of American Fordism, the housing and highway programs of the federal government took center stage. These programs pumped billions of dollars into the cities and created the framework for the period of urbanization after World War II. In the area of housing, the federal government attempted, beginning in 1932, to activate dormant mortgage financing (Federal Home Loan Bank Act). In 1934 the federal Savings and Loan Insurance Corporation was established as an insurance system for mortgage banks. The policy measures of the New Deal in the 1930s, which were accompanied by widespread social struggles, peaked in the housing legislation of 1937, the Wagner–Steagall Act. From this legislation emerged the tradition of a dual system of subsidies for homebuilders in the suburbs and public housing for the peripheral working class of the inner city (Florida and Feldmann, 1988: 191f.)[4]

After World War II, the Housing Act of 1949, with its mortgage insurance program for war veterans and civilians, became the most important legal pre-condition for suburbanization. The program was administered through the FHA and the VA. Until the late 1980s, 47% of all mortgaged homes were built under this program (Marcuse and Hartman, 1988; Gilderbloom and Appelbaum, 1988). An even larger influence on the 'suburban solution' was the practice of offering tax rebates for private home construction. Such subsidies had reached $25 billion in 1985 alone (Marcuse and Hartman, 1988).

The second strategy for housing provision after the Housing Act of 1937 was public housing. Along with urban renewal, which took off in the 1950s, public housing became the inner-city counterpart to the 'suburban solution'.[5] Measures pertaining to the inner city never reached the degree of significance in terms of housing policy and macroeconomic impact that the suburban expansion attained. In the latter case a specific sociospatial complex for the linkage of mass production and mass consumption emerged. The inner-city policies were more effective than suburban subsidization in concentrating and restructuring the central functions of productive services in the downtown. Moreover, the contradictions of American Fordism – which systematically excluded important segments of the working class from production and consumption – were most visibly reflected in the sociospatial opposition of city core and suburbia (Florida and Feldmann, 1988: 188). In the urban crisis felt since the early 1970s, the local mode of regulation burst at the seams of this specific inner-city version of American housing Fordism. Social struggles against the destruction of housing through urban renewal formed the core of the urban social movements of the 1960s and 1970s (Marcuse and Hartman, 1988). Public housing projects became centers of African American urban rebellion.

A more effective instrument of change in the built environment of the American city were the expenditures of the federal government for highways (Walker, 1977: 595; Friedland, 1983). The Interstate Highway program, initiated with the 1956 Highway Act, was the largest infrastructure project of modern history. Highway construction did not just facilitate commuting between suburbia and city core with the family automobile; it also supported the decentralization of transportation and of commerce. Like the Haussmannian boulevards of nineteenth century Paris, highway construction cut violently through urban neighborhoods, destroyed more housing units than urban renewal, and drastically reduced the quality of life in the communities (Walker, 1977: 598). During the construction of the Hollywood Freeway in Los Angeles, 60% of the land used for the road had not been vacant and had to be reimbursed or cleared (Nelson, 1983: 282).

Fordist urban development forced previously unexperienced expenditures for collective consumption on the capitalist state (Aglietta, 1979: 236). The production of a social infrastructure became a central precondition for the maintenance of the nexus between continuous capital accumulation and the necessary level of consumption of the middle and working classes. This social infrastructure, which included educational and research facilities, as well as institutions to facilitate the reproduction of labor power and cultural affairs, affected the conditions of class struggle – labor relations and the legal framework for production and exchange – and entailed surveillance and repression (Harvey, 1982).

As the world's policeman, the United States carried giant military expenditures (Aglietta, 1979: 236). Between 1946 and 1965, the country spent 62% of its federal budget ($776 billion dollars) in this sector (Clayton, 1967: 449). The internal economic functions of defense expenditures as a fiscal policy are as relevant as their military effects on the 'class struggle on a world scale' (Aglietta, 1979) itself. The geography and politics of these payments become an important parameter for the emergence of specific places and regions (Clayton, 1967: 449). The federal funds not only created jobs in the defense sector but built an entirely new infrastructure. The locational decisions of the defense industry during World War II also influenced housing construction, as did the location of later cold-war industries. In addition, the strategic military value of infrastructural measures in the cities of Fordism should not be underestimated.[6]

Los Angeles was produced as a city in Fordism through the external dynamics sketched above. Economically, the expansion of the military sector changed the region into a 'martial metropolis' (Lotchin, 1984; Bloch, 1987). The war machine was grafted onto the existing aerospace industries and onto the branch-plant economy of the prewar period. As a center of heavy and consumer industries, of oil production and processing, of tourism and of the movie industry, Southern California was a prime example of an economy built on and through urbanization in Fordism. The particularly active history of the real estate sector in the city was no obstacle to filling the suburban landscapes of previous periods with bungalows, double garages and swimming pools. The urban area, which at the beginning of the 1930s had already been a 'fragmented metropolis' (Fogelson, 1967), had never experienced dense urbanization in the style of the nineteenth century. Its social space, however, functionally fell apart into downtown and suburbia much like other American cities of the same period. The difference between Los Angeles and cities in the East consisted merely in the fact that in Southern California, suburbanization meant primary urbanization and was not a decentralized wave of urbanization that followed historically the centralized form of urbanization (cf. Foster, 1971: 172ff.).[7] Relative to those of other US cities, the core of Los Angeles played a minor role in the historiography of the urban region.

The projection of those general trends of urbanization in Fordism onto Los Angeles, however, tells only half the story. The next section, therefore, will roughly outline how the general development of Fordist structures was translated into Los Angeles.

## Los Angeles: Fordist City

It is not that politics seems futile or ugly or threatening to the Angelenos; to most of them, politics seems unnecessary (Carney, 1964: 117).

No major group is disarmed and without access (Carney, 1964: 110).

Burn, Baby, Burn (Slogan, Watts riots 1965).

The emergence of a new period of urbanization always comes with the elimination and modification of obstacles erected in the built environment and social structure in previous periods of urbanization (Harvey, 1985b: 265). The following sections explore how local politics and policies in Los Angeles supported the urban area's social and economic development as well as its built environment. It will be shown – using the concept of 'paraFordism' – how some of these local developments predated the emergence of Fordism as a national regime of accumulation.

### Primitive Accumulation

The city was able to stand up to the competition of its neighbors – San Diego in the south and San Francisco in the north – at the time because the local bourgeoisie successfully tied its profit-maximizing strategies to the growth of the city itself. These strategies consisted of first lowering the relative cost of labor power and suppressing the trade unions; second, spending more money on infrastructure measures than had been the case up to that point; and third, drawing large amounts of capital into the city from outside. Finally, they created a large enough regional market to support the development of the urban region. In the rivalry with San Francisco, Los Angeles was successful because the strategies of its local bourgeoisie gave the city a relative advantage over its competitors. Between 1890 and 1910, the wages in Los Angeles were from 20 to 40% lower than in San Francisco. The growth of Los Angeles as an industrial center rested on this significant difference (McWilliams, 1979: 277; Davis, 1990).

Fueled by open-shop policies, a dual labor market structure emerged in Los Angeles. Immigrants from Asia, Southern and Eastern Europe and Latin America provided the labor power for the city's industrial expansion, establishing a pattern which was to influence the labor markets of Los Angeles later on: the constant supply of cheap labor in the city. Next to this regulation of the price of the commodity labor power in favor of the interests of the local bourgeoisie, other measures taken by local boosters pale in comparison. But their effect on the development of Los Angeles should not be underestimated. Two measures in particular stand out: the water imperialism of the central city vis-à-vis the regional hinterland; and the aggressive pursuit of a port to which the landlocked city could be tied.

## The Economy of Para-Fordist Los Angeles

Some essential structural elements of the Fordist 'long wave' which was soon to roll over the country era had already been in existence in Los Angeles due to fortunate circumstances and a good deal of local boosterism by the 1920s. The production of oil had a decisive impact on the creation of a local 'para-Fordism' in Southern California. The oil boom allowed Los Angeles to erect modern urban and industrial infrastructure. Los Angeles was the first city in the world which was entirely lit electrically: 'Los Angeles entered its industrial and metropolitan age at the most advanced possible stage, the so-called 'second technological-scientific revolution' (Davis, 1990: 39).

Capital reached Southern California mostly in the pockets of its owners. The immigration of thousands of farmers and small-town people from the Midwest made Los Angeles demographically the most American of all big American cities; their savings came into the region as fuel for the local real estate industry. As late as 1930, the social structure of the region was characterized by migration from the geographical heartland of the US. It was called 'the seacoast of Iowa'. Its population was the most Protestant, the whitest, and oldest of all American cities. During this period, Los Angeles grew on the surplus accumulated in other regions of the country. In spite of this drainage of funds from elsewhere, up until World War II, the city suffered from a capital deficit due to the dominance of both consumerism, and the real estate and construction sectors. This deficit was an obstacle to a Fordist economy built on industrial manufacturing. As Davis writes, Los Angeles was a 'city of the petty bourgeoisie and its servants' (Davis, 1990: 74).

The para-Fordist economy of Los Angeles had five large sectors in 1930. Ranked by sales in each individual sector, these were housing and real estate, food and agriculture, oil, Hollywood and automobiles and tires. From these incomplete roots, one of the nerve centers of Fordist production in America was to develop. These roots were incomplete because the city suffered from insufficient linkages to the national economy. Therefore, the Great Depression of the 1930s appeared as an inversion of the situation in other American cities. While in the large industrial centers like Chicago or Detroit the connection of mass production with mass consumption had not been developed, Los Angeles had already laid out the structure for mass consumption (suburbs, automobiles, etc.) without possessing a corresponding productive apparatus (Davis, 1990).

## Fordist Industrialization

While Los Angeles had emerged as an automobile and suburban 'artifact for consumption' and had actually been relatively deindustrialized during the 1920s, the city's industrialization picked up during the 1930s. In spite of the relative decrease in manufacturing's significance during the 1920s, the foundations for a comprehensive industrialization of the region had been laid. In part, this development sprang directly from the decisions of the large corporations in the East and in the Midwest to decentralize their production – for example, Ford's decision to build branch plants in Los Angeles and other cities (Fogelson, 1967: 128). The

**Plate 4.2** *South Gate: city of pride, progress and prosperity (Roger Keil)*

concentration of Fordist mass industries had progressed so far that local entrepreneurs hardly dared to compete with the large companies: 'Even if local entrepreneurs were convinced that rubber could be profitably produced in Los Angeles, they lacked the resources and skills to compete with the Akron oligopoly' (Fogelson, 1967: 127).

The conditions for the implementation of a pro-growth strategy had been prepared in the expansive phase of the 1920s when the growth of the Los Angeles consumer market had attracted branch plants in the automobile industry (Morales, 1986).[8] In the 1930s, an industrialized area developed along the Los Angeles River, stretching from Vernon in the north to Long Beach in the south, from Alameda Street in the west to Pico Rivera in the east. In its heavy industrial and consumer goods plants, particularly in the steel, rubber and auto complex, hundreds of thousands of workers were employed for decades after 1930 (Donahoe, 1987: 4–6).

The wealth of Los Angeles and its sectoral specialization (e.g. aerospace) allowed the city to get through the Great Depression better than other cities. While elsewhere in the US plants were closed, the Californian factories maintained and even expanded their production. In 1939, there were one-fifth more industrial workers in Los Angeles than in 1929. During World War II this situation stabilized. Southern California at the time produced one third of all American war planes. From 1939 to 1944, employment in airplane construction grew from 1000 to 280 000. In total, the number of workers in the plants and docks of the urban region grew from 205 000 to 638 000 between 1939 and 1943 (Clark, 1983: 283). After the war, suburbanization fueled production in the mass industries once again and a new wave of branch plants was established in Southern California. Los Angeles maintained its second place in automobile production after Detroit through the 1950s. Seven large assembly plants with an annual capacity of 650 000 cars were present in the area at the time (Morales, 1986).

The production process in film bore similarities to the mass-production processes in consumer goods industries. Studios were organized like assembly lines: the production process was completely standardized and movies were turned out by the yard. Vertical integration of the industry lowered risk as the film companies owned most distribution points all the way to the theaters. The 'studio system' was intact until 1940 when it was supplemented and later replaced by other forms of production (Christopherson and Storper, 1986).

It has already been noted that the establishment of an industrial base had been the policy of the local growth machine since the 1920s. Robin Bloch (1987) has demonstrated how the aerospace industry took a foothold in Los Angeles because local place entrepreneurs had created appropriate conditions for the location of this industry in the Los Angeles area. This is particularly significant since aerospace is an industry which is commonly viewed most clearly as a direct product of national political decisions and international crises. During the war years, the Southern Californian economy was integrated into the national economy on the basis of aerospace and other defense industries:

> On this basis, elements of the regional bourgeoisie – often in conflict with other regional bourgeoisies and, of course, not without intra-regional class and group conflict – were able to propel themselves and the region into the future on the broad shoulders of the aerospace industry, thus leading the way (if not, in fact, *forcing* the pace) for large parts of the rest of the US (Bloch, 1987: 77)

One consequence of this local and regional urban development effort was the emergence of the urban region as a 'base camp' (Clark, 1983: 282) for the US aerospace industry. The new managers of the electronics, aerospace and real estate industries directed local plants and offices but their interests were more oriented towards Washington and international markets. Their ambitious plans were contradicted by the parochial chamber of commerce mentality of the old power elite (Wiley and Gottlieb, 1982: 110; Carney, 1964: 118). Due to its national orientation, Fordist industrialization ultimately undermined its locally specific conditions of accumulation, conditions that had given the area a competitive advantage over other regions. With increasing industrialization, the history of Los Angeles as 'the citadel of the open shop' ended – at least in the core sectors of manufacturing (Fogelson, 1967: 130). After 1940, a previously unexperienced growth of unionization occurred, and in 1955, 90% of the workers in the local aerospace industry were members of a trade union (Clark, 1983: 282).

## TRANSIT AND AUTOMOBILIZATION

Most American cities expanded after World War II along the highways to and through the suburbs. Los Angeles had preempted this development by at least one generation. In fact, the settlement pattern of Los Angeles had been in existence long before the 1930s; the city had already grown alongside the rail tracks and street corridors between the boom of the 1880s and the boom of 1919–23.[9] The automobile was only partly responsible for the territorial expansion of Los Angeles:

'Various transportation systems have operated successively, and the main city-extension anticipated the model T Ford' (Marchand, 1986: 115). Thus, the freeways can equally be understood as a *response* to rather than as a *reason* for the decentralization of the city (Wachs, 1984: 297). Nevertheless, cars played an important role in the emergence of para-Fordist Los Angeles. Their use and accommodation in the urban structure foreshadowed similar developments in the rest of the nation.

Los Angeles experienced its most extensive growth during the 1920s. During this time, the diffusion of automobiles exploded as well. By the end of the decade, already one out of three Angelenos owned a car (Wachs, 1984).[10] To the degree that in Los Angeles urbanization meant what came to be called *disurbanization* elsewhere, the rail-bound public transit lines became superfluous. The automobile companies were instrumental in ridding the region of its pre-Fordist (rail-oriented) infrastructure.[11]

Local growth strategists who expected the catalytic effect of the private automobile on other economic processes in the urban region were the key movers in the automobilization of Los Angeles. As Bottles (1987) has shown, the most diverse interests were united in celebrating the automobile. Dramatic traffic jams in the early 1920s had led to the Major Traffic Street Plan for Los Angeles in 1924. This plan called for the construction, expansion and straightening of new and existing roads. More than 30 years before the federal highway program, the plan demanded the city embark on expressway construction. Only a fraction of the proposed program was realized, however.

In 1937, a new beginning was made. The Central Business District Association provided the local version of a New Deal-type measure and was subsidized by the federal Public Works Administration and by the city with an amount of $110 000 for a new traffic study. The organization feared further dispersion of economic activity in the city and damage to their inner-city business interests. After a year of research, a citizen committee tabled a study which contained the proposal of an expressway system whose original plans can be seen as the skeleton for the current freeway grid (Bottles, 1987: 218). Many years before it became federal policy, a piece of Fordist infrastructure had emerged as the product of the political activity of the local growth machine. As indicated earlier, the war stopped the implementation of the plans. But the development could not be reversed. What seemed unique and merely tailored to solve urban traffic problems in 1937, turned out, in hindsight, to be one of the central elements of Fordist urbanism in general. During World War II confidence in the relevance of freeways was unbroken but local agents lacked a financing option. This option was created in 1947 with the California Collier–Burns Act which provided $300 million for the metropolitan freeway system of Los Angeles alone (Bottles, 1987: 230).[12]

The Pasadena (or Arroyo Seco) Parkway was opened in 1940[13] and supplemented later with the Hollywood, San Bernadino, Santa Ana and Harbor Freeways to form a radial system that was meant to service the downtown (Warner, 1972: 141; Clark, 1983: 273). World War II, however, changed this planning logic in a decisive way because the military industry was more interested in suburban locations and favored the maintenance of the grid system on which Los Angeles had grown:

68

*Plate 4.3*  *Fordist streetscape, downtown Los Angeles (Roger Keil)*

*Plate 4.4*  *Dismantling rail: abandoned tracks in West Los Angeles (Roger Keil)*

**Plate 4.5**  *The Arroyo Seco Parkway (Photo by 'Dick' Whittington, Courtesy of the Henry E. Huntington Library)*

> The grid pattern, based on overspeculation, combined with population growth to create what one analyst called a 'flexible labor market', which permitted the new wartime industries to set themselves up in outlying areas, beyond the business central district. This perimeter development and the vast auto-supportive highway program, the first and largest of any American city, allowed managerial and factory personnel to live considerable distances from both their places of work and the central city (Wiley and Gottlieb, 1982: 111).

The conflict of interest between the downtown bourgeoisie, which favored central development, and the military and civil entrepreneurs of the emerging Fordist complex (street and housing construction, shopping malls, suburban industries) was indicative of the years to come. Often, however, it was the same property owners and speculators who, in their effort to decentralize their interests by moving their activities to suburbia, endangered their downtown profits. This insight eventually led to attempts by the traditional downtown growth coalition to increase property values in the downtown by investment in an infrastructure for high culture (Wiley and Gottlieb, 1982: 111; Gottlieb and Wolt, 1976).

The grid system that had emerged from the contradictory local dynamics of competing growth coalitions became a model for California freeway planning after the passing of the Interstate Highway Act of 1956 (Warner, 1972: 141). Los Angeles still remained unique in many respects: while in American cities today between one fourth and one-third of the entire urban area is used by traffic (freeways, streets, parking lots), this share is 50% in Los Angeles, the city with the highest per capita car use in the world. The automobile thus is given as much space as all other human activities in the city (Marchand, 1986: 106–107).

The struggle over the regulation of traffic in Los Angeles was by no means restricted to road construction. As much as transportation planning is less concerned with rapid movement than with reaching places, territorial coalitions, concerned about the profitability of their property, fight over the most lucrative connection of their protectorate into the main streams of labor power and consumer capacity. These territorial coalitions can be seen as competing subsidiaries of the regional growth machine. Since the 1920s Los Angeles has witnessed a continuous tug-of-war between the place entrepreneurs of the inner city, who prefer a 'neocolonial' radial transportation system, with the downtown as its center of gravity, and business coalitions of the suburbs, who hope to smash the 'imperial chains' of the inner-city coalition in order to pursue their own business interests (Adler, 1986).

It is interesting to note in this context that the idea of a central–radial public transit system in Los Angeles became the focal point of a typical New Deal coalition as it existed in almost all American cities after the 1930s, and through which place entrepreneurs, politicians and labor unionists joined to carry out urban renewal and redevelopment. The strategies of the various coalitions reflected different aspects and versions of the concept of the Fordist city: centralization and decentralization; public and private ownership of collective consumption enterprises; collective and private consumption were the main lines of struggle. The most important agents in this struggle were the traditional downtown coalition, various government levels implicated through investments into public transit, transit labor unions, commuters, the transit-dependent poor who did not own cars, and the numerous suburban growth coalitions. The decision-making powers of the public transit authority of Southern California (SCRTD) were historically curtailed because it had to constitute its position in the highly politicized field of tension among these agents (Adler, 1986).

The debates and struggles over public transit and automobile traffic have been structured by contradictions between various territorial and sectoral factions of the ruling elite. The history of transit in Los Angeles was part of local conditions of which the city became a key element of the emergence of Fordism overall.

## HOUSING

The history of housing provision in Los Angeles also identifies the city as a place where Fordist elements emerged earlier than elsewhere in the United States. In 1930, single-family homes made up 94% of the entire housing supply. Ironically, this figure decreased at the same time as this housing form began its victory parade in the US. In 1960, only 72% of housing units in Los Angeles were single-family homes. The decentralized project of the 1920s could not survive in the face of the centralization and agglomeration tendencies of the local Fordist economic miracle.[14] The more Los Angeles expanded, the more it grew vertically. In 1956, at the top of the wave of suburbanization, the city's voters lifted the height limit on skyscrapers, a limit which had persisted as an expression of both earthquake scare and the dominant planning ideology of decentralization (Foster, 1971: iii). This measure signalled the opening of the sky for the absorption of capital after the near-total settlement of the Southern California plain.

Suburbanization and the hunger for space were still unbroken: 'The suburbs at first jumped over farmlands, creating curious checkerboard patterns with houses planted among orange groves, but as the real estate beneath the orchards became too valuable for growing oranges, developers sometimes uprooted a thousand trees a day' (Clark, 1983: 289). While the construction of housing had almost stopped during the war years, and the few new apartments had quickly been occupied by defense workers who streamed into the city in large numbers, a building boom hit the city after 1945. Around 1950, the market began to stabilize. The new inhabitants of Los Angeles were willing consumers of the Fordist showcase product: the single-family home. In 1948 a suburbanite could purchase a small but comfortable house for a monthly instalment of $50. The homeownership rate rose between 1940 and 1950 from 40 to 53%; the single-family home was the favorite housing form. In 1960 there were 2.4 million housing units in Los Angeles, two and a half times more than in 1940. In 1963 a quarter of all construction activity in the US occurred in Southern California; and a quarter of all real estate agents in the country had their seat in Los Angeles. After 1960, however, the relative share of multi-family buildings grew. Already in 1958, the number of built apartments was bigger than that of single-family homes. This trend finally led to a situation where, between 1970 and 1973, 92% of all constructed housing units were apartments: a spectacular example of a 'spatial fix' through intensification of investments (Marchand, 1986: 71–73; Clark, 1983).

In Los Angeles, like elsewhere, the American Dream was built on credit. Between two-thirds and three-quarters of the housing units were mortgaged in 1960. This number was higher than the national average and also higher than the figure for comparable cities. Between 1950 and 1960, the total debt of homeowners in the city rose from $2.4 to $6 billion (in 1986 values; the rise in constant prices was from $2 to $4.9 billion). The tradition of external financing of Southern California real estate which had started in earlier boom times continued in this period because the rate of return was higher in the American West than it was in the East. 'From this viewpoint Los Angeles appears not as a local product but as a national endeavor, concentrating interests and hopes from the whole nation' (Marchand, 1986: 155). And, despite its remarkable peculiarities and despite its 'headstart' into Fordism, Los Angeles does not defy national trends of housing provision after 1945.

Public housing was the inner-city version of Fordist housing provision. It had come into existence due to working-class pressure during the New Deal period. In 1949 Los Angeles was the first American city to obtain an allocation of federal funds for public housing after the new Housing Act which had been passed that same year (Marcuse and Hartman, 1988). This allocation was largely due to the political lobbying of Los Angeles mayor Fletcher Bowron who felt pressure from his working-class constituencies. The Federal Housing Authority allocated 10 000 units to the city. The City Council ratified the contract in 1950 with a large majority. Only one year later, however, political power relationships in the city had shifted, and the political majority for public housing began to wane. The fact that part of the housing units were to be newly constructed buildings on suburban sites was important in triggering the resistance of the conservative council members: without the legitimizing element of the elimination of inner-city slum areas, they felt, all that remained was sheer socialism. Consequently, a bitter struggle – drenched in McCarthyist cacophonies – ensued around the project (Parson, 1985: 93). The opponents of public housing finally gained the majority in the City Council, won their case in a plebiscite and toppled Mayor Bowron, the 'champion of public housing', in 1953. He was replaced by the conservative Republican Norris Poulson, the handpicked candidate of the powerful inner-city bourgeoisie (Hines, 1982: 139; Parson, 1985: 98). The defeat of the forces in support of public housing who were represented by the municipal housing authority meant that between 1953 and 1955 fewer than half of the 10 000 allocated housing units were built (Hines, 1982: 140; Parson, 1985: 12). By 1955 the era of public housing in Los Angeles was over. While the private suburban solution became the main strategy of Fordist housing provision, the inner city was anticipating the ravages of urban renewal (Parson, 1985: 101).

## Politics

In spite of the fragmentation of the urban region, the structured coherence of Fordist Los Angeles can be explained mostly from the perspective of the political hegemony of the center. Los Angeles in the 1930s came close to the cliché image of a corrupt, violent and ungovernable American metropolis. The setting in which the lone PI of noirish detective novels was caught between a corrupt urban administration and the underworld found its real-life correspondence in the urban politics of Southern California where corruption and brutality ruled the political process. The conducting of political business by a club of older white gentlemen mostly from the traditional downtown bourgeoisie, and its 'foot soldiers', recruited in the right-leaning Midwestern petty bourgeoisie, lends credence to all kinds of conspiracy theories of urban government. After the effective elimination of democratic, socialist and progressive[15] alternatives in the beginning of the century, the local state had become a powerful tool of the central city place entrepreneurs who had rallied politically around the *Los Angeles Times* empire (Gottlieb and Wolt, 1977).

The mayor of Los Angeles from 1933 to 1938 was Frank Shaw – a Republican and a New Deal supporter. His 'interest group liberalism' was weighted toward the center of the political spectrum, which put him at odds with liberals, leftists and conservative moral reformers. This unlikely coalition accused (overzealously and perhaps hypocritically) the Shaw administration of being corrupt and graft-ridden. Shaw's tenure ended in scandal, following the bombing of the car of a detective who was supposed to examine corruption in local politics. A 1938 recall[16] vote brought Justice Fletcher Bowron – described by the *Times* as an 'honest reformer who has become the unwitting dupe of the CIO, the Communists, and certain crackpot reformers' – into the mayoral office.

Under Bowron the urban restructuring of the New Deal coalition – public housing and its evil twin of urban renewal – began to take shape. But when public housing and Bowron were defeated, the social aspects of this project evaporated.

The Bunker Hill urban renewal project, approved by the City Council in 1959, opened the door for a comprehensive valorization of space in the central city (Friedman, 1978; Gottlieb and Wolt, 1977; Parson, 1993). The Central City Committee, appointed by Mayor Poulson in 1957, developed a general plan for the inner-city district in cooperation with the city's planning commission and business representatives.

Poulson's mayorality was characterized by the creation of good business conditions for that part of the regional bourgeoisie with interests in the inner city; Poulson himself was '[the old elite's] perfect foil' (Wiley and Gottlieb, 1982: 112). The strategy of cultural upgrading in the inner city as a lever of urban development, the political elimination of a social form of housing provision, and the unscrupulous implementation of urban renewal measures against the existing inner-city population were the leading phenomena in the politics of the 1950s.[17]

The establishment of the hegemony of the central city was never a linear process. The electoral militancy of the Mexican population with Armenians, Russians, African Americans and Jews on the Eastside had led to the election of Ed Roybal, the first City Councilman of Mexican American origin since 1881. Through the McCarthy period and until his resignation from the council in 1962, Roybal remained a critical voice in an era of conservative hegemony. Earlier than in comparable cities in the US, African Americans became Los Angeles City Council members in the 1950s. The McCarthyism and anticommunism of the cold war saw the subjugation of formal party politics to the postwar productivity deal while sowing the ground for the antistatist movement politics of the following decade (Parson, 1985).

Cracks in the structured coherence of Fordist Los Angeles appeared in the urban periphery. The revolt of the suburban districts of the city of Los Angeles against the hegemony of the downtown found its political expression in 1961 when Sam Yorty was elected mayor. His tirades against the 'downtown machine' secured Yorty decisive electoral margins in the semirural San Fernando Valley, and his bow towards the black population on the question of police brutality gave him votes which his opponent Poulson did not control anymore (Gottlieb and Wolt, 1977).

In essential questions like urban development policies, police violence, economic development, etc., the local state under Yorty was little more than the executive committee of regional capital. Soon after having been elected on a populist and antielitist ticket, the mayor had made his peace with the 'downtown machine'. Until his reelection against the liberal Jimmy Roosevelt, who had campaigned explicitly against the business interests of the inner city, Yorty had changed from being the 'champion of the little man' to a representative of the existing order supported by the waning yet still noticeable influence of the *Los Angeles Times*.

The modernized populist despotism of capital over the urban political process, which Yorty represented, experienced the beginning of its end with the Watts rebellion in 1965. The summer of that year saw an urban explosion which was one of the most intense black riots of the decade. The bigoted and racist position of Yorty (and of his police apparatus) was repeatedly criticized in the wake of the Watts uprising and reached a final climax in the election campaign of 1969. Based on the conservatism of his constituency in the suburban San Fernando Valley,

Yorty was able to mount a smear campaign against (the former policeman) Tom Bradley on the terrain of internal security. Up until the middle of the 1960s, all essential pillars of what was to become the Bradley coalition were politically marginalized: neither African Americans, nor Jews, nor the suburban Westside had noticeable impact on the urban political process. The institutionalized labor movement also had no significant share of power. Carney (1964: 118) wrote: 'Organized labor has still the stigma of the parvenu. . . . [It] has not been a major power in the city either. At best, labor has been one of the competing influence groups.'

The municipal government of Yorty neither presented a lasting solution for the incorporation of the contradictions of the imminent restructuring processes nor held the complete trust of the elite for the implementation of their ambitious plans for the downtown. Two days before the mayoral election of 1969, the *LAT* wrote an editorial about Yorty:

> The city of Los Angeles is approaching a choice at the polls that will determine the quality of its future for years to come. . . . The incumbent, Sam Yorty, has an eight-year record of bickering and weak leadership, racial divisiveness and clowning absenteeism on world-wide junkets, collusion and bribery among his appointed commissioners, and tirades against the agencies of justice in metropolitan Los Angeles. . . . The *Times* believes that the future of this city lies not in dividing into antagonistic factions those who will live in it the coming decades, but Mayor Yorty has willfully done that (quoted in Gottlieb and Wolt, 1977: 406).

It was only Tom Bradley's rise at the beginning of the 1970s that proved that the traditional political regulation which Yorty stood for was no longer appropriate for the demands posed by the development of Los Angeles. Southern California was on the threshold of becoming a world city region. Two characteristics of the emerging Bradley regime accounted for these changing circumstances: the (incomplete) incorporation of racial and ethnic minorities as well as the working class into the regime; and the programmatic commitment to the erection of the world city citadel.

Bradley's insight into the necessity for corporatist recruitment of both the core working class and the relevant civil rights organizations into the project of urban restructuring signified a break with the elite policy of exclusion which had characterized both Poulson and Yorty. The Bradley regime guaranteed an interim integration of the centrifugal forces of the Fordist social structure and expressed a willingness to lend political profile to the expansionary drive of capital. Bradley, then, became on one hand the temporary solution for the coherence of the Fordist city, and on the other, the political engineer of post-Fordist restructuring in the world city. For the national and international corporations which made Los Angeles their location, as well as for the local place entrepreneurs of the downtown and of the larger region, Bradley's statesmanlike appearance served their needs for an appropriate representation of their plans for the production of an international place.

How Bradley's appearance and political savvy were complemented by a clear program to develop a world class city will be subject of the following chapter. Ironically, Bradley bought the temporary political stability of the structured

**Plate 4.6**  *Fordist sunset in East Los Angeles (Roger Keil)*

coherence represented by his administration with the integration of unstable political fiefdoms: '. . . the Jewish west side, the black south-central area, the conservative San Fernando Valley, and, of course, downtown, represented by a black city councilman who delighted in acting as the court jester while vociferously defending his downtown clients' (Wiley and Gottlieb, 1982: 114). New political groups could intervene in this empire of fiefdoms only when the Bradley coalition collapsed. This process sealed the fate of Fordist Los Angeles and triggered the genesis of the world city.

# CHAPTER 5

# IMPOSSIBLE DREAM

Former policeman and African American political activist Tom Bradley was elected mayor of Los Angeles in 1973. He had run unsuccessfully against conservative incumbent Sam Yorty four years earlier at a time when the aftermath of the Watts rebellion of 1965 had turned Los Angeles into a racialized political battleground. Predictions for black political power in the City of Angels were accordingly grim during the time (Scoble, 1967). Thus, when he took office in 1973 as the first elected African American mayor in any major US city, Bradley symbolized a turn in urban politics in both Los Angeles and the United States. The period was characterized by the big questions that the 'urban crisis' of the 1960s had posed: social policy, urban renewal, environment, racism etc. (Bollens and Geyer, 1973). Los Angeles, at the time, was not much different from other American cities, except perhaps that it seemed much less important than places like New York, Chicago or San Francisco. It had little more to offer than the charm of a regional center which attempted – once again – to revive a seemingly nonexistent down-town core through a half-hearted urban renewal program. Little more than one decade later, in 1984, Tom Bradley's city presented itself as the proud host of the financially and propagandistically wildly successful Olympic Games, and a hopeful contender for the crown of the world cities on the Pacific Rim. Not much of the cow-town modesty of the post-World War II era was left. Los Angeles had learned to use the American art of boosterism as a weapon in international interurban competition. Los Angeles was poised to become the 'world capital of the twenty-first century'. This project was supported by various factions of urban elites and pushed ahead politically by Tom Bradley. It came to a sudden – but perhaps only temporary – halt on April 29, 1992 when the most violent and pervasive urban unrest in America during this century called into question the viability of the 'world class city'.

## THE BRADLEY REGIME

There have been at least two ways of conceptualizing the construction of power in Los Angeles: in the first view, Los Angeles has always had a 'permanent govern-ment' of a mostly landed bourgeoisie (from the old rancher aristocracy to the real estate tycoons of today). Voting and popular struggles have rarely been able to influence the course of the city's development charted by this ruling elite; in the second view, the ruling of Los Angeles has been conceived as a function of class struggles in space. Governing coalitions have been dependent both on the power of permanent elite factions and on some degree of popular consent. I would argue that both interpretations hold some truth. They are complementary explanations rather than exclusive stories.

78

***Plate 5.1*** *Los Angeles City Hall/John's Burger (Roger Keil)*

Complex urban regions like Los Angeles are not governable by just one ruling bloc, yet there are competing factions within both the ruling elites and the popular classes. One of the most important ongoing struggles inside Los Angeles' ruling class, for example, has been the fight between the center-oriented and the sub-urban real-estate based bourgeoisie, marked in past decades by the shift in the regional power structure from the downtown *Times* hegemony to the emergent and implanted aerospace- and automobile-related, federally subsidized capital factions that industrialized the suburbs after World War II. That the power between these two major blocs has been kept largely in balance can be discerned from the form of the city itself: Los Angeles is, as one observer put it, the first American city to be urban, suburban and exurban at once.

Although they did not *invent* a revitalization strategy (plans like that had existed since the 1940s and had been implemented since the 1950s), the Bradley regime was the ideal medium to make good on these plans. Bradley made a pact not just with the traditional downtown bourgeoisie but also with their Westside competitors. In addition, he pulled significant portions of the international real estate capital flowing into the city into his coalition by using the local political process both in procedural terms and on philosophical grounds: he extended affirmative action to Chinese bankers and defended Japanese real estate and other investors against what he (probably correctly) considered racist attacks on foreign

investment. Over a long period of time, Bradley was also a believable representative of 'community concerns', however controversial they might have appeared
at certain times; he was one of the first big city black mayors; he appealed to the
white middle class with his stated 'environmentalism'; and he served not only parts
of the African American community but also various petty bourgeois elements in
several newly immigrated communities with his creation of public jobs and the
support for small business. He managed to become the 'teflon mayor' because of
unbroken popular support.

Bradley was never just the creature of one ruling class faction but the
(malleable and flexible) product of social and political class struggles that pushed
him and his regime all over the political landscape during his years in office. Like
other black mayors (in Newark, Gary, etc.) Bradley came to power at the height of
the 'urban crisis' and had to deal with similar problems. Unlike these mayors,
however, Bradley came to preside over the most spectacular internationalized
growth of any big city in North America, symbolized by the Olympics in 1984, and
the resurgence of the corporate downtown (among other things). Bradley's way out
of the 'urban crisis' was a growth strategy which propelled the city into 'world class
city' status.

There have been two major interpretations of the Bradley regime. One has
attempted to view Bradley's reign as the successful incorporation of minority
voters into the existing system of local political power (Sonenshein, 1993); the
other has been largely critical of the politics of the mayor's administration in the
context of larger restructuring processes (Davis, 1990).

While Davis – like Sonenshein – considers the support of supralocal Jewish
politicians in the Democratic Party (the Berman–Waxman machine) a key element
of the local coalition in Los Angeles, he emphasizes the exploding aspects of the
increasing cleavage between Jewish (Westside) voters and inner-city communities
of color fueled by the ideological battle cry of 'slow growth'. Historically, the
political leadership of the Berman–Waxman machine (and their strategic connection to Zev Yaroslavsky, the former Westside councilman) played a decisive
role in this tension. While Sonenshein stresses the stabilization of the coalition
through Bradley's skills in attracting federal monies (Saltzstein, S Ostrow, 1986),
Davis points out the deficiencies of Bradley's social policy. Instead of using
municipal funds to address social problems Bradley's administration shifted the
responsibility for social ills to the federal government and to the county. In terms
of urban development, Bradley's policies, which were directed at internationalizing
and redeveloping the downtown, could be read as a pacification strategy signaling
to the Westside that growth would be concentrated elsewhere. But they also
amounted to a disinvestment policy in south-central and east Los Angeles. To
Davis, the purely arithmetic electoral Bradley coalition, therefore, was mostly
superficial and not an example of successful incorporation. During the crisis of the
Bradley regime in the late 1980s, Westside homeowners were stepping up their
demand for slow-growth policies as developers were attempting to sway public
opinion in minority neighborhoods by catering to fears of job loss and economic
decline if growth controls went into effect. Representatives of rapid development
and high densities often clad their projects in a rhetoric of class struggle and
populism by suggesting the job-creation and housing benefits of their practices.

The Bradley coalition, therefore, dissolved neatly along the racial and class lines which had divided constituencies before the mayor's five consecutive mandates. While the white middle classes emerged as winners in this process, the working classes in the inner city – marginalized, impoverished and suppressed during Bradley's quest for the 'world class city' – remained 'a sleeping dragon' (Davis, 1987).[1]

The Bradley coalition became the local political instrument of the globalization of Los Angeles. But the successful implementation of Bradley's program was dependent on the modification of the very coalition that brought him to, and held him in, power. Bradley's political decision in favor of the expansion of the 'world class city' was no feasible program for the social regulation of the world city. The Bradley coalition, prime mover of local internationalization strategies, was itself transformed in the process. International investment and continued immigration exploded the structured coherence in which the coalition had a safe and powerful place.

The hegemony of the Bradley coalition in Los Angeles during the 1970s and 1980s could not have worked without a foundation of popular support.[2] Even the colossal and out-of-control Community Redevelopment Agency (CRA), which has been operating in the interests of international capital and the local real estate industry, was subject to popular influences over the years. It was typical of Bradley's style (which set him miles apart from his predecessors) to incorporate powerful social groups into his coalition. The best example – and hardly a token appointment – was County labor leader[3] James Wood's tenure as the chairman of the board of the CRA. Yet, the inclusiveness of Bradley's coalition distinguished itself significantly from the exclusive and elite way the 'permanent government' of Los Angeles had run the city through most of its history.

Bradley was a contradictory figure, a mediator between the 'permanent government' and the popular classes of Los Angeles, between global capital and local communities. He had to represent a variety of ruling-class interests and mediate them with a variety of popular demands. One way to conceptualize this is by imagining Bradley as the mayor simultaneously of a Santa Barbara, a Detroit, the 24th ward of Tokyo, a Seattle, a Tijuana, a Palo Alto and a few more cities. Each of these 'cities' have ruling classes and class structures, cultural heritages, political traditions of their own. Who becomes hegemonic in this process is a function not just of economic power but of the social, cultural and political struggles articulating this economic power within local civil society.

## BRADLEY'S PLAN FOR LOS ANGELES: THE IMPOSSIBLE DREAM

Some politicians find it fashionable to rail against foreign investment – to conjure up images of foreign takeovers. . . . At its best, this is nothing but political grandstanding. But at its worst, this is a dangerous strain of racism that must be rebutted (Tom Bradley quoted in Harris, 1989).

We will always stand firm against those among us who could sow the seeds of disharmony. We must not tolerate calls for a halt or a reduction in foreign investment in our city. We will remain vigilant against narrow-minded interests who would exploit fears and promote prejudice in a bid to drive foreign investors from our community. We welcome foreign investment because we know it creates new jobs for our workers and new tax revenue for our city. It is because of Japanese investments in Los Angeles that over 150 000 jobs have been created in the Los Angeles area (Bradley, 1989: 6).

> To a greater extent than any other municipal leader . . . Bradley has integrated foreign capital into the top rungs of his coalition. Although no one can recall the mayor making strenuous efforts to defend the 50 000 local high-wage manufacturing jobs wiped out by imports since 1975, he has been unflagging in his promotion of the movement of free capital across the Pacific while denouncing critics of Japanese power as 'racists'. His administration has kept landing fees at LAX amongst the lowest in the world, vastly expanded port facilities, given special zoning exemptions and development-right subsidies to foreign investors Downtown (especially Shuwa), and made expatriate bankers the recipients of 'affirmative action' (Davis, 1990: 136–137).

Tom Bradley's success was based on his programmatic commitment to the 'impossible dream'[4] of transforming Los Angeles from a secondary, non-concentrated, socially and spatially segregated national metropolis into one of the great centers of international finance, production and commerce of the waning twentieth century. However clear this vision might appear in historical hindsight, Bradley's first steps after his inauguration were not so farsighted, and grew rather from the logic of every political decision. Internationally oriented economic development, the application to host the Olympics, and urban redevelopment were processes that were already in place when Bradley came in and revitalized them. Getting the Olympics back to Southern California (after the world sports event had put Los Angeles on the map of international metropoles in 1932) had been on the wish list of urban elites since 1939 when the Southern California Committee for the Olympic Games was founded. Bradley recognized that the combination of the Olympic idea with his urban management methods promised to be a 'goldmine' for the city (Payne and Ratzan, 1987). Urban renewal had been a continuous theme in local politics since the 1950s but had not led to many tangible results beyond the destruction of housing units, the construction of a cultural center on Bunker Hill and the erection of Dodger Stadium in Chavez Ravine. In terms of urban and economic development, the stated goal of a boom fueled by international investment and foreign labor was not achievable until such investment actually occurred as a consequence of the boosterism of the Bradley administration.

Interestingly enough, early political statements by Bradley did not make it apparent that he would pursue the internationalization of Los Angeles actively. The mayor's inauguration took place at a time when President Nixon, declaring the urban crisis over, prepared his New Federalism; a time when cities everywhere in the United States were in dire financial straits. Bradley's 1973 program and rhetoric were characterized by related events: the retreat of the federal government from responsibility for the cities (New Federalism); the local fiscal crisis, unemployment, etc.; and the plunge of the inner city into total meaninglessness (Woody, 1982; Bradley, 1974). Bradley advocated strong federal subsidies to the cities, argued against a 'throw-away-mentality' with regard to the inner cities, propagated new management techniques in the local state, and implemented a local form of corporatism which got 'some of the country's most outstanding leaders from labor unions, industry, finance, law, and academia' working together 'on active citizen committees to promote the economic development program of the city' (Bradley, 1979: 135).

Bradley's initial economic program focused on the link between the city and the federal government. That was how solutions to 'the urban crisis' were envisioned at the time. Only after he had come to power did he move into full gear to convince the city's traditional economic elites of his ability to maintain and develop the city as a profitable business location. He hired Fred Schnell, the president of a big insurance company, as an economic consultant to the city. In consultation with leaders of the economic interest groups in the city, Schnell proposed an Economic Development Office for the city, which was established in 1975. In the years to come, Brad Crowe, the head of this office, became instrumental in increasing the allocation of federal funds to the city. As Bradley's biographers report laconically: 'Thus began a relationship that would change the skyline and the make-up of Downtown Los Angeles' (Payne and Ratzan, 1987: 141).

But Bradley's initial and rapid success in turning the city around was not just a function of his economic finesse. He also managed to maintain popular support. When he transcended the racialized discourse that Sam Yorty had forced on him in the 1969 and 1973 campaigns, Tom Bradley entered City Hall as a 'peacemaker' and 'integrator'. Bradley's ability to smooth out the waves of social unrest in Los Angeles during that time enabled new concepts of an urban future to surface, and opened the space of the city to the fantasies of (Westside) developers who had their eyes on the downtown prize. In this context, the concept of the world class city emerged during the 1970s as a more or less deliberate attempt to fight the sticky reputation of Los Angeles as a 'cowtown populated by wannabes and hillbillies'. In imaginary competition with New York City, Los Angeles, under the leadership of the Bradley coalition, was to reinvent itself. The availability of space in Los Angeles, as well as the more flexible social structures and residential markets, were considered key assets in that competition for primacy in the US urban system.[5]

Early in Bradley's tenure as mayor, Los Angeles became a beneficiary of the tightly knit relationship between the cities and the federal government of the United States. Predominantly due to the activities of Bradley's administration, Los Angeles – once an underaverage recipient of federal transfer funds – after 1973 received more federal monies for social and urban development programs than most other cities in the USA. Between 1971 and 1980, the sum of federal transfer payments tripled. From less than $100 million in 1972, these payments rose to $320 million in 1978–79, an expression of the Bradley administration's expertise in riding the carousel of federal aid. Originally elected on a platform that promised to counteract the defunding and destruction of the inner-city communities after Watts, 1965, Bradley now strove to come through on his promise while taking the city into the orbit of world city formation. Bradley, whose practice of relying on federal funds meant a departure from Sam Yorty's reluctance in such matters, turned the city's growing dependency on federal transfers into political power for himself by directing the flow of money into the structures of his bureaucracy and con-stituencies. For instance, the number of staff in the office of the mayor grew from 275 to over 600 under Bradley. Most of these new employees – like many aides of council members – were hired directly with federal funding. In this context, Bradley countered allegations of building a political machine with the establishment in 1976 of a quasi-independent Community Development Department designed to administer the housing and community block grants of the federal government. Over the years, Bradley's interest shifted towards large transfer payments for urban development and infrastructure projects, eventually eclipsing entirely the initial social and community development aspects of his program (Saltzstein, Sonenshein and Ostrow, 1986).

After the elections of 1977, when the 'increase in foreign trade' was still of lesser importance to policy programs in Los Angeles (Bradley, 1979), the internationalization of the city remained one of the continuous – and never uncontroversial – themes of local political discourse. For the first time, Bradley had to justify his trips to foreign countries. The strategy of justification gave him the opportunity to introduce the political postulate to make Los Angeles 'a truly international city'. Bradley made it known that he considered it his mandate to foster the reputation of the city as the 'gateway to the Pacific Rim'. Behind Washington, Los Angeles became the place in the United States most favored by visiting foreign dignitaries. Bradley returned many of these visits and advertised Los Angeles as a business location and tourist spot in Europe, Asia and Africa (Payne and Ratzan, 1987). Between 1983 and 1989, he spent a total of 15 weeks on official trips to foreign countries (*LAT*, September 6, 1989, II, 2). On these travels, he personally represented a world city cosmopolitanism that he wished for as a feature of his city. Bradley was considered a 'world class citizen' who was well-liked and very effective applying his 'silent diplomacy' in the countries of Europe, Africa and along the Pacific Rim.

One focus of the internationalization strategy that played a big role in boosting the city was the expansion of urban infrastructures, such as the port and the airport, as keystones to stepping up international trade. As a result of Bradley's strategies to make Los Angeles 'the financial and commercial capital of the Pacific Rim' (Bradley, n.d.: 3), the city had trade offices in Japanese and Chinese cities. The 71 national governments represented in Los Angeles made the consulate corps the second largest of its kind in the United States (Payne and Ratzan, 1987).

With the success of the urban development strategy – expressed in the growth of the skyline of Los Angeles – the internationalization of the city became a self-fulfilling prophecy: the more local development attracted global capital and international workers, the more this characteristic became the integral fuel of urban politics. The internal logic of the world class city doctrine was the conviction that the central and internationally oriented urban development policy would contribute to the improvement of the social situation of the majority of citizens in Los Angeles. In this instance, the ideology of the world class city most clearly diverged from the social reality of world city formation, which presented itself in a dynamics of fragmentation, polarization and pauperization.

Beginning in the 1980s, but particularly after the successful 'pilot strategy' of the 1984 Olympics, the Bradley government hardly hid its desire to further an unfettered internationalization of the city. Reaching out over the Pacific Ocean became a new 'Manifest Destiny', as a predetermined fate of American national history, which was now embodied by Los Angeles and which implied the 'legitimate' leadership of the city and of the nation on the Pacific Rim:

**Plate 5.2**  *Home Boy Tacos #1, McArthur Park area Los Angeles (Roger Keil)*

Los Angeles is standing on the very brink of her great destiny. Through the vision and industry of her people, Los Angeles should be prepared to lead America into the twenty-first century. Los Angeles is the future because the world's future will be in the Pacific Rim. Just as the Atlantic was the ocean of the twentieth century, the Pacific will be the ocean of the twenty-first. Los Angeles, as the gateway city to the Pacific Rim nations, sits astride the travel and trade routes between the United States and the Pacific Rim. The opening of the Pacific Rim will change human history in many profound ways, and Los Angeles is poised on the edge of these dramatic changes (Bradley, n.d.: 1).

Bradley did not leave room for any doubts that he would also demand the leadership role of Los Angeles domestically: 'Los Angeles will continue to lead America in World Economic Competition' (Bradley, 1989).

## THE END OF THE DREAM: THE CRISIS OF THE BRADLEY REGIME

Indeed, there is the widespread feeling that the Growth Machine – the business–labor–real-estate complex and its political allies – is responsible for ignoring the impact of economic change on the daily lives of the city's residents (Shearer, 1988).

Like all ideology, 'slow growth' and its 'pro-growth' antipode must be understood as much from the standpoint of the questions absent, as those posed. The debate between affluent homeowners and mega-developers is, after all, waged in the language of *Alice in Wonderland*, with both camps conspiring to preserve false opposites, 'growth' versus 'neighborhood quality'. It is symptomatic of the current distribution of power – that the appalling destruction and misery within Los Angeles's inner city areas became the great non-issue during the 1980s, while the impact of growth upon affluent neighborhoods occupied center stage (Davis, 1990).

During Tom Bradley's fourth term in office after 1985, the political hegemony of his regime began to wane. The more it fulfilled itself, the less acceptable Bradley's concept of unlimited development in the world city citadel became. It started to become obvious that many of the social, economic, spatial and environmental problems from which the urban region suffered had been caused by the specific course of internationalization that the elites of the city followed. Social and economic polarization and fragmentation corresponded to the disintegration of the political alliances on which the Bradley coalition rested.

From 1986 on, this disintegration was most visible in two areas: first, a redrawing of council district boundaries in Los Angeles showed the cracks that had appeared in the city's structured coherence due to immigration and internationalization. The black–white–Jewish coalition that had carried the Bradley regime was now being questioned by both newly emerging economic elites and by regrouping popular forces. Second, the coalition was falling apart over issues in which the economic interests of its members increasingly clashed due to the process of internationalization.

A lawsuit by the Department of Justice in Washington against the city of Los Angeles in November of 1985 necessitated a redrawing of the city's council districts. The Latino population, which at the time was estimated to be at least 30% of the city's total, was represented only by Richard Alatorre in the 15-member City Council. Redistricting was intended to make the election of a second Hispanic council member possible, thereby increasing Latino representation numerically from 6.5 to 13%. The original redistricting plan for the city was drafted by Richard Alatorre. It would have placed Michael Woo, the first Chinese American council-man in Los Angeles, into a district which would have included Chinatown but which – with its 65% Latino majority – would have made the reelection of an Asian American unrealistic. Political maneuvering in City Council finally ended up leaving Woo in Hollywood and creating a mostly Latino district at the expense of the northern, white districts (Keil, 1987a). In the election of February 3, 1987, Gloria Molina, a Chicana politician, was elected in this district as a new council member (Clayton, 1987a, b).[6]

The constantly shifting proportional representation of parts of the polity due to changing demographic realities can only be a 'solution' of very limited duration. In addition, demographic change only incompletely expressed the structural shift in political power in Los Angeles. The Bradley coalition fell under the influence of several important dynamics which exploded this structure: the crisis of African American political power; the growing influence of Latino and Asian politicians in California; the increase in Jewish political power in Los Angeles.[7] These changes in representation had centrifugal effects because they were expressions of the growing dissimilarity of social realities for individual communities in Los Angeles. They called into question the fabric of political power and economic stability in Los Angeles. The political coalition of mostly African American and Jewish voters which had determined most of the politics during the 1970s and 1980s became porous. It showed that the connection of the social question with civil rights issues turned out to be more difficult when the wealth of the Westside could be considered as functionally related to the misery in the east and the south of the City. Bradley's 'impossible dream', his strategy of linking the growth of the world class city to improvements in the low-income communities, failed because, in reality, it led to a deepening of the social divide. The crisis of the Bradley coalition, which had rested on a specific spatial and territorial system of power, also entailed a crisis of political space in the city. Geographical terms such as 'Westside', 'East LA', and 'South Central' came to stand in for socially, economically and politically opposed versions of world-city politics.[8] When the old black-and-white order of power in Los Angeles began to erode, the world class city concept of the Bradley regime began to fall apart.

Although Bradley stuck to his strategy and welcomed further internationalization in Los Angeles, he experienced great difficulties, from 1986 on, in joining the different members of his coalition under a single project (Boyarsky, 1987c). On the other hand, the new social problems had surfaced so vehemently that a linking of social policy to the continued expansion of global city functions could not be propagated plausibly anymore. Bradley's lack of a strategy of pacification and welfare for the impoverished and internationalized inner-city neighborhoods was congruent with the feeling among political observers that Bradley's policies were out of touch with the neighborhoods whose loyalty had stabilized his regime over many years (Boyarsky, 1987b; Bunting, 1988a, b). Moreover, the crisis of the Bradley regime could be interpreted as an overall crisis of black power whose promise had mostly been to turn civil rights politics into tangible improvements in the lives of African Americans (Clayton, 1989; Cockburn, 1989; Decker, 1989). When this problem became clear to Bradley, the mayor drastically changed his policy. He hoped to add profile to his administration by hiring Mike Gage as his personal deputee. Gage countered the loss of the public's trust in Bradley with a political about-face in four areas considered central by the mayor's strategists: environmental policy (recycling, a ban of heavy truck traffic in city areas during specific times, a strategy to solve the city's sewage crisis and the clean-up of Santa Monica Bay); social policy (with an emphasis on children, youth, the handicapped and the elderly as well as on child care and after-school care); housing (where Bradley made community activist Gary Squier the author of his housing policy); and security (more police but without tax hikes).

On the other side of the political spectrum within his coalition, Bradley had to struggle with those white politicians who were turning their backs on the center and who had read the success of the 1986 slow-growth initiative 'Proposition U' as a sign that they were on the right track. These politicians were able to bind some of the traditional Bradley supporters in the liberal and Jewish camp. A pivotal event in this shift was the surprising election of liberal urban planner Ruth Galanter in Venice in 1987 against incumbent Pat Russell who had been endorsed by Bradley (Boyarsky, 1987a; interview Bickhart). The debate about controlled growth in the city was a dominant factor in the implosion of the political center in Los Angeles. An *LAT* poll found in 1987 that the controversy around growth was considered the biggest potential disruption of the 'period of racial harmony' that had characterized the city since Bradley's election in 1973 (Roderick, 1987). This discourse proved to be an increasingly unmanageable field for those world-city boosters who – like Bradley himself – wanted to leave the development of world city space to the unfettered forces of international capital. Problems of air and other pollution, of traffic and transit, crime and police brutality, sprawl and densification, pushed to the fore in the disparate neighborhoods of Los Angeles and cried out for more interventionist solutions on the part of the local state. Such demands typically took one of two forms: first, the reformist demand for growth restrictions of all kinds; and second, the formation of new alliances in resistance to specific projects. On the one hand, the formal call for an expansion of grassroots political and planning reform was linked to the substantial demand for growth restrictions of all kinds and defined the political space in which local politicians were able to operate.[9] On the other hand – despite the widely heard assumption that slow growth was 'the liberalism of the privileged' among conservatives and progressives alike (Will, 1987)[10] – new forms of movement politics emerged that brought together previously separated fragments. This politics had its most visible expression in the struggle against the LANCER incinerator project in south-central Los Angeles which was stopped due to the concerted efforts of 'Westside environmentalists' and environmental justice and community activists from communities of color in the inner city.

In the prelude to the 1989 mayoral election, the different political agendas of two preeminent candidates, incumbent Tom Bradley and his challenger from the 5th District on the Westside, Zev Yaroslavsky, expressed the diverging positions within the former coalition of blacks and Jews. Yaroslavsky, who had to quit the race later due to a political scandal involving his campaign managers, championed a development concept for Los Angeles which in several important areas departed from the path that the Bradley coalition had laid out over the previous 20 years.[11] While Zev Yaroslavsky could hardly have built a social agenda that would have outdone Bradley, he developed his platform around the question of slow growth. At the beginning of 1988, Yaroslavsky proclaimed that he considered long-term uncontrolled growth as the main reason for the crisis of the Bradley regime and of the city overall (Chorneau, 1988a). Instead of the preference for the downtown, Yaroslavsky, like other place entrepreneurs on the affluent Westside, pursued a multicentral strategy intended not just to distribute growth but also to prevent traffic collapse. 'Managed growth' was the slogan used to push this strategy. The pivot point of Yaroslavsky's position was the notion that many of those in the west of the city who had benefitted from the growth of the citadel were now increasingly voicing their concerns about having to live in what the world city had to offer. Calls for a new urban form became louder. Citizen groups declared that Los Angeles was 'not yet New York'.[12] The pervasive and long-nurtured image of Los Angeles as a low-density, single-family-home urban space in a paradisal, subtropic environment came in handy as a ready-made conceptive ideology of alternative world city development exactly when the urban region was choking from centralized downtown growth and all its uncontrolled social and environmental effects. As was true of petty bourgeois movements in the earlier part of this century, private homeownership and urban form were inextricably merged into one distinctive view of Los Angeles. The task at hand in the 1980s and 1990s was to adjust the private consumption of space to the new dynamics of inter-nationalization. Many representatives of 'slow growth' wanted the best of both worlds – wanted to have their cake and eat it, too. For his mayoral strategy, Yaroslavsky had relied on an 'octopus-network' which pretended to renounce the big donations from 'downtown'. The key to the systematic critique of centralist growth in the Yaroslavsky campaign was his opposition to the activities of the CRA which bore the stamp of Tom Bradley. But it also signaled a more profound crisis of political consensus in Los Angeles. The programmatic statements of incumbent Bradley and original challenger Yaroslavsky reveal typical political strategies and decisions in Los Angeles. The two candidates symbolized the dissociation of the African American and Jewish political machines into two, clearly discernible positions, personified in Bradley and Yaroslavsky (Didion, 1989).[13]

## THE ELECTION OF 1989 AND THE CRISIS OF URBAN CONSENSUS

Maybe a hundred people in Los Angeles, besides the handful of reporters assigned to City Hall, actually follow city and county politics. (Didion, 1989: 99)

There is no mechanism in Los Angeles to foster consensus or coalition. (Kayden, 1991)

In the mayoral primary elections of April 11, 1989, Bradley received 52% of the vote and was able to stay in office. Among the other candidates, Nate Holden, a surprisingly strong contender, received 28% support from the electorate (Boyarsky, 1989b). Arithmetically, the 1989 election was the least important such event since the early 1950s at least. Fewer than a quarter of those eligible bothered to cast their vote. In the primary of 1969, when Sam Yorty won over Tom Bradley, 66% had voted; in the pursuant runoff election that same year an impressive 76% turnout was registered. In 1973, when Bradley turned the tables on Yorty, the turnout was 57 and 64% respectively. Clearly then, the low turnout in 1989 has to be interpreted as a sign of the decreasing significance attached to mayoral elections by the political public.

Discussions about the form of urban government were triggered by the debate on political ethics in the wake of the 'Far East Bank-Scandal', and by the political conflict between the Police Commission and the City Council that ensued after the beating of African American Rodney G. King by Los Angeles police officers.[14] By the early 1990s the core institutions of the local state were put to the test under pressure by the formation of the world city. Los Angeles, which was the whitest, most Anglo-Saxon and Protestant city in the United States between the 1870s and the 1920s, became the most ethnically diverse city of the country during the remainder of the twentieth century (Kayden, 1991). It was recognized that changes in the fundamental demographic and economic conditions of the regional mode of regulation would now have to be considered in any discussion of political reform in Los Angeles. The direction of such reform could be the politicization of local representative organs, which could call into question the technical administrative approach at the base of the progressivist city charter (Schockman, 1996). In the center of the struggle are 40 commissions which have jurisdictions as diverse as animal rescue and the port. The members of the commissions are appointed by the mayor who thus exerts political control outside of the electoral process. This arrangement has reflected the progressivist conviction that 'right-minded citizens' – usually a stand-in for white middle-class males – should run the political process in the city.[15] The recognition of a lack of political consensus (which had simply been assumed to exist in previous periods) necessitated a new political culture of debate and discourse which would end up allocating new roles to old institutions in Los Angeles. But before the implosion of political power could be countered with consensus strategies capable of redirecting the creation of hegemony back into the conflict structure of the city, Los Angeles exploded in an urban rebellion.

## RIORDAN RISING: REPUBLICAN URBANISM OR URBAN REPUBLIC?

> Rioting [in 1992] erupted at a crossroads with mythic meaning: Florence and Normandie – the first a capital of the Rennaissance, the other a bloody battlefield. Toward which future is Los Angeles gravitating – renaissance or death? (Hayden, 1993)

In 1993, after 20 years in office, Tom Bradley was not a candidate for mayor anymore. He stepped back and created the possibility for a city divided by the Rodney King beating and the rebellion of 1992 to redefine its leadership as it attempted to heal itself. In a field of initially over 50 candidates in the mayoral race of 1993, Councilman Mike Woo came closest to carrying the torch of the waning Bradley coalition in a redefined multicultural alliance. Yet Woo's campaign ultimately went under with the former coalition itself. The winner of the June 1993 election was multimillionaire businessman and lawyer Richard 'Dick' Riordan. The new mayor had long been a major mover and shaker behind the political front lines in Los Angeles. His lavish campaign contributions had kept many political campaigns afloat in California. Riordan being a Republican, most of these contributions went to politicians who were of his party. But Riordan, who calls himself 'a liberal with a small L' (Stewart, 1992: 19), is not easy to categorize. Many see in him a local version of a new breed of populist politicians which Ross Perot has defined for this decade in national American politics. Rich, conservative, philanthropic and dedicated to a philosophy of problem-solving, Riordan – who admittedly has read every single speech given by Perot – looks like a perfect emulation of the erratic politician from Texas. But there is more to him. Steeped in Catholic social gospel, Riordan sometimes comes across as a champion of the poor whom he does not know but seeks to better: 'Everything in my thinking starts with poor people', he said before he was first elected (Stewart, 1992).

And there is the other Riordan whose entire professional life seems like a preparation for office. He was an insider of Los Angeles politics without ever having held public office. He has been part of the most powerful circles of permanent government in Southern California for decades. A long-time supporter of Tom Bradley, both politically and financially, Riordan had landed powerful appointments on city commissions before he finally turned away from Bradley when his associate, Bill Wardlaw, a conservative Democrat, persuaded him to run for mayor (Merl, 1995: 10). The new mayor's displayed populism vies for prominence with his equally unmistakable elitism which often reeks of benevolent paternalism more reminiscent of feudal than modern democratic societies. His populism is also strictly selective in its outreach and effect. While having obvious appeal with many voters in majority white and Republican areas of the city, Riordan has not been able to break into the African American vote.

Bradley's governing coalition had initially been a consequence of social upheaval and democratic grassroots initiative, a reaction to a racially divided and racist city after the Watts riots. Through Bradley, the city came together. Riordan, on the other hand, is hardly a symbol of renewal and social change. He has been a truly reactionary figure of stagnation and retrenchment in social terms, and an uncompromising economic reformer whose sense of civic culture is fundamentally defined by his business persona. In fact, in Riordan's world, citizenship has been mostly recast as entrepreneurship; the powerful civic multiculture of Los Angeles has withered into a purely economic asset: 'We are home of the most ethnically diverse people in the world. Together, Angelenos make up the most colorful mosaic of entrepreneurs anywhere' (City of Los Angeles, 1994: 2). Social movements are contextualized in an economic universe in which language and concepts are without exception those of the market: 'Given room at the economic table, business, government, labor and environmentalists can bring about win–win situations' (City of Los Angeles, 1994: 3). Whereas Bradley's vision of building a 'world class city' had been inspired by more than monetary considerations, Riordan's neoliberal ideas of economic and administrative reform in Los Angeles – put to work by his chief of staff, UCLA business professor William Ouchi – echo the general *Zeitgeist* of a period of downsizing and lean corporations (Merl, 1995: 10). Where Bradley meant to build global *grandesse*, Riordan strives to mold Los Angeles into a competitive business organization able to hold its own in a globalized world: 'Companies and industries are succeeding in Los Angeles because they have remade themselves to compete in the new global economy. So, too, must city government' (City of Los Angeles, 1994: 1). In addition to administrative reform, the mayor has pushed expansion of the port and airport in Los Angeles, supported a $1.8 billion public works project in the Alameda corridor, and overseen a major overhaul of the city's permit system intended to streamline development in the city.

Challenged by veteran Democrat Tom Hayden in the 1997 election, Riordan needed to do more than talk about economic growth, deregulation and streamlining government. As Xandra Kayden, a UCLA political scientist and major voice in the city's debate on charter reform, reminded us before the election: 'The mayoral campaign should be an opportunity to think about Los Angeles as a place to live and as a player in the global economy. Regrettably, the image of the city is now one of racial division, of wildly disparate socio-economic classes living in isolation from each other' (Kayden, 1996: M6). Riordan has spent much effort transforming a public city – born in the Progressivism of the early twentieth century and matured through the social struggles of Fordism and the contradictions of world city formation – into a private corporation in which citizenship has begun to resemble consumer capacity. The public space of the city has finally been brought in line with the image of Los Angeles as a private place of individual dream seekers.

> There cannot be a sense of community if everyone sits in their own back yard. This sense of community is also important for the economy. The Riordan administration has placed considerable emphasis on economic growth, but there is more to the economic vitality of an international city than rules and regulations. The single greatest asset the city has is its diversity. There are substantial populations in Los Angeles from every part of the globe. That means markets, trade and investment. But it will not happen if we are unable to project the image of a whole community (Kayden, 1996: M6).

Richard Riordan was reelected on April 8, 1997 with a landslide majority. He will be the mayor to lead the city past the millennium. The campaign had offered a clear choice to voters: the competition between challenger Tom Hayden and incumbent Riordan was interpreted as a 'left–right showdown in City of Angels' (Fraser, 1997). Hayden, a 1960s student radical, progressive Democratic state assemblyman and senator, high profile environmentalist and social justice spokesperson, represents everything Riordan did not. As it turned out, the voters rejected the alternative offered by Hayden with a margin of 61 to 34%. There were two noteworthy facts about this otherwise uninspiring mayoral campaign. First, voter participation sank to an all-time low of 20%. City elections have now lost their draw with almost all but the most politicized sections of the population. Didion's observations about the general lack of interest in municipal affairs seem, once again, confirmed. Second, and more surprisingly, among the few who voted, the Latino voters emerged as a new political force (Boyarsky, 1997). Latinos comprised 15% of all voters (up from 10% in the 1993 runoff) while Anglo voters were 65% (down from 72% in the 1993 runoff). Black voters, who had been 12% of the voters in the 1993 runoff, were at 13% in 1997 (Jeffe, 1997). A strong vote among white and Latino voters for Riordan decided the race. A *Los Angeles Times* exit poll suggests that while support for Riordan was strongest among whites and weakest among black voters, the incumbent received 60% of the Latino vote and 62% of the Asian vote (*LAT*, April 10, 1997: A27).

Although Riordan managed to be reelected in 1997, the restructuring of Los Angeles after the relatively stable Bradley coalition has only begun. With about 40% of the city's voters being Latin, there will certainly be other options for political coalitions in the future. In 1993, before Riordan was elected, Tom Hayden had outlined the challenges the city would face during that period: 'The stakes are grave. Abandoned by state and federal politicians seeking suburban votes, megacities like Los Angeles are on their own, boiling with all the crises of the planet in one caldron. If Los Angeles cannot address its crises through more self government, where is hope'? (Hayden, 1993). At the end of the twentieth century, Los Angeles faces the crossroads of Republican urbanism or of an alternative urban republic.

# PART III

GLOBALIZING THE LOCAL

# CHAPTER 6
# POLITICAL ECONOMY

One can find in Los Angeles not only the high technology industrial complexes of the Silicon Valley and the erratic sunbelt economy of Houston, but also the far-reaching industrial decline and bankrupt urban neighborhoods of rust-belted Detroit or Cleveland. There is a Boston in Los Angeles, a Lower Manhattan and a South Bronx, a Sao Paolo and a Singapore. There may be no other comparable urban region which presents so vividly such a composite assemblage and articulation of urban restructuring processes. Los Angeles seems to be conjugating the recent history of capitalist urbanization in virtually all its inflectional forms (Soja, 1989: 193).

Recent years have witnessed a moderate rebound in economic growth in Los Angeles, in the wake of the severe downturn of the early 1990s. The upswing in activity, however, has occurred in the context of a costly and continuing restructuring of the L.A. Economy. . . . The substantial weakness evidenced in the Southern California economy during the early 1990s derived from a combination of cyclical downturn and structural economic change (Gabriel, 1996: 25–26).

## THE CRISIS OF FORDISM, SPACE AND INTERNATIONALIZATION[1]

The restructuring of Los Angeles has its roots in the crisis of the Fordist formation. First internationalization, and later globalization are at the core of this crisis and its aftermath. American Fordism used to be characterized by solving its crises and contradictions not through an external thermostat but through internal measures (Lipietz, 1982). At the same time, however, it was the distribution of American methods of mass production and consumption that created the structural fissures along which US hegemony started to break down after the 1960s. In the United States, globalization has had two main geographical effects: a shift in the national system of cities on one hand and a trend towards a bicoastal economy. A few large urban areas have become the primary centers of the newly inter-nationalized American economy. Foreign direct investment into the United States has been found to favor southwestern and coastal areas in the country (Sassen-Koob, 1987b: 78; Glickman, 1987). Equally, the new 'fourth wave' of mostly Latin-American and Asian immigration has been concentrated in the metropolitan centers of the two coasts and – for obvious reasons – on the MexAmerican border (Muller and Espenshade, 1985; Light and Bonacich, 1988; Waldinger and Bozorgmehr, 1996a).

In this context, the rise of Los Angeles to global significance occurred. The situation in Southern California has reflected the development of American Fordism during war and peace since the 1930s. From the 1960s on, 'Los Angeles has shifted from being a highly specialized industrial center focussed on aircraft production to a more diversified and decentralized industrial/financial metropolis' (Soja, Morales and Wolff, 1983: 211). In his characterization of post-Fordist urbanization, Alain Lipietz locates Los Angeles as a place in transition between the former Fordist core and the periphery: London and Paris emulate Los Angeles while the Southern California metropolis takes on the profile of São Paolo and Mexico City, which themselves begin to resemble Calcutta (Lipietz, 1992a: 108). Towards the end of the 1990s, the fertile chaos described by Soja above – a puzzle with diverse but rather rigid pieces – has congealed into a new urban form while its constitutive parts are losing their singular referents in the First, Third or Fourth worlds. The 'world capital of the twenty-first century' has already suffered through major recessions, an uprising and a series of natural catastrophes which have put the model to a serious test. While the pillars of Southern California's economy have mostly withstood the pressures of these economic, political and natural upheavals, much of the corporate enthusiasm of the 1980s as well as the sensationalist description of Los Angeles as a Dickensian hell have waned and given way to a more sober assessment of a stagnating, crisis-ridden but functioning economy. While the hegemonic agenda of conquering the world via the Pacific Rim has been toned down to the defensive strategy 'beyond declinism' (The New Vision Council, 1994: I–17), the often hyperbolic and catastrophic critical descriptions of Los Angeles as a Third World hellhole have been largely substituted by a sense of pragmatism.[2] Muddling through has replaced the bravado of the previous decade.

## FROM FORDISM TO POST-FORDISM AND BEYOND

The economy of Los Angeles in the 1990s stratifies itself along the trajectories of two processes that determine post-Fordist urbanization: *flexibilization* and *globalization*. Urban and regional development has changed shape in the restructuring process. It has been argued that in contrast to earlier branch-plant industrial development, there is now a discernible formation of a set of 'industrial districts' with a developmental logic of their own. As part of a pronounced strategy of internationalization and recentralization during the crisis of the 1970s, the traditional industrial sectors of the period of mass production were almost completely eliminated. Like in other parts of the US, the Fordist mass worker was abandoned by national capital. Although total employment rose in the region, a selective deindustrialization took place. This led, on one hand, to the loss of 75% of the local auto, tire, steel and civilian aircraft industries – that is, 70 000 well-paid jobs, most of them unionized – between 1978 and 1983. Most of these losses were suffered in the industrial belt along the Long Beach Freeway, which used to be the largest contiguous industrial area after the Ruhr in Germany (Soja, Morales and Wolff, 1983).

On the other hand, in the five southern Californian counties – Los Angeles, Orange, Riverside, San Bernardino and Ventura – 1.3 million new jobs were created between 1970 and 1980. Interestingly enough, many of these jobs were in manufacturing. In the 1970s, Los Angeles County was the biggest industrial town on earth with almost 1 million manufacturing jobs. While in the entire US employment rose by less than 1 million jobs in industrial production between 1970 and 1980, the Los Angeles region contributed 225 000 new positions. In Los

Angeles County, one-third of the jobs created were in manufacturing. The economists of the Los Angeles Economic Roundtable calculated an increase in employment of 29.3% in Los Angeles County for the period of 1972–84, making the city the largest job machine in the country. In total the area added 846 000 jobs (Los Angeles Economic Roundtable, 1986: 8). Most of the new jobs were in high-tech sectors (predominantly aircraft and aerospace), in production services, and in low-wage sectors such as garment work and personal services (Soja, Morales and Wolff, 1983). The growth of these sectors and their integration into the national economy were supported by the region's exceptional 'communications and transportation infrastructure' (Los Angeles Economic Roundtable, 1986: 5). The influx of federal military expenditure, in spite of its decline, remained critical for the regional economy.

## LABOR MARKETS

Growth and restructuring of the urban economy today are linked to globalization in Southern California, where the pace of restructuring over the past two decades has been determined largely by the steady supply of offshore capital and immigrant labor. In this context, Sassen-Koob (1984b) talks about 'new industrial zones for world capital'. She mentions three groups of reasons for the emergence of such new zones.

First, there are technical and economic considerations, including the advantages of vertically disintegrated agglomeration economies and the diversified labor market structure necessary for them. As a destination of immigrant workers on both the high and low ends of the labor market, Southern California is provided with cheap labor on the one hand and highly skilled specialists on the other. Second, difficult conditions for investment in the Third World have improved the status of 'location USA' in relative terms. Some sectors, including the garment sector, have pulled production of certain items (e.g. sportswear) from Third World production sites into Los Angeles (Olney, 1987a). And thirdly, access to US markets is an important factor in the locational decisions of foreign investors. In sum, regions like Southern California have been characterized by three traits: the simultaneous availability of highly skilled labor and steady flow of low-wage labor; the simultaneous access to space for industrial facilities and for research and development (be it in recycled inner-city areas or on the agricultural or desert frontier); plus regional development directed towards the expansion of industrial production.

Throughout the 1980s and into the 1990s, Southern California has been seen as one of the regional success stories of American capitalism, particularly in terms of job growth. Yet, 'job growth is not evenly distributed throughout industries in Los Angeles. And more importantly, high levels of hiring do not translate into high wages' (Wolff, 1991). Job growth does not mean better jobs in terms of job security, health and safety. The polarized globalization of local labor markets has been at the center of this development. A significant factor in local labor market formation is the emergence of Los Angeles as a global city, an international control center on the Pacific Rim which calls for a stratum of professional specialists. The immigration of highly skilled professionals to US growth centers like Los Angeles has led to a brain drain from Europe, Canada, the former Eastern bloc and the Third World. In addition to undocumented professionals who use their position as students at California universities and their English proficiency to blend into the local labor market, there is also a class of specialists who are imported by multinational corporations from abroad on temporary visas.

But the emergence of the global city also enhances the presence of low-wage labor like janitorial work. Much of this labor market segment is directly fed by immigration. In three areas immigrant (undocumented) labor is particularly important: first, sub-minimum-wage employment (such as in the garment industry); second, employment at just above minimum wage (e.g. jobs taken by migrant farm workers); and third, the flexible employment of undocumented workers in the core sectors such as automobile manufacturing (Soja, Morales and Wolff, 1983).

After 1970, 70% of all legal immigrants (and 75% of all Mexicans) who came to California settled in the Los Angeles area. This 70% figure can probably be assumed to apply to undocumented immigrants as well. Immigrants, and mostly immigrant women, are the proletariat in the growth industries of the world city. In the mid-1980s in Los Angeles County (where half of all manufacturing jobs of California are concentrated), 57% of all Hispanics were unskilled workers, workers in service firms or factory workers. In the services alone the number was 65%. Of all jobs held by Hispanics, 43% could be associated with the massive industrial growth in Los Angeles (Sassen-Koob, 1987b: 81).

Certainly, the important insight from the studies of economic geographers of Southern California is that polarized labor markets do not just occur because the workers in low-skill manufacturing industries (e.g. the garment industry) cannot compete in a postindustrial, knowledge-based society, or because low-wage service industries (e.g. janitorial work, catering) support the core sectors of the economy. Rather, the Los Angeles case shows that polarization of labor markets is neither a thing of the past nor just a characteristic feature of the new social division of labor in the internationalized post-Fordist city, but is a *mainstay* of future-oriented industrial growth sectors such as high technology. Allen Scott has identified these polarized conditions for the high-technology industrial complex of Southern California. Looking both at engineering and scientific employees and at low-wage workers in electronics assembly subcontract shops, he maintains that these groups are representative of 'the two dominant labor-market factions that characterize the complex; namely, on the one side, skilled professional workers, and on the other side, a group of unskilled and predominantly immigrant workers' (Scott, 1993a: 157).

## ECONOMIC STRUCTURES

The reemergence or the strengthening of existing crafts production and the high-tech sector have been associated particularly with the growing vertical disintegration of the social division of labor. This shift implies a more fluid configuration of products and processes as well as flexible labor markets. These processes, which

can be studied closely in Los Angeles, have been the criteria for the restructuring of capitalism worldwide. There are arguments as to the pervasiveness of the changes, the novelty of the changes, the meaning of these changes for working people and certainly about whether the sum total of the new forms of labor organization warrant the designation of a new period of capitalist regulation after Fordism.[3] Los Angeles has been considered both the testing ground for post-Fordist innovation and a discursive object in the analysis that has determined the scholarly debate for more than a decade.

In line with this debate, Allen Scott (1988b) differentiates three main pillars on which the Southern California economy rests: services; high tech; crafts production. In many ways these pillars are also the foundations of the global restructuring of industrial capitalism overall (Figure 6.1).

## SERVICES

In 1989, the service sector[4] in Los Angeles County employed about 1 176 700 people. Employment in this sector grew by 434 000 between 1979 and 1990. Between 1972 and 1984 alone, employment in services grew by 63.5% from 571 000 to 934 200 (Wolff, 1991; Los Angeles Economic Roundtable, 1986). Services are the fastest growing sector in the economy. A big part of this sector involves business services linked to the control functions of the global city. In 1986, these business services accounted for one fourth of all services (260 000). Work relationships, labor markets and internal structures in these often new businesses form a flexibilized network considered typical for the post-Fordist economy. One-fifth of the employees in this area work for private employment agencies which enable corporations to cover their employment needs with temporary workers without having to pay benefits. Vertical disintegration and the subcontracting of work characterize virtually all growth sectors from private security firms to janitorial services, building management, computer and data processing as well as consulting and accounting. There is a strong indication of vertical disintegration in these various industries since many companies contract out with external firms for process management, security, data processing and other business services. Whatever the glossy image of the service industry is, many workers, in fact, face a much more insecure – often part-time, nonbenefit – work reality than either traditional manufacturing or traditional service workers. Other business services (including building cleaning, guard services), retail/personal services (including restaurants and beauty shops), and nongovernmental social services (like daycare, residential care) added 87 000 jobs in 1988 and 1989 (representing 56% of total job growth); yet they were also in industries with average annual wages of $16 600 or less (Wolff, 1991).

In FIRE (finance, insurance and real estate) there was a total of 292 000 jobs in 1989 and an increase of 68 300 jobs between 1979 and 1990 (Wolff, 1991). In the financial industry, which had 128 000 workers in 1984, Los Angeles' rapid rise to the top of the international financial system has been particularly visible. Between 1972, when it had 81 000 employees, and 1984 this sector grew by 56%; total employment during the same period rose by only 29%. In the beginning of the

GOVERNORS STATE UNIVERSITY
UNIVERSITY PARK
IL 60466

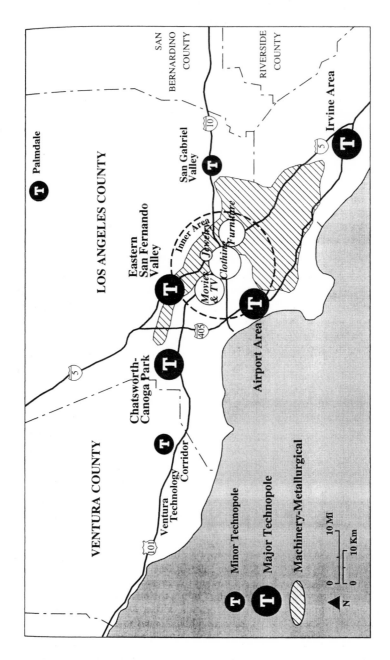

**Figure 6.1** *Schematic view of the industrial geography of metropolitan Los Angeles. Major freeways are shown (Source: Soja and Scott, 1996: 13; courtesy of the authors)*

1980s, Cohen (1981) classified Los Angeles as a regional financial center; Thrift (1987) called Los Angeles a secondary international financial center. Since then, Los Angeles has surpassed San Francisco as the most important financial center on the American West Coast. Today, though, much of the bullish self-confidence of the 1980s, which earned Los Angeles the label of an international 'capital of capitals', whose significance along the Pacific Rim was surpassed only by Tokyo (Soja, 1989: 192), has disappeared:

> Soja's prediction of less than a decade ago has failed to materialize. The experience of California banks with overseas lending proved singularly unsuccessful. Security Pacific's aggressive strategy at participating in global foreign exchange and securities markets failed in 1991, and it was taken over by Bank of America. Los Angeles remains, however, the home of some of the largest thrifts and mortgage companies in the United States – which only highlights Southern California's importance in the realm of consumer banking (Dymski and Veitch, 1996: 47).

Los Angeles is still also an important center of international banking. Approximately 150 international banks are active in Los Angeles, putting Los Angeles into second place after New York in the USA. Japanese banks have played a particularly important role in the emergence of an international banking center in downtown Los Angeles. At times the strength of the giant Japanese banking companies – 6 out of the 10 largest banks in the world are Japanese – has been considered an omen for the expectation that Los Angeles would eventually rival New York for the top spot in the American banking hierarchy. In the late 1980s, more than one-third of all foreign-owned American banks were Japanese. Over 13% of the California credit market, as well as 3 out of the 10 largest banks in the state, were in Japanese control. In contrast to other parts of the USA, Japanese banks in California are not confined to the 'ghetto' of exclusive service to Japanese. In the late 1980s, for example, 90% of the customers and 99% of the employees of the Japanese-owned California First Bank were Americans. The bankers from the Far East were intent not just to catch up with, but to bypass the California banks. While insiders cautioned against too rapid expansion ('We can't extend credit everywhere from earth to moon'), Los Angeles was considered a prime location in this attempt. With more than 800 branch offices of Japanese firms in Southern California, the urban region presented itself as the '24th ward' of Tokyo: 117 000 Southern Californians were Japanese Americans, 200 000 possessed a Japanese passport in 1987 (Kotkin and Kishimoto, 1987).

The internationalization of the banking sector in Los Angeles is by no means just a result of the citadel function of its downtown in the global financial networks. For while California subsidiaries of international Japanese banks have targeted the – mostly big – business with Americans and commercial customers, it is interesting to note that local banks owned by Asian immigrants to Los Angeles concentrate on ethnically defined markets (Kristof, 1987). This strategy of 'small fish', as a Korean banker in Los Angeles called it, rests on the detailed knowledge of exotic and traditional business practices of the respective group of immigrants. This knowledge is considered crucial for the functioning of the newly internationalized ethnic communities of Los Angeles. Besides knowing the social customs of a given immigrant group, ethnic bankers have relatively easy access to personal information on customers in the community which they serve. A good reputation in the community is a criterion for a customer's credit rating, and a bad reputation – even if it originates in the home country of an immigrant – might mean a lowering of the rating (Unger, 1988).

The financing of small businesses through Korean banks is only *one* socio-economic channel through which capital streams from the Far East are transmitted into the banks, production facilities, real estate markets, food and liquor stores as well as gas stations of Los Angeles (others including existing capital, community credit sources (or *kyes*), private lenders, credit sharks as well as Korean–American savings and loans and credit unions) (Light and Bonacich, 1988). These various business practices shed light on the diversification in structure and agency of the urban internationalization processes between local and global economic horizons. And the capitalization of the internationalized economies of post-Fordist Los Angeles is, at least partly, determined by non-economic – that is social and political – factors on the local level.

The leading role of Los Angeles in finance (over the traditionally stronger San Francisco) stems from the increased capacity of international trade flowing through Southern California. The case of Los Angeles confirms, without doubt, the relevancy of internationalized commercial capital, which is held partly responsible for the growth of global financial centers. All four groups of commercial capital as identified by Thrift (1987) – mediating the exchange of commodities, mediating money exchange, dealing in securities and selling corporate services – are of significance in Los Angeles. Strategically located at the crossroads of rising streams of capital from the Pacific Rim, the money managers of Southern California administered $100 billion in 1986. Together with the roughly $50 billion managed by local banks and insurance companies, this amounted to an 88% increase over two years. Roughly 140 firms competed for these funds. Only a handful of them were more than 20 years old. Many of them had been created in the wake of the early successes of junk bond czar Michael Milken and targeted the treasures of the international casino capitalism of the late Reagan years specializing in junk bonds, takeovers and other services. Although there have been few integrative internationalization tendencies of the industry – Japanese investors in the USA, for example, continue to prefer Japanese financial consultants – the trend is towards an 'ordered segmentation' in the globalization of the financial center Los Angeles.

The growth of finance in Los Angeles is almost synonymous with the internationalization of Southern California. Los Angeles has been made into a completely globalized artifact for the consumption and processing of manufactured commodities and raw materials from around the world. The ports in Los Angeles and Long Beach have allowed Asian commodities easy and inexpensive access to the huge Southern California consumer markets where two-thirds of the buying power of the state are concentrated. In addition, the relatively low fees at Los Angeles International Airport have strengthened the city's commercial location. In 1983, air transport accounted for half of the total value of goods coming through Southern California, and its share was rising. Between 1970 and 1987, international trade's share of the gross regional product increased from 13 to 25% (SCAG, 1987: 1). Almost half of North American trans-Pacific trade went through the ports of Los Angeles and Long Beach in the late 1980s (Soja, 1989: 192). Japan topped the list both in imports and exports to and from the Southern California economy. The Los Angeles customs district is considered the busiest in the United States (Gabriel, 1996: 28).

Among the internationalized business services which concentrate in Los Angeles are advertising and building management. The high dependence of the local advertising industry on the international economy makes local agencies particularly vulnerable to shifting international ad accounts. Many firms in the advertising business in Los Angeles have been kept alive through the accounts of Japanese corporations; those who have had these funds withdrawn have failed. Four of the companies with the largest ad accounts in the United States are car makers Toyota, Nissan, Honda and Mazda, all of whom have their headquarters in the Los Angeles area. Together, they spent $600 annually for advertising in the late 1980s. In addition, other sectors, including the electronics industry, and computer and office automation producers, also pump millions into the local advertising industry (Howard, 1987b). To international corporations, Los Angeles is a bridge-head for the United States and a marketplace in its own right. The advertising industry in Los Angeles profits from this situation and helps expand local world-city functions by using its expertise to convey the marketing needs of the trans-national production system into locally specific markets. While the advertising industry itself is hard to internationalize, due to the relevance of local conditions, it serves the function of crafting vital local–global relationships of the world city economy.

A similar case is in building management. This industry has largely resisted direct internationalization; only a few foreign management firms, including British companies James Lang Wooton and Richard Ellis, have located in Los Angeles. Yet the lateral international entanglements of the industry have been becoming more important (Thrift, 1987: 226). That is, while it is mostly local managers who take care of buildings (since they know the local business conditions best), these managers are increasingly entering into contractual relationships with interna-tional owners and cleaning firms who, in turn, employ a largely internationalized workforce. A vertical disintegration then occurs, resulting in the separation of building owners, management, cleaning firms and janitors. At each point of this vertical structure, international firms and workers are present.[5] The internatio-nalization of local real estate markets has also accelerated the transition from the management of the buildings by the owners themselves to fee management. Thus, the internationalization process has virtually created a new service industry by professionalizing management. The Building Owners and Managers Association, which was, originally after its inception in 1915, an association of individual building owners, now serves large companies as an organ of political representa-tion. Since membership in the association is by individual building, a growing number of foreign owners automatically participate.

An essential task of the building management industry is the cleaning of office towers, which is accomplished mostly through contract firms. Whereas at the beginning of the 1980s no transnational corporations were present in the United States cleaning industry, today they are dominant in this sector of the economy. In Los Angeles, these contract firms take their workers from an internationalized pool of laborers who clean office buildings at night, mostly for minimum wage. In the

United States overall, this once largely African American and male niche of the labor market has become mostly a domain of Central American women and men. Nationally, between 1975 and 1987 janitorial employment rose from 2.3 million to 2.9 million. The number of American contract cleaners in commercial office buildings rose from 390 000 to 850 000 (*Update*, 1987). As a growing sector of the economy, the cleaning industry is immediately tied into the expansion of the citadel functions of the world city. In Los Angeles, 95% of the janitors are Latin; 50% of them are women. With the growing success of the real estate industry in Los Angeles' office centers, the social situation of these workers worsened steadily (Schimek, 1989).

It is not just the business services mentioned here that have expanded in the world city economy. Other services, like the hotel business, tourism and recreation, health services, legal services, engineering services, architecture and accounting, also grew throughout the 1980s. An excellent example of this trend is the expansion of giant law firms in Southern California into the Far East. Increases also occurred in the personal services sector, which had 35 400 employees in 1972 and 39 200 in 1985 (Los Angeles Area Chamber of Commerce, 1985).

The emergence of citadel functions in Los Angeles seems to have come with a general pattern of labor market fragmentation and polarization as exemplified in the building management and cleaning industries. A study of the University of Southern California found in 1987 that while certain jobs – including high-paying ones in the main service sectors; part-time, low-paying jobs; and those in precarious lines of work – had increased during the 1980s mid-level positions in production had declined. It did not come as a surprise that increases in low-wage employment are correlated to the internationalization and feminization of labor markets in these industries (Core Laboratory Workshop, 1987: 92; see also Gabriel, 1996).

## CRAFTS PRODUCTION

Mostly in the old inner-city industrial areas, but also in newer suburban locations, several crafts industries have recently experienced a renaissance. Among them are the movie, furniture, food processing, metalworking, paper, plastics, textiles[6] and garment industries.[7] Since the deindustrialization of major mass-producing sectors like auto, steel and increasingly aerospace, these crafts-based industries have become virtually synonymous with the manufacturing complex of Los Angeles (Los Angeles Manufacturing Action Project, 1995). The relative stability of the crafts sector helped Los Angeles remain the largest industrial city in the nation through the 1980s, a decade during which other manufacturing centers in America experienced sharp declines. During this period, Los Angeles balanced the loss of nearly 100 000 jobs in traditional heavy industry durable manufacturing (such as glass, steel, fabricated metal products, automobiles) (Wolff, 1991). Most of these industries are thoroughly internationalized both in capital stock and workforce. Entrepreneurs as well as workers in the workshops and sewing shops of this crafts-based economy are often new immigrants.

Perhaps nowhere else in the economy are the differences between image and reality more pronounced than in the crafts-based sector. The definition of this sector in Los Angeles is difficult because traditional sectoral statistics tend to overlook or misrepresent the realities, particularly in newer sectors. One of those sectors which has a strong foothold in crafts-type industries and production is environmental consulting and equipment manufacturing: 'Like entertainment and textiles, the environmental industries in Southern California are largely invisible, obscured by inconsistent government statistical reporting, outmoded SIC categories, and rapidly changing regulations and technologies' (The New Vision Business Council, 1994: III-14).[8] 'Crafts' is almost a chaotic term which attempts to capture the most developed and sophisticated specialized professions in film as well as routine, yet seemingly pre-Fordist work realities in garment or food production. On one hand, small-batch, custom-made production has been wedded to new technologies and novel materials; on the other hand, standardized, yet flexible, mass production is performed in the most 'primitive' technical fashion, with relatively unskilled, individual workers performing piecework in a nonunionized, often unsafe, environment. In the latter case, innovation happens mostly in management and in the organization of work processes where – under the umbrella of vertical disintegration – global market demand and local work conditions are tailored to fit increasingly fragmented and diversified marketplaces. No wonder, then, that in the crafts industries there may be the highest cross-industry wage and income differentials. While the entertainment industry has the highest annual average wages overall ($45 600), the nondurable manufacturing sector (including the garment industry) has only about half this average ($24 100). In addition, intrasectoral differentiations, of course, also need to be taken into account. Inside the film industry, for example, the salary of an international star or of a film director bears not even a distant relationship to that of a stage hand (Wolff, 1991).

The largest of the crafts sectors, and the only one that was growing significantly through the 1980s, was the apparel sector, which had 94 000 employees in 1989 (up 13 400 since 1979 – a rise of 16.5%).[9] Between 1972 and 1982, when national employment in apparel sank by 19%, California added 13% more jobs. Of California's garment jobs, 80% are in Los Angeles County and the majority of these are in downtown Los Angeles (Olney, 1987a; Scott, 1984a). As Allen Scott and his researchers noted in the early 1980s, the women's dress industry in Los Angeles, for example, is an extremely work intensive and static industry in terms of organization. It relies on archaic work technologies using rudimentary mechanical devices such as knives and sewing machines (Scott, 1984a: 4). Vertical disintegration and contract work are normal in an industry that recruits its workforce mostly among Asian and Latin American women. With the cooperation of various social classes of immigrant communities, a complex new inner-city industrial center has come into existence.

Garment production was brought to Los Angeles from New York in the 1920s mostly by Jewish entrepreneurs looking for a nonunion environment for their companies. Over the past two decades, the industry has been revived by the infusion of mostly family capital from Korea and China and by the influx of 'cheap labor' from Latin America and Asia. While nationally, employment in the garment sector was decreasing by 19% between 1972 and 1982, the rag trade of Los Angeles was expanding and was rivaled only by New York City's. In California, apparel jobs

*Plate 6.1* *Fashion district, Los Angeles (Roger Keil)*

grew by 13% during the same period; most of this growth occurred in Los Angeles, where 80% of the state's industry is concentrated. By the end of the 1980s union officials estimated that up to 120 000 workers (mostly women) were employed in minimum-wage positions in Southern California's sweatshops (Olney, 1987a).

A production structure characterized by an 'organizational disintegration of production' has made the industry one of the local success stories of the emerging flexible regime of accumulation. The basis of this flexibilization and vertical disintegration is the so-called 'jobber–contractor mode of production'. Vertical disintegration refers to the organizational and technical fragmentation of the production process between the treatment of the raw materials and the finished product, and stands in contrast to the more integrated Fordist models of labor process organization. Outsourcing, risk-sharing and subcontracting are the hallmarks of vertical disintegration. In the case of the garment sector, jobbers produce their own designs, buy the raw materials and arrange the sale of the finished product. Contractors obtain bundles of cut garment parts from the jobbers and sew them together to produce garments. In California, the jobber–contractor mode of production is more widespread than in other US regions. Another indication of disintegration is the small company size; there are on average 26 employees per company in California, as opposed to 40 employees on average nationally (Olney, 1987a).

While the main factor for the boom of the garment industry was the existence of cheap labor, the market success of the local sector can also be credited to its flexible structure which allowed it to react fast (faster even than the competition from developing countries) to the six annual cycles of the fashion industry. The low rate of capitalization that characterizes the local garment sector strengthened this position and made entrepreneurs more mobile. The combination of these local advantages helped the Los Angeles garment sector to carve out a fairly stable niche in the middle segment of the international clothing sector. It holds a middle position between the mass factories of the Third World (which, for example, produce men's dress shirts) and the *haute couture* from New York, Paris and Milan. The Southland's specialization is in women's and children's apparel as well as in beach- and sportswear (Olney, 1987b).

The division of labor in the garment industry is largely social, as opposed to technical (in one factory). Contract work lowers risks given the volatile and chaotic marketplace and global competition. The social environment of the garment industry – the immigrant community – is crucial for the survival of the sector in this situation. The garment industry uses immigrant communities as a source and regulatory system of exploitable labor while immigrant communities tie into the entrepreneurial opportunities for scattered capital and jobs for unskilled workers. These structures are confirmed in the emergence of ethnic contractor associations which express the presence of strong ethnic subgroups of garment capitalists. In the late 1980s, four groups had founded such organizations: Anglos, Latinos, Chinese and Koreans (Olney, 1987a). While these associations are ethnically organized, in critical areas they work together for the entire class of garment manufacturers in the Confederated Clothing Contractors of America and in the Coalition of the Apparel Industry of California.[10]

The mechanics of internationalization in the garment industry suggest that the construction of the crafts-based pillar of the post-Fordist economy of Los Angeles is being achieved by complex local social, economic and political processes. On one hand, there is the characteristic emergence of ethnically and nationally segmented production areas where a mixture of hyperexploitation and paternalism dominates. Seemingly precapitalist social ties are being used to organize and regulate one of the growth sectors of the current capitalist economy. Since in Los Angeles this occurs with Third World immigrant labor and offshore capital, the barriers between the global core and the global periphery are torn down and reconfigured: the Third World regulates a part of post-Fordist capitalism in Los Angeles. Class interests are overdetermined in many ways by the contradictions of core and periphery and by community ethnicity in this situation.

On the other hand, the economic and political forms of organization of garment factories – and their workers in the labor unions – leave no doubt that the integration of the newly internationalized realities of production in the crafts industries into the structured coherence of Los Angeles occurs along class lines. Internationalization materializes in a field of tension between universal (global) class interests which are played out and modified locally in an environment of ethnic and national niches.

One crafts industry which is often considered 'nonmanufacturing' but which really produces quite tangible items is the entertainment and movie industry. Christopherson and Storper (1986) have shown its exemplary development from a Fordist, studio-centered, Taylorist and vertically integrated mass industry into a flexibly specialized, internationalized, vertically disintegrated sector. A business study of Los Angeles County found:

> To cope with the new risks and costs of high-quality production, once insular, studio-dominated Hollywood began to fragment. New investors, partners, and other players from outside the industry were actively courted to share the financial burdens of film

108

*Plate 6.2   Garment factory, Los Angeles (Roger Keil)*

production. Vertically-integrated studios gradually phased out internal production
capabilities and long-term contracts in favor of subcontracting all parts of cinematic
production on a project-by-project basis to independent production teams (The New
Vision Business Council, 1994: III-6).

The same was shown for the animated movies industry, where some work processes – perhaps up to half of all work involved – are farmed out regularly to low-
wage countries. This puts pressure on local labor markets in a highly unionized
sector of the economy in Los Angeles. Yet, it also creates opportunities for East
Asian entrepreneurs involved in branch plant production abroad to establish
bridgeheads in Hollywood designed to enter the US marketplace (Scott, 1984b).
Many special services, like scriptwriting, photographic services, musical composition, special effects, and, of course, acting, are available in Los Angeles. In 1990,
93 600 people in Los Angeles County worked in the motion picture industry
(Wolff, 1991). While in 1975, there existed only 1142 companies in motion picture
production and services in Los Angeles, by 1991 their number had risen to 3790
(The New Vision Business Council, 1994: III-6).

As in the movie and entertainment industry, production conditions in furniture
illustrate paradigmatically the characteristics of the new accumulation regime in
Los Angeles.[11] In 1986, 54 371 employees worked in 1171 shops in Southern

California; 39 000 of these workers were in Los Angeles County, 10 000 in Orange County. In 1979, 35% of the workers were Mexican immigrants. Competition with the maquiladoras along the MexAmerican border meant a direct clash with production conditions in a Third World country – both in terms of wages and environmental standards (Bloch, 1989). This competition can be held largely responsible for the drop in employment since the mid-1980s: in Los Angeles County, in 1990, only 35 700 jobs remained in this industry (Wolff, 1991). By comparison with furniture companies in the East of the United States, the firms in Los Angeles are mostly small; many of them are family businesses. The trend towards flexibilization and subcontracting, which is prevalent in all crafts industries, however, has led to a weakening of niche firms and towards a strengthening of the well-capitalized and adaptable large companies (Bloch, 1989). The social composition of the segmented and fragmented markets has a direct influence on the structure of the local industry. The supply of cheap residential furniture for the endless stream of in-migrants into Los Angeles – partly through imported goods and partly through locally produced goods by imported firms – and a high-end designer market for residential and office furniture mark the two extremes of the industry spectrum (Bloch and Keil, 1991).

## HIGH TECH

Finally, there is the high technology sector. Much of this is in aerospace which remained untouched by the 1982/83 recession and only started to erode after 1986 with the decline in defense spending. Aerospace (that is, transportation equipment) supported 156 000 jobs in 1990. High tech/aerospace lost 12 600 well-paying jobs in 1988 and 1989 alone as things continued to slide downward in this industry (Wolff, 1991). It is foreseeable, though, that Los Angeles will remain an important location for both research and development, as well as manufacturing for the international high-technology industry.

Since World War II, the Los Angeles area has had a strong position in this sector nationally. The aerospace industry in suburban Southern California has been the core of an agglomeration of electronics and communication technology firms predominantly in Orange County and in the San Fernando Valley (Hall and Markusen, 1985). Hall *et al.* (1985) have shown that in 1974 Los Angeles (four counties) contributed 50% of all California jobs in computer services, software production and data processing. California, at the time, claimed roughly 18%, 20% and 7% of total US employment in these sectors respectively. Although Los Angeles lost ground to its competitor, San Francisco, after 1979, the urban region maintained its dominant position in high tech in California during the 1980s (Hall *et al.*, 1985: 60). Moreover, as Soja has assumed, Southern California had then the largest concentration of high-tech industries anywhere. Between 1972 and 1979, regional employment in electronics and aerospace (SIC 372, 376, 357, 365, 366, 367, 382) grew by more than 110 000. A federal statistic revealed in 1985 that in Los Angeles County alone, more than 250 000 workers were in high tech (Soja, 1989: 204).

A large part of the high-tech success story can be traced back to the politics of land and economic development in Orange County. In contrast to the crafts industries, which can be found in the polluted and congested areas of traditional urban centers, high tech tends to locate in relatively unspoiled suburban areas, often in neo-industrialized locations where there are no strong unions and where there is a business climate uninhibited by large-scale production and Fordist production relationships (Scott, 1988a). In Southern California, accordingly, Allen Scott identifies five major high-technology industrial districts (San Diego, Northern Orange County, El Segundo, Chatsworth–Canoga Park, Burbank–Glendale) and five minor districts, none of which are located in old industrial areas (as along the Alameda corridor in Los Angeles County) (Scott, 1993a: 13).

This shift of new technologies away from the inner city (a shift which has exacerbated the postwar suburban shift of industries) is a significant fact of the new geography of employment, residence and consumption in Los Angeles; new technologies are often centered near the best residential areas – in this case, the South Bay Beach communities. Castells and Hall have written that 'the defense technopoles of Southern California first emerged from entrepreneurialism and innovation linked to a new kind of urban culture' (supported by the warfare state, R.K.) (Castells and Hall, 1994: 188). In fact, it can be noted that the success of the specific kind of innovative milieu as described by Scott (1993a) was immediately connected to the success of a new type of urbanism that was allegedly going to conquer the world's metropolitan peripheries from Orange County outward: 'Orange County presents itself as a foretaste of the future, a genuine re-creation of everyday life in a brilliantly recombinant postmodern world, beyond Oz, beyond even the utopic late-Modernisms of Disney. It claims to have taken the lead in the new competition for the Happiest Place on Earth, and if anyplace else is still running, it is purely through faithful simulation of the original' (Soja, 1992: 95). The inscription of a high-technology complex in Southern California, thus, seems to have been embedded into a nonurban, posturban or exurban landscape whose built and social environments breathed the air of innovation and novelty just as much as the awe-inspiring products of McDonnell Douglas, Martin-Marietta or TRW. Yet, as Castells and Hall also admit:

> In this interactive process between an innovative city, an innovative industry, and a supportive Warfare State, the Los Angeles-centered megapolis emerged as a new spatial form – a form characterized by endless decentralization of the various technopoles, the productive building blocks of the system, and a resulting polycentric structure linked by the network of freeways. Through its media industries Southern California went on to project its image, massively and successfully, to the entire world; but behind it, at the core of its real estate and advanced services businesses, the defense industry provided the real dynamo of growth (Castells and Hall, 1994: 188).

More important in the context of my narrative of Los Angeles than the spatial–economic interplay highlighted by Soja and others are the trialectics of local, national and international aspects of the development of the Southern California technopole. In their brief and sketchy description of the area, Castells and Hall (1994: 182–188) give a number of reasons for the concentration of engineering and entrepreneurialism in aviation there. In a similar argument as Bloch's (1987; see Chapter 4), Castells and Hall stress the 'considerable help and support from Los

Angeles business and civic groups' (1994: 186). Local civic, economic and political boosterism for high technology industries was complemented by the activities of the local military establishment who braided the streams of national defense expenditures into the regional research and development complex which included such reputed organizations as the Jet Propulsion laboratory of Pasadena and the RAND Corporation in Santa Monica (Castells and Hall, 1994: 186). These local efforts to attract high-tech capital and talent to Southern California were tied neatly into the national and global defense priorities of the United States and into the Pacific Rim orientation of the national economy since the 1940s.

The full extent to which local industrial complexes in high tech will be integrated into global markets will be seen in the near future. In the past, the global, external character of the industry has been expressed in its (admittedly questionable and perhaps immoral) use value for the America's world-hegemonic position during the Fordist age and for global warfare. The 'long-term structural problems' identified by Scott (1993a: 254) for the high-tech region of Southern California – declining Department of Defense expenditures and the rising tide of foreign competition in aerospace and electronics – have already started to trigger change in industry goals, performance and structure. In the center of these changes is a new adaptation by the local business culture to 'the hard realities of commercial (and internationalized) markets' (Scott, 1993a: 254). While the use values of the products of the Southern California technopole have long been global, their exchange value was always protected by the shield of the national military–industrial complex in the United States. It was an industrial success story that thrived largely in an overpriced dream-world of artificial long-term economic stability.

The defense-related pseudo-stability of the post-World War II decades which produced a classical Fordist work environment of long-range, unionized, well-paid (and often white male) employment also hid another story which has now come to the fore. The predominance of the Fordist industrial complex has all but eclipsed the growing and thriving reality of a 'relentlessly cutthroat and virtually unregulated competitive environment [which] has led to the development of an immense and expanding sweatshop system in many of the industries serving core high-technology producers, e.g., in electronics assembly, printed circuits production, plastics molding, metal fabrication, machining and so on' (Scott, 1993a: 254). The much-touted future orientation of high tech – often advertised with messianic overtones – also reveals a certain propensity to reproduce more archaic work relationships as described earlier for the 'low-technology, labor-intensive industries of the region such as furniture, clothing, and jewelry. Within this system, low skills, low wages and price gouging are the watchwords, and in many cases outputs compete to an ever-increasing degree not with the world's highest quality producers, but with the lowest' (Scott, 1993a: 254).[12] In the absence of concerted political, economic and civic measures to deal with some of the most rampant excesses of the crisis in high tech, Scott assumes a 'Dickensian' future for Southern California's high-tech complexes. This 'possible scenario of future trends might envisage massive closure of defense-industry plants combined with the ascendancy of a hyperflexible production complex characterized by a widening circle of sweatshops, deteriorating work conditions, erosion of the region's skill

base, and continued falling wage rates for the majority of industrial workers'
(Scott, 1993a: 255). If this drama were to be played out in Southern California in
the future, it would surely involve a further globalization of the economy, one in
which internationalized labor and capital would play a central role.

# CHAPTER 7

# IMMIGRANT WORLDS

Spanish-speaking Los Angeles – the second-largest Mexican, Guatemalan and Salvadorean city in the hemisphere – has far in excess of the necessary critical mass of institutions and media to define its own distinctive urbanity: a different, more 'classical' way of living in the city based on gregarious, communitarian uses of markets, boulevards, parks and so on. The great Latino shopping streets – Broadway in Downtown and Brooklyn in Boyle Heights – have more in common with the early twentieth-century city, with the culture of Ragtime, than they do with a deathwish 'postmodernity' (Davis, 1987: 79).

[E]thnic minority cultures play an important role in this postmodern culture. Their exclusion from political power and cultural recognition has enabled them to cultivate a sophisticated capacity for ambiguity, juxtaposition, and irony – all key qualities in the postmodern aesthetic (Lipsitz, 1986/7: 159).

## PARADISE INCORPORATED: CALIFORNIA AS A GLOBAL PRODUCT

Since its Spanish American beginnings, California has been a turnstile for international capital and immigration. The last Mexican Governor of California, Pio Pico, said in the 1840s: 'We find ourselves suddenly threatened by hordes of Yankee emigrants who have already begun to flock into our country, and whose progress we cannot arrest' (California Department of Commerce, 1987: i). The goldrush which rolled over the state in the same decade was one of the earliest examples of a complete internationalization of a region, of the investment of foreign capital and of the production of an internationalized proletariat (Finzsch, 1982).

The Yankees brought capital into the backward and mostly isolated American region. But capital scarcity prevailed throughout the century and was only periodically lessened by booms like the one in the 1880s. While most merchandise and people reached California through the port of San Francisco, capital for real estate and other development tended to be piggybacked into the state by sun-searching Midwesterners and ailing Eastcoasters. The United States generally also served as a field for the absorption of British capital surpluses in the nineteenth century. Most of these investments flowed into railway construction, which helped to tie the California economy in with the rest of the nation in the second half of the century. Tourists, fortune hunters and prospectors came by train or boat from the East. In return, enabled by the emergent technology of refrigeration, wagons filled with agricultural products went out from California (McWilliams, 1979; Starr, 1985; Cleland and Hardy, 1929). Early on, local entrepreneurs attempted to turn the disadvantage of being relatively isolated from both the continental and the transatlantic economies into a virtue. Especially in Southern California – even more distant than the Bay Area – an early version of pan-Pacific megalomania took hold which imagined Los Angeles as the nodal point of a Pacific economy which would be independent from Europe. Railway tycoon Henry Huntington said at the end of the nineteenth century: 'I am a foresighted man, and I believe that Los Angeles is destined to become the most important city in this country, if not in the world. It can extend in any direction as far as you like. Its front door opens on the Pacific, the ocean of the future. Europe can supply her own wants; we shall supply the wants of Asia. There is nothing that cannot be made and few things that will not grow in Southern California' (Henry Huntington, quoted in McWilliams, 1979: 133–134). Like Pico's premonition, Huntington's vision described a real historical trend. Yet it was reversed as time went on. Today it is Asia with its car plants, its electronic industry and its capital that satisfies the needs of Californians.

Despite this rich history, we can only meaningfully speak of an internationalization by foreign capital investment in the strict sense since the 1970s. In 1984, 11.7% of California's real estate, production facilities and equipment were owned by foreign investors. The state was the target area of 25% of all Japanese investments and of 44.4% of investment from the rest of Asia, Africa and the Pacific. In 1987 foreign direct investment to the United States was concentrated in California ($42 billion), Texas ($41 billion) and New York ($23 billion) (*LAT*, June 28, 1989a, IV: 1). Manufacturing made up 47% of the total volume of jobs created by foreign direct investment (California Department of Commerce, 1987). Total employment by foreign subsidiaries concentrated in production and retailing was highest among all American states in 1989 (California: 324 000 jobs; New York: 300 100; Texas: 207 000) (*LAT*, June 28, 1989a). The government of California pursued an aggressive recruitment policy in Asia throughout the 1980s. In 1987, Governor George Deukmejian reported that a newly founded Californian trade office in Japan had already led to investments of $100 million and to the creation of 2000 jobs in the Golden State. The state also had trade offices in London and Mexico City and intended to open similar institutions in Hong Kong and Frankfurt in 1990. Los Angeles was the center for the investments from the Asian-Pacific region; these investments were concentrated in real estate, manufacturing and oil production. In 1985, 21 of 105 officially registered international investment transactions mentioning a specific target city occurred in Los Angeles. The Los Angeles Basin was the destination of 54 investment actions which moved capital into Irvine, Tustin, Long Beach, Torrance, Corona and Ontario (California Department of Commerce, 1987). This trend of increasing internationalization tied in with genuine globalization dynamics in the 1990s.

Globalization has meant the emergence of a new social and spatial structure. California became the epitomic site of the new global economy populated with venture capitalists, broken labor unions, flexibilized wages, and new service and high-technology jobs (Stephens, 1986). As Allen Scott (1988a, b) has shown for various industrial sectors in Los Angeles and Orange counties, current international investment in California has come with distinctly new industrial districts with a new set of globally induced local problems. In order to remain competitive in the 'Pacific Century', the state, its regions and cities renounced many egalitarian aspects of the American Dream and accepted or even fostered the creation of an ethnically and class-divided society. In the core of this development –fueled by government policy and economic activity of all sorts – is an unprecedented complexity of social and economic realities, a two-tracked economy with Asians and non-Latino whites competing for well-paying, high-status jobs, while Latinos and African Americans vie for poorly paid jobs, mostly in services. In the end, many see a Third World economy with a clear separation of poverty and prosperity emerging as the region's future (Soja and Scott, 1996).

## INTERNATIONAL WORKING CLASS

While California has played the role of foreshadowing developments that would later happen in other parts of the USA, it has also retained much of its individuality. It is particularly the continuing presence of an internationalized working class that makes California distinct even by American standards. Since the nineteenth century immigration from China and Japan as well as Mexico provided an unending stream of workers for agriculture, railway construction and industries. Immigration to California was marked by specific characteristics consisting of the state's geographical location on the Pacific Ocean, its relative isolation from the rest of the American continent by its inland mountains, its proximity to Mexico, and its abundance of natural resources (Muller and Espenshade, 1985: 18). In 1852, four years after the gold rush, which had made the population of California soar to 200 000, the Chinese made up 10% of all Californians. In the three following decades until the passage of the Chinese Exclusion Act in 1882 about 335 000 Chinese emigrated to California. Thousands of Japanese came first from Hawaii and later, after Japanese emigration restrictions were lifted in 1886, directly from Japan. Immigration from Asia stopped around the turn of the century due to the racial–ethnic bias of American immigration policies. During the first two decades of the twentieth century, Mexican immigration rose sharply. In the 1920s, Mexicans made up 40% of all legal immigrants and an estimated larger proportion of illegal immigrants. Of the 368 000 Mexicans who lived in California in 1930 (representing 4.5% of the state's population) 40% lived in Los Angeles County. California Mexicans were a mostly urban population. Only the Depression, with its program of repatriation, which demanded that all Mexicans who did not possess dual citizenship had to leave the country, changed this trend (Muller and Espenshade, 1985: 18–23).

The next significant – in this case internal – wave of migration was the one that brought African Americans from the South to California during the boom of the war years in the 1940s. Between 1941 and 1945, the number of black Californians grew from 124 000 to almost half a million (Muller and Espenshade, 1985: 23). The influx of both Mexicans and African Americans into the region was related to the expansion of the industrial base of Los Angeles (including agribusiness) during the middle decades of the twentieth century. But gaining a foothold in the new industries, particularly after Pearl Harbor, proved hard for both groups because of racial discrimination, leading to difficult logistics of work and home: 'In 1940, most Mexicans still lived in Central and East Los Angeles, which were several miles away from the burgeoning industrial neighborhoods of Maywood, Pico Rivera,

South Gate, and Vernon. Mexicans could not purchase homes in these districts because of the racially exclusive housing covenants' (Laslett, 1996: 55). African Americans faced similar obstacles in getting established in Los Angeles. These difficulties were 'symptomatic of a more general increase in racial tensions during this period, as whites struggled to confine people of color to unskilled jobs, segregated schools and swimming pools, and certain well-defined parts of the city' (Laslett, 1996: 57). These tensions erupted most violently during the 'Zoot Suit' riots of 1943 when white servicemen hunted Mexican youth clad in these oversized fashion statements expressive of jazz culture and subcultural refusal (Laslett, 1996: 57). The impact of black and Latino immigration during this time changed the face of Los Angeles irreversibly, but there was still a long way to go before it would become today's 'plural city' (Waldinger, 1996). 'Despite the impressive growth of the Hispanic and African American populations between 1930 and 1960, Los Angeles remained an essentially Anglo metropolis' (Sabagh and Bozorgmehr, 1996: 87).

Let me pause here before describing the developments of the past 30 years and return to the early decades of the century. While Mexican immigration and African American in-migration were dominant demographic tendencies during that time, they were not the only trends foreshadowing today's multicultural population mix. The Japanese population of Los Angeles County grew from 40 to 8536 from 1890 to 1920, a significant number which compares to German, Russian, Italian and African American in-migration to Los Angeles during the same period (see Table 7.1). Like other people of color, the Japanese suffered from the racist under-currents of Los Angeles (and American) society. In their particular case, war-related internment of about 40 000 people stood out as a major example of racial tension in the period (Laslett, 1996: 57–58).

## AFTER 1965: THE NEW IMMIGRATION

After the reform of immigration policies following the passage of the Hart–Celler Act in 1965,[1] the number of Asian immigrants rose dramatically again; they have been consistently high ever since. California has continued to draw large numbers of legal and undocumented immigrants from all destinations. Controls, like the ones instituted by the Simpson–Rodino Bill of 1986, have proved largely unsuccessful. Yet, particularly after the 1992 rebellion in Los Angeles, a strong nativist mood which resulted in Proposition 187 has made life for immigrants in the state increasingly difficult (Waldinger, 1996: 446–447).

Increasing and changing immigration after 1965 has had profound impacts on the demographics of California. In 1989 alone, almost half of all US immigrants named California as their intended residence. More than half of all immigrants to California, 244 818 individuals, came from Mexico. Of all immigrants to the state, 262 805 were admitted to Los Angeles County (US Immigration and Naturalization Service, 1990: 32–38). Together with Miami and New York, Los Angeles has become one of the prime gateway cities[2] in the United States. In 1988, 13.7% of all new immigrants to the United States chose Los Angeles as their new home; in the post-amnesty years of 1989–90, this number rose to 27.3%. In 1930, 22.1% of

**Table 7.1** African Americans and foreign-born by selected country of origin, Los Angeles County, 1870–1920

| | Mexico[1] | Great Britain | Ireland | France | Germany | Russia | Italy | China | Japan | African American |
|---|---|---|---|---|---|---|---|---|---|---|
| 1870 | 1 886 | 113 | 471 | 317 | 635 | 48 | 60 | 233 | N/A | 149 |
| 1880 | 1 721 | 843 | 725 | 603 | 1 075 | 69 | 249 | 1 144 | N/A | 870 |
| 1890 | 493 | 2 198 | 1 322 | 724 | 2 767 | 73 | 447 | 1 831 | 40 | 1 202 |
| 1900 | 817 | 3 746 | 1 720 | 993 | 4 023 | 293 | 763 | 1 885 | 152 | 2 419 |
| 1910 | 5 632 | 9 584 | 3 878 | 1 916 | 9 604 | 4 758 | 3 802 | 1 481 | 3 931 | 6 821 |
| 1920 | 21 653 | 14 287 | 4 932 | 2 685 | 10 563 | 9 775 | 7 931 | 1 792 | 8 536 | 8 841 |

1. It is hard to explain the reasons behind the drop in the number of Mexicans in 1890 and 1900 because the US–Mexican border was extremely porous at the time, and as a result these numbers are estimated.

Source: Laslett (1996).

the population of Los Angeles County was foreign-born – this was about twice the average of the United States in total. In 1990, this figure had risen to 32.7% – four times the American average (Muller, 1993: 112, Table 4-1).

The restructuring of the economic base of Southern California has made the region a 'paradigmatic example for a city of the Third World on North American territory' (Lieser, 1985: 404) or even, as one East Coast observer wrote (with a bit too much hyperbole), 'the capital of the Third World' (Rieff, 1993). Large parts of the so-called 'fourth wave' (Muller and Espenshade, 1985) of immigrants to California are attracted to this urban region and absorbed into a huge economy under the conditions of the post-Fordist polarization of labor and consumption markets. The demographic profile of the region shows that a majority of the population in Southern California has been nonwhite since the 1980s. In 1990, the SCAG five-county area had 49.7% non-Hispanic whites, 33.1% Hispanics, 8% blacks and 9.2% Asians and others. In the same statistics it was estimated that in the year 2010, 44.3% of the population will be Hispanic, 36.1% white, 8.1% black and 11.5% Asian and others (SCAG, 1993). While this estimate is probably conservative, the categories used also gloss over the increasing globalized fragmentation of Los Angeles to which classical census logic hardly does justice.

## CREATING IMMIGRANT COMMUNITIES

Immigration has developed dynamics of its own. A large immigrant population, particularly when it is clustered in complex urban communities, engenders a demand for the immigration of further workers of different professions – from medical doctors, priests or lawyers to personal servants from their home country (Sassen-Koob, 1987b: 73). The immigrant communities of Los Angeles, thus, emerge as genuine world city communities which bear the external characteristics of their original culture (language, food, music, etc.), but represent an 'emerging ethnicity' specific to the world city. Ethnicity becomes a 'continuous variable' (Yancey, Ericksen and Juliani, 1976: 397–399) of a local political economy, geography and sociology which – as products of globalization – are themselves subject to constant change. This suggests that the conditions of existence for ethnic communities depends on their ability to integrate into the world city economy. One of these conditions of integration in Los Angeles has been the inclusion of immigrant labor into the mushrooming low-wage economy. The underemployed and underpaid international working class of Los Angeles County made up one quarter of the total employment of that county in 1986. Three-quarters of the new immigrants at that point could be found in the low-wage categories; that is, they earned four dollars or less per hour. In the same year, the annual income of at least 900 000 workers was less than $10 000. This corresponds to a numerical increase of 50% since 1973, when 600 000 workers had such little income. At the same time, poverty in Los Angeles was increasingly 'hispanic-ized'. One-quarter to one-third of all Hispanic workers could be counted under the working poor. For the economy and social structure of Los Angeles it is interesting to note that the city resisted the national trend towards the reduction of industrial jobs since local industries could rely on the availability of these workers.

*Plate 7.1*   *Koreatown (Roger Keil)*

Neo-industrialization and postindustrialization in Los Angeles coincided with a Latinization of a population of working poor (Cole, 1988; Ong, 1988; Ong and Morales, 1988).

## ENTREPRENEURIAL IMMIGRATION

Since the 1970s, Los Angeles has become the stage for a previously and elsewhere unknown internationalized accumulation of capital through immigrant small capital owners, primarily from the Third World. There is anecdotal evidence of interest by European investors in small and medium-size firms in Southern California (Cole, 1987); but the lion's share of small-scale capital immigration comes from Asia. In a study of Korean small entrepreneurs, Light and Bonacich (1988) describe how an economically highly successful Third World colony has emerged at the margins of American society. The Koreans in Los Angeles are the latest link in a long chain in the tradition of American urbanism: since the census of 1880, new immigrants have a higher degree of entrepreneurship and self-employment than other groups in the population. The Koreans, however, like the Cubans in Miami, are an exception in the sense that they have developed a comprehensive and coherent ethnic economy (Light and Bonacich, 1988: 8–10).

By the late 1980s, Koreans who had come to Los Angeles since the 1960s accounted for just 1% of the total population of Los Angeles County. Yet, between 1967 and 1977, they founded 5.5% of all new firms in the area. Thus, they did not just fill gaps or niches in the world city economy, but increased the share of entrepreneurs in the total population through immigrant capital and internationalization. The Koreans who have come to Los Angeles have had mostly excellent preconditions: 'Koreans were highly educated in their country of origin, often well endowed with money upon their arrival in the United States, and commonly middle or upper middle class in social origin' (Light and Bonacich, 1988: 19). From this position, they have played quite a specific role in the construction of the world-city economy: Korean immigrants have stabilized neighborhoods (an essential aspect in the attempt to reverse tumbling real estate prices on the fringes of the world city citadel); have improved the public education system (a remarkable achievement in a school system in which almost half of all high school students drop out before graduation); have fought against street violence (Koreatown has become the *cordon sanitaire* between the ghetto on the one hand and the central business district and the 'better' residential areas on the other); and have injected new capital and entrepreneurial energy into the economy of Los Angeles County (Light and Bonacich, 1988: 6–7).[3] When Los Angeles went up in flames on April 29, 1992, the function of the security corridor provided by Koreatown became obvious. At least 1867 Korean shops and businesses were burnt down or looted. Korean businesspeople suffered total property damages of $347 million (Kwong, 1992: 88). The Koreans who settled down as small entrepreneurs in Los Angeles completed the national economic cycle of an international economic process which had been started decades earlier in the United States when they exported capital, technology and military power onto the Korean peninsula. The Americans, conclude Light and Bonacich (1988: 27–67), had used Korean entrepreneurs to avoid stricter labor laws at home and to take advantage of cheaper labor in Korea. This inverted history now allows two hypotheses with regard to the economy of Los Angeles: first, a place emerges where global contradictions from the Fordist period are now played out in the social and built environment of a new period of urbanization; second, it is being confirmed that the world city is a microscopic version of global tendencies. It is not just their mirror reflection; world city formation is the urbanization of global restructuring.

## REPRODUCING THE WORLD CITY

The social structure of the world city tends to be congruent with the fragmentation of its economy (Ross and Trachte, 1983). In fact, patterns of social stratification by consumption capacity, life-styles, etc. belong to the core of the mode of regulation which emerges in the world city. Their intricate and complex web of exchange relationships is a central structural element of the emerging political economy of the global city (Sassen, 1991). New kinds of reproduction also engender new productive relationships. The economic polarization and internationalized social fragmentation of Los Angeles simultaneously provide the starting point for, and represent the result of, a huge spectrum of state, entrepreneurial, collective and individual practices on a completely globalized urban terrain. In contrast to the situation in the Fordist city – which was built on the equalizing tendencies of mass production and consumption – diversified forms of production, distribution and consumption of commodities now become the social and economic elements of regulation of an extremely rugged urban ecology.

In the following section, I will briefly look at housing and social welfare in globalized Los Angeles. Towards the end of this chapter, I will offer a typology of entrepreneurial practices in the new world city economy of Los Angeles with which I will begin to describe the kinds of realignments of urban consumption that I consider typical for cities like Los Angeles. While this typology has some descriptive and analytical value and helps introduce the subject matter, I do not, by any means, claim that the four categories I use are exclusive or complete.

## HOUSING

The housing problem in Southern California – that is, the lack of affordable housing or the lack of access to it – and the problem of overcrowding are directly linked to immigration in the public discourse. Most immigrants are employed in low-wage sectors and consequently contribute to the pressures on the low end of the housing market. In this sense, we see, in Los Angeles, yet another case of immigrants bearing the brunt of the urban housing crisis, a phenomenon typical of capitalist cities at least since the days of Engels' famous description of the misery among Irish immigrants to England in the 1840s (Engels, 1971: 48). Simultaneously, immigrants have begun to redefine the standards of housing and housing provision in California in a way that questions the rationality of housing policy in the state. The settlement patterns of the new migration call into question the viability of traditional construction and housing standards, the zoning plans, and other local instruments of regulation. The new immigration challenges the traditional knowledge of such instruments itself and the viability of housing reform (Baer, 1986).

In a general climate of restructuring and welfare state retreat (Wolch, 1996), increased immigration during the 1980s had a visible impact on the provision and quality of available housing and on the rising homelessness in Los Angeles. While demand rose constantly for affordable housing, the number of housing units – 1.2 million in the city of Los Angeles – remained stable (City of Los Angeles Blue Ribbon Committee on Affordable Housing, 1988). In Los Angeles County, the 'collapse of affordable housing' was mostly due to upward filtering of existing units, demolition and insufficient rebuilding of multi-family units (Wolch, 1996: 400–406). A closed system of housing provision made it difficult for new immigrants to break into the housing market. Since the existing housing stock was not sufficient, immigrants have tended to live in overcrowded conditions and to convert nonstandard units into living space: 40 000 families, that is up to 200 000, were estimated to live in garages during the 1980s (Squier, 1988). Overcrowding is a phenomenon which affects immigrant and minority communities disproportionately. More than 40% of Asian and almost 55% of Hispanic households lived in crowded conditions in Los Angeles County in 1990 (Dear, 1996a: 15). Of typically low income earning immigrants, 44% paid more than 30% of their income for housing. Overcrowding and heightened demand for affordable housing increased the pressure particularly in the downtown where minority and immigrant communities tend to be concentrated (Baer, 1986). In traditionally African American communities, this has led to processes of displacement and increased residential densities (Oliver and Johnson, 1984; Oliver, Johnson, and Farrell, 1993; Vergara, 1997).

The internationalization of Los Angeles changes the common standards of housing. Existing local building codes and zoning plans carried with them an implicit program of social control and of social exclusion against the 'dangerous classes' – both potentially restricting factors for new immigrants. Baer (1986: 348), however, has argued that immigrants entered the Southern California housing market when Californians were more willing to put housing standards up for debate. In this situation, Third World housing practices started to influence and redefine what housing meant in an American city like Los Angeles. At the interface of local and global developments in Los Angeles, the concept of 'housing' has been redefined by all participants but particularly by the immigrant communities themselves. Defending housing as a central use value is the imperative of the acculturation of Third World immigrants. They build their living spaces in a process of negotiating state regulation, state regression, poverty and community standards imported during immigration. A recent observer has described this process as follows:

> The largest housing program in Los Angeles is taking place in backyards, often without city permits. The lot is a unit where families of different income levels share space. The house facing the street is the largest, best built and most comfortable, and living conditions often deteriorate as one moves closer to the alley.
>
> With the help of contractors, family members and friends, as their resources allow it, people erect structures and add extra space to existing buildings. From the alley side, in the backyard, one frequently finds additional units of housing – one of them typically an old trailer that can be bought for about $1000. . . . Small old trailers are often used to house undocumented immigrants while they work and repay their fees to 'coyotes' those who bring 'illegales' into the country.
>
> While suburban living is still possible throughout most low-income areas of LA, a view from the alleys reveals that the lots have lost much of their garden quality. The back yard and often even the front yard is a piece of land used to serve the needs of the family and friends and for economic survival. Cages full of chickens and rabbits (and once I saw a horse) bear witness to a rural lifestyle. Tamed nature exists in patches, often having to take second place to the needs of children, cars, work, storage, dogs, and barnyard animals. The good life represented by a few small trees, potted plants, cactuses and chiles, sharing space with watch dogs and their dog houses (Vergara, 1997: 3–4).[4]

## GLOBALIZING SOCIAL WELFARE

The regression of the welfare state in the period of globalization in Los Angeles was not restricted to housing (Wolch, 1996). A 'shadow state' of more than 8500 nonprofit organizations in Los Angeles County grew alongside and in partial replacement of the traditional social welfare institutions of the local state (Wolch, 1989; Geiger and Wolch, 1986). First, the imbrication of urban and global economies in Los Angeles coincided with a subordination of social concerns under the dynamics of urban economic development; second, globalization and immigration have increased the use of the voluntary sector in solving social problems.

The official narrative of globalization maintains that economic growth will benefit everyone in the urban area. While critics of world city formation point out

**Plate 7.2**  *Toy district, Skid Row (Roger Keil)*

that social problems seem to increase rather than decrease in the process of the city's internationalization, the American Dream is sold to immigrants as the guide to the theater of the world city. In this sense, the Community Development Department (CDD) of the city of Los Angeles took over responsibilities of basic social welfare provision such as food, housing and job-training, specifically targeting new immigrant workers mostly from Central America and Mexico as well as bridging services for immigrant entrepreneurs. Churches, community self-help and similar organizations offer a variety of services to complement the local state's (diminishing) activities. With regard to the local state, struggles over the distribution of dwindling resources among established social groups and new immigrants are not as common as one might expect because new immigrant communities tend to rely heavily on family or community resources for the solution of social problems. New immigrants tend to be more hesitant to use state services than nonimmigrants. There is, however, a growing number of social programs specifically directed at new immigrants. This growth is partly a result of community demands on the local state. Social policy is used by local state bureaucracies to sew together the sociospatial fragments of the world city into a pacified patchwork. This is, for example, the case in the area east of the downtown where CDD and other agencies provide bridging and mediating services between Little Tokyo businesses, Chinese toy wholesalers and the homeless of Skid Row.

One social service organization, the Pacific Asian Consortium of Employment (PACE), has provided services to new immigrants from Pacific Asian countries since the late 1970s. Pacific Asians who live or work in the area were offered vocational training, retraining and skill training, services for the elderly and the handicapped. PACE had programs informing people about housing, and providing construction aid, energy-saving, economic and technical assistance for small business. All services were linked to the spatial integration of the area. As part of

*124*

**Plate 7.3** *Homeless 'bed' in the doorway of a social service agency and luxury car across the street*

the economic development strategy of the city of Los Angeles, and in close cooperation with its Economic Development Department, PACE also acted as a medium for the attraction of foreign capital into the New Asian Corridor. The measures and programs offered by the local state which were meant to assist the integration of immigration and foreign investment into the city are complemented by the internal social forms of organization in the ethnic communities and by demands for the recognition of new spatiopolitical forms.[5]

The strategic planning of the local social welfare state relies heavily on the informal social networks of the familial, community and voluntary structures of the immigrant communities. In addition, some service providers in the shadow state have specialized in servicing the international population. These organizations include institutionalized forms of communitarian self-help, ethnic churches, and large traditional service providers. Among them is the United Way of Los Angeles, an organization which has thrown itself keenly into the challenges posed by world city formation. United Way publications since the mid-1980s have embraced a language and analysis that portray Los Angeles as a global city and multiracial and multiethnic metropolis (United Way, 1986; Torres-Gil, n.d.). While ethnic diversity was introduced as a positive value, the United Way's policies were geared towards bringing new immigrants into the center of American society:

> Los Angeles' growing role as a center for Pacific Rim trade will make it a continuing magnet not only for international business, but also for the constant flow of immigrants. The long term consequences of actively drawing immigrants and refugees into the mainstream, rather than allowing independent and isolated ethnic enclaves to develop, are worth everyone's time and action today (United Way of Los Angeles, 1987: iii).

George F. Moody, president of Security Pacific Corporation and co-campaign chairman of United Way in 1987, elaborates on the deliberate attempt by this organization to integrate 'problem groups' into the mythological middle of American society. United Way and its ethnic councils, in Moody's view, were to 'serve as both antennae and conduits to the public':

> The Los Angeles area is the country's new Ellis Island. We comprise the number one destination for legal immigration in North America. Some 50 foreign banking offices serve Pacific Rim businesses in our community. There is a great potential for good and prosperity in the presence of these businesses. As a continuing magnet for international business, we also are attracting a constant flow of immigrants.
>
> The long-term consequences of actively drawing immigrants and refugees into the mainstream, rather than allowing independent and isolated enclaves to develop, are worth everyone's time and action. In the fast lane of today's global economy, Los Angeles must ensure that culturally appropriate health and human services are accessible for New Americans (Moody, 1987: 13).

The social movements and nonprofit organizations in ethnic communities are once again seen as the nuclei of the activities in the social welfare area. Proactive policies facilitate the articulation of the influx of immigrants with the structure of local service provision.[6] The United Way, for example, founded Asian, Hispanic and black 'Leadership Councils' which were to coordinate voluntary social service in these communities and to allocate and distribute funds and services (United Way, 1987).

Those policies and institutions can, however, only partly contain the contradictions they have to deal with. Immigrant communities have consistently tested and challenged the boundaries of the social welfare state. And despite their innovative character, the efforts of the local welfare state, and of its shadow in civil society, have not been able to successfully stem the tide of social problems Los Angeles has faced in the 1990s. This became more than obvious in the uprising of 1992 and the discussions in its aftermath.

## CONSUMPTION

The emergence of a numerically strong Latino population with steadily increasing buying power has led to marketing strategies by American mass-producing corporations that include some form of targeting of these consumer groups. In a first stage, the 'Fordization' of the American society has been expanded to integrate the formerly disregarded ethnic markets. Chicanos in Los Angeles have become drivers of Chevrolets and consumers of mass-produced American food such as Spam and McDonald's fast food. National advertising budgets have begun to reflect the relevance of these newly 'Fordized' Latino customers. Ad campaigns emphasize what is considered an extremely traditional and family-oriented life-style in the Latino communities. Food, beverages, tobacco products and automobiles are the leading products for which Latinos are especially targeted. In the 1980s the 'Los Angeles Marketing Area' (Los Angeles–Long Beach, Anaheim–Santa

126

**Plate 7.4**  *Marketing in immigrant communities (Roger Keil)*

Ana–Garden Grove) with its 2.3 million inhabitants who have the 'Spanish language and certain historical and cultural traditions' in common, presented the largest 'Hispanic' media market in the United States. In 1985 alone, $59.2 million were spent in that area there for advertising in the printed media as well as in radio and television (*Los Angeles Times* Marketing Research, 1986). In regular market surveys which the *Los Angeles Times* put together during the 1980s to help focus their advertising, the emergence of a non-Anglo mass market for consumption goods was registered. It was noted that Los Angeles was the largest Asian and Latin and the third largest African American market area in the United States (*Los Angeles Times* Marketing Research, 1986: 2). While targeted marketing for these ethnic groups was generally considered difficult in Los Angeles, the methods used by the advertising industry have improved, adapting to the demands of a world city economic environment (*Los Angeles Times* Marketing Research, 1986). The advertising industry made its response to the different ethnic segments of the Los Angeles market its growth strategy for the 1990s (Howard, 1988). In addition to the traditional (and continuing) hegemonic strategies of the large food companies, of automobile producers, etc. for incorporating the growing buying power of Los Angeles' ethnic communities, there are also marketing opportunities created by new forms of individualized consumption that are typical for the social structure of the world city.

# THE ETHNIC SUPERMARKET: NEO-FORDISM IN THE BARRIO

Supermarket and shopping center were the core elements of the mass consumption-oriented Fordist retail industry, relay stations in the reproduction of the 'Fordist subject' (Hirsch and Roth, 1986: 53–64). They were like factories in which the congruency of individualization and mass conditioning were produced. Their product mix and their marketing strategies were directed towards uniformity and the equalization of tastes, a tendency which finally – ironically, as a consequence of sinking buying power in the Fordist crisis – found its peak expression in the advent of 'generic products'. Since the 1980s, however, a different trend has been noticeable: the markets are increasingly differentiated due to social and economic criteria.

On one hand, the overconsumption of the new middle classes has been provided with a new reproductive infrastructure. Generic products are taken from the supermarket shelves and replaced by new designer products and gourmet foods (Zwahlen, 1988). Genetic engineering and buying power surpluses have prepared the ground for the expansion of a product-differentiated agriculture which lives up to the demands of the new markets. Southern California is considered a prime market for new designer products and international luxury products.[7] On the other hand, the retail industry, constantly haunted by processes of concentration and restructuring, has been aggressively reorganizing its sales strategies under the pressure of an increasingly internationalized consumption structure.[8]

Next to this differentiating equalization of the Fordist city, by which Anglo food was brought to non-Anglo communities, there is now a new strategy which does not derive from the postulate of a generally even supply of the means of reproduction but has the difference of the internationalized populations of the world city as its presupposition. Starting with a marketing idea of the Vons chain – with a market share of 25% in 1983–84, the second largest of its kind in Southern California – retail corporations have created ethnically focused marketing strategies which have fragmented the supply of consumption goods in the urban area along the freshly drawn and changing lines of international populations. In the middle of the 1980s, the marketing strategists of the Vons chain noticed a surprising weakness in its supermarkets in majority Latino areas.[9] While Vons usually controlled 65% of food sales in a two-mile radius around its stores, this was not the case in Latino neighborhoods. In areas with high immigration, the sales of most supermarkets tended even to go down. The result of this insight was the development of a supermarket format which was meant to specifically target the Spanish-speaking population of Los Angeles, a new chain of stores with the name Tianguis, which is the Spanish adaptation of an Aztec term for marketplace.[10] The stores were to be placed into the community as important centers seeking to reflect the original meaning of their name. The social function of creating a 'marketplace' reminiscent of Central American shopping practices was complemented by the urbanist element of creating La Placita, an open space in front of each market (where American supermarkets would only see parking spaces). La Placita was accordingly sold as part of the concept as a perfect place for customers

**Plate 7.5**  *Tianguis Market (Roger Keil)*

to relax before or after shopping. Half of the interior was dominated by the loud colors of the store's logo in order to create an illusionary Central American ambience, while the other half was furnished and decorated like a 'normal' American supermarket.

The first Tianguis store was opened on January 30, 1987 in Montebello, east of Los Angeles. At the time, 90% of the Latinos in Montebello were Mexican. Of the 300 employees of the market, 98% were Latinos; 80% were bilingual. Signage and packaging were in Spanish; all checks were accepted in order to make the place accessible to the main target group, the new immigrants. For the second, 'moderately acculturated' target group the store's homemade tortillas were to evoke a certain nostalgia. Totally acculturated Mexican Americans were not considered a main target group.

Von's strategy of product differentiation – including the upscale Pavillion markets – was copied by other chains such as Boys and Ralphs, with varying success. Tim Hammond, the speaker of a large American commercial association, the Food Market Institute, confirmed in 1987, that the industry expected that the trend of retailers catering to ethnically and territorially bound groups in Los Angeles would prevail in the 1990s. The strategies of the large supermarket chains would change in the process. In the 1990s, Vons has abandoned its Tianguis strategy. Strategies of the major chains have also been complemented increasingly by the emerging Fordization of the individual ethnic groups themselves: in Chinese Monterey Park, customers have been able to choose between several local supermarkets, among them two Hoa Binh stores. In the Armenian part of Hollywood, Ron's Market, a converted Vons store, has become the center of a growing immigrant community from the former Soviet Union. Perhaps the most impressive single example for the emergence of ethnic supermarkets has been the El Tapatio store in southeast Los Angeles where a tortilla factory is the centerpiece of a

**Plate 7.6** *El Tapatio Mercado (Roger Keil)*

bustling Mexican market and where La Placita is replete with food booths and features a market-owned shuttle service that takes carless customers and their full shopping bags to their homes (Lehrer, 1995).

## MINIMALLS: PRIMITIVE ACCUMULATION AT THE STREET CORNER

Wherever immigrants are concentrated geographically in large numbers, the opportunity emerges for reproduction through businesses and stores of the respective culture or nationality. This has been the case, for example, with the Central Americans (mostly from Guatemala, El Salvador and Nicaragua) in the Westlake and Pico Union areas of Los Angeles. An estimated 40% of all Central American immigrants in the USA live in Los Angeles.[11] In catering to the specific needs of their fellow immigrants, Central American business people in Los Angeles have created a completely novel part of the local economy. Most immigrant businesses are founded only after arrival in Southern California. They are, once established, the signs of a relatively stable, permanent international subeconomy of the world city. In contrast to the 'colonialist' strategies of the supermarket chains which transpose the dominance of the 'white' Fordist economy onto the

130

*Plate 7.7* Minimall (Roger Keil)

fragmented, post-Fordist communities of the globalized urban fabric, immigrant entrepreneurs have developed a culture of consumption which rises endogenously from the *Barrio*. Many businesses born out of these immigrant cultures are central to an ethnically defined system of reproduction. They are also an element of 'primitive accumulation' in the immigrant communities. In Los Angeles, the creation of a new spatiality of consumption was particularly conducive to this process. Minimalls, usually two-storey buildings that enclose street corners in an L-shape, became the locations of choice for immigrant businesses and consequently for the reproduction of immigrant communities. By the end of the 1980s, 2000 such minimalls existed in Southern California. William Hayes, a construction firm owner who has built 125 minimalls in Southern California, estimated the share of new immigrants among the tenants of the commercial space in these malls at 75%. Appropriately, the *Los Angeles Times* called them 'stores of opportunity' (J. Sanchez, 1987a).[12]

While minimalls have had a high reputation among immigrants and represent the foundation of an immigrant petty bourgeoisie, its aesthetic and urbanist value has been the subject of heated discussions in Los Angeles. Opponents of minimalls claim that they further traffic and crime problems in residential neighborhoods. Due to strong support for this position in the general public, the city of Los Angeles temporarily placed a moratorium on the construction of the malls. Yet, overall, the reactions of the local state towards the market-led internationalization of the street corners and of the consumption patterns in the urban region have remained ambiguous. While the director of the Office for Small Business with the mayor of Los Angeles considered the moratorium a disadvantage to business starts (J. Sanchez, 1987a), other bureaucrats regarded the minimalls as future problem areas.[13] The seemingly anarchic internationalization of street corners and storefronts has been accomplished by a globalized petty bourgeoisie who makes their family property the basis of a new phase of primitive accumulation. Each investment into a mini mall store tends to range between $50 000 and $75 000 and comes mostly out of savings and family loans; rents for the store are paid through the exploitation of family members and 16-hour working days. This process amounts to a significant international capital influx into the local economy of Los Angeles. Investments tend to be successful where there is an integration into the reproductive cycle of the internationalized urban communities (J. Sanchez, 1987a). When they fear that market anarchy will exceed the efficiency of the reproduction of ethnic communities, planning authorities will intervene and, as one official put it, opt for surgical and responsible growth, a euphemism for the curtailment of minimalls. Despite the rhetoric of slow growth advocates and words of caution from city officials, the anarchic development of minimalls has been ultimately embedded in a system of planning controls. Thus, it has been complementary to the larger project of the 'world class city' as espoused by the Los Angeles elites since the 1970s. Minimalls are proof of the emergence of new forms of social reproduction that are typical of the social stratification and political economy of the world city – regardless of more critical aesthetic or urban planning considerations.

## TACO TRUCKS: THE AUTOMOBILIZATION OF ACCULTURATED CONSUMPTION

In Los Angeles, the built environment of reproduction can hardly be separated from the automobile. Reyner Banham's observation still holds that the freeway system (and the car in all its apparent forms) 'is now a single comprehensible place, a coherent state of mind, a complete way of life, the fourth ecology of the Angeleno. (. . .) The freeway is where the Angelenos live a large part of their lives' (Banham, 1971: 213–214).[14] The internationalization of Los Angeles, consequently, includes the automobilization of the immigrant population and of its reproductive systems. Automobile culture is one of the important entry gates into the economy of Los Angeles. Thousands of new immigrants work in car washes or work as valet parking drivers, operate parking lots, pump gasoline or fill the peripheral labor market segments in the automobile or supply industries (Morales, 1983).

One specific sector of the automobilized immigrant economy of Los Angeles is the food catering business. In Southern California, an estimated number of 4300 so-called taco trucks are on the streets every day. Up to 8000 people are believed to work in this sector of the economy. The medium-sized delivery trucks with kitchen and side counter sell mostly tacos, hamburgers, hot dogs and soft drinks to predominantly Latino customers around the city. While other nationalities (e.g. Vietnamese, Armenians) are also involved in the catering business, the Mexicans with their taco trucks are the majority. Supervised by the County Health Department, these trucks are a major link in the reproduction of new immigrant communities – both for caterers and customers. These fast food outlets on wheels can usually be seen in most Latino areas of the city; they sit at the curb in front of

*132*

**Plate 7.8**  *Taco trucks (Roger Keil)*

factory gates and schools (J. Sanchez, 1987b; Murphy, 1990). The presence of taco trucks means the expansion of the street culture of Los Angeles into the immigrant communities and the rooting of immigrants in the fast food culture of the city.

In contrast to traditional catering trucks, most taco trucks have semi-fixed locations which they rent from the owners of Latino nightclubs, from gas stations and parking lots. Taco trucks operate in a constantly changing legal environment. Urban regulations regarding times and places of operation are subject to neighborhood politics and standards of public order. Los Angeles City Council has repeatedly had taco truck regulations on its agenda, mostly in regard to citizen demands for more restrictive policies. In January of 1990, 50 drivers demonstrated with their trucks in front of City Hall against harassment and against threats to their existence caused by arbitrary regulations (Murphy, 1990).

The taco trucks, which operate in the border region of established and contingent business cultures, on the threshold between the built city and the mobile urbanites, are products of the specific formation processes of the world city in Los Angeles. Taco trucks are a Los Angeles phenomenon, an example of immigrant adaptation to an automobilized society (J. Sanchez, 1987b). In turn, this automobilized acculturation is ultimately the peripheralization of automobile culture in Los Angeles. In line with the analysis that George Lipsitz (1986/7) has offered regarding popular culture in east Los Angeles, taco trucks can be seen as part of a postmodern culture that has its origin in the restructuring of the social fabric of the internationalized city and the creativeness of its inhabitants. The case of the automobilization of acculturation is one element of the production of a new urban culture and economy that takes its origin from the national Fordist form but transcends it in an innovative, place-specific and peculiar way.

***Plate 7.9*** *Cash for cans: recycling economy (Roger Keil)*

## TAKING IT TO THE STREET

The fourth type of consumptive economy I would like to introduce in this typology is also related to the culture of the street in Los Angeles: roadside vendors who offer plastic bags of fruit and nuts to drivers at busy intersections from shopping carts parked on traffic islands; and street vendors who sell socks, tapes, children's clothes, sweets, fruit and other merchandise from cardboard boxes or blankets on the sidewalk to passers-by (R. Sanchez, 1987). In the late 1980s, estimates as to how many such vendors were selling merchandise in Los Angeles' downtown and immigrant communities as well as at intersections across the city ran as high as 2000 individuals. Those who work as vendors are mostly poor, do not have a good formal education, or are too old to compete even in the low-wage economy of the city (R. Sanchez, 1987; Schneider, 1987; Citron, 1989).

Like the minimalls and the taco trucks, the street and roadside vendors belong to the informal economy which has direct connections to immigrant economies (Portes and Sassen-Koob, 1987). In the area of street trade, tax evasion, black market activity and exploitation of family members has become the rule, and the informal quality of these occupations has become the essential feature of this increasingly important sector of the world city economy. In sum, the consumption supply of the street economy represents a growing section of the total

**Plate 7.10**   *Street vendor (Roger Keil)*

consumption of the internationalized neighborhoods of the world city, and a persistent, and semi-reliable self-employment opportunity on the lowest rung of the urban economy. Informalization does not contradict regulation through the state. Rather, its extent and character are defined by regulatory and police measures of the local state. In 1989, the local government stopped prosecuting undocumented day laborers who assembled at street corners around the city each morning to be hired by entrepreneurs or private persons in construction or gardening. Moreover, the city designated certain places in the urban area where they were allowed to stand and look for work. A Latina coordinator was employed by the city to organize the process of matching workers with employers at the street level (Tobar, 1989a, b).

By the end of the 1980s, though, when Los Angeles had become the paradig-matic example of a metropolis that relied on immigrant labor, the city still had the strictest laws against street vending in any big American city. Under the laws at the time, only a few commodities, such as flowers and hot dogs, could be sold freely (Citron, 1989). Between January and August 1987 alone, 238 street vendors were sentenced; this was more than in all of 1986 (R. Sanchez, 1987). Constant police activity in the inner city kept vendors on their toes at all times; they were arrested, their merchandise and personal belongings were frequently confiscated and they became victims of police brutality (Palazzo, 1989; Citron, 1989). At any point in time, plainclothes police could be observed in the downtown arresting and harassing vendors who did not have licences. On the surface, the rigid attitude of the local state against such a 'Third World' street economy was legitimized publicly by pointing to the competition it constituted to established businesses. The street vendors responded with the demand that their activities be legalized and licensed, too, which they thought would benefit the entire urban economy (R. Sanchez, 1987; Martínez, 1991).

Yet, the discussion around street vending was not just about legality and tax evasion. The vendors and the economy they represented became the subject of a discourse on the meaning of the city which questioned traditional ideas about Los Angeles as an American metropolis and began to legitimize a new period of urbanization. There is the model of an internationalized city which represents directly the functional contradiction of citadel and ghetto. In this model, the marginalized labor force of the immigrants is subjected to the reproductive and aesthetic needs of the culture of the citadel. The discursive battle cry in this context is 'cosmopolitanism'. Street vending is touted as a 'cosmopolitan event', where, for example, downtown workers can buy croissants from niche caterers on their way to their offices (Palazzo, 1989). When Los Angeles city councilman Mike Woo initiated a taskforce to eliminate the restrictive legislation on street vending in Los Angeles, he called the existing laws 'absurd', because in his eyes, regulated street vending contributed to the general vitality of the city and offered employment to immigrants (Citron, 1989). Between the metaphorical 'croissant' and the regulation of its sale, we can spot a program for a new form of urban production and consumption which combines the folklore elements of an internationalized street culture with allusions to the 'American Dream' to become the dominant image of the misery of a subsistence culture and of the horror of a Third World city.

This positive reevaluation of street vending by some urban elites contradicted traditional fears over the image of the city which, as some urban officials believed, was sullied by vending. In particular, it was feared that Los Angeles might be associated with the 'backwardness' of Third World cities (R. Sanchez, 1987). What seemed to be at issue was certainly whether street vending would be accepted as a possible cheap source of service labor for downtown office workers or whether it would retain its character as a link in the chain of immigrant economies. The fact that street vendors enjoyed a growing role in immigrant communities seemed to shield them from being reduced to a mere cheap labor pool for the needs of the citadel (R. Sanchez, 1987). While this also meant that their position in the discourse about the meaning of the city was noticeable and important and although the *vendedores ambulantes* have formed a Street Vendors Association (Martínez, 1991), the public attack on immigrants after the 1992 rebellion and in the wake of Proposition 187 will probably weaken the social position of immigrant street entrepreneurs in the near future. The meaning of this type of consumption to the entire fabric of the world city will remain subject to debate (Rutton, 1992b).

## CONCLUSION

The social production of reproduction in the internationalized city is a lively expression of the restructuring of social relationships in a period of new and changing immigration patterns. New productive relationships emerge alongside new patterns of consumption and welfare. The deregulation and flexibilization in the world of work correspond to the equivalent phenomena in the world of reproduction and consumption. In a triangle between (1) the control functions of the

*Plate 7.11*  Police raid on street vendors, downtown Los Angeles (Roger Keil)

local state in zoning, economic activities and other fields, (2) a 'glocalized' marketplace, and (3) the creative survival strategies of immigrant communities' civil societies, a tenuous social structure of settlement takes hold. Constantly threatened by competing demands of the world city community, often disenfranchised, brutalized and economically exploited, most immigrant communities have learned how to take up a sophisticated fight for their survival in the context of an ever-changing world-city landscape (see Valle and Torres, 1994). There is a dialectic of construction and constitution of community which characterizes immigrant social collectives in Los Angeles: old cultural and social identities are given up in favor of a new universe of identities which is characteristic of the globalized city and resting on an increasingly diverse social reality.

# CHAPTER 8
# BUILDING THE WORLD CITY

Well, here we are entering a new decade and quite a new world as well. Our planet has been undergoing quite a change. Demands for freedom becoming reality in many different countries. Global economy becoming more intertwined everyday. Peace between the super powers replacing the cold war. And through all these changes one thing remains a constant; Southern California Real Estate! (A San Diego real estate agent in 1990).

At the mouths of the Hudson and of the Mississippi, at the confluence of Allegheny and Monongahela, on Lake Michigan and on the Bay of San Francisco even another nation would have seen the rise of great cities. . . . Los Angeles, however, that city of millions, is an artificial product which has the American psyche as a precondition (Wagner, 1935: 159).

The world city is the specific political economy of place in the space of global capitalism. As such it is the product both of global and local political and economic processes. The internationalized real estate market of cities, in combination with public redevelopment schemes and public–private partnerships which act as 'transmission belts', have been considered important ways in which large capital surpluses have been absorbed by the production of urban space (Harvey, 1989a). The 'creative destruction' which characterizes this process is accompanied by a specific unevenness: on the one hand, a withdrawal of capital to the periphery takes place, leading to deindustrialization and urban decline; on the other hand, productive capital and real estate capital are being pumped into the centers as well as the edges of global cities (Ross and Trachte, 1983). Part of this stream flows into the citadel functions of the inner city and into the new nodes of development like research and industrial parks, airports and the like; another part feeds the low-wage industries and services that spring up as Third World enclaves in core countries. These capital streams increase *relative* surplus value by replacing living labor through labor-saving technologies; it also increases *absolute* surplus value by introducing sweatshop work conditions. In cities like Los Angeles, local actors translate the globally dimensioned capital movements into a place-specific built environment and social structure through locally defined political and social processes. The complexities of these global and local activities in the production of internationalized space are the subject of this chapter.

Strategies to replan downtown Los Angeles as a center first for national, later for international, capital go back to the 1940s, and superseded plans for a revitalization of the existing but run-down regional center functions of the inner city (Haas and Heskin, 1981: 548). Now, close to the end of the twentieth century, after a hunt by international real estate capital for the prime parcels of Southern California, aided by relentless political support for redevelopment, Los Angeles has become a thoroughly globalized space. The purely *statistical* internationalization is matched by the common perception and the ideological construction of the global city: while a constant flow of foreign real estate capital entered the city in the mid to late 1980s, this trend received much attention only as a result of some spectacular deals by Japanese investors. The internationalization of Los Angeles was noted through a xenophobic discourse. Alarm over spectacular sales of office towers, hotels and golf courses – all of them objects of the representative business and life worlds of the internationalized bourgeoisie in the citadel of the world city – to Japanese investors posed the question of American sovereignty. Frantz and Collins wrote accordingly:

> The question is what this expansion will mean for the American real estate industry. Will real estate go the route of the consumer electronics industry or the auto industry? Can the Japanese capture enough of the decentralized market to become a dominant force, setting rents and determining housing costs for a nation of tenants? By using the growing power of Japanese-owned banks and influencing policy through their cadre of lobbyists, can they affect zoning laws and wide-ranging government policies? (Frantz and Collins, 1989: 246).

To most people these were rhetorical questions. Popular depictions of the Japanization of urban space could be read as a neonationalist call to arms. This apocalyptical vision was widely discussed in the public sphere of Los Angeles but found little support. In a direct response to a newspaper article by Catherine Collins in which she asked about American sovereignty (Collins, 1989), Ivan Faggen, globally responsible director of the real estate consulting firm Arthur Andersen & Co., maintained that the real estate sector was 'the best place for Japanese money'. Owning large parts of the American market, Faggen continued, hardly enabled the Japanese to gain control over rent and cost for services to the tenants because these are determined by local competition (Faggen, 1989: VIII, 3). In reference to the direct influence of Japanese investors on the municipal political and planning process, a skeptical attitude prevailed.

In a study of six Los Angeles neighborhoods, Dymski and Veitch (1992) have shown that the financial dynamics of urban growth has been closely linked to the spatial division of race, ethnicity and power in the city. They criticize the common image of Los Angeles as a Fay Wray who is mangled by a King Kong of foreign investment and immigration, maintaining instead that '[s]ince capital and development in L.A. has historically been controlled by Anglo elites, the King Kong image is more accurate when inverted. The helpless Anglo "We" is not broadly besieged by the King Kong "Other": Fay Wray controls the resources needed for the Other to survive' (1992: 133).

Foreign investors are rarely active on the municipal political level. They leave this task to local representatives and enter all kinds of joint ventures with them. Possible partners include real estate firms, construction companies, developers, financial institutes, business and professional associations, chambers of commerce, private planning and consulting firms and individual politicians. In linkage contracts, complex political connections with political and social organizations in the local sphere – especially those that are territorially dependent – come into existence.[1]

Thus, in a situation of the growing internationalization of the market, the confrontation of 'indigenous' versus 'foreign' agents in the real estate business is,

***Plate 8.1*** *Pershing Square and First Interstate Tower (Roger Keil)*

in the first place, an ideological maneuver. Instead of becoming an issue of confrontation between competing nations, doing business with urban space has been internationalized using the help of 'local' actors. In Los Angeles, for example, this was the case when Sumitomo Real Estate, the largest Japanese real estate firm, entered a business relationship with Los Angeles real estate giant Fred Sands. Thus both companies linked their respective 'indigenous' with their 'global' interests. Using a 'video-tour', the agencies delivered southern Californian real estate offers into Japanese homes and offices (*LABJ*, May 14, 1989: 2).[2]

Transnational real estate firms or local consulting firms (often one and the same) assume the role of transmitters. In the late 1980s, one such organization was Acquest International, located in Los Angeles. Its main business was to bring capital for commercial projects from overseas to the western United States. International investors would use the firm to help them find lucrative buildings at a location in whose favor they had already made a decision. The investors did not directly get involved in the local political process but took its results for granted. In cases of political indecisiveness or generally unclear conditions, investors consider the risk too high and renounce their investment. Building height restrictions, traffic studies and environmental impact assessments increase the risk for the investor and make it necessary for local mediators to get involved. While transnationals look for local partners in real estate deals, they do not automatically make their projects subject to negotiation with the local community or groups critical of their development proposals. They also tend to 'learn quickly, setting up local subsidiaries or simply gaining the experience to take on additional projects on a full ownership basis' (Knox, 1993: 7). The arrival of transnational corporations on the local real estate market does not occur without changes in the local political system.

International investment still encounters many obstacles on the local level. Whereas in the 1980s local governments wanted to attract investment at any price, the pressure from groups critical of growth and development led to a variety of building restrictions that made the construction of big projects a time-consuming and expensive process in which the expertise of local place entrepreneurs became an important skill which the foreign investors were forced to acquire. Real estate management firms, developers as well as individual consultants, began to play an ever more important role in this situation. In an environment that appears to make it more difficult for developers to get their way without meeting community resistance, consulting provides the social and legal software for the physical planning process. According to one consultant, in contrast to earlier periods in Los Angeles' history, 'almost every project is held hostage today' (Garcia, quoted in the *LABJ*, C, July 24, 1989).

Consultants emerge as the main actors of the urban development game. They tend to appear as free-floating agents between City Hall, 'the community' and the developers. They are, however, typically employed by the latter and provided with ideological and legal armaments by real estate think tanks like the Urban Land Institute. The guild's shining stars in Southern California are political heavy-weights, usually with a public sector background and a law degree.[3] Bill Boyarski of the *Los Angeles Times* has described the workday of Art Snyder, a consultant in City Hall:

> [Snyder] does it all for a client – legal matters, planning advice, the works. You could see it . . . when he appeared before the Planning Committee for a hearing on Watt's [City West] project. He had loose-leaf books for the committee members, containing the complete description of the project, plus a supporting legal analysis. Snyder even provided his draft of a proposed final ordinance that the council could adopt, once it decided to approve the project.
>
> All this work is usually done by the planning department and the city attorney's office. Snyder has saved them the trouble – and the taxpayers some money. Grateful, the two committee members present, Chairman Hal Bernson and Michael Woo, approved the project as written by Snyder. . . .
>
> Then Snyder literally followed the measure through City Hall, to see that it wasn't changed. On Friday morning, he attended a meeting between representatives of the city attorney and city clerk as the final ordinance was drawn.
>
> His job was far from finished. He visited every council office, spending half an hour or more with each representative. He was at it again the morning of the vote, starting his rounds of council offices at 8:30 a.m. The vote itself was anticlimactic (the Council approved the project by 14 : 1; *Los Angeles Times*, December 15, 1989: B2).

This work introduced a new dimension of *Realpolitik* into the politics of development in Los Angeles. In the grey areas of linkage, consulting and public/private partnerships, single projects of urban development sometimes replace and sometimes supplement the general vision of planning and urban development. In downtown Los Angeles, the First Interstate World Center, the tallest tower in the American West, was built – after lengthy negotiations – with the air rights of the central library which had burnt out. It stands as a swaying monument of linkage mania in Southern California. Especially on the Westside of Los Angeles, in the triangle between West Hollywood, Santa Monica and the International Airport, where middle-class communities have learned to turn their economic and cultural capital into positions of power at the bargaining table, every single development project becomes an exercise in idiosyncratic micropolitics. A semiprivatized form of urban planning and urban politics is taking hold which differs from earlier forms of urban politics in both substance and form. The political resources of the public process of urban politics are now shifted into an elusive private space where urbanism is a business effort by definition, subjected to the monadic and nomadic ethos of the movement of capital in space.

The shift towards privatization tends to weaken those communities that do not have sufficient material or cultural resources to organize themselves effectively, since from the start they operate on the mercantile terrain of private real estate capital. Social responsibility – allegedly guaranteed by 'linkages' – becomes an adjunct of the profit interests and tax considerations of the investors and the local states. The supply of affordable housing, welfare or jobs – once considered social services – is turned into the scrap product of a market-regulated process of negotiations on the urban micro level. In middle-class neighborhoods this can lead to considerable improvements in the community. But the deregulation of urban politics tends to lead to the defeat of the poor communities: the living quarters of the working classes are condemned to be use values of a lower order for their inhabitants, precisely owing to their lack of exchange value, which translates into a less powerful political position in a privatized political arena. The various micropolitical projects and urban utopias are different versions of postmodern politics, and rest on the monetarization and privatization of political spaces. The city – once hailed as the epitome of public *space* – becomes a mere collection of private *places*. In Los Angeles, the shift from the public to the private and from the social to the economic spheres is exacerbated by the growing fragmentation of the political system into political fiefdoms segregated and separated by class, race and nationality – particularly after the collapse of the once unifying, yet now extinct, Bradley coalition.

Of course, the internationalization of the production of space does not necessarily differ from the earlier periods of real estate development. Decisions about development were almost always quite removed from the community level even before globalization brought in a new set of players and widened the playing field. Process and result of the production of space have hardly changed: 'One must be aware of the positive general disposition of state, county and city government in California to investment capital and development activities, a disposition which is not altered by reason of the foreign source of the capital', writes Robert E. Duffy, a leading real estate attorney in Los Angeles (Duffy, 1989). The place entrepreneurs experience this positive disposition on the side of the local state as a structural advantage. It is expressed in the 'positive general disposition' of the institutions of the state with regards to growth. Hence, the mobilization of local–global harmony has to be understood primarily as an attempt to align foreign and indigenous place entrepreneurs in order to both unify them behind a common growth project and leave them enough space to pursue competitive business objectives. The relationship of internationalized investment to the local community is predetermined in the sense that growth itself – whether locally or globally induced – is not fundamentally up for debate but is merely modified in a specific framework commonly referred to as 'growth management'. The relationship of place entrepreneurs and communities remains structured in favor of growth in the period of increased internationalization: the local community is expected to act not as a decision-making agency but only as a moderator of developments which are prescribed in the existing institutional relationships of power in the city.

The positive attitude of the local state towards investment from overseas is crucial. Duffy (1989) points out the particular openness of Southern California's local politicians towards Japanese capital. He cites as examples the activities of former Mayor Tom Bradley and former County Supervisor Kenneth Hahn in the Japan–Los Angeles Partnership Forum: 'At those assemblies, Los Angeles county and city officials have extended a warm hand of cooperation to the Japanese investor and businessman, asking in return only that the Japanese be aware of the need to be good and responsible "corporate citizens" of the city and county – meaning an involvement in local civic, cultural and social affairs' (Duffy, 1989).

During the 1980s, this intervention increasingly happened by way of political donations from foreign investors and companies to local politicians. Mayor Bradley's campaign coffers, for example, were filled by such contributions for many years. Much of his political strength came from Bradley's capacity to receive both electoral and financial support from the members of his 'coalition' of Jewish, black and other liberal voters (Sonenshein, 1993: 186). Among these were many Asians and Asian Americans. In 1989, the mayor was almost driven from office by a scandal that involved the Far East National Bank which gave Bradley an annual stipend in exchange for 'lucrative deposits of city funds' (Sonenshein, 1993: 206). Between 1984 and 1988, Bradley, one of the most well-known and most respected American politicians in Japan, received more than $200 000 from more than a dozen Japanese real estate firms, banks and other companies. These payments from corporations such as Nissan Motor or Sumitomo were hardly worth mentioning in comparison with national campaign contributions, but locally they were quite influential. Bradley could use this influence in his (ultimately unsuccessful) bid for the governor's position in California and in his successful reelection as mayor in 1989 (*Newsweek*, July 11, 1988).[4]

Real estate insider Duffy advised both American skeptics and Japanese investors that their cooperation would be advantageous to them. He particularly suggested that the investors be sensitive, show good will, perform good property management and respect the wishes of the local community. He concluded that it was important to 'consider formation of relationships with domestic developers and consultants who, aside from their expertise, naturally lend a public relations buffer' (Duffy, 1989). The 'new sensitivity' of the foreign investors replaced the earlier practice of 'brutal landgrab' without any consideration for local conditions. Participants at a Japan–America conference in Los Angeles in May of 1989 saw harmony and mutual understanding of investors and local communities as their

major concern. Social aspects of real estate investment and the investors' integration into an ethnically and racially mixed urban society were deliberately
included in discussions of investment strategies (see *LABJ* special issues during the
conference, May 14–18, 1989). Mayor Bradley reminded the participants of the
growing respect of Japanese investors for the local community: '[There] is a
growing sensitivity to the issue. And I think Japanese companies have been trying
to respond to our expressions of concern and are trying to be sensitive to all
minorities – all the way from hiring to (contracting out) services to minority firms'
(quoted in Shiver, 1989).[5] The 'sensitive' method of mediation of global interests
into the local space rests on the general understanding by the local place
entrepreneurs that the process of land valorization and land use in the city is – as
Stone (1982) has shown – systemically structured in their favor. In addition, it is
important to note that the grafting of a globalized financial and investment structure onto a local financial system happens in an environment that is prestructured
by class and racial divisions. Dymski and Veitch write accordingly:

> Communities' growth is facilitated or checked by financial dynamics – that is, path-
> dependent, cumulative decisions about capital, credit and banking service flows. The
> character of financial dynamics, and hence of overall growth, depends on the locus of
> capital control and the adequacy of financial infrastructure. An examination of L.A.
> growth patterns reveals the ethnocentricity of capital: financial dynamics are most
> robust in areas heavily populated by ethnic groups with control over capital (Dymski
> and Veitch, 1992: 133).

In the increasingly globalized space of Los Angeles, national and ethnic connections have become important media of global processes. This has created new
roles for the economic and political elites of immigrant or local ethnic communities. Chinese American Michael Woo, a one-time contender for the mayoral
position in the election of 1993, and city councilman in Los Angeles between 1985
and 1993, became a central mediating figure between Asian investors and local
communities – first in his home turf, the Hollywood district, and later throughout
the city. Although Woo did not consider the designation 'Asian' as sufficiently clear
to describe the wealth of cultures and nationalities that have immigrated to Los
Angeles from Asia, he became the leading representative and sometimes spokes-
man of the disparate communities of Asian immigrants. Individual activities of
politicians and planners are complemented by more institutionalized and
organized processes which facilitate the structural integration of different ethnic
real estate and investment capitals as well as immigrants in Los Angeles.

The incorporation of Los Angeles into the global economy is supported by the
sociospatial organization of the city's internationalized neighborhoods. A comprehensive process of community building and destruction has been experienced by
many downtown Los Angeles neighborhoods in the globalization process.
Especially the growth sectors of the post-Fordist urban economy have expanded
in the classical residential and commercial neighborhoods of the downtown. The
east of the downtown has become the location of choice (assisted by planning
decisions) for the toy, flower and seafood wholesale markets. A strong lobby of
area businesspeople – the Central City East Association and the Little Tokyo
Merchants Assocation in the northeast – has aggressively sought to control or even

displace Skid Row homeless people and their service organizations from what they consider their territory. In the south of the downtown, the jewelry and garment sectors have increasingly dominated the use of space. Garment has moved away from its traditional base along 8th Street towards the north along Spring Street and south along Maple Avenue. As a consequence of consecutive proposals to develop Central City West, the expansive activities of the wholesale and crafts industries have also put pressure on residential neighborhoods west of the Harbor Freeway. In Chinatown and Little Tokyo, the urban development process worked as a transmission belt moving East Asian capital into a clearly defined and culturally (as well as legally) produced space in the city. The case of Koreatown is special in the sense that 'its resurgence, most obviously manifested in the booming commercial edifices on Olympic and Vermont Avenues, has come without Anglo in-migration. It has also come largely without local (Anglo) banks' money. It is a new model – a healthy financial dynamic not controlled by Anglo elites or their banks' (Dymski and Veitch, 1992: 151). The production of an ethnically defined space comes with a respective system of social and technical infrastructure. In the New Asian corridor between Echo Park, La Brea and the Santa Monica and the Harbor freeways, in whose center lies Koreatown, a wide range of public and private service agencies have located, regulating the globalization process locally (see also Chapter 7).

These processes of cultural and political integration of immigrants into the space of the world city are a form of 'incorporation' of a place into the global economy (Sokolovsky, 1985). They create the locally specific conditions, a political economy of place. Global place entrepreneurs clearly recognize this kind of incorporation as the sociospatial precondition for the success of their investment and consider them instrumental to their decision-making process: 'Besides the economic strength of the Southern California Market, Asian investors feel comfortable in the region's multicultural environment. Los Angeles has the largest Japanese, Chinese, Korean, Vietnamese and Philippine populations outside their own country', notes an important consulting study of the Los Angeles real estate market (Acquest, 1987: 30).

Multiculturality here means the existence of national cultures in a foreign place. Their existence makes it possible for investors and immigrants to create links to Los Angeles through well-known and familiar structures, or at least, structures that resemble those left behind in their country of origin. That is, the internationalization of the political economy through the local control of global capital flows happens in a way that hides the process of the formation of a multicultural world city from the view of the external observer. Instead, Los Angeles appears on this level as the projection of familiar and 'acceptable' new cultural forms; undesired aspects of the process are often concealed or played down. In place of the cultural diversity of the urban region, either a lily-white or an 'acceptable' (that is, familiar), but always unicultural Los Angeles is presented.[6] To Japanese investors, Los Angeles appears as a Westernized version of Japan; to Chinese or Korean immigrants, the recognition of the cultural mix of the city has been cushioned in the security of knowing that the relevant relationships immigrants might expect in Los Angeles are inside their own ethnic culture. This image was shattered to no small degree in the uprising of 1992.

On the whole, despite the foregrounding of the cultural aspects of international investment and migration, the creation of world city spaces is mostly an economic process that is mediated and differentiated through cultural dynamics. It reflects the conditions of the urban and regional division of labor which have emerged from a historical and geographical development process in consecutive periods of urbanization. This spatial pattern has proven to be *relatively* stable and has served as a system of fixed points in the process of creative destruction which the urban space is always undergoing.[7] Even in the phase of increased globalization, the existing sociospatial hierarchies seem generally to have been stabilized. This confirmation of the existing larger spatial structure through the onslaught of globalization, however, has often come at the expense of the destruction of individual microstructures, and has also not precluded, by any means, the continuous reconstruction and deconstruction of urban space and its meanings.[8]

The dialectics of the existing and the emerging spatial division of labor are among the permanent themes that place entrepreneurs concern themselves with. In terms of their spatial direction, the interventions of foreign capital in Los Angeles first follow and confirm the existing dynamics. The differentiated supply of the specific political economies of individual places in the structured coherence of Los Angeles predetermines the way in which investments are distributed spatially. In the 1980s and early 1990s, it was mostly assumed that the continuing influx of business from the Pacific Rim would lead to a further concentration in the inner city: 'During the past two decades the shift of business activity from Europe to New York has changed dramatically. Now the major exchange of goods and services takes place between the Pacific Rim and Los Angeles, due in large part to the rapid economic growth of Japan, Korea, Singapore and Taiwan' (Ortiz, 1987: S-32). Much of this optimism was dampened later on when Asian economics shared severe signs of crisis and investment flows ebbed.

Not too long ago, Los Angeles was marketed as the 'world's most exciting city today' and downtown Los Angeles was described as 'the major target of intelligent businessmen looking for long-term real estate opportunities and, of course, the perfect business climate' (Ortiz, 1987).[9] The growth of international investment in the downtown has been linked mostly to the insurance and the financial sectors at that location; these functions also spread into existing but growing secondary locations, such as the 'horizontal downtown' of Wilshire Boulevard: 'The increase of Asian business in Los Angeles has created an amplified focus on expansion of space for service companies already located in the Mid-Wilshire area. These firms, accounting, legal and insurance, are finding the chance to support their larger corporate clients in downtown and surrounding areas, while simultaneously being close to their labor pool' (Merrit, 1987: S-22).

Thus, the globalization of urban space does not occur in a historical, spatial or political void. The specific historical and geographical conditions that have defined a place before or during its internationalization are crucially important for place-specific restructuring. In Los Angeles, as in other cities, this is true for the traditional political and spatial contradiction of centralization and decentralization. Under the hegemony of centrality, suburban or exurban place entrepreneurs attempt to add peripheral growth centers to the potential shopping list of overseas capital. Such spaces have been used mostly for production and storage, as well as for the headquarters of some international companies. Even the boosters of the downtown economy acknowledge that instead of a sole concentration on the downtown a dialectical division of labor between centers and peripheries determines the real estate market in the age of globalization.

Although statistically it appears as if global capital is moving through cities like an invader from outer space, local space entrepreneurs (who can be themselves head offices of the subsidiaries of transnational firms) provide the necessary means to facilitate the spatial and social integration of these investments locally. They do this by using the local political and planning process as a mediating instrument. This insistence on the necessity for transnational investment and development corporations to immerse themselves in the local places they buy, sell and develop is not meant to underrate the desire of the development industry to free itself from both political and local constraints. Much of what used to be considered the responsibilities of municipal governments and planning institutions has been shifted to the development industry. This industry, which includes, on the one hand, those maverick entrepreneurs who go from rags to riches and back to oblivion again in the space of a few years, and on the other hand, large traditional corporations, has shown that it despises government control of its activities. However, since these organizations are operating 'within the tight constraints of the economic system' (Sudjic, 1992: 44) and want to avoid possible performance disasters in local markets, they are forced to get involved in on-site research, planning and even politics. The type of transnational real estate development firm that emerged in the 1980s and found its most pronounced expression in the ill-fated Olympia and York of Toronto, acts 'like a hybrid of an old-fashioned landed estate and a civic planning authority, albeit one geared up to maximizing financial returns. To succeed it must involve itself more and more in issues such as transport planning, and long-term economic forecasting. It has to co-opt the kind of people who would once have worked in public city planning offices' (Sudjic, 1992: 46). Such internalization of previously public functions into the privatized sphere of development is, in fact, one powerful way to create strategic links between the interests of the global corporation and the place where the investment occurs.

These changes in the structure of the development industry and in their relationships with public and local decision-making and planning beg the question of how class hegemony is formed in and through space. Consider class formation in space a process of the spatial diffusion and concentration of power. The consequence of such processes of spatial differentiation are a complex net of spatial contradictions within and between classes. We need to remind ourselves in assessing the effects of internationalization on urban space in Southern California that the main spatial contradiction does not occur between global capital and the local bourgeoisie. Rather, the main contradiction of urban space consists of the fundamental rupture between the use of space for the reproduction of capital (and of the international capitalist class) on the one hand and the (re)production of labor power (and of the working class and their spaces) on the other. This is primarily a contradiction of exchange value versus use value. While this contradiction has been typical of capitalism in general, globalization takes it to a new level.

While the internationalization of urban space proceeds with the help of local place entrepreneurs, the local political process of the production of space is altered as well. First, due to the arrival of international investors and developers, the center of local power is shifted increasingly from the locally dependent bourgeoisie to the national and international bourgeoisie. This is the main source of intraclass contradiction among the bourgeoisie in the world city. Second, however, the local face of power changes precisely through the dialectics of local opposition to and cooperation with these new global agents. The implementation of international capitalist hegemony in urban space is reflected through the prism of, and checked by the activities and opposition of, local groups. These local political, social and economic agents hold up their particular interests in the use value of their neighborhoods (or in locally defined economic structures) against the globally defined exchange value interests in urban space. It can be taken for granted that the local decision-making process is systemically structured in favor of the global rather than the local actors: this is not because these actors are international but because this is how the planning and political process in capitalist cities usually works. Thus, here one does not find fundamental contradictions but merely individual conflicts of interest among the local and foreign place entrepreneurs. On the political level, however, the international agents are forced to engage with the local community. As such, the internationalization of urban space appears as class conflict in space.

The preexisting distribution of urban space in Los Angeles is an important starting point for the internationalization process. The institutional framework of planning and politics, the differential designation and boosting of investment zones of specific character, the traditional praxis of the place entrepreneurs, the ethnically segmented spatial division of labor, and local political opposition of use-value oriented groups against the speculative valorization of their neighborhoods are factors that influence the globalization process. While the attention of local actors and boosters switches from one to the next object of speculative desire (from Bunker Hill to South Park, from Central City West to Central City North, etc.), the investment practices of the external, international agents also shift in response to local action. An excellent example of this strong local power of regulation is the continuing discussion of planning committees and development authorities about the expansion of the downtown core towards the north, the west and the east. Local political and planning decisions determine the frame – and never the detailed process – of future development of the citadel in Los Angeles. The fact that there is no singular plan but often parallel and competing projects does not weaken the local capacity to regulate but increases the differentiation and segregation of capitals by nationality, sectors and size. In this way entire cities emerge *within* cities, and places develop identities in urban space. Japanese capital invests in Little Tokyo; Chinese investors concentrate on Chinatown and the new Chinese communities in the San Gabriel Valley; Korean capital colonizes Koreatown. The creation of such segregated internationalized subspaces in the world city transplants foreign practices of production and consumption from the countries of origin into the world city and offers a laboratory for post-Fordist (more flexible and more internationalized) practices of production and consumption.

Various factions and groups of place entrepreneurs compete for valuable parts of the world city. The contradiction of centrality and decentrality, for example, which often dominates debates about the urban area as a whole, is a dogged fight over achievable differential ground rents and profit rates. There are variations in the praxis of the local and the global place entrepreneurs who appear sometimes as complementary users of urban space and sometimes as competitors. Japanese investors are often thought of as preferring fully leased buildings for which they pay top prices and which they plan to keep for long periods. Their prime targets are so-called 'corporate brochure buildings' with high symbolic and representational value (Acquest, 1987: 30). Chinese real estate capital is believed to be more speculative and more willing to enter risky arrangements. While Los Angeles was the target of large-scale investments from the United States, Canada, Great Britain and from other European countries in the 1970s, (*LAT*, May 13, 1979; September 3, 1979; October 7, 1979), most of the capital during the 1980s and early 1990s came from Asia, mostly from Japan (Acquest, 1987: 40). A large part of the Japanese real estate investment has come from large corporations like Shuwa or Mitsui Fudosan who have bought or built entire office and business complexes – often paid for by massive accumulated small-scale savings of Japanese citizens. The key sale in this category during the 1980s was the acquisition of the ARCO Towers in downtown Los Angeles by Shuwa for $600 million in 1986. By stressing the showpiece aspect of their real estate acquisitions, the Japanese buyers – perhaps unintentionally – supported the centrality of the world city citadel as an internationally produced place. By buying into the local place entrepreneurial strategy of boosting the role of Los Angeles as the capital of the Pacific Rim, the 'Far East' became a captive client.[10]

In this respect, the production of the world city citadel reminds one of the towns that were built by prospectors: they are both the result of self-fulfilling prophecy. The investments are presented as options for a qualitatively new future of urban space in Los Angeles. The production of the world city citadel thus simultaneously means a spatial practice and the creation of a mythological place where the magical forces of the thrust of globalization are being tied together and transformed speculatively and concretely into a built environment. Yet in the age of telecommunications and television it is not the rumors of gold finds that entice the political economy of place: the landscape of the United States dominates the cerebral and imaginative maps of Japanese investors not just because of abstract statistical calculations but also through the existence of an odd category of 'television cities' that offer their skylines as a backdrop to serial productions of the studios in Burbank and Hollywood (*LABJ*, October 12, 1987). Los Angeles is one of these cities. Along with the prospect of stable profits, the city offers images of success and grandiosity. The Japanese concentration on showpiece objects is open to this lure of acquiring a piece of a dream world as a windfall of the profitable real estate deal. The two processes cannot be separated; they determine the interface between local and global actors. It was in this way, up until the real estate crisis, that Los Angeles absorbed part of the overaccumulation of the Japanese economic miracle. At the same time, this process created a new place: downtown Los Angeles as we know it today. This place became a chip in globalized casino capitalism.

In the globalization process, there is a shift from the uniformly zoned Fordist use of space and time to post-Fordist differentiation and flexibility. Everything now is potentially being used in every possible way and around the clock. Externally, space and time in Los Angeles are increasingly determined through the position of the city in the 24-hour carousel of financial trade between the markets in Europe and Asia. This combination of globally significant location and boundless time management changes the position of Los Angeles in the global city network. Internally, the expansion of the downtown citadel from an 8-hour-a-day office container, which separated its functions both spatially and temporally, into a 24-hour city, now rejoins these functions flexibly into a new reality. The planning in the late 1980s for a 'world-class center' (which at the same time is supposed to be an 'urban village' for the South Park area of the central city) made such interventions into space and time programmatic items: rental apartments and condominiums, offices, shops and hotel in one single complex were to facilitate the use of the inner city around the clock (Ryon, 1988). This temporal flexibilization in particular was one of the main objectives of the Community Redevelopment Agency:

> One of the major goals of the Agency is to see the city develop it's [sic] 24-hour nature. Under it's [sic] direction Los Angeles has, over the last eleven years [since 1978], developed the solid financial base which will allow them to pursue the expansion of the 24-hour character of the city. 'The challenge' [CRA Chairman James Wood] said, 'is to ensure that any new development contains 24-hour uses, as opposed to just 8 to 5'. Theaters, restaurants, hotels, retail stores, and residential areas all help to draw people into the city in hours other than just during the day, Monday through Friday (Laganiere, 1989).

The totalization of temporal use supplements the program of the globalization of urban space and makes the production of Los Angeles as a world city a spatially and temporally unlimited process. This explodes the given space of local politics. From the unionization of Latina janitors who work on contract for a Danish cleaning firm and a German building management company to maintain Japanese-owned office towers, to the struggles of communities against the megaplans of international investors, we can talk intelligently about local politics as a category only if we ground its meaning in the globalization of space and time in the world city.

Finally, the internationalization of Los Angeles at least symbolically marks a turning point in the historical geography of the capitalist world system and in the role of the United States in this system. When Shuwa bought the ARCO Towers in 1986, the senior of the corporation, Shiberu Kobayashi, gave the mayor of Los Angeles, Tom Bradley, a check of $100 000. This sum was to be used to erect a monument to greet and honor immigrants, as the Statue of Liberty does in New York City, but this time for immigrants who arrive on the West Coast. In contrast to the Statue of Liberty, which was designed to celebrate the national position of the USA (and its ideals of freedom and democracy), the monument of Los Angeles – for which a bizarre 'steel cloud' above the Harbor Freeway was one suggested design – was intended to be the symbol of the dynamics of the Pacific Rim. In this interpretation, Los Angeles would be constructed as a deterritorialized international place rather than an American city, a fact that remained true after many

Japanese investors offloaded overpriced property in the mid-1990s. While some local place entrepreneurs lifted their heads in the sale of prime real estate, the built environment of Los Angeles was now thoroughly a global commodity, never to return to the glory days of the railway barons, the *Los Angeles Times* empire or the local sports tycoons. Los Angeles is irreversibly global.[11]

# PART IV

LOCALIZING THE GLOBAL

# CHAPTER 9

# REDEVELOPMENT

Redeveloped with public tax increments under the aegis of the powerful and largely unaccountable Community Redevelopment Agency, the Downtown project is one of the largest postwar urban designs in North America. Site assemblage and clearing on a vast scale, with little mobilized opposition, have resurrected land values, upon which big developers and off-shore capital (increasingly Japanese) have planted a series of billion-dollar, block-square megastructures: Crocker Center, the Bonaventure Hotel and Shopping Mall, the World Trade Center, the Broadway Plaza, Arco Center, CitiCorp Plaza, California Plaza, and so on. With historical landscapes erased, with megastructures and superblocks as primary components, and with an increasingly dense and self-contained circulation system, the new financial district is best conceived as a single demonically self-referential hyperstructure, a Miesian skyscape raised to dementia (Davis, 1990: 228–229).

The [community redevelopment, R.K.] agency lacks a clear mission. The City Council is expanding redevelopment through adoption of new civil disturbance and earthquake recovery areas, while the Mayor is focusing on economic development programs, and the Agency is currently emphasizing affordable housing programs. Accordingly, it is not surprising to find CRA staff confused about program goals and priorities. . . . The agency has an inconsistent track record in working effectively with and *empowering* the communities served by the Agency (Los Angeles City Council, 1995: 4).

Between Mike Davis' acerbic assessment of the record of the Los Angeles Community Redevelopment Agency (CRA) and the rather uncompromising dismissal of that agency's role in rebuilding the city expressed in an audit half a decade later, lies a period of dramatic change in Los Angeles redevelopment. In the four decades before 1990 the CRA, more than any other institution in Los Angeles, had changed the city's skyline and urban form. During the 1990s, the project of redevelopment almost came to a total halt. This chapter narrates and analyzes some aspects of the rise and demise of the agency, which is one of the largest quasi-governmental organizations Los Angeles has seen in its 200-year history. Community redevelopment has been in the center of the institutionalized forms of mediation between global and local dynamics. Through most of its history, the CRA has been the most important political institution to moderate, modify and execute the process of world city formation in Los Angeles. In 1995, the CRA had 'eighteen redevelopment project areas encompassing more than 6600 acres of land in the City of Los Angeles' (Los Angeles City Council, 1995: 41). An additional 18 areas with a total acreage of 21 311 were the subject of studies, or revitalization projects or were disaster recovery project areas (Los Angeles City Council, 1995: 42) (Figure 9.1). They are – to varying degrees – locations of international investment and migration; the enormous agency which has administered these areas has worked as a giant transmitter of local fiscal authority and tax increment – originally meant to serve the public good – into the development budget of local, national and transnational corporations.

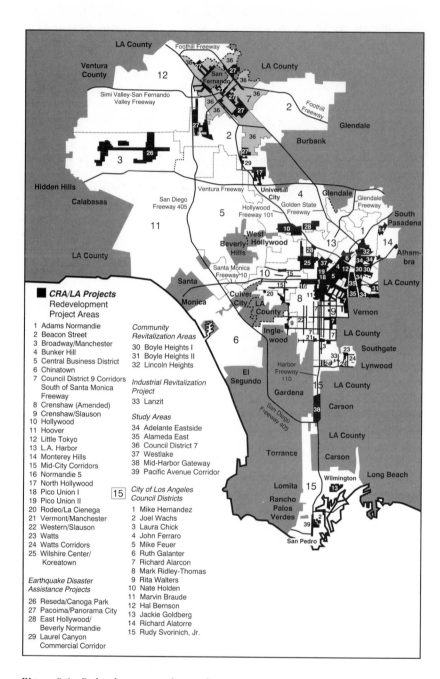

**Figure 9.1** *Redevelopment and revitalization areas in Los Angeles, 1997 (courtesy of the Community Redevelopment Agency, Los Angeles)*

Redevelopment and urban renewal were central concerns of federal urban policy after World War II. Laws regulating redevelopment were passed between 1937 and 1949 federally and in individual states. This legislation initially breathed the air of social welfare and economic reform typical of the Keynesian New Deal state. Its impetus was the creation of public and affordable housing in the inner cities, whose increasing social and physical decomposition was to be countered by large-scale reform measures (Marcuse and Hartman, 1988; Parson, 1985). In the 1950s, a gradual but steady redefinition of urban renewal and redevelopment occurred. The meaning of 'blight' was identified more and more with a decrease in local tax bases and less with the physical or social situation in individual neighborhoods. Since the suburbanization of the white middle class had 'left behind' concentrations of poverty in inner cities largely inhabited by people of color, contemporaries of the first waves of urban renewal experienced this redevelopment process as the removal of African Americans, of the poor and the elderly from downtown residential neighborhoods. Under the political and ideological influence of real estate associations and the building industry, the mandate of housing construction disappeared from the redevelopment process almost entirely.[1]

The framework in which the CRA has operated in Los Angeles is defined by urban redevelopment legislation, which is part of the Health and Safety Code of the state of California. It was passed by the Legislature in 1945 and activated in Los Angeles in 1948 through the founding of the CRA by City Council. Established as a quasi-local state agency, the CRA has two major purposes: the development of low- and moderate-income housing and the revitalization of blighted areas (Los Angeles County Grand Jury, 1988/89). Economic development and job creation can be added as the other major mandates of the CRA.[2] Particularly in the 1980s, the CRA also assumed a role as a provider of social services, for instance in Skid Row, where the CRA financed services for the homeless.

The central term in the redevelopment process is 'blight'. When a neighborhood is deemed blighted, the process of renewal can be considered started. This characterization can be applied to any piece of land inside the city or out, inhabited or not, built up or not. The definition of blight is political in character. Its justification can be technical, hygienic, economic or social. The goal of redevelopment is always the improvement or reestablishment of the municipal tax base. Enlarging the tax base itself provides the main source of the CRA funds. Economically, the so-called 'tax increment financing' allows the CRA to use estimated increases in tax income in a given area for redevelopment before these increases have occurred. Redevelopment, thus, is intended to finance itself through its expected results. This means that the CRA can divert funds from the allocation process of local taxes – which would normally be earmarked for schools, social services, etc. – in order to finance the social and technical infrastructure, the planning process and other measures necessary for the redevelopment of a given area. In the concrete case of the internationalization of Los Angeles, this has resulted in subsidizing foreign investors – often multinational corporations – through local tax dollars.[3]

The successful application of tax increment financing presupposes territorial powers, since the CRA must have jurisdiction over the redevelopment zones. The

*Plate 9.1* *The Museum of Contemporary Art, Los Angeles (Roger Keil)*

CRA has, in fact, been given the power of eminent domain, which allows it to expropriate property from individual owners, to assemble parcels of land and to ready them for construction. Eminent domain is a powerful tool for changing the political economy of place and urban land use and was used to prepare the ground for international investment. With the help of the real estate industry and other place entrepreneurs the CRA has been punching out the pattern of expected rents and profits from the land which it oversees.

Just as the designation of redevelopment project areas is politically defined so is the allocation of funds to the CRA. The latter is governed by a board of commissioners whose members are appointed by the mayor. Formally and substantially, the Board is a representative of the political regime at any given moment. This is equally true for the administration of the CRA. Thus, both are sensitive to political change in the regime. Jim Wood, former chairman of the board, believed that the CRA was, therefore, the 'political tool' of competing groups in the city.[4] Indeed, the decision-making process in the CRA is subject to modifications due to changing relationships of political and economic power in the city. Political organization has been a main factor in this process.

From its inception in the 1940s, community redevelopment in downtown Los Angeles has been in the hands of inner-city place entrepreneurs, with the predominant one being the Central City Association (Haas and Heskin, 1981). In supporting downtown redevelopment, these place entrepreneurs have paradoxically undermined their traditional control of downtown Los Angeles. The process of redevelopment changed urban property relationships. Large national corporations (monopoly capital) became the owners of the assembled parcels in the downtown. In 1955, property capital owned 89% of the parcels on Bunker Hill, while after redevelopment it only owned 9%; monopoly capital – split fairly evenly into industrial and financial sectors – owned the rest (Friedman, 1978: 132). Yet this shift from local property ownership to the dominance of monopoly capital in downtown landownership was only an interim step on the way to the consolidation of the globalized citadel. Increasingly, the owners of land and buildings in the emerging world city are American and foreign transnational corporations. In the activities of the CRA, several levels of world city formation come together: local vision, planning and preparing of the ground on the one hand, and international investment on the other. Since the 1970s, 'multinational business interests in modern Los Angeles have been able to employ the CRA as their bulldozer, financier, and scapegoat' (Haas and Heskin, 1981: 550).

For the past two decades, the CRA has been characterized by a new governance structure more in line with the growing complexity of the urban region. In the 1980s, the CRA tied together the cliquish, and hardly institutionalized, downtown power structures into a quasi-corporatist system adapted to the growing tasks of a rapidly internationalizing city. An 'informal communication network' came into existence connecting the economic place entrepreneurs of Los Angeles with each other and tieing them into the system of political power. Using city commissions as arenas of action and in tune with the quiet, behind-the-scenes style common to former mayor Tom Bradley, the CRA expanded power from the traditional economic elite to other social groups (Scott, 1982). At first glance, the shift from the old to the new regime looks like a democratization of autocratic structures of earlier periods, when a handpicked clique of place entrepreneurs with almost unlimited power over the political process governed urban development and redevelopment. At second sight, however, this shift can be better described as a structural and procedural adaptation to changing urban realities. Instead of establishing more democratic control structures, this shift fostered a closer linkage of the old and new elites with the global and local economic actors in the formation of the world city. In lieu of a strengthening of civil society in the planning and redevelopment process, local economic interests were made more compatible with the incipient globalization process. The almost complete disregard for political opposition was replaced by an incorporation and cooptation of old and new resistances. At the time this was seen as a logical response to the growing sophistication of Los Angeles with its diversifying economic interests, exploding foreign investments and expanding immigrant communities (Scott, 1982).

This shift established the institutional centerpiece of a decidedly internationally oriented mode of local political and social regulation. In the first phase urban redevelopment remained a 'political tool' of the city's powerful property owners and their international business partners. From the first redevelopment project – which started on Bunker Hill with the displacement of 6000 residents and ended with the erection of part of the world city citadel of office towers and palaces of high culture – up to the projects of the early 1980s, the redevelopment process was characterized by a brutal predominance of exchange-value oriented uses of urban space. Up to 1988, the CRA had destroyed 11 240 affordable housing units and rebuilt only 10,700. In most cases earlier affordable rent levels were not maintained in this new construction (Stewart, 1988). Inner-city residential neighborhoods like the one around the projected urban freeway Route 2, as well as Skid Row, Pico Union and Little Tokyo, were *relatively* irrelevant factors in redevelopment (Haas and Heskin, 1981). Only more recently, when a new wave of globalization washed over the city, did formal cooptation or even outright disregard evolve into a substantial incorporation of oppositional forces. In the following section, I will explore three project areas in detail.

## Little Tokyo

The Little Tokyo redevelopment project area comprises 66 acres southeast of the government district in downtown Los Angeles. The area has been the traditional neighborhood of Japanese immigrants since the beginning of the twentieth century. It flourished in the decades before World War II when it was the cultural and economic center of Los Angeles County's Japanese population. Most of the 35 000 Japanese who lived in Los Angeles County in 1930 had their residence within a circle of 5 kilometers around Little Tokyo. Internment of Japanese Americans during World War II nearly eliminated the traditional life and character of 'J-Town'. After 1945, Little Tokyo never regained the lustre of the prewar years. Many Japanese Americans preferred suburban residential locations like Gardena in the South Bay when they returned from the camps. As a consequence, the population of Little Tokyo became statistically older and poorer, while the area remained the cultural and symbolic center of the Japanese community (Doi et al., 1986).

In the 1960s, the Little Tokyo Redevelopment Association (LTRA), an initiative of local businesspeople and residents, attempted to stem the threatening expansion of the administrative center in the northwest of Little Tokyo and to have a redevelopment project area designated. This designation finally occurred in 1970 (Doi et al., 1986). Originally, the CRA plan for the area was considered a model of citizen-oriented redevelopment. But already by 1973, critical voices had begun to emerge in the community. Many residents started to believe that redevelopment in their neighborhood would take place at their expense. They feared that Little Tokyo would be transformed from a neighborhood with many affordable housing units, with businesses and cultural institutions servicing the local population, into an investment zone for Japanese and American capital (Condas et al., 1984).

This shift was symbolized in particular by the investments of the Japanese construction giant Kajima International. The Kajima building, constructed in 1967, was the first investment of Japanese capital in Little Tokyo. In 1972, this fourth largest construction company in the world, obtained the commission (over a group of local business people, Asiamerica, Inc.) to build a luxury hotel in Little Tokyo. Richard G. Mitchell, chief administrator of the CRA, announced that Kajima won the day because it had already established itself in the area and had shown 'a great personal interest' in Little Tokyo (quoted in Doi et al., 1986: 13). The subsequent construction of the New Otani hotel highrise, the demolition of a complex of buildings used by many social, cultural and political organizations in the community to make space for the Weller Court Shopping Center, as well as the continuing eviction of residents from their apartments due to redevelopment, escalated the struggles between the residents of the neighborhood and their political organizations on the one side and the investors, the city and the CRA on the other. In 1976, in order to help tenants fight the evictions for the Weller Court

**Plate 9.2**  *Little Tokyo (Roger Keil)*

project, the Little Tokyo People's Rights Organization (LTPRO) was founded. A lively and activist community culture was established which had its home in the Sun Building in Little Tokyo, where community organizations rented rooms and offices. After the demolition of the Sun Building, these organizations found a new home in the 1980s in the Japanese American Cultural and Community Center (JACCC) (Doi *et al.*, 1986).

The majority of the 600 residential units left in Little Tokyo in 1970 fell prey to redevelopment. Some of the evicted tenants found a new home in the Little Tokyo Towers or in Miyako Gardens where a total of 400 new units were built. While about 50 affordable units were rehabilitated and returned to the market, and 167 condominiums were constructed, critics of the CRA noted that only a minority of these units were used by people who had lost their apartments in Little Tokyo.[5]

Urban redevelopment in Little Tokyo was exemplary of the first wave of activities of the CRA in Los Angeles. Redevelopment was formally understood as a large-scale process wherein entire neighborhoods were bulldozed and rebuilt against the protest of the extant residential population. The city and the CRA were politically willing and able to push through their plans for the area and to legitimate it in the interest of metropolitan planning. Following the general plan of the city in 1965, a so-called 'international zone' – including Little Tokyo, Chinatown and the Mexican center Olvera Street – was to be built (Little Tokyo Anti Eviction Task Force, 1976). In the planning document *Silverbook* of 1972, Little Tokyo's future was designated as a Japanese American commercial, cultural and residential neighborhood; redevelopment was presented as an essential step in that direction. In the eyes of the residents and of the opponents of redevelopment, the process opened the doors for the destruction of the traditional community structure and for the opening of the neighborhood for external attractions catering to tourists and convention visitors rather than to local residents (Murase, 1983: 23).

The original redevelopment strategy of the CRA and of the city in the 1960s aimed at a redesign of the area's urban form and economy in the interest of expanding Japanese capital. Little Tokyo was to be developed consistent with the image that Japanese capital had of itself. This included the construction of high rises and hotels and the erection of a globally representative cultural and tourist center (Condas *et al.*, 1984). Little Tokyo, therefore, was 'freed' from its marginal position as part of the impoverished core of Fordist Los Angeles in order to become both a diversified, commercialized piece of the puzzle that makes up the citadel of Los Angeles and ultimately, functionally, a part of Japan. The residents felt attacked from both sides. On one hand, the population of Little Tokyo felt the pressure of the expansion of the hegemonic Anglo city, expressed in several attempts by City Hall to transform the area north of First Street into an administrative center. On the other hand, the inhabitants of Little Tokyo felt under pressure from Japanese capital ('the Japanese Japanese'), who attempted not just to demonstrate their newly gained economic power but to reestablish the political and social influence which they had in the Los Angeles Japanese community before World War II (Matsuoka, 1971). While the official position of the CRA questioned the survivability of the traditional working-class neighborhood (Little Tokyo in the case of no redevelopment), the critics considered redevelopment itself the actual enemy of the survival of what one activist called 'traditional proletarian lifestyles'.

The resistance of the population, represented by the LTPRO, against the destruction of their apartments and of their social infrastructure led, after 1970, to a confrontation which attracted the attention of the entire city. The vision favored by radical antiredevelopment activists for their neighborhood differed sharply from the emergent hegemonic discourse of world city formation. They countered the concept of an 'international zone' with a concept of 'Third World unity' (Little Tokyo Anti Eviction Task Force, 1976: 333). The opposition by the 'street politicians' – a term used by a CRA official – to the plans for their neighborhood stalled evictions and demolitions temporarily, but they could not establish a political alternative. As a symbolic counterdiscourse, this opposition had a strong impact, however, on the formation and the politics of new redevelopment projects.

This change was personified in Cooke Sunoo, long-time director of the Little Tokyo project area. Sunoo was appointed by Mayor Bradley as a liaison between the local community and the CRA during the bitter confrontations in the early 1970s. He fulfilled this role from 1974 to 1988; between 1978 and 1988, he oversaw the project area for the CRA. As a moderate critic of redevelopment, Sunoo was able both to express his conviction that redevelopment had to be a process that worked from the inside out and to guarantee that the selective integration of the population into the renewal process would happen under the umbrella of the existing hegemony.[6] Under Sunoo's project directorship, the attitude of the CRA in the area changed from complete disregard of the population to partial acknowledgement of oppositional demands. In the new zoning plan for the area north of First Street, discussed and adopted in the late 1980s, the maintenance of existing housing stock and of the – historically valuable – San Pedro Firm building and the establishment of cultural institutions were included. This cooptation of the opposition occurred with the exclusion of fundamental opponents to redevelopment whose voices had been silenced in the decade before. Redevelopment changed face in two ways. It became both more flexible in dealing with community concerns and it opened itself to new kinds of market-driven growth which replaced the culture of unmediated corporate power – expressed in the New Otani Hotel – with postmodern images of spectacle and consumption.[7]

# CHINATOWN[8]

Redevelopment in Little Tokyo set the tone for future fundamental criticism of the CRA. Little Tokyo's experience was seen as a warning sign by communities in other project areas. Such was the case in Chinatown. The 303 acres project, which was created in January 1980, housed 8600 people in the late 1980s, a marked rise of 80% since 1970. Redevelopment opponents in Chinatown made direct reference to Little Tokyo when they began their struggle against the CRA. While there was initial support in Chinatown both from business and residents for redevelopment, its disadvantages to the community quickly became obvious: the threat of destruction of existing residential units and of small business; and political disempowerment. The lesson learned from the Little Tokyo experience by activists in Chinatown was expressed in their demand – raised directly after the designation of the project area – to maintain affordable housing for families and the elderly, and to maintain the communitarian structure of the neighborhood. The Project Area Committee (PAC), the consulting organ of the local population in the redevelopment process, spoke out against evictions and for the use of vacant land for new construction. Indeed, as one advocate of the community reported, only 35 families were driven from their homes in Chinatown. The partial taming of the destructive dynamics of redevelopment in Chinatown was a product of intense political struggles at different levels. Both the CRA and local councilman Gil Lindsay attempted to push through their traditional model of redevelopment. Lindsay even disbanded the elected PAC in 1985 to replace it with a Community Advisory Committee whose members were appointed by the councilman himself. In contrast to Little Tokyo, however, the formal political disempowerment of the local community did not lead to large-scale demolition and renewal. Rather, the CRA in part fulfilled the request for the retention of affordable housing.

CRA policies aimed at revitalizing the area with the help of large-scale private investment. Consequently, the CRA fostered economic activities which would turn Chinatown – like Little Tokyo before it – into an appendix of the globalized Pacific Rim citadel and into a tourist destination. The alternative model favored by activists was to preserve Chinatown as a balanced community with municipal services and housing. All political actors in Chinatown – capitalists from China, Hong Kong and Taiwan, local Chinese capital, Vietnamese-Chinese petty bourgeois, municipal politicians with world city ambitions, the CRA administration, and the internationalized residential population – were operating in a swiftly shifting context. Direct investment of Chinese capital in Chinatown, which is adjacent to the central business district (CBD) and to Bunker Hill, led to rising costs for commercial and residential leases. At the same time the neighborhood experienced rapid population change. More than 20% of the area's population is now Hispanic, and the composition of the Asian population has been altered over the past two decades due to the influx of new ethnic groups from South East Asia. In particular, Vietnamese Chinese challenged the social, economic and political hegemony of traditional 'ethnic Chinese' from China, Taiwan and Hong Kong. By the middle of the 1980s, Vietnamese Chinese owned 700 of the 1400 stores and firms in Chinatown (Day, 1985: 33).

The biggest political contradiction in redeveloped Chinatown has been the one between the local and international place entrepreneurs on one hand and the residents on the other. Small business – itself endangered by rising rents due to globalized land markets – has typically sided with the latter in this conflict (Day, 1985). The concerns of the CRA's critics were heard insofar as Chinatown did not experience large-scale destruction of housing for redevelopment and that area saw the maintenance and new construction of affordable housing for families and the elderly. Thus, the attrition of the local population was avoided or at least slowed down. This shift marked a general change in policy by the CRA which was pressured to actively integrate community demands into redevelopment. The high level and sustained awareness of possibly detrimental consequences of redevelopment among the area's residents made it difficult for investors to blast a trail through the community with bulldozers. In addition, externally induced attempts to take over parts of Chinatown were often less successful than development efforts by local Chinese investors who knew the political economy of place more intimately.

## HOLLYWOOD

Bunker Hill – with its gleaming office and hotel towers as well as with its cultural temple, the Museum of Contemporary Art, and its unfinished Disney Concert Hall – and the CBD at all times were the most important CRA project areas. When the Hollywood project area was designated in 1986, however, a possible spatial competitor to the downtown was brought into play and a new kind of redevelopment policy was introduced aggressively.

Hollywood was designated a redevelopment project in April 1986 and was named a project area in June of the same year. Under the political aegis of Councilman Michael Woo, who had been elected in 1985 to represent a district which contained Hollywood, the area claimed more central functions for the entire urban region. Some place entrepreneurs even considered Hollywood as potentially a second downtown. This notion was built on two assumptions: first, Hollywood was considered predestined to attract investment from global capital markets because of its locational advantages as an internationally well-known tourist site and because of its developed urban structure;[9] second, it was hoped that the Hollywood subway line which connects downtown and Hollywood along Hollywood Boulevard, will create an axis between the competing urban cores.[10] By the mid-1990s, these dreams have mostly failed to materialize as Hollywood has not been able to capture a significant slice of international corporate investment and as Hollywood Boulevard continues to represent the seedy downside of mass tourism rather than the glitz of a world city. The Hollywood subway, marred by severe construction problems as well as corruption, has not yet become the incubator of renewal as was hoped in the original redevelopment design.[11] The dreams about redevelopment in Hollywood continue unabated. In the spring of 1997, a Toronto-based company, TrizecHahn, made public plans for a $145-million retail and entertainment center to the east of the historic Chinese Theater on Hollywood Boulevard. This project of 300 000 square feet of entertainment and retail space, restaurants and public space is to be developed under the auspices of the CRA (Boxall and Gordon, 1997: B1 and B10).

Despite its lack of success in creating a second downtown, the Hollywood project area's significance in the context of this discussion of redevelopment has been in the career of its political institutions. Councilman Michael Woo, a planner by training and well-advised by a progressive and competent staff, initially attempted to create a system of political representation in Hollywood markedly different from previous CRA practice. The PAC, made up partly of elected representatives and partly of appointees of the councilman, was meant to play a significant role in the public decision-making process. The original intention to create an open and democratic process and 'human' redevelopment was corrupted, when, in 1989, the PAC was disbanded (after the end of the legally binding period) by decree of Michael Woo. Hollywood's activist community subsequently split into those who accepted the hegemonic redevelopment discourse as determining for the entire local political process, and those who vehemently defied this. The former group was organized in the Community Advisory Council appointed by Woo, while the CRA opponents continued to meet in the disempowered and disenfranchised PAC. Woo and the new project area manager, Cooke Sunoo, defined the redevelopment discourse as a constructive act. Their political opponents emphasized the destructive elements of redevelopment. The consequence of this split was that fundamental critique of redevelopment began to equal powerlessness; the discourse of redevelopment became largely self-referential and the democratic public political process – originally favored by Woo and his office – was overshadowed through administrative dominance. After more than 10 years of failed attempts to 'regain some of its long-faded luster' (Boxall and Gordon, 1997: B1), the once most democratically legitimized of all redevelopment project areas seems to have come full circle. Opposition to projected development has been marginalized and is considered insignificant. The TrizecHahn entertainment complex east of Mann's Chinese Theater would, in the words of Councilwoman Goldberg, be opposed only by 'the same five or 10 people who think everything is no good' (quoted in Boxall and Gordon, 1997: B10).

## THE CRA AS A TOOL OF POLITICAL DISCOURSE

How do these cases fit into the larger picture? Between 1986 and 1990, CRA politics changed under the pressure of shifting political conditions in Los Angeles. In view of the growing gap between their mandate and the result of their activities, the CRA, from the early 1980s on, had looked for legitimation strategies in order to be able to continue its redevelopment activity primarily in the downtown. Most commonly, such strategies took the form of social linkages of investments in CRA areas. Developers were held to enter contracts with firms owned by women and/or minorities. Linkage arrangements also entailed traffic improvements to deal with flows increased by redevelopment; and 1% of investment sums had to be spent on art (an issue which was of particular importance to anchor the project in Hollywood) (Clifford, 1991).[12] In levying such measures, the CRA had several legal and technical options including imposing a fee for the transfer of air and development rights which is possible in a given area if the total density is maintained. Income from such fees have to be spent for 'public use' (Chorneau, 1988b).[13]

During the 1980s, the CRA increasingly tied the changes it initiated in the built environment to new forms of social regulation. Always concerned about its political and social influence in project areas, the agency, in fact, took over some of the social services which – due to a loss of revenues as a consequence of tax increment financing – could not be financed by traditional agencies of the local social welfare state: homes for the homeless, psychiatric care, social work. During the Reagan/Bush era, when federal and county administrations tried to shed their responsibility for such programs, the CRA became one of the most important providers of services in Los Angeles. CRA officials tended to downplay or deny their intention to assume a larger role in social welfare provision beyond creating the social infrastructure for such services. Yet there is plenty of evidence to the contrary, such as the CRA's support for the Skid Row Development Corporation, an institution mandated to rehabilitate homeless people. Another example was the founding in 1984 of the Single Room Occupancy Housing Corporation which restores old hotels in Skid Row for the homeless and for former substance abusers. In 1988, the organization ran 1000 of the 10 000 hotel rooms of this kind in the east of the city (Stewart, 1988). By regulating homelessness and by limiting its impact to designated areas in the city, the CRA attempted to keep 'the problem' out of the emerging investment zones. The creation of a 'livable environment' for the homeless in the east of the downtown was intended to prevent the 'commute' between the survival structures of the downtown (panhandling, food, parks, etc.) and the church missions and SROs (Single Room Occupancy Hotels) of Skid Row.[14] In all of these attempts to play a bigger role in service provision, the CRA had to establish itself as a political actor moderating the different interests of the place entrepreneurs. For example, the centralization of homeless services in one part of the city always met with fierce resistance. In Skid Row, fish and toy wholesalers – mostly new immigrant entrepreneurs from Japan, Korea and China, who viewed the area as a window of economic opportunity – as well as the more established businesses in Little Tokyo just north of the area, were particularly vocal in their resistance against CRA-sponsored increases in homeless services there. The decentralized 'solution' also pitted residents against the CRA in those areas that had been earmarked as locations for homeless trailers purchased from a mega-construction site in Utah to be used as homeless quarters around the city.

The social and cultural component of CRA activity also had external effects. While specific programs such as those delivering homeless services could co-opt and spatially regulate potentially resistant social collectives internally, another group of CRA policies enhanced the image of Los Angeles in the arena of global interurban competition and improved the political position of the CRA relative to other political powers in the city. Jo-Anne Berelowitz has researched the specific significance of the cultural aspects of redevelopment using the example of the Museum of Contemporary Art (MOCA) in the Bunker Hill redevelopment project area:

> From its earliest conception, the Museum of Contemporary Art was regarded as a crucial component of the redevelopment of Downtown; for the City's power structure realized that for Los Angeles to qualify as a 'world city' it would need more than big buildings, busy trade, and apartment complexes. It would also need *Culture.*
>
> Clearly intended as more than merely a showcase for art, more than merely the signifier of its own function, MOCA serves also as climate creator for international finance; as catalyst for developing a 'real' downtown; as gathering place; a generator of intriguing experimentalism; a social adventure; a demarcator of innovation; engenderer of honor, attention, business and jobs; monument; destination; and L.A.'s first step toward urbanism (Berelowitz, 1990: 211, 213).

The social and cultural aspects of the redevelopment process which had been crafted to foster the image of Los Angeles as a world class city internationally outweighed those that could have had a real improvement in the conditions of life for the people in the project areas. The latter were effectively neutralized by the continuing dynamic expansion of the downtown and the pursuant effects of gentrification.

The CRA's leadership had begun to grasp that it was necessary to accept both internal reform and more flexible and inclusive political tactics if the agency was to remain in business beyond the end of the century. Notwithstanding these changes, critics of redevelopment formed an effective political opposition by the end of the 1980s and began to push the CRA even further. Traditionally, two main currents could be distinguished in this opposition. First, there was the conservative position of suburban politicians who fought against the expenses of inner-city revitalization which, in their eyes, subsidized a development which was taking place even without the help of the CRA while funds for projects in other parts of the city were not available when they were needed. Second, there was the radical position of inner-city neighborhood and labor groups who opposed redevelopment for social justice reasons and often espoused an ideology critical of capitalist urban development in general.

## Moderate Critique and Careful Reforms

Former Los Angeles Councilman Ernani Bernardi from the northern San Fernando Valley was the most articulate representative of an angry but politically moderate critique of the CRA. As far back as 1977, Bernardi, in a lawsuit, blocked the automatic increase of the spending horizon of the CRA in its CBD project area. He was joined in this suit by Los Angeles County which feared for a loss of tax income as a consequence of redevelopment (Stewart, 1988). Bernardi identified three problems with the redevelopment process:

1.  The option of defining an area as blighted without having to apply clear guidelines invites arbitrary decisions on the side of urban governments and

their redevelopment agencies. He cited cases from smaller communities in the San Gabriel Valley east of Los Angeles where gravel pits and vacant land had been declared redevelopment areas.

2. In the CBD of Los Angeles, the largest CRA project, economic growth would also have been possible without taxpayers' subsidies. It can be added that subsidizing central office functions does not create jobs where most people live but where capital is concentrated.

3. In the shift of taxes by tax increment financing to the benefit of the CRA is an irresponsible real cut of expenses for social welfare and education.

At the beginning of the 1990s, the CRA's moderate critics received support from Mayor Tom Bradley and the City Council, who, after practically decades of noncritical backing of developers and investors in the project areas, began to champion social aspects of urban redevelopment. Partly, at least, this can be attributed to the growing popular resistance against the CRA and to political demands for a redistribution of redevelopment funds. In a process that tied the activities of neighborhood and community-based groups into the political process, Mayor Bradley and the City Council entered a phase of democratization and politicization of the autocratic and technological redevelopment process. While there had always been latent resistance in the City Council against the CRA, the mayor's policy shift regarding redevelopment was significant and can be interpreted as part of Bradley's search for new political and social coalitions in Los Angeles. In 1988, for example, he favored a comprehensive day care program which he wanted to see connected to the redevelopment process; he invited Carlyle Hall, a moderate opponent of redevelopment, to become a member of the CRA's board; and he appointed Michael Bodaken, a tenant activist, coordinator of the municipal affordable housing programs. Hall was the founder of the Center for Law in the Public Interest and had worked previously as a mediator for the city to deal with 'angry citizens groups' who had voiced their opposition to Bradley's downtown redevelopment. Bodaken replaced long-time activist Gary Squier who had become the acting director of the city's Housing Authority. Bodaken was a lawyer with the Legal Aid Foundation of Los Angeles and an explicit critic of the destruction of rental housing by the city and the CRA.[15] Thus, Hall's appointment was interpreted as Bradley's attempt to stabilize the position of the CRA by finding a political majority for the redesignation of funds that could potentially be freed if the cap on downtown redevelopment was lifted – even if this meant an acceptance of development foes into the fold (Stewart, 1990a; 1990b). The change in Bradley's almost unconditional pro-growth position was not restricted to the redevelopment process. Towards the end of 1989, the mayor baffled the public of Los Angeles by unexpectedly expressing criticism of large-scale developments in the San Fernando Valley and at the border with Santa Monica. This was seen as a strategy for regaining control over both the urban development process and politically discontented voters in the west of the city (Clifford, 1990).

In the meantime, after a long period of inaction and failed attempts to obtain full control over the board of the CRA, which was appointed by the mayor, the City Council formed a committee whose only purpose was to monitor the CRA. The activities of the mayor and of this committee eventually led to the disclosure of a series of improper business practices on the side of the CRA (Clifford and Fritsch, 1990). In the past, the City Council had turned down control over the board mostly because individual project areas could only be designated if this process was initiated by the respective representative of the council district in question. The designation and administration of project areas, thus, was mainly seen as a territorially autonomous affair of individual council members, of which other councillors would steer clear. However, with the increasing political importance of slow growth, particularly in the west of the city, the need was felt to achieve some sort of control over the entire development policy of the CRA. Successive attempts to subordinate the CRA directly to the City Council ultimately failed in June 1989, in July 1990 and February 1991; in the latter case the attempt failed even though a majority of 7 over 6 politicians had voted for the proposal of Zev Yaroslavsky, a long-time proponent of stricter controls on the CRA (Stewart, 1991).

In 1989, appointments to the Community Redevelopment and Housing Committee of the City Council – Gloria Molina, Richard Alatorre and Zev Yaroslavsky – put the opposition both in the poor and Latino east and in the more wealthy but anti-growth west in a powerful position relative to the CRA. Molina was the most aggressive critic of the CRA in the City Council.[16] At the event of the passage of a legal package intended to reform the CRA in 1991, which gave the public and elected politicians more control over the CRA, Molina said: 'What we are dealing with is the most resistant, arrogant city agency. They are not going to pull their sneaky kinds of deals anymore' (quoted in Stewart, 1991: A1).[17] The City Council extended direct review authority over the CRA to District Attorney Jim Hahn and to City Controller Rick Tuttle and made it legally possible for it to recall CRA board members and to reject a wide variety of CRA decisions by a two-thirds majority (Stewart, 1991).[18]

Next to the structural reforms, the opposition of former Councilman Zev Yaroslavsky to CRA Chair Jim Wood was the most distinctive feature of the moderate strand of anti-redevelopment politics in Los Angeles in the late 1980s and early 1990s.[19] The antagonism between the two politicians – who had fought each other in public for more than a decade – signalled more than just personal strife. It was the expression of some of the most visible lines of conflict to cross Los Angeles in the 1980s and early 1990s. It signified vastly divergent concepts for the built environment and the social space of the world city. While Jim Wood is mentioned in one breath with Tom Bradley as the builder and architect of Los Angeles' modern downtown, Yaroslavsky is known as a vehement critic of growth and centralization. In April 1990, when the respective City Council Committee had spoken out against a reappointment of Wood as chairman of the CRA board, Yaroslavsky told his perennial opponent: 'You want to create a dense urban core in downtown Los Angeles. Incredible. I cannot share that vision' (quoted in Fritsch and Stewart, 1990: B1). Together with Marvin Braude, Yaroslavsky was the most vocal proponent of growth control policies on Los Angeles City Council throughout the 1980s. These two politicians were the authors of the most influential growth control ordinance of the decade: Proposition U was passed in November 1986 by referendum and reduced the scope of new commercial construction in the entire urban area by half of their originally projected density – with the exception of some designated centers.[20] Like the different concepts of space that dominated the oppositional relationship of Yaroslavsky and Wood, their diverging class interests were determining factors in their conflict. As a representative of the major labor unions, Wood was a proponent of a policy that secured construction jobs by constantly fueling the market while Yaroslavsky represented the residential and neighborhood interests of the middle class in the west of the city.

## Community Politics: from Exchange Value to Use Value

The redevelopment process was, from the beginning, subject to critique by radical groups. Individual projects had been fought by local organizations at many points, but in the late 1980s, the CRA's policies drew a city-wide reaction. When the CRA planned to lift its court-imposed spending cap in the CBD project area from $750 million to $5 billion, they triggered a strong reaction from radical community and social justice groups. The tenant organization Housing Los Angeles published a bilingual brochure in 1988 which demanded a public hearing on the shift in the CRA's spending policy. The organization demanded that instead of continuing to foster real estate speculation and overdevelopment in the downtown, all tax gains created by redevelopment should be made available to neighborhoods of the poor and that a nonprofit housing program be developed (Housing Los Angeles, 1988).

During the following year, some of the most important neighborhood organizations and labor unions of the city formed a coalition under the aegis of the Campaign for Critical Needs,[21] which attacked CRA policies head-on. The coalition partners looked at redevelopment from their respective interest position: the housing and tenant organizations demanded primarily an increase in the expenses for public and social housing; Jobs With Peace fought for better day care programs, a position also represented in the compromise package offered by the mayor's office.[22] In a widely read commentary in the *Los Angeles Sunday Times*, representatives of the coalition presented their position on urban redevelopment. Besides demanding a democratization of the redevelopment process, the authors discussed the options of a reform-oriented redevelopment strategy:

> If you had the power to decide how to spend $4.25 billion, what programs would you fund? Advocates for the poor insist that all of the money should go for critical needs: affordable housing and shelters for the homeless; decent and affordable health and child care; better education for our children and job training for the unemployed. Others take a different view, saying that half of the money should be used for CRA-built housing and the other $2 billion spent subsidizing CRA's pet downtown projects (Bodaken, Gross and Thigpen, 1989).

In October of 1989, delegates of this broad community coalition met in a school in downtown Los Angeles for a summit meeting on urban planning and development.[23] The conference participants agreed on two things: the activities of the CRA in the past had been detrimental to working-class neighborhoods and communities of color. Some participants stressed the destruction of inner-city neighborhoods and jobs through the CRA. They showed little inclination to compromise with the apparatus of redevelopment. Others attempted to redefine the rules of redevelopment, in order to achieve increased spending for communities. This position aimed for cooperation between city council members such as Gloria Molina, who were critical of the current policies of the CRA, and other public institutions interested in redistributing redevelopment dollars. In both cases, the activities envisioned a strategic and tactical merging of labor and community issues. The participants of the summit had no doubt that there was an immediate connection between the construction of new high rises, the destruction of affordable housing, the creation of specifically new labor markets (for example in janitorial services) and the privatization of public services. The CRA and the campaign against their policies became the central focus of the convergence of the politics of labor and the politics of community. An important demand that came out of the meeting was for support of community economic development.[24]

At the beginning of the 1990s, the efforts of the coalition and other critics bore first fruits. In the wake of a violent labor struggle between janitors and their employers in the Century City office center in June of 1990, the mayor and the CRA accepted a proposal for a new policy which had its roots in union demands: in March 1991, they agreed to make wages and benefits for low-income earners in all new office buildings and hotels in CRA project areas subject to negotiation between the CRA and the developers.[25] This policy change affected janitors, room service workers, kitchen aides, valet parkers, gardeners and private security personnel. The CRA was thus forced to become a regulatory institution for work relations in the project areas. Consequently, the CRA was able to influence minimum wages, medical care, job security, and grievance and arbitration. In the agreement was the requirement that developers and operators of the new office and hotel spaces provide funding for education in English-as-a-second-language for the mostly Latin personnel. And an easing of the conditions for union-organizing drives in the new buildings was also part of the policy package. The Los Angeles Chamber of Commerce and the Central City Association, longtime boosters of CRA downtown expansion, opposed the intended policy changes as one-sided preferential treatment of labor interests.[26] Indeed, local observers agreed that by the early 1990s, the influence of the unions of immigrant workers on urban policy in Los Angeles had grown. This had much to do with a shift internal to the labor movement. While linkage contracts used to be common in the construction industry and its established labor unions – tieing construction in CRA projects to union labor – such contracts were now being sought for the first time for workers in low-wage sectors (Clifford, 1991).

These new policies could be understood as a 'social-democratic' reversal of traditional practices. They imbricated capital accumulation in space and economic expansion with a kind of social responsibility, and the creation of wealth with the satisfaction of critical needs. 'Social-democratic' offers itself as a label because the local policies in Los Angeles, with their implication of the Bradley coalition and their corporatist integration of organized labor, together with pressuring international capital into committing to social responsibility for the redeveloped areas, contradicted the dominant market liberalism of the time. The fact that the redevelopment process had run into serious opposition – even before the rebellion

***Plate 9.3*** *Angels Flight, Bunker Hill (Roger Keil)*

of 1992 laid open the larger divides of the urban region – is an important aspect of this development. The resistance of community activists and labor organizers to the dictates of internationalized restructuring proved partly successful and stood as testimony that the internationalization of space in Los Angeles occurred in a context of struggle.

## REDESIGNING REDEVELOPMENT

By the mid-1990s, while it still received about $150 million a year in property taxes, the CRA was considered by many observers to be only a shadow of its former self (Fulton, 1994). Virtually reduced from its former privileged position to the status of a regular city department, the CRA, in an official audit of its management practices, was found lacking in the entrepreneurial capacities necessary to remain an effective developer of urban real estate (Los Angeles City Council, 1995: 35). The major findings of the audit were welcomed even by CRA management, even though it put them in an uncomfortable position. Daniel P. Garcia, who had just been named Chair of the CRA's board, commented on the audit: 'It creates a more objective environment to discuss with the City Council and the mayor what the focus [of the CRA] ought to be' (quoted in Merl, 1995).

While the CRA had been focussed in its development mission during the Bradley years, a combination of factors now caused confusion and contradiction in its goals and strategies. First, there was no agreement among the city's political class as to what direction redevelopment would take. Mayor Richard Riordan did not hide his critical stance towards traditional redevelopment. The corporatist machine, which had functioned smoothly in tandem with the Bradley coalition, did not fit well with Riordan's new emphasis on markets, flexibility and downsizing. As one author remarked in 1994, when the mayor presented his budget to the Los Angeles public, 'Riordan wants to kill old-fashioned redevelopment and harvest its organs for use by his streamlined city government' (Fulton, 1994: M6). The mayor was pushing for a replacement of (real estate based) redevelopment by other types of economic development and job creation. At the same time, Los Angeles City Council, which has powers to oversee the CRA, was contemplating an expanded redevelopment mandate, while CRA management itself was extending the CRA's role as a provider of affordable housing (Los Angeles City Council, 1995: 36). Second, the CRA had been remaking itself in the face of natural disaster and social unrest. After the rebellion of 1992, it had started to study 'the feasibility of civil disturbance recovery and/or neighborhood revitalization in 12 areas comprising 20 103 acres of the City' (Los Angeles City Council, 1995: 36); after the 1994 Northridge earthquake, the City Council established five earthquake recovery areas encompassing 6944 acres (Los Angeles City Council, 1995: 36). At the same time, it started to provide housing in increasing numbers. In the first half of the 1990s, the CRA consistently exceeded the statutory requirement of using at least 20% of tax increment financing for affordable housing (Los Angeles City Council, 1995: 32). Redevelopment became a mixed bag of real estate development, social service delivery and emergency relief. And third, the CRA continued to be under attack for its autocratic management style. In particular, the 1995 audit found that '[A]lthough CRA devotes a substantial amount of . . . time and energy to community outreach and public participation, the Agency has an inconsistent track record in working effectively with and *empowering* the communities served by the Agency' (Los Angeles City Council, 1995: 4). Finally, the whole project of redevelopment had fallen on hard times during and since the recession of the early 1990s when a commentator wrote in the *Los Angeles Times*: '[T]he redevelopment of Downtown is over. A bad real-estate market and money problems have all but killed an ambitious redevelopment plan for Hollywood. Lingering distrust has blocked the CRA from pursuing the long-delayed task of assisting inner-city neighborhoods, especially in South Central' (Fulton, 1994: M6). As Los Angeles entered the final years of the century, its downtown, once the pride of the redevelopment effort, seemed of less significance than ever. In the shadows of the downtown office towers which had mushroomed partly due to the path beaten by the CRA, a series of megaprojects continues to occupy the phantasies of Los Angeles' downtown-centered elites. While, during the Bradley years, the assumption was that the rest of the city should support what went on at the center of the city because it would affect the well-being of those elsewhere, the question now is: does anyone care?

# CHAPTER 10

# LOCAL STATES

No matter the scale, global economics must still function in local landscapes. More-over, global enterprises seek comparative advantages provided by the ability of local governments to transfer social wealth into the hands of private capital. Thus capital's globalizing reach becomes most vulnerable when it encounters democratic initiatives that emerge from local landscapes (Valle and Torres, 1994: 4).

From its pre-Columbian beginnings, through the colonial period, from the era of Mexican rule to the American present, several overlapping dynamics have created a layered political space in Southern California. During this century, the emerging and waning Fordist model of political–spatial regulation and the globalization and flexibilization of political spaces have been the two most pervasive tendencies in structuring local states in Southern California. In this chapter, I briefly sketch the historical geography of these dynamics, and then look at the emergence of specific strategies used by local states in the Los Angeles region to deal with the global-ization of the city.

## FORDIST POLITICAL LANDSCAPES: FRAGMENTED SUBURBANIZATION

The main sociospatial contradiction in Los Angeles during Fordism was the bipolarity of urban center and suburbia. The Fordist landscape of Los Angeles was partly a product of local political decisions to support early automobile-based transit and decentralized homeownership, which shifted the nature of transit from that of a collective good to that of private consumption and divided the city's working class sociospatially through industrial and residential suburbanization. Politically, these dynamics were reflected in a mode of regulation that kept the major contradiction of center and periphery in check until 1965, and took on a form of marginal 'incorporation' (Browning, Marshall and Tabb, 1984) after 1965. In 1965, the Watts rebellion challenged the sociospatial inequalities that were enshrined through such political boundary-setting. The upheaval of the inner-city population can be interpreted as being directed against the entire Fordist spatial mode of regulation, which, to a growing number of urban residents, had meant political and economic exclusion. Eventually, the Bradley coalition in Los Angeles became the centerpiece of regional governance (see Chapter 11).

The goal of urban planning in Los Angeles was to avoid the density of traditional urbanization (Wachs, 1984: 306; Fogelson, 1967; Foster, 1971). Urbanization thus took place under the tutelage of an 'antiurban' growth machine. This was not due to the immigration of rural people from the Midwest seeking to re-create a small-town atmosphere, nor to the existence of an expanded rail-based transportation system. Rather, decentralization was primarily a consequence of dispersed indus-trial patterns. The extractive industry in particular was instrumental as oil discoveries led to an early incorporation of scattered 'black gold suburbs'. Oil drew other industries in its wake and industrialization in the region really took off with 'the arrival of the Goodyear Tire and Rubber Company' in 1919 (Viehe, 1981: 13). During the following decade, the region experienced a first wave of large investment into industrial production facilities: oil processing (and related means of production); tires; furniture; steel and glass; aerospace; auto; chemicals; street transportation. The industrialization of the suburbs stopped the annexation strategy of Los Angeles because it improved the economic basis of the suburban net (Viehe, 1981).

Consequently, a new metropolitan configuration emerged in Los Angeles: 'Instead of developing an industrial urban core surrounded by residential suburbs, the city developed an administrative–residential core surrounded by an industrial suburban network' (Viehe 1981: 14). The settlement pattern of the fragmented and politically splintered working class in the suburbs – filling the fragmented spaces between the oil fields and the industrial plants – improved the relative position of the central city (Viehe, 1981: 18).

The formation of local municipalities accentuated the spatial separation of social classes and gave it distinct political form. In Los Angeles County, a middle-class dominated incorporation movement fragmented this central contradiction into concrete spatial entities following the Lakewood Plan in 1954, which allowed the subcontracting of services in individual cities with the county (Hoch, 1981, 1984; Miller, 1981). Between 1950 and 1970, municipal borderlines in the south and east of Los Angeles increasingly served the purpose of separating people by race and income (Miller, 1981: 172). The new incorporations were socially more uniform – mostly white and relatively wealthy – while the African American and Latino populations were concentrated in the city of Los Angeles and in the older suburbs of the Eastside. Incorporations in the San Gabriel Valley beginning in the 1950s created a politically sanctioned system of segregation, the intentional product of the political organizations of the regional bourgeoisie and of certain local middle-class factions (Hoch, 1981). The specifically American autonomy of the local state (home rule) facilitated the fragmentation of the political and social structure of the city as a central moment of class rule (Hoch, 1981: 5). The class relationships of mid-century Los Angeles were molded in the jurisdictional–political topography of the region as territorial relationships.

This segregation of industrial and residential suburbs came close to being an ideal landscape of separated working and living spaces connected by the auto-mobile. Some of the cities that were incorporated after World War II (e.g. Vernon, Commerce and Industry) were purely industrial areas with only a few inhabitants; other communities were purely residential and had a negligible tax base. Facilitating the incorporation of residential communities, Los Angeles County, as well as large neighboring cities, sold urban services to newly incorporated towns for a lower fee than the towns would have charged had they provided these services themselves. The first contract of this sort – the Lakewood Plan – became the template of spatial regulation in Los Angeles County for the post-World War II era (Miller, 1981: 104–105). Between 1954 and 1973, 33 of the more than 80 cities in Los Angeles County were incorporated, many of them through an arrangement akin to the Lakewood Plan.[1]

As in other cities of the same period, urban space in Los Angeles was fragmented into an inner city populated by people of color, and a mainly white suburban belt. The incorporation of white suburban working-class enclaves under the hegemony of bourgeois interests separated these core workers of the labor market spatially from the more marginalized black and Latino segments. While the black working class expanded its residential area along Central Avenue in Los Angeles, Mexican immigrants concentrated mostly in the nonincorporated areas in the urban region. East Los Angeles, with its more than 100 000 inhabitants, is the largest non-incorporated community in California and the center of Chicano culture in Los Angeles. South-Central Los Angeles encompasses the incorporated areas to the south of downtown, including various communities within Los Angeles City, such as Watts and Willowbrook. During the 1980s, Los Angeles lost 53% of its manufacturing jobs, most of which were located in the industrial belt stretching from downtown to Long Beach. This was a severe blow to workers in south Los Angeles, many of whom were people of color. With the collapse of the traditional industrial sector of Fordism, combined with the demise of Keynesian fiscal intervention, workers' ability to earn a substantive income via wage employment was drastically reduced, leaving a combination of minimum-wage service jobs, the black market, and declining welfare payments as a way to eke out a living. Accordingly, the political clout of these communities was equally diminished.

On the other side of the urban region, neighborhood groups from affluent communities have become very powerful on the local political scene in recent years, receiving their impetus from the 1978 Proposition 13 which severely restrained the spending powers of local government. Seeking to preserve a 'homogeneity of race, class and, especially, home values' (Davis 1990: 153), a patchwork of suburban fiefdoms, the product of homeowners' associations, have been established to prevent the erosion of property values. In the 1990s, there has been a plethora of community name changes led by homeowner associations resisting both pro-growth forces as well as the burgeoning low-income ethnic and immigrant populations which threaten to burst out of the ghettos and barrios into the low-density gentility of the suburbs.[2]

## INTERNATIONALIZATION

As a world city, Los Angeles has built on the fragmented and increasingly privatized structure created in earlier decades. Local states in the region have been integrated into the spatial and political logic of the region's 'structured coherence' (Harvey, 1989a) on the basis of distinct politics and policies which have granted them special status in the spatial division of labor. Southern California's fragmented structure – which had helped to organize the regional space of a Fordist production/consumption complex – was retooled in a way that helped integrate the region into the newly globalized economy.

The individual municipal governments, the county boards of supervisors, and the special districts make up a complex patchwork of local governance. In the five-county region, there are 177 cities, 88 in Los Angeles County alone (Dear, 1996a:

68). Each represents special combinations of ruling-class strategies and popular opposition; each has its own 'territorial approach'. These fissures have kept residences separated from industries, the middle class from the working class, African Americans from Chicanos and Central Americans, etc. Formerly white areas – such as the hub cities of Bell and Cudahy (see below) – have become ports of entry for Central Americans. 'Black' South Central has become Latino, too, while formerly white and Hispanic areas to the north of the hub cities – e.g. Monterey Park (Horton, 1995) – now have a prominent Asian population. The implications of these shifts need to be discussed with regard to the role of local government and local struggles with these governments. In the remainder of this chapter, I will use case studies to examine how individual local states have dealt with globalization.

In California, specifically, local governments – though admittedly creatures of the state – do, in fact, as incorporated units, have a grassroots-type autonomy. This autonomy has led to a fragmentation unknown elsewhere. Fragmentation and incorporation along class lines have segregated American urban regions almost beyond recognizability as one urban unit of governance. Most incorporations are conservative and middle-class led; where they are proletarian, they have often meant the incorporation of poverty and environmental pollution. On top of wide-spread fragmentation, cities like Los Angeles with their imperialist annexing power have created metropolitan inequalities that have no equivalent in other industrial countries. Historically, neighborhood-based territorial politics in the United States, particularly in the form of homeowners' associations, have rarely been a base for urban progressivism or progressive metropolitan alternatives.

Progressive local politics has always faced an uphill battle in Los Angeles. Municipal socialism was defeated before World War II (Davis, 1990). The public housing wars during the cold war were lost by the progressive coalition (Parson, 1985), and the Bradley coalition in Los Angeles was increasingly unable to live up to the initial promises it seemed to have made. No progressive political project seemed equipped to carry beyond the racial divide. Ghettoization and forced segregation have been immediately translated into racialized politics, the aspects of which have been by no means always progressive. In addition, the class character of incorporation, together with the Fordist practice of zoning, has rarely made ethnically uniform residential communities (such as Chicano east Los Angeles) strong enough to incorporate successfully.

While Democratic regimes have governed the city through many of the years since the 1960s without forming a classical political machine, the racialization of politics has led to a confirmation of, rather than a challenge to, the status quo. Although people of color now have far better representation, they have hardly changed the political agenda except as it relates to racism and police brutality.

In Southern California, local governments have pursued the project of the world city by weaving the rhetoric of world city *grandesse* into a new political economy of place. Cities have attempted to deal with the pressure of internationalization on their communities with similar, yet significantly varied, policy responses and rhetoric. In the following sections, I will look more closely at five areas in Los Angeles County: West Hollywood, Santa Monica, the hub cities, Carson and Compton.[3]

***Plate 10.1*** *West Hollywood parking lot (Roger Keil)*

## WEST HOLLYWOOD

> We live in an extraordinary time. Los Angeles has become the creative collision point
> between the First and Third Worlds, the Next City in the decade before the Next
> Century. At the center of this new center is West Hollywood (Cole, 1989a: 7).

West Hollywood was incorporated in 1984 after resisting earlier attempts at
annexation by Los Angeles, and after three earlier runs at founding an independent
city (Moos, 1989; Haas, 1986). The urban enclave, wedged between Los Angeles
and Beverly Hills (see Figure 10.1), finally succeeded in city building because of
the peculiar mix of an activist homosexual population[4] with a majority tenant
population, mostly elderly people.[5]

West Hollywood's incorporation campaign was driven by the goal of local self-
government. However, the coalition of gay and tenant movements led the
campaign to success. Organized in the Coalition for Economic Survival (CES),
tenants were the strongest political bloc in the electoral system of the new city. No
one could have been elected to the City Council against the recommendation of
the CES. As a result, West Hollywood passed one of the strictest rent control laws
in the United States. The structure of West Hollywood enabled the politically
active gay and tenant movements to shape the foundation of the city in response
to their specific interests. The strength of this solution was not so much in the
pursuit of particular interests (like gay rights or tenants' rights), but in the
coalition itself (Moos, 1989).[6]

How do these developments relate to restructuring and internationalization in
the Los Angeles region? West Hollywood pursued an aggressive marketing and
economic development strategy, consciously attempting to integrate itself into the
global economy. In addition, through the first years of its existence, West Hollywood was able to manage social problems resulting from its specific history and

178

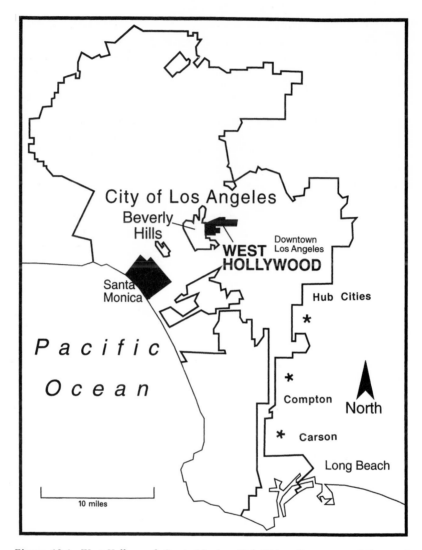

**Figure 10.1** *West Hollywood, Santa Monica, Hub Cities, Compton and Carson in the Los Angeles region (adapted from Foster, 1995: 139; courtesy of the author and Pion Press)*

from the restructuring that took place in Southern California through the 1980s. This municipal democracy was maintained by 'a symbiotic relationship of business and liberalism' (Waldman, 1988).

## WEST HOLLYWOOD: THE CREATIVE CITY

In September of 1987, West Hollywood began to market itself as an 'avant-garde, culturally sophisticated, creative city' (Howard, 1987a). The concept of the 'creative city' as an advertising slogan intended to generate urban development was developed by the nonprofit West Hollywood Marketing Corporation. Founded in 1986, this was a cooperative public–private partnership which, together with the local chamber of commerce (with which it shared an office in the chic designer district of the city), functioned as the most important economic development instrument of West Hollywood.

The 'creative city' campaign was intended to give the newly founded city high visibility in the local and global marketplace, articulating its own image production with the contextual rhetoric of the world class city. The adjective 'creative' was derived from the fact that more than 40% of the economic activity in the city takes place in 'creative' industries: fashion, design, food, movies and so forth (Citron, 1988). There were obvious cross-references to the construction of an urban and a gay identity in this process: 'Creativity was a prevalent theme in the gay press throughout the incorporation campaign. Articles sometimes directly stated that gays are more creative than nongays (. . .) Creativity is spoken of in a general way, creating the impresssion that the type of creativity needed to run a city is the same type of creativity used in artistic projects. Such references to creativity comprise part of a "constitutive narrative" of West Hollywood, a narrative which sought to embody gay identity' (Forest, 1995: 143–144). It is significant that the formation of local identity and the insertion of the local creative, flexible and crafts-based sectors into the global economy operated within the same symbolic lexicon during these years.

Rick Cole, the first director of the West Hollywood Marketing Corporation, said in 1987: 'Much of what people associate with Los Angeles – which is this newly self-conscious world capital – emanates from West Hollywood' (in Howard, 1987a). Plugging itself into the regional process of world city formation, West Hollywood sold itself to the world with an 'innovative strategy' as a 'unique community' (West Hollywood Marketing Corporation, 1988). The geographical territories of Southern California were thus transformed into 'images of the mind', adding to the earlier transformation process which turned nonincorporated areas into a political territory. It was assumed that the image of a city could be 'the most important factor in the life of a community' (West Hollywood Marketing Corporation, 1988). The relevant aspect of this reincarnation of traditional boosterism is the self-confident evocation of uniqueness in an *international* and *world-historic* ambience as stated in the opening quote: 'in an extraordinary time'; 'the creative collision point between the First and Third Worlds'; 'the Next City in the decade before the Next Century'. And finally: 'At the center of this new center is West Hollywood' (Cole, 1989a: 7), site of the production of a 'historical moment':

> Throughout our Twentieth Century, the most dazzling cabarets have always been a sideshow to the upheavals of history. The titanic shifts of world trade and wealth, the cataclysms that wrench apart nations and peoples – these are the forces that lend a special sparkle and poignance to the unforgettable cafés of our age:
> . . . the bistros of the Left Bank in Paris after the Great War and before the Crash,
> . . . the nightclubs of the exotic casbah in Vichy Casablanca following the Fall of France,
> . . . the sidewalk trattoria of the Via Veneto in Roma at the time of 'la dolce vita' after the Second World War,
> . . . the coffee houses of Bohemian Greenwich Village in the Empire City during Pax Americana,

. . . and the sidewalk cafes and restaurants of West Hollywood at the dawn of the Pacific Century (Cole, 1989a: 7).

West Hollywood has characterized itself as the melting pot of those national and international cultures that have been thrown from marginality into the spotlight of a postmodern multiculture: accelerated Russian immigration to West Hollywood redefined what (food) consumption meant in this community; the gay movement functioned as a catalyst for a new aesthetic culture of corporeality and perfection; the globalization of the economy brought 'the refinement of Europe, the productivity of Asia and the ambition of the Middle East to the nearby Avenues of Design. From Kracow and Haifa, Tehran and Omaha, Bangkok and Milan, Chihuahua and Cleveland, the Tides of History have carried the resourceful to West Hollywood' (Cole, 1989a: 7).

While falling partly for the sweet temptation of the boundless universe of the postmodern condition, the marketing of West Hollywood has knowingly defied the simulated postmodern synchronicity that characterizes the Los Angeles region in the eyes of many observers. The production of place in West Hollywood has led to the concrete materiality of a local state in an emerging post-Fordist world city economy: a materialized built environment and social infrastructure of 'hyper-reality'. In the end, it is not a real or a historical city that serves as a model for the image that West Hollywood has created for itself, but the Casablanca of the movie by the same name: the 'creative city' appears as a 'script and a perpetual motion picture' (Baudrillard: 1983: 26). The many cultures of West Hollywood 'coexist in restive proximity, like the scene in "Casablanca" where Victor Laslo directs the house band in a stirring version of "*La Marseillaise*" while Major Strosser and his officers bellow out the "*Horst Wessel*"-song' (Cole, 1989a: 7). The reflection of the imaginary of the 'creative city' onto this embryonic switching station of the world city is now complete: the 'creative city' itself became a productive force in securing a niche in the global economic environment of Southern California.

The sale of the city 'on its own terms' (Waldman, 1988: 542) was also anchored in the draft General Plan, prepared by a consulting firm, stating the connection between urban image and urban economy. West Hollywood was presented as a new city which would generate innovation in business and through high 'imageability', uniqueness, a spectrum of attractions and commercial services. Babyboomers were considered a particular target group due to their high incomes and consumerism (City of West Hollywood, 1987). In the plan that was ultimately passed by the City Council on June 20, 1988, this canon of possibilities was transformed into a municipal policy program.[7] In this context, the 'creative industries' of West Hollywood were put to work: the city secured them a location in the chaos of the global economy and did not shy away from using its power in structuring the newly incorporated economic base of the municipality. West Hollywood's design industry, for example, emerged in the backyards and alleys of an unregulated county territory in small flexible and creative workshops (Cole, 1989b: 35). Increased regulation after incorporation led to tensions with some of these firms (West Hollywood Marketing Corporation, 1988). Similarly, West Hollywood provoked anger among real estate investors when the city replaced the traditional permissiveness in zoning with more sensitive plans, including height restrictions that limited buildings to 45 feet. Stringent design standards were also put into place (Waldman, 1988; City of West Hollywood, 1988). In general, however, local business entered with consent into the new social contract created by the formation of the local state in West Hollywood and so did its population. They supported the assumptions about the place that led the city marketers to boost the unique character of the urban enclave (Law, 1994: iv).

## WEST HOLLYWOOD: CITY OF ECONOMIC SURVIVAL[8]

The 'creative city' was the term that symbolized the means by which post-Fordist urban development and marketing strategies of the 1980s were welded together with social movement activity. The main groups involved in this process were quite heterogeneous. Although both the tenant movement and the gay and lesbian movement had roots in the peak time of social movement activity during the 1960s, the incorporation was not an unambiguous founding of a 'progressive' community. The homosexual population is highly differentiated and hardly 'progressively' minded on all issues. As Kirby has pointed out correctly, 'it is both naive and presumptuous to argue that a collective defined in terms of sexual orientation should act monolithically to accept the "map of meaning" defined by those with a different political agenda' (Kirby, 1993: 75).[9] The groups participating in the coalition for incorporation acted in their own interest and did not share many political goals beyond the founding of the city.[10]

The local state in West Hollywood was brought to life through these disparate social movements. Insofar as they have maintained their political presence in West Hollywood beyond incorporation, the local state has proved to be more responsive to their special demands than other cities might have been. From the beginning, the distribution of political power on the City Council was viewed as representative of all groups which had supported incorporation. Their social and political organizations – the Campaign for Economic Survival, the Stonewall Gay and Lesbian Democratic Club – determined political discourse in the new city. It was never possible, however, to speak of a clear dominance of progressive forces. In the appointments of citizen committees, proportional representation of progressives and conservatives was strictly adhered to. However, the high degree of civil organization of the politically relevant groups in West Hollywood along their special interests meant also that political representatives of the local state usually encountered challenges only in the fields of gay/lesbian and tenant rights.

Rent control and the question of political representation by homosexuals were considered the most pressing social problems in West Hollywood at the time of incorporation. During the formation of the local state the urban government took significant steps to address these problems. Homosexuals found political representation, and the city passed a number of measures which improved the social status of its gay and lesbian citizens (e.g. the domestic partnership program, bylaws against discrimination). In addition, the city passed one of the strictest rent control laws in the United States (Gilderbloom and Appelbaum, 1988: 131; Haas, 1986). In its section on 'Human services', the city's General Plan provided clear guidelines for the distribution of these services.

**Plate 10.2** David Hockney, 'Hancock Street West Hollywood without Sun,' Cover of West Hollywood Magazine, 1989 (Reproduced by permission of the artist).

Citizen participation in policymaking, planning and implementation as well as evaluation of the services was a prominent goal of the municipal social welfare system (City of West Hollywood, 1988: 169–173). The city explicitly sought to create and implement a progressive and humane social policy. Particularly in the area of care for AIDS patients, West Hollywood has played a leading role in municipal social welfare provision.[11] A community needs assessment in 1994 found that the general population of West Hollywood rated the following five services as most important in the community: information about AIDS, HIV testing, information on all services, library services and protection against discrimination (Law, 1994: iii). The peculiar mixture of a local 'war on poverty' with innovative contractual policies involving private service providers points to the constitution of a new type of local welfare state which combines private-sector methods of a post-welfare state capitalism with the community mandate of social responsibility. The very local character of this initiative is remarkable in itself.

The 'creative city' and the 'city of economic survival' were twin responses to the demands placed on West Hollywood by the role of the area in the regional world city formation process. It remains to be seen how compatible these responses will be in the future as pressures of gentrification and competition with neighboring communities rise, and to what degree the specific mix that led to the foundation and formation of West Hollywood as a city will be sustainable over time. On the one hand, West Hollywood has continued to be a symbol and a significant place in the construction of gay community and identity. However, as Forest has reminded us: 'The connection between West Hollywood and gays tends to disguise the constructed nature of gay identity. Thus the use of place encourages the "common-sense" perception that gays are a social group as natural, and therefore as legitimate, as ethnicities. (. . .) Place (. . .) plays a fundamental role in the creation of a particular "normative ideal" of gay identity' (Forest, 1995: 151–152). The economic and social potential of the gay community has clearly been recognized beyond the boundaries of the small city. Comparing the gay community to new immigrant and ethnic communities in Los Angeles, Joel Kotkin has written: 'West Hollywood's economic success, most insiders agree, directly stems from its large concentration of gays and lesbians, who represent about one-third of its population. In many ways, they anchor the city's economic growth much as the Chinese do in the San Gabriel Valley or the Jews in the Pico-Robertson district of Los Angeles' (Kotkin, 1995a: M1).[12]

## SANTA MONICA: MOSCOW BY THE SEA[13]

Santa Monica is a coastal city of 86 905 people (1990) located west of Los Angeles (see Figure 10.1). The combination of a large tenant population (80% of residents) and a young, liberal middle class provided the sociological basis for a 'quiche-and-perrier-radicalism' (Shearer, 1984) and a 'progressive' majority on the City Council in 1981. The success of the 'progressive' coalition in the municipal election was predated by a referendum that had introduced a strict local rent-control law in 1979. Tenants had formed the Santa Monica Fair Housing Alliance and established themselves as 'a class for themselves' (Heskin, 1983). The fusion of organized tenants with the Campaign for Economic Democracy (CED) led by (then) Democratic California assemblyman and 1960s activist Tom Hayden into an organization called Santa Monicans for Renters' Rights (SMRR) formed the foundation on which both the referendum and the municipal elections were won by the progressives.

The new municipal government, which thought of itself as social-democratic and liberal, espoused direct democracy and citizen participation as the main aspects of their political activity. Task forces, new urban commissions on culture and women, and a directly elected rent control board were instituted. Neighborhood groups were to be supported directly through nondiscriminatory distribution of federal funds. 'Human-oriented' urban planning became the core of the new municipal policy (Shearer, 1984; Kann, 1986; Clavel, 1986).[14]

Western coastal communities in Southern California have been shown to have a particularly young, mostly white and well-paid population (see Soja, 1989: 211). The politics and policies of the progressive Santa Monica coalition can be interpreted as a specific set of actions by liberal 'place entrepreneurs' to sustain the privileges of a particular stratum of professionals on this Westside of Los Angeles. In this sense, the 'radical' program of the white young urban professionals of Santa Monica was an instance of typical clientele politics which provided municipal services to a specific segment of the fragmented society of world city Los Angeles.[15]

184

***Plate 10.3*** Pacific coast, Santa Monica (Roger Keil)

## THE REORGANIZATION OF URBAN DISCOURSE: REFORM IN SANTA MONICA

The local reform government under SMRR reorganized the urban political process in Santa Monica mostly in the areas of social policy, rent control, urban development and urban growth. The introduction of a socially defined zoning and urban development policy was a core item on the program of the liberal populist alliance. The municipal government pursued this strategy in two ways. First, the planning process in Santa Monica was democratized. Citizen participation became the main aspect of land-use planning. Public forums were held and planning review instruments were introduced in order to create a neighborhood-based planning process. The redevelopment process replaced large-scale demolition of poor neighborhoods and aloof administration with direct funding for 'geographically designated democratic neighborhood organizations' (Shearer, 1984: 577). Second, the planning and development process in Santa Monica was redefined in order to incorporate positions in the community that were critical of growth. The cost of urban development and the change in property values were juxtaposed to changes in local quality of life. The city stopped rubberstamping investors' projects and assumed a strict regulating role in development. The goals of these policies were congruent with the vision of 'a city as a livable human-scale environment where people of all incomes and races can live and interact' (Shearer, 1984: 579).

An important aspect of this policy change was inclusionary zoning, and the linkage of affordable housing and development projects.[16] Redrawing the zoning plan of the city was thus a central element of reform. This included new height and density limits, the designation of certain areas for the creation of industrial and office space, and the linking of social services to private development projects. These policies were aimed at slowing gentrification and maintaining a socially diversified community. They also signified the pioneering of a new kind of planning in Southern California.[17]

The reformed urban development process in Santa Monica can ultimately be understood as an attempt to articulate the pressures put on the coastal community by the expansion of the world city economy in light of the socioeconomic status and liberal political beliefs of a majority population of middle-class tenants. Since this articulation is necessarily contradictory, the new planning instruments were ambiguous in their political meaning. While fundamental debates on issues like growth had loomed large in the initial phase of the formation of SMRR, the real-political process of channelling investment pressures into a community critical of growth occurred on a more concrete and pragmatic level – e.g. during the discussion of planning legislation. It is possible to characterize this movement from the fundamental to the pragmatic as a function of the movement of activists into the state. By the mid-1980s, the movement into the state had reached a critical point: the middle-class based local state had difficulties legitimizing its actions before the emerging and self-confident middle-class based civil society of Santa Monica.[18] The solutions to this legitimation crisis were as innovative as the reform approach itself. The confrontation between the SMRR rank and file, who continued to be strongly antigrowth, and the more compromising politicians in City Hall (like former Mayor James Conn and Derek Shearer), who favored moderate growth, was transformed into a new consensus in the second half of the decade. This consensus implied a fundamental agreement over democracy in the planning process, and an acknowledgement of the necessity for public–private development contracts between the city, the neighborhoods and the investors.

In theoretical terms, this consensus represented the institutionalization of a postmodern mode of regulation in that the abandonment of a potentially universal political solution, which was initially present in the programmatic statements of the radical reformers, led to a socially and territorially partial solution. The city engineered a new local social compromise which included the opposition – most notably the associations of landlords and developers. For the pragmatists, who came to outnumber the representatives of verbal and activist radicalism in Santa Monica, the establishment of adaptive planning and development instruments by the local state became a question of 'normalizing' relationships with capital forces whose investment pressures on the city were strongly felt. They stopped questioning the legitimacy of capital to control accumulation and investment, and offered themselves as predictable actors who preferred negotiations over the kind of frontal attacks that had been potentially present in SMRR's ideology (Kann, 1986: 187).

## ECONOMIC DEVELOPMENT: FROM MOSCOW BY THE SEA TO JAPANESE SEASIDE RESORT

In contrast to almost all municipalities in the United States, Santa Monica need not fear a lack of investment. Territorial and social structural advantages guarantee that economic development and tax base enhancing capital infusion will occur on a constant basis in this community. These advantages put the city into a situation in which they are able to exact fees from development. Economic development in Santa Monica can be viewed as a successful linking of selective consumerism with the elements of a local postindustrialism. This was the basis for the functional incorporation of Santa Monica and of the cultural particularism of the local middle class into the internationalizing Los Angeles region. The middle class should not, however, be seen as spared by the crisis but should be considered a winner in the restructuring game, all part of a move which the entire American society underwent during the Reagan/Bush years towards a consumption-oriented middle-class culture. An important part of this shift has been the growing emphasis on culture and education as a means to give local youth a headstart into a middle-class world of tomorrow (Kann, 1986: 6–7; Davis, 1986).

While hardly intended by the liberal municipal government, the price of prosperity was the gentrification of the economic and social structure.[19] This process was most pronounced in the revitalization of the pedestrian area Third Street Mall which was taken up after 1987. The mall had been a strip of stores mostly in the low-price consumption range. The regeneration of Third Street was to turn the area into an entertainment and shopping zone fit to compete for international tourist dollars with upscale Rodeo Drive in Beverly Hills. The establishment of such a specialized retail market was an intended consequence of the city's imbrication into the economy of the Pacific Rim and Santa Monica's position on the map of the Japanese tourist industry. Third Street Mall has now become one of the most important globalized spaces of conspicuous consumption next to Beverly Hills, Little Tokyo and certain areas of West Hollywood. At any day or evening masses of pedestrians spill from adjacent parking garages and from the Santa Monica Place Mall onto the palm-tree-lined streetscape. Upscale restaurants and chain stores have replaced the indigent culture of years past. Bicycle policemen enforce a modicum of order in the interest of the new market culture, but Third Street Mall has also become one of the surprising new counterintuitive public spaces of Los Angeles: 'Third Street Promenade is a pedestrian promenade with formalized vendor's kiosks, seating and ornamental plantings. (. . .) [It is a] public space in the traditional sense, open not just to shoppers but to loiterers, street performers and, for the moment, the homeless' (Flusty, 1994: 53).

Economic development in Santa Monica under the progressive regime integrated community concerns with business interests. In recognition of the growth pressures in the entire region which are felt particularly strongly in cities like Santa Monica, the compromises between developers and neighborhood groups focus on the consequences of growth to local communities.[20]

## RENTERS' REPUBLIC AND HOMELESS PARADISE? SOCIAL DEMOCRACY AND THE LOCAL WELFARE STATE IN SANTA MONICA

As an integral part of the Los Angeles region, Santa Monica could only partly fend off the negative effects of world city growth. From sewage treatment to homelessness and crime, the environmental and social problems of the world city entered

***Plate 10.4***   *Third Street Promenade (Roger Keil)*

the privileged space of the small city on the Pacific. The city, therefore, had to devise a local social policy which dealt with these overspill problems. The core of the alternative social policy of Santa Monica was the reform of rent control.[21] The establishment of strong rent control – including vacancy control – led to a substantial income redistribution between landlords and tenants in favor of the latter since 1979. The share of rent in the overall income of households was expected to be reduced from 23 to 17% on average. Without rent control, this share would have climbed to about 30% (Gilderbloom and Appelbaum, 1988).[22]

The struggle between the tenants and landlords occurred after 1979 under the political hegemony of the advocates of rent control. Any attempt by oppositional forces to break the power of SMRR could only be successful if these forces supported rent control.[23] Thus, the struggle over tenants' rights had central significance for the reform process overall (Citron, 1986; Wilkinson, 1989d). The political con-sensus – whether as real concession or lip service – over the legitimacy of rent control, however, never covered the deep chasm between the political actors in this conflict.[24] The well-documented academic debate on rent control in Santa Monica has mirrored the conflicts between tenants and landlords in more or less polemical form (Heskin, 1983; Kann, 1986; Clavel, 1986; Gilderbloom and Appelbaum, 1988).

In the summer of 1989, a committee made up of members of the local rent control board and representatives of landlords proposed a compromise which was to change the regulation in relevant respects. The new law was to allow landlords to raise rents in some buildings substantially, if they were willing to provide affordable housing elsewhere (Moran, 1989a). This proposal was viewed as a major breakthrough in the hardened fronts on the issue of housing in Santa Monica. The publicly displayed happiness over the agreement did not last long, though. Soon after it was reached, the representative organs of the two conflicting parties threw out the agreement for the same reasons that had kept them on two sides of the political barricades for years before. Despite this setback for those forces who were aiming for political consensus in Santa Monica, the development of such a strategy meant a fundamental reversal of the politics of a sharply antagonistic social conflict in housing. Since the mid 1980s, SMRR and the All Santa Monica Coalition in the City Council attempted to find consensual solutions to political conflicts beyond the issue of rent control. One signal of a move in that direction was SMRR member and former mayor James Conn's consent to the development of Colorado Place. This new politics of compromise was possible precisely because the political public of Santa Monica had fundamentally accepted the program of SMRR, which had led to the nickname 'people's republic of Santa Monica' in the early 1980s (Citron, 1987). From this base, a politics of balance was articulated and began to marginalize the traditional left-wing ideological contents of this same program in favor of a more ambivalently postmodern and pragmatic pluralism. In the course of this trend, the compromise over rent control had to be understood. Although it was ultimately overturned, it was a continuation rather than an end to the dialogue between the conflicting parties. The discourse on rent control – born out of a sense of attack on the traditional American political system – was deflected into a discourse on securing the privileges of the local middle class with a social touch (Kann, 1986: 182).

The municipality was forced into a paradoxical policy constellation in which middle-class politicians, conscious of the need to protect their privileges, continued to pursue alternative social policies. Next to rent control, the city's policies on homelessness have been significant in this respect. Before harsh control policies were reintroduced, Santa Monica spent one-third of its social service budget on care for the homeless who were congregating on the city's beaches and streets. The local police, for many years, did not harass homeless people unless they committed a violent crime; the city allowed homeless people to camp out in front of City Hall.[25] The city's policies became a model for the devolution of general social responsibility onto individual local actors after 10 years of cuts in the area of social services under Presidents Reagan and Bush. It was also consistent with the fragmentations of social policy through postmodern pluralism which were intended to achieve a new correlation between the economic strength of the urban community and its political flexibility.

## THE MOVEMENT INTO THE STATE

Santa Monica and West Hollywood have been the centers of new forms of politics which have their basis in the organizational and economic strength of the middle class. Relative social security (although precarious at the margins of the middle class) and high political presence and flexibility melt into a place-specific sociocultural basis for the cities' adaptation to the needs of world city formation. The implementation of liberal or radical projects coming out of previous periods of social movement activity – that is, the politics of social responsibility – now takes place through its metamorphosis into post-Fordist, fragmented and diversified forms of politics. Alternative social projects and 'social democracy', whose points of reference were the national political space, are localized and fragmented, and spatially segregated in this process. At the same time, these projects lost some of their antisystemic critical thrust. The movement into the state in Santa Monica – the taking of power by the middle class – was a place-specific transformation of local state practice which has to be contextualized in the larger restructuring of the world city region. The program and politics of SMRR were both a redefinition and a rejection of traditional left and liberal projects of change as America had known them since the New Deal. Localization and flexibilization were the strongest characteristics of this shift. They became the precondition for the emergence of what I would call the post-Fordist local state in these communities.

Differences in perspective and in the results of local state policies in Santa Monica and West Hollywood can be explained by the specific dynamics of local class structures and political cultures. In Santa Monica, a materially secure and politically left-leaning middle class who also belong to the political class of the United States have come to power (Kann, 1986). In West Hollywood the success of progressive politics has rested on the mobilization of the special interests of specific middle-class fragments: homosexuals and tenants. The middle-class fragments of West Hollywood belong neither potentially nor really to the hegemonic bloc of American society: their middle-class culture is marginal in spite of their connection to the cultural acropolis of Hollywood.[26]

There are also differences in the organizational form of the 'movement into the state'. SMRR and CED in Santa Monica were endogenous organizations which arose from the social structural changes of the community in the 1970s and grew to the degree that the consumption habits and privileges of the new middle classes combined with the social beliefs of the 1960s (Kann, 1986: 75). SMRR and CED were original organizations of a reurbanized middle class. In West Hollywood, on the other hand, only the political activity of CES – a cadre organization which stood for racial and ethnic equality and for the protection of the conditions of reproduction of the urban working class – kickstarted the local movement. CES orchestrated the unity of the gay movement, which had been less than interested in local issues, with the tenant movement, while the local autonomists, who had followers in all political camps, functioned as catalysts.

Despite these differences, both middle-class movements into the state were successful in integrating those segments of the population which they represented into the structured coherence of the world city. Their significance has continued to be in providing arenas of alternative policy formation in an era of severe austerity and state withdrawal. In doing this, the progressive governments of West Hollywood and Santa Monica have avoided falling into a strictly defensive mode and have been able to remain a challenge to the status quo.[27]

## CARSON: FUTURE UNLIMITED

Cities are what men make them
On land that is given by God
(Anonymous; quoted in Jerrils, 1972: vi).

Carson, a city of 85 000 (1993) in the south of the Los Angeles Basin, north of Long Beach and east of Torrance in the South Bay, capitalizes on the opportunities that have sprung up through the northward expansion of the harbor economy along the Long Beach and Harbor freeways. The operative logo the community has chosen for itself is 'Future Unlimited'. 'As a community of the twenty-first century, Carson is a place where futures begin' (City of Carson, 1987). Carson's explicit development strategy – heavily influenced by the city's leading place entrepreneur, the Watson Land Company – is to provide a safe ground for international (i.e. mostly Japanese) investment.

Carson incorporated by plebiscite as the 77th independent community of Los Angeles County in 1968. Incorporation was preceded by a lively history which was mostly determined by the breaking up of the giant landed properties of the Dominguez family on Rancho San Pedro. To this day this family's heirs manage and develop a large part of the city's lands through Dominguez Properties and the Watson Land Company. The city's name goes back to George Henry Carson, the son-in-law of Don Manuel Dominguez who was credited with initiating the transformation of the Mexican rancho into American real estate capital. In the 1920s oil was found in the Dominguez Hills, and Carson became the site of refineries and chemical industries which still today characterize the image of parts of the city. Carson's development, thus, has been largely a product of the entangled interests of (inter-)national capital and of local real estate capital, specifically the oil companies Shell and Arco, and the Watson Land Company, respectively.

The internationalization of the Los Angeles urban region lent a new quality to this relationship: Carson became a turnstile for the integration of global economic tendencies into the local urban structure. As a 'unique industrial city, which cleans itself' (in the words of one city official), Carson strives to remake itself into an important part of the subeconomy of the South Bay based on world trade and high technology. High-tech production took hold, for example, in an industrial park owned by Watson Land where the Japanese corporation Pioneer produced laser disks for videos in a nonunionized plant. In the 1980s among the Fortune 500 companies Shell Oil, TRW, McDonnell-Douglas, Pepsi-Cola Bottling, Borden Chemicals, Bridgestone Tires, Atlantic Richfield, the American Can Co., K-Mart, Nissan, Tomy Toys, Fuji Photo Film, Elixir Corporation, Mercedes Benz of North America and Peugeot of America had all established their US headquarters in Carson (City of Carson, n.d.). In the city's official development policy, traditional industrialization was intended to play a minor role because it was believed to cause too many long-term problems. Instead, only high-technology 'clean' production – such as the manufacturing of computer chips – has been considered desirable. Because of its history in oil and chemicals, the city that had 124 car junk yards, several waste dumps and eight refineries in the late 1980s has

**Plate 10.5** *Carson: Future Unlimited (Roger Keil)*

embarked on a strategy of ecological modernization reimaging itself as sensitive to environmental concerns.

Carson's geographical position – in the center of several freeway interchanges, close to the port and to downtown Los Angeles – has frequently been cited by municipal officials and business representatives as an important locational advantage (Stelpflug in *South Coast Business*, 1986). Other structural locational advantages include the availability of undeveloped land, the activities of a business-friendly municipal development authority, the absence of local property taxes and the existence of a highly skilled and stable local reservoir of labor. Visibility is an important factor in the sale of Carson as a business location: the dominant presence of the Nissan headquarters at the intersection of the Harbor and San Diego freeways and the characteristic Goodyear blimp often hovering above the city mark Carson as a recognizable place in the Los Angeles Basin. That the visibility of international headquarters has begun to eclipse the city's traditional notoriety for refineries can only be considered advantageous from the point of view of local place entrepreneurs.

Carson's role as a forerunner in regional cities' efforts to open their economies to global investment can largely be credited to the political willingness of local actors to fundamentally alter the economic base of their town. Although there has been no official municipal strategy to attract foreign capital, it is possible to identify relevant interests who pursue such a strategy. Watson Land, the largest developer of industrial complexes in Los Angeles County, and one of the largest of its kind in the United States, functions as an active transmission belt transporting the capital and economic energy of the Pacific Rim into the local economy. Watson Land has thus been able to achieve two things: first, its aggressive expansionary strategy built on investment from abroad has thrown previously underutilized land into the process of land development; second, the corporation has replaced earlier land uses in favor of more future-oriented economic activities. Watson Land has shown interest in

**Plate 10.6**  *The Goodyear Blimp, Carson (Ute Lehrer)*

predominantly Japanese investment in Carson. About 25–30% of the company's properties were leased to Japanese clients by the late 1980s. The Japanese corporations American Honda, Meiko Warehousing, Bridgestone Tire Company, Kenwood USA Corporation, Maruzen of America, Mitsui-Soko (USA), Nakano Warehouse, Pioneer Electronics, Pioneer Video, Tomy Coleco and Toyota Motors shared 2 million square feet of land leased by Watson Land. Among the developments in Carson, three stand out for their size and significance: the Watson Industrial Center South, with an area of almost 10 million square feet; the Watson Corporate Center, with 1.3 million square feet; and the Watson Intermodal Center, with 700 000 square feet. A company brochure written in Japanese presented Carson's locational advantages to potential investors from the Far East. Watson Land representatives, including the company's chair of the board of directors and its president, have participated in official trade missions of the County Economic Development Division to Japan (Watson Land, n.d.).

Watson Land's aggressive outward-oriented strategy has been complemented by its involvement in local politics. The company observes, accompanies and consults the local political decision-making process. Watson Land has consistently provided financial support for local candidates running on a platform of free enterprise and economic growth. The company created a political liaison position to lobby and influence the city administration and local council in planning and policy matters.

Typically, land-use conflicts between Carson's residential population and its economic enterprises were predominant among local political issues. For example, the spaces designated for container storage and the regulation of heavy truck traffic have become indicative of the pressure of restructuring linked mostly to the expansion of the port and warehousing economy. In issues like these, local political activity regulates and negotiates the insertion of globally oriented economic interests into the local space of the community. Any restrictions on truck traffic and container storage would seriously inhibit the expansionary strategies of local place entrepreneurs. Political activity on the part of Watson Land is not strategically and comprehensively orchestrated, but depends on individual issues through which the local place entrepreneur attempts to determine the ways in which its interests can be entwined with global dynamics and foreign investment patterns.

Next to the direct involvement of companies, it is the semiofficial associations such as the local chamber of commerce who are most significant in the internationalization of Carson's economy. The chamber selects and coordinates the interests of various capital groups in the city and provides a common forum for local and international capital to streamline their interests before they encounter the municipal political arena. For foreign (e.g. Japanese) firms, the chamber of commerce provides the opportunity for an initiation into the local community and into the local political process. The personal network of the 'good old boys' who used to run the city is consequently expanded into the global realm. Such relationships are considered an imperative for firms seeking to guarantee their insertion into the local economy. This impression is confirmed by a representative of Nissan Motor Company in Carson: 'In the past, we've been somewhat segmented. . . . Not that there wasn't a good relationship, it was more of a do-your-own-thing situation then. What I find interesting now is that we all want to get involved. We have shown a greater interest in the community and they, in turn, have shown a greater interest in us' (Stelpflug in *South Coast Business*, 1986).

The formation of an integrated 'glocalized' political economy which presents itself as an integration of international firms into the local (business) community ultimately becomes the program of the local state. Carson is presented as a magnet for international investment and a continuous boomtown[28] with an unbroken genealogy from the days of the ranchos to the era of globalization: 'In many ways, Carson represents the oldest and newest of California. From the rich historical heritage of the Rancho San Pedro legacy to its modern, high-tech business parks and centers, Carson is rapidly living up to its motto, "Future Unlimited"' (Stelpflug in *South Coast Business*, 1986).

Certainly, Carson is especially vocal in its attempts to attract business by any means possible. A recent mayor unequivocally claimed in 1994: 'We are prepared to do whatever it takes to attract and retain business. From an organizational and policy standpoint we have streamlined every process, we have kept fees low and we continue to exist as a no-local-property-tax, no-utility-tax city. If there is one message that we send it's that we don't *say* we're "business friendly" – we *are* business friendly' (Mayor Michael Mitoma, quoted in Stelpflug, 1994: 5; emphasis added, R.K.). Yet, in contrast to purely industrial or commercial cities in Los Angeles County, Carson is also a residential city with the most 'ethnically diverse population in the United States' (Allen and Turner, 1997: 243). In 1993, Carson's population was almost evenly distributed among the region's major ethnic groups: 27.4% were Hispanic, 25.9% Black, 24.0% Asian, and 22.1% white.[29] One of the challenges the city with the 'future unlimited' will surely face in the next generation, is to find ways in which the globalized local economy will interact with this mixed population base. In the present, the community seems to be able to hold the balance. Diversity is seen as congruent with the goal of economic growth as long as citizenship is defined as operating in the global marketplace of interurban competition.[30]

## THE HUB CITIES: CLASS SOLIDARITY AND GAMBLING

> Any effort to make local government more accountable and democratic must factor in the Latino community as both a voting and, more importantly, a working population upon which Southern California's present and future economic regime is being built (Valle and Torres, 1994: 5).

Another set of local circumstances has characterized the local state's role in restructuring in the eastern working-class suburbs and industrial communities of Los Angeles. Hit particularly hard by deindustrialization (Davis, 1991b), the communities of this Fordist landscape of mass production have reacted to the economic crisis they experienced in the 1970s with innovative politics based in traditions of working-class militancy and neighborhood activism. In the east of Los Angeles, along the Santa Ana Freeway, a small ribbon of cities defines the heart of the old industrial economy of Southern California. These cities, also sometimes called 'hub cities', are the industrial communities Vernon and Commerce and the mixed, or residential, communities of Bell, Bell Gardens, Cudahy, Huntington Park, Lynwood, Maywood and Southgate.

The hub cities have been considered losers in local interurban competition. They have taken the brunt of the deindustrialization, impoverishment and housing crisis encountered in the region overall. Between 1978 and 1982 the southeast of Los Angeles lost more than 75 000 jobs, mostly through plant closures in basic manufacturing industries and related sectors. Compared with the prosperous middle-class cities of west Los Angeles, the recent history of the eastern cities is a sad version of the general trend of the destruction of Fordist and pre-Fordist industrial landscapes in developed capitalist countries. The common narrative of deindustrialization usually paints a picture of victimization of working-class communities and underrates the survivability and innovative capacities of such communities in their search for a future after deindustrialization. In the following sections I will challenge this common narrative by presenting the hub cities as an example of a working-class-induced process of community reinvention.

The working-class suburbs east of Los Angeles were predominantly white by the middle of the century. Only since the 1950s have they become increasingly the residence of Chicanos and Spanish-speaking immigrants. In 1980, southeast Los

***Plate 10.7*** *Welcome to Commerce: The Model City (Roger Keil)*

Angeles could be considered a port of entry for immigrants from Latin America and Asia for the entire region. At the same time, the southeast became more native: the area has the highest concentration of native Americans anywhere in the urban region. In 1983 the Hispanic population of the southeastern communities was between 45 and 85% of the total populations in these individual cities. The resident Chicano population has recently been increasingly replaced by new Latin American immigrants. Commercial enterprises in the area have gone the same route: stores catering to a mostly Anglo or Chicano clientele have made way for Asian and Central American establishments. This trend has also been reflected in political shifts away from the rule of white politicians (mostly old men) towards greater Latino representation. Deindustrialization and new immigration have been coupled with a visible tendency towards industrial restructuring, during which service industries, small office parks, small warehouses and light industry as well as mini steel mills and garment factories have emerged as indicators of a changing industrial base in a formerly heavy industrial area. Most of these new enterprises are nonunionized; most pay lower wages than common in traditional Fordist industries and employ mostly minorities, women and undocumented workers (Donahoe, 1987: Chapter 3).

As their degree of mechanization increased, the branch plants of the mass industries in the hub cities began hiring ethnic minorities, African Americans and women. These same groups were to become the main victims of layoffs due to plant closings in the late 1970s and early 1980s (Donahoe, 1987: Chapter 5). The workforce at Bethlehem Steel South Gate was highly integrated compared to the steel mills of the American East: at the time of its closing 25% were Anglo, 30% African American and the rest predominantly Hispanic. The closure of plants in these communities thus contributed to denying new immigrants participation in the prosperity of the American Dream. It was also interpreted by some as a

196

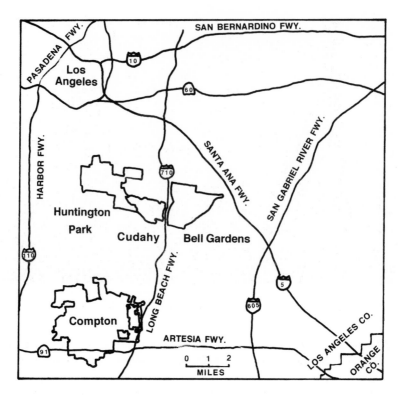

*Figure 10.2* Poorest suburbs in Los Angeles (Source: Los Angeles Times, June 6, 1989; Graphics Ute Lehrer)

consequence of consciously racist decision-making. Where there had been unionized jobs with good wages in the post-World War II decades, only low-paying employment in garment sweatshops and services remained in the 1980s and 1990s. Large-scale impoverishment was the consequence of this tendency. By the late 1980s, three of the hub cities, Cudahy (second poorest), Bell Gardens (third) and Huntington Park (seventh) were among the poorest suburbs in the United States; two more cities in the south and in the east of Los Angeles, Compton (12th) and South El Monte (15th) made it on this chart of misery (*LAT*, June 6, 1989: II, 1) (see Figure 10.2).

The history of labor disputes and the continuing demographic internationaliza-tion of the southeast of Los Angeles during the past decades created a specific political situation which determined the path of restructuring in the hub cities. In the struggles against plant closures, documented in detail by Myrna Donahoe, the nuclei for a redefinition of local politics in the southeast can be found. First, in their struggles against the closures of steel, tire and auto plants, workers learned that their traditional fixation on shopfloor activism was an insufficient base for the defense of their interests against corporations (Donahoe, 1987, Chapter 8: 30). An emerging antiplant closure movement included an alliance of local unionized workers and New Left activists whose communal strategy aimed for local autonomy. The grassroots groups allied loosely in the organization 'Los Angeles

**Plate 10.8** *Deindustrialization on Los Angeles' Eastside (Roger Keil)*

Coalition against Plant Closures' (later 'Californians against Plant Shut Downs') deliberately addressed their isolation and attempted to create new structures of solidarity (Donahoe, 1987, Chapter 8: 30). The most essential political guidelines growing out of this redefinition of urban community along class lines included the understanding that corporations could be held responsible for workers and their communities rather than allowed to make unilateral decisions about profits, investments and production (Donahoe, 1987).

Local governments themselves originally contributed little to the struggles of the workers in the plants.[31] In contrast to the lethargy of elected governments, which were hardly representative anymore of the increasingly ethnically diverse and politicized population, the workers and their communities created institutions of communal solidarity in reaction to the plant closings. Members of the United Steel Workers Local 1845 of Bethlehem Steel founded the Steelworkers Oldtimers Foundation in South Gate which organized a food bank in their local in 1983. More than 10 000 families from the southeast of Los Angeles obtained assistance through this food bank each month in the mid-1980s.[32] The union hall became the community center, the symbolic and physical place of working-class solidarity, and a venue for informational meetings on related struggles.

Besides the class solidarity of the workers' communities around the closed plants, there have also been signs of change in the local political arena. By the 1980s, the movement against plant closings started to make inroads into local state institutions, and the system of political representation in the communities began to feel the impact of demographic internationalization. First, activists were able to gain local political influence and use it to further the cause of the local working-class community. The most important success of this strategy was the election of steel worker George Cole in 1983 as a city councillor in the city of Bell. Cole had run for office because local governments up to that time had not done anything to stem the wave of plant closings in the area. Secondly, more and more Latino politicians were able to obtain seats on their local councils which had previously been mostly white. In 1988 the first Hispanic city councillor of Cudahy, Wilfred 'Bill' Colon, became also the first Hispanic mayor of that city, a city whose population was more than 70% Hispanic at the time. Many of these Latino residents, however, remain excluded from the formal political process because they are nondocumented immigrants.[33]

The altered political landscape in the hub cities has led to reforms and new policy approaches, which in part grew directly out of the protest demands of the local population. Cole himself pleaded for effective regional economic planning and for an image of the small cities as one subregion. He pointed out that the money necessary for a revitalization of this subregion was not flowing into the communities. Rational planning on the subregional level has been hindered by the tax system which has fueled competition among cities for sales tax income. This situation was exacerbated through cuts in funding from the federal government to the cities. Coordination of strategies to deal with the economic and social crisis have stopped short of territorial consolidation mostly because the identities of residents are tied to the political autonomy of their cities and because they consider proximity to local politicians an advantage that would be lost with consolidation.

In office, George Cole fought for concerted action by the hub cities to build a skill training and retraining program under the Job Training Partnership Act of the state of California. A Hub Cities Joint Powers Authority was founded by the cities of Bell, Cudahy, Huntington Park, Lynwood, Maywood and South Gate. The agency gave the hub cities partial, subregional autonomy in the allocation of funds for vocational training and retraining which otherwise would have been administered by the county (*The Cudahy News Letter*, March/April, 1988). The impetus of local autonomy was eminent because the involved cities – all of them with high unemployment figures – felt neglected by the county administration. The hub cities failed to get recognition as an autonomous service delivery area. Instead, the county gave them the status of prime agent, meaning that monies continued to be administered by the county while local institutions decided their allocation. The training programs targeted jobs that paid more than the poverty line, but particular occupations were not predetermined. Vocational and skills training, retraining and specialization of skilled workers and the teaching of general knowledge were meant to help workers adapt to the changed economic structure of the southeast. Programs included skill development for workers in high-tech production in the aerospace industry (lasers, computers), and basic skills for the workers of the new Southern California mass industries like garments (literary skills, English as a second language). The programs that were partly administered by organizations such as the United Automobile Workers (UAW) focussed on the needs of both laid-off industrial workers in the region and the new immigrant Latino segments of the local working class. The hub cities thus created a kind of subregional crisis management in the form of concerted actions by corporatist actors. Simultaneously, they produced the core of a subregional planning strategy which attempted to approach the common problems of the small cities in the deindustrialization belt. The cooperation of the various cities around job training was considered a model for the consolidation of further urban services.

Another strategy used by the cities was an aggressive urban redevelopment program. In the eyes of Councillor Cole, redevelopment created a new bargaining position for the communities which demanded more flexibility, but gave them the opportunity to deal directly with investors and developers and thus participate in regional growth. Although developers are often able to dictate conditions of investment strategies or play cities against each other in locational decisions, municipalities can also at times achieve through skillful negotiation that their interests are written into development agreements. In one case in Bell the urban government was able to insist that investors commit themselves to annual minimum tax payments regardless of their sales. In another urban redevelopment project under the Community Redevelopment Act the city retained its property title in order to add income through redevelopment to the expected rise in sales taxes on the premises. In this special context the urban redevelopment process, which so often is destructive to working-class and poor communities, became a potentially creative instrument organized and supported by the political representatives of both the workers in the closed plants and their social movement allies. But this counterhegemonic tendency met with considerable resistance from the usual place entrepreneurs in the urban process (and the destruction of housing has been part of redevelopment in the hub cities as much as elsewhere).

Urban redevelopment has taken a curious and exotic turn since 1980. On the basis of a law still existing from the nineteenth century, allowing gambling in certain communities, a poker club opened its doors in the city of Bell. At the time, this club, with its 100 tables, was the largest of its kind in the world. During its best years, it brought $2 million in taxes into the city coffers – roughly a quarter of the city's total budget. Other cities in the area followed suit, and more casinos have opened since. The Bicycle Club casino in Bell Gardens had an annual gross income of $100 million (Davis, 1991c).[34] During the 1980s, the casinos became a bizarre site of ethnic gambling cultures and a showcase of the globalized population of the subregion. Formally, they were a reaction both to decreased public incomes in the wake of Proposition 13 (which had limited the ability of cities to raise tax money) and to the consequences of deindustrialization. Substantively, they were a result of the area's increasing internationalization. Historically, all clubs have had problems with crime and corruption. One club in Bell was consequently taken over by the municipality through the procedure of 'eminent domain' in order to retain the profitable income for the city. Not surprisingly, the clubs also became a focus of interurban competition among the hub cities. It was important which city first was granted permission to allow certain kinds of gambling in its borders. Specific games are associated with specific cultures and specific traditions and organizations of crime. The legalization of Chinese gambling in Huntington Park brought Chinese gangs and crime clans to that city.

From the point of view of smaller communities, the poker club strategy appears more rational than reindustrialization because the latter does not offer any incentives to the city's budget. The trucking and transportation business, for example, has often been mentioned as a sector that could possibly make its home in the hub cities. However, cities are not particularly interested in this business because it does not generate income through sales tax, yet it puts an additional burden on local infrastructures. Lacking large municipal budgets, the poor communities in

***Plate 10.9*** *Shop in Huntington Park – Home of Huntington Park Casino (Roger Keil)*

the southeast of Los Angeles – in contrast to their industrial neighbors Vernon and Commerce – are not able to provide social programs similar to those in Santa Monica or West Hollywood. However, the small cities have sometimes come up with remarkable policy innovations to achieve social support through other means (besides the communal solidarity of the workers themselves).

The cases discussed here are no paradisal islands of working-class territorial and political autonomy. The communities in the east of Los Angeles are sites of contradiction. On the one hand they are real but impure responses to years of political activity and workers' resistance to plant closures in the area. They are a lively example of the – admittedly limited – capacity of urban working-class communities to survive the restructuring process. Instead of being thrown on the scrap heap of deindustrialization, the entire area has retooled itself as a part of the periphery of the world city. On the other hand, they are the product of relatively unfettered globalized market processes with ties into the underground and criminal economy. The cities of the southeast immerse themselves self-confidently into the uneven structured coherence of Los Angeles. The regional universe in which the local states of the hub cities circulate is not designed in their favor. An east–west divide clearly separates the different worlds of Los Angeles. To para-phrase anti-plant-closing activist and city councillor George Cole, there is a regional rift that rests on the economy and has created a rigidly segregated social and environmental landscape in which one finds all waste incinerators, most of the solid waste, and all of the planned prisons on the eastern half of the divide while prosperity and cleaner environments are found in the west.[35]

It has only begun to dawn on the inhabitants of Los Angeles' Westside, where the boosterist narratives of the region originate, that the deprived inhabitants of the east of the urban area have started to organize themselves as autonomous agents in the restructuring process. The east is objecting more and more to becoming the literal garbage dump of Southern California. The local state and movement-based politics in the hub cities described in this section may be a model for this reorientation. The activities of the local governments of West Hollywood and Santa Monica are limited in their autonomy more by the enormous growth pressure on their communities through international capital than by the pressures imposed by the local structured coherence. Cities like Bell or Cudahy tell a different story. Here the regional political and economic structure operates as a spatialized regulating institution which structures the entire urban area in favor of the bourgeois hegemony of the Westside and to the detriment of the Eastside. Internationalization in the east does not mean investment from the Far East or Europe into glittering office complexes but massive immigration from the Third World, gambling casinos, multinational crime. Whereas in the west the internationalization of the networks of capital, transportation and telecommunications threaten existing community-based urban infrastructures, the east is under the threat of becoming a giant garbage dump and sink for pollution as well as an emergency ward for the infrastructure crisis of the urban region. Where they are not themselves part of the globalized power structure of the capitalist mega-economy, the middle classes of the west fulfill a veritable comprador function in relation to the east.

## EPILOGUE: THIS IS COMPTON

In the widely differentiated global marketplace of interurban competition, local states use the Olympics, cultural palaces or creative industries in order to increase their market value. The entrepreneurialism governing city politics today has legitimated almost any means for cities to put themselves onto the maps of global recognition. The city of Compton, south of Los Angeles, and number 12 on the list of the poorest suburbs in the United States, has entered the fray on a different note. The city is hardly capable of cutting a competitive edge for itself via innovative city marketing in hypercompetitive Southern California. The municipality – notorious gang territory with a murder rate rivalling that of Detroit and Miami – spends 70% of its budget on 'public safety'. The police force of Compton, which is financed through this money, has gained a reputation as bad as the one of the LAPD in Los Angeles proper. Police brutality has been an ongoing issue in the Latino, Samoan and African American communities. Devoid of an industrial base, the city's main source of revenue has been an ever-increasing property tax rate which makes the city a clear loser in the region's municipal universe (structured after the Lakewood Plan). A series of political corruption cases and shady redevelopment schemes have not helped to improve the reputation of Compton in Southern California and in the world (Davis, 1994b).[36]

Compton's place on our urban map owes itself less to the policies of the local state than to its economic success on the world market, which forced widespread recognition of the city's socioeconomic realities. As a murderous center of gang activity,[37] where Crips and Bloods and related gangs (African American, Latino and Samoan) are fighting for the control of territory and markets, Compton has

*Plate 10.10* Compton Fashion Center (Roger Keil)

become the unrivalled world headquarters of hiphop music, particularly in its 'gangsta rap' version. When the rap group N(iggers) W(ith) A(ttitude) from Compton sold half a million copies of its album 'Straight Outta Compton' in the summer of 1989 without much radio play, a flood of defiant self-stylization was triggered in the world-forsaken community. The creation of communal identity was achieved through a decidedly antiestablishmentarian attitude which expressed itself in blunt realist style and with an unapologetically capitalist sales strategy. Jumping on the NWA bandwagon, other bands like Above the Law and Compton's Most Wanted cemented the image of Compton as the ultimate gangster haven. NWA individual career spinoffs of the late Eazy E. and Ice Cube helped create an entire industry of inverted Compton marketing. In neighboring communities, a multicultural hiphop scene developed with Samoans Boo-Yaa TRIBE and Chicano Kid Frost contributing to the early hype of the south and east of Los Angeles. In contrast to the conscious simulacra of the marketing strategies of West Hollywood and Santa Monica, and in contrast to the class-based community strategy of the hub cities, the rappers of Compton have subscribed to an allegedly unmediated representation of stark reality and truth meant to give identity to the inhabitants and to the place of Compton. This strategy of the specific place is able to create positive identity from the deliberately delinquent life of the 'gangsta'. Mirroring the territorial logic of gangland, the hiphop strategy is ultimately an exercise in claiming space in the territorial jungle of the world city whose hegemony is structured against the population and the local state of Compton: 'I claim Compton', runs one line in Compton's Most Wanted's 'This Is Compton'. The reality strategy aims towards the production of visibility in a situation of complete marginalization and criminalization. It is the inversion of Compton's southern neighbor Carson's internationalization strategy which targets global business investment with images of a peaceful multinational community. In Compton, distinction is achieved through claiming the hood as the natural home territory of horror. While other local states have marketed themselves as localities of innovation, stability and success, Compton's global music market handlers sell the city as the home of the drive-by-shooting: 'It's the Compton Thang'.[38]

# CHAPTER 11
# POLITICS AND RIOTS

Men at arms shout, 'Who goes there?'
We have journeyed far from here
Armed with bibles make us swear

. . .

Flags are flying dollar bills,
From the heights of concrete hills
you can see the pinnacles

. . .

In the streets of many walls
Here the peasants come and crawl
You can hear their numbers called

. . .

Screaming people fly so fast
In their shiny metal cars
through the woods of steel and glass

The Rolling Stones, 'Citadel'

## REBELLION: RIOT IS THE LANGUAGE OF THE UNHEARD

Tom Bradley's impossible dream ended in the afternoon of the April 29, 1992. In Simi Valley, in the north of Los Angeles, a jury consisting entirely of whites, with the exception of one Asian man, acquitted four white policemen, who on the night of March 3, 1991, had beaten African American Rodney King so brutally he almost died. The beating had been caught on tape by an amateur videographer and would soon be broadcast to millions of people around the world. Warren Christopher, a lawyer who was chair of a commission on the Los Angeles Police Department (later called the Christopher Commission), wrote in his diary on that fateful April afternoon in 1992 that the verdict was unbelievable, and riots could be expected (Dunne, 1991). As we now know, Christopher's premonitions proved to be correct: in the four days following the verdict, Los Angeles erupted into the gravest civil unrest the city has seen in this century.

On May 4, after almost all of the 623 documented fires had been extinguished (initial press reports had spoken of 5000 fires), 60 people had been killed (perhaps 'only' 45 of them in immediate connection to the violence in the street), 10 having been killed by security forces and another 2383 people counted as injured. The estimated damage was $1 billion. In Koreatown alone, more than 300 stores had been set on fire or looted. Twenty thousand jobs had disappeared; 5000 were considered long-term losses. Eight hundred and fifty families had been made homeless as a consequence of the rioting (*LAT*, 1992; ACLU, 1992). Between April 29 and May 5, 12 545 arrests were reported; 51% of those arraigned were Latino, 36% were African American.

The police forces of the city and the county were joined by the National Guard and by the Marines in their effort to control the imposed curfew (ACLU, 1992). Mike Davis, who experienced the riots as an eyewitness, estimated that 40 000– 50 000 persons participated actively and 200 000 passively in the uprising (Davis, 1992b: 17). Many thousands helped in the rebuilding efforts right after the event and more than 30 000 people joined in a peace march through Koreatown.

There have been countless explanations, experiences, anecdotes, statistics and polemics in the wake of the uprising. I will touch on only a few of them in the following section. This discussion is guided by the question of whether the discourse on the formation of a world city in Los Angeles, as discussed throughout this book, has anything to offer by way of an explanation for the riots in 1992.

## PROGRESSIVE POLITICS AND SOCIAL MOVEMENTS: LABOR, COMMUNITY, ENVIRONMENT

> The immigrant working class does not simply submit to the city for the purposes of capital, it is not merely the collective victim of 'urban crisis'; it also strives to transform and create the city, its praxis is a material force, however unrecognized or invisible in most accounts of contemporary Los Angeles (Davis, 1987: 78).

> 'The worker as a victim' was a concept the Campaign came across in all its work and angrily and aggressively worked to combat. . . . It was the workers' political decision that an aggressive, confident stance – 'the worker as an organizer, the worker as fighter, the UAW taking on General Motors', and not 'the worker as victim' – that would attract the allies necessary to challenge the corporation (Mann, 1987: 176–178).

Press reports on the 1992 riots depicted a situation of destruction of both the built environment and the civility of Los Angeles. In the popular media, the impression of an epidemic social pathology was nurtured. The end of the American Dream of multiculturalism had already been stated before the Rodney King verdict. Los Angeles, which had just advanced from the position of trendsetter to paradigmatic laboratory of urban research, receded practically overnight to its previously held niche as the poorly understood, inexplicable Moloch at the margins of American history (Wilkinson, 1991; Reinhold, 1992; Campbell, 1992a, b). The repeated representation of Los Angeles as the protoplasm of urban pathology and violence in this context served – perhaps not without intention – to eclipse the humanistic aspects of civil society in Los Angeles. There was little discussion, at the time, about how it was possible that a society as diverse as that of Los Angeles had been able to sustain itself in the pressure cooker of globalization and restructuring without erupting into full-scale social violence before 1992. In all common depictions, Angelenos/as as social activists, everyday antiracists, class-conscious trade unionists or defenders of their living environments were completely disregarded. This chapter is dedicated to those people who are instrumental in maintaining the latent antihegemonic civility and quotidian humanity of the urban region.

In the Fordist mass industries, as well as in the new (or renewed) 'crafts industries' of Los Angeles, workers have expressed their interests collectively during the restructuring processes of the past two decades and have influenced the trajectory of this process. They have often done so using innovative strategies of organizing and action. One has been a new brand of social unionism created by linking the concerns of the labor movement with those of oppressed communities. These strategies challenge the specific rupture in the complementary arrangements of city and factory caused by the crisis of Fordism. As conditions in workplaces and neighborhoods have changed, so have the lines of social struggle and social compromise. In particular, the internationalization of the working class during this period of restructuring has increased the need for new forms of social regulation. In the course of this development, the characteristically American separation of the politics of the workplace from the politics of community has also been questioned.

Social movements, community groups, neighborhood associations and labor unions have contributed to politicize and civilize the terrain in Los Angeles. In particular, the convergence of territorial and workplace-related movement segments in Los Angeles during the 1980s and 1990s, the struggle of a labor and community coalition against the closing of the General Motors (GM) plant in Van Nuys, the community-oriented strategy of labor organizers in the garment industry during the late 1980s in downtown Los Angeles, the movement for community economic development tied to the struggle against the destruction of housing in south Los Angeles, and the environmental justice activism of the 1990s can be cited as movements against the grain of restructuring, racism, oppression and injustice – the very causes of the 1992 rebellion.

At the root of these experiences is the distinctive experience of American society 'that the linguistic, cultural, and institutional meaning given to the differentiation of work and community, a characteristic of all industrial capitalist societies, has taken a sharply divided form, and that it has done so for a very long time' (Katznelson, 1981: 19). Yet, over the past two decades in Los Angeles, there was also a countervailing force which created much interethnic solidarity and interracial unity usually unnoticed by the common depiction of the 1992 events. One such experience was the struggle of labor and community groups in Van Nuys, in the north of the city, to keep the local GM plant open. The disappearance of jobs in the automobile industry of Los Angeles since the 1970s did not occur without the resistance of workers and industrial communities (Haas and Morales, 1986; Haas, 1985). An extensive social movement against the closures modified or even halted the local effects of what had become known as the 'deindustrialization of America' (Bluestone and Harrison, 1982). Workers realized that the total elimination of the tire or steel industries in Los Angeles could be averted only if local movements overcame the traditional separation of individual workplaces in specific plants. The need for more cooperation among locals was exacerbated by the continuously decreasing degree of organization in Southern California: the labor movement was caught in the double dynamics of receding unionized Fordist employment and increasing nonunion operations of the new economy. While defending their jobs, workers had to come to grips with the end of Fordist mass production in its traditional form, a change which left industrial sociologists and organizers alike scrambling for alternatives.

Two main trends developed from the struggle of individual locals against the closures of the first big wave of deindustrialization in the United States: first, the economic crisis drove the labor movement from its traditional arena of the workplace into the community. Second, in this process the role of labor unions as social agents was extended. They changed from being narrowly defined collective bargaining institutions to being initiators of economic development. During the first phase of plant closings, the labor movement became active in community economic development primarily in order to maintain traditional standards in the community and on the shop floor. This phase was also characterized by the readiness of unions to make concessions and the pressure of blackmail through ultimatums by corporations threatening to pack up and leave. Only hesitantly did workers start to develop common strategies of resistance with local institutions and local government. More effective forms of resistance and more positive demands were directed at the corporations (Haas and Morales, 1986: 23–26).

In 1982 in Van Nuys, the threat by GM that it would shut down its local assembly plant, which had been in the community since 1948, brought forth strong local resistance. The Labor/Community Coalition to Keep GM Van Nuys Open went beyond the more defensive tactics of the previous movements in Los Angeles. In Van Nuys, activists were deliberate in their attempt to counter what they considered a 'retreat lifted to the level of strategy' in other plant-closing fights. A militant group of workers and community leaders decided to take on the fight with GM. At the Van Nuys plant during the mid-1980s, 4800 workers assembled Camaros and Firebirds – cars which enjoyed continuing success on the marketplace despite their traditional gas-guzzling design. Until its closure in the summer of 1992 the factory was the last entirely American auto production in California (at one time the second-most important production location in the United States after Michigan).[1]

Locally, resistance against GM gained momentum quickly after the 1982 announcement. In only a few months, the Coalition to Keep GM Van Nuys Open emerged on a broad base of community and shop-floor support. Next to the workers stood more than 200 well-known individuals from churches, the labor movement and minority groups. This coalition rejected the plant closing and possible concessions and threatened GM with preventive activities and a possible boycott of GM products in the Southland in the event of a closure. In addition, they demanded that GM keep open the Van Nuys factory for at least 10 more years (Mann, 1987: 10), when production of Camaros and Firebirds moved entirely to GM's location in St Thérèse, Quebec.

The Coalition to Keep GM Van Nuys Open reacted offensively and directly to the threat of the plant closing. By organizing 'community' along class lines, the coalition superseded the specific spatial conditions of reproduction typical of the area's Fordist past which had taken workers united on the shop floor and segregated them in fractured communities outside of the plant.

Emphasizing the civil rights aspects of the campaign was a reaction both to the traditional practice of segregation in the labor movement itself and to the changing material situation that the movement had to confront in Los Angeles in the 1980s. The internationalized character of the workforce determined the politics of civil rights at the workplace and in the neighborhood. The campaign defined 'community' in a way that exploded the narrow spatial and ethnic connotations usually associated with the term. By realizing that it was practically impossible to

**Plate 11.1**   *Demonstration against plant closing Van Nuys, 1986 (Roger Keil)*

define the spatial dimensions of community radially or in any other pattern *around* the plant when a large number of workers commuted from places up to 60 miles away, the campaign activists created a new understanding of the space of community as the region. The multiethnic and multiracial composition of the workers made it necessary to think of 'community' as a concept that *transcended* the sociospatial patchwork of Southern California rather than *reproducing* it. 'The core of the movement was the alliance between the GM workers and the black and Chicano communities. It was the successful integration of the issues of class and race that gave the coalition its vitality and power (. . .) In every city, regardless of the specific objectives and demands, the ability of workers, many of whom are themselves black, Latino, or Asian, to ally with minority communities and organizations is critical' (Mann, 1987: 376–377). This way the campaign could overcome some of the traditional American exceptionalist separations of residence and workplace which had been exacerbated by Fordism. The narrow, and sometimes parochial, concept of 'community', typical of many struggles in the United States, was, in the case of the campaign, exchanged for a more inclusive socioterritorial concept of urban struggles. Finally, the coalition acted as regional planners from below in that it did not restrict its politics to the narrow issue of job loss, but approached the problem of the plant closing in a more comprehensive fashion.

## LABOR AND LIVING: SOCIAL UNIONISM IN THE GARMENT INDUSTRY OF LOS ANGELES COUNTY

One of the crafts-based and flexibilized production sectors of Southern California that expanded in the 1980s and consolidated its position in the 1990s is the garment industry, concentrated in downtown Los Angeles. For decades after it was introduced into the region, the garment sector in Los Angeles was a relatively stable industry, locationally and socially. But its internationalization and restructuring confronted the union with a host of new problems. Decreasing organization rates reflected the national trend, and the changing composition of the local working class negatively affected the conditions for successful labor union activity of the traditional kind (formerly composed mostly of Jewish-European skilled craftsmen and women, the industry had come to be dominated by a predominantly female, unskilled workforce of immigrants from Latin America, China, Vietnam and Korea). Whereas in the 1940s, when total employment in this sector was only 19 000, the International Ladies' Garment Workers Union (ILGWU) had 15 000 members in 1987 (Ferraro, 1988), only 2000 workers (1200 of whom were directly employed in the garment sector) were under contract with this union (Olney, 1987a). In 1995 the ILGWU joined forces nationally with the Amalgamated Clothing and Textile Workers Union to form UNITE, the Union of Needletraders, Industrial and Textile Employees, and had merely about 4000–5000 members in all of the western states (Mulligan, 1995). Union foes even claimed that 'among L.A.'s approximately 150 000 garment workers' in 1997, 'Unite has no more than 500 members in the entire region' (Kotkin, 1997: 3). The idea of the 'unorganizability' of poor, female, immigrant workers took hold, and was nurtured by theoretical and academic considerations which focussed on the labor market situation and on the legal vulnerability of undocumented workers. Immigrant workers were widely considered to be easily manipulable and fair game for ravenous employers in a volatile marketplace (Soja, Morales and Wolff, 1983: 219). Union organizers in Los Angeles did not accept this interpretation. While it is correct that the garment sector recruits its workforce from the vulnerable pool of immigrant labor, the assumption that these workers are unorganizable and easily manipulated does not necessarily hold. Nevertheless, the organization of workers of different nationalities and cultures and varying (or nonexistent) traditions of workplace militancy is a difficult and long-term challenge (Olney, 1987b: 24).

Even a minimum program of union organization within sectors having a strong immigrant workforce needed to address more than just work-related issues. It included demands for health insurance for workers and their families, for affordable housing, for an amnesty for undocumented immigrants and a raised minimum wage (Olney and Keil, 1988). In each of these areas, the labor union was dependent on support from the communities that sustained the industry. One example was the statewide campaign to raise the minimum wage in California to $5.01 which had the support of local labor movement activists and from neighborhood-based groups in Los Angeles. Much of the dynamics of this activism came from three local groups of the Industrial Areas Foundation (founded by Saul Alinsky) which were firmly rooted in Latino and African American inner-city neighborhoods and churches. The Alinsky organizations – the South Central Organizing Committee (SCOC), the United Neighborhood Organization (UNO) and the East Valley Organization (EVO) – represented more than 130 000 churchgoers, most of them from East Los Angeles. They were politically independent and aspired to be multiracial and multiclass in their composition. Yet, the majority of their members resided in the Latino east and the African American south of Los

Angeles. Of the members of SCOC, 98% were African American or Latino, a reflection of the residential population of the neighborhoods where SCOC was active. The Alinsky groups had built their argument for an increase of the minimum wage mostly on the fact that a family of three with an annual income based on the previous minimum wage of $3.35 had to live on an income that fell $2100 below the official poverty line. The statewide campaign to increase the minimum wage was accompanied by local demonstrations and other direct actions that attempted to influence employers in affected industries.

The work of labor unions in the internationalized low-wage sectors is directed towards those urban communities where their members and potential members live, where their children go to school and where they satisfy their social needs like health care. This way, they participate in creating the social structures of the world city. In both cases, in the barely organized garment industry and in the struggle against the closure of GM Van Nuys, the redefinition of the relationship of workplace and residence (or class and community) was a central feature of the forms of resistance against the policies of the local state apparatus (from the school district to settlement agencies) and exploitative employers. Rather, in paraphrasing Eric Mann, one can conclude that the architects of global capitalism in the centers of economic power and in the citadels of the world cities will have to reckon with the worker as organizer, the worker as fighter and the unions as serious opponents. This strategic strength of workers in the global city is complemented by the active role of social movements and political groups in the neighborhood.

## THE BULLDOZERS STOP HERE: IN DEFENSE OF NEIGHBORHOOD

> From the point of view of residents, the creation and defense of the use values of neighborhood is the central urban question (Logan and Molotch, 1987: 99).

The influx of redevelopment-assisted international capital into downtown Los Angeles has equalled an attack on the residences of thousands of working-class and middle-class people.[2] The limited power of disconnected community struggles to influence the dominant power of global capitalist companies in their insatiable hunger for horizontal and vertical space has usually been taken for granted. Some of the communities (Little Tokyo, Pico Union, Skid Row and Route 2) that had taken up the fight against elimination through downtown expansion 'have served as unwitting land banks for future corporate development schemes, and are struggling to stay afloat in the wake of their irrelevance to present corporate needs' (Haas and Heskin, 1981: 550). Yet there is more to this story.

The northern stretches of south-central Los Angeles have been going through struggles over proposed and real changes in land use. An area which stretches from the Santa Monica Freeway in the north to 41st Street and Martin-Luther-King-Jr Boulevard in the south and from Figueroa Street in the west to Alameda Street in the east, was designated by the state of California as an enterprise zone in 1986 (Figure 11.1). The enterprise zone was meant to attract businesses, preferably light

212

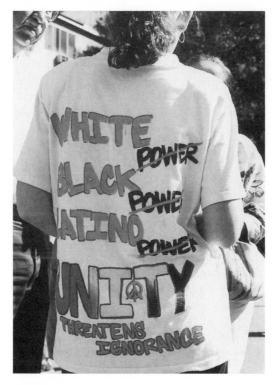

***Plate 11.2***   *Unity Threatens Ignorance (Roger Keil)*

industry. The zone's location near downtown and near the campus of the University of Southern California (USC) has made the area particularly interesting to high-technology development. USC has in many ways been involved in the restructuring of the area: they are a major landowner south of downtown, they provide research staff and even rooms for the coordinator of the enterprise zone. Many people in the community have referred to the zone as 'USC's enterprise zone'. The Central City Enterprise Zone was meant to be integrated into an internationally oriented economy through its emphasis on an industrial growth sector.

Although there is a clear mismatch between the traditional blue-collar work-force resident in the area and the high-tech approach, the labor force – as far as it will be recruited from the area – is part of the new global working class of Los Angeles. The designation of the Central City Enterprise Zone stirred up considerable uneasiness with the area's residents over the future of their neighborhood. In 1987 members of the Saint Vincent de Paul Church in the West Adams area, a chapter of the Alinsky-style SCOC, got together with local residents in the Maple Avenue neighborhood which is part of the enterprise zone to fight a proposed zone change that would have allowed residential land to be turned over to the construction of a garment factory. The zone change, the so-called Maple Avenue Plan Amendment, was introduced by the late City Councilman Gilbert Lindsay, who deemed it necessary 'in order to provide for

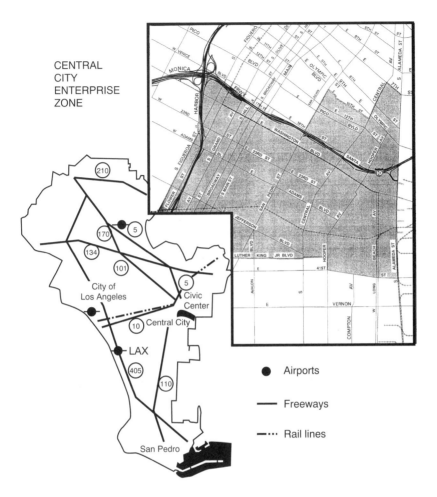

**Figure 11.1**  *Central City Enterprise Zone (Courtesy Community Development Department, City of Los Angeles)*

the economic survival of the garment manufacturing business within the City of Los Angeles' (quoted in Harris, 1987a). The concrete project that had made the council office become active was the plan of the Kluger garment factory to relocate from their downtown production site into the Maple Avenue area. The proposal took two beatings by the City Planning Commission in 1986 and 1987 and was finally withdrawn by the councilman in February 1988, when 1000 people showed up to protest at a Planning and Environment Committee meeting of Los Angeles City Council.

The office of the city councilman and the coordinator of the enterprise zone stressed the necessity of an expansion of space for existing downtown industries and new investment (Harris, 1987a). In stark contrast to what was conceived by the proponents of such growth as a grand design to cope with inner-city problems of unemployment and poverty, officials detected a NIMBY attitude among local residents. Yet, opponents of the city's plans, facing the possibility of 3000 homes lost through the implementation of the enterprise zone, changed the discourse of the conflict. Instead of taking a defensive stance of 'homes versus jobs', they demanded a comprehensive understanding of their neighborhood as a live/work community: 'We, the St. Vincent/SCOC want to have a say/input about the *kind of factories* and economic development that will come into the Enterprise Zone and *where* those developments will be located' (St Vincent de Paul Church, 1987).

These were two differing concepts regarding the use of urban space. Local residents claimed a voice in *how* their area was to be integrated into the new globalized space-economy of Los Angeles. The mostly Latino working-class community in the Maple Avenue area succeeded in changing the course and the discourse of the conflict, stopping the plan amendment that would have destroyed many of their homes. They established themselves as a political force which the grand architects of the global city had to reckon with.

## THE STRUGGLE FOR ENVIRONMENTAL JUSTICE

More recently, Los Angeles has become one of the major sites for the nascent environmental justice movement in the United States (see Pulido, 1996b). One of the major organizations to focus on the relationship of social class, race and gender to environmental and human health has been the Labor/Community Watchdog, founded by the Labor/Community Strategy Center. This group has been very successful in contextualizing issues of political emancipation and economic justice in environmental discourses. Since publishing the study *L.A.'s Lethal Air* (Mann, 1991), the Watchdog has become a fixture in urban environmental politics in Los Angeles. This book casts the struggle against the proposals of the 1989 Air Quality Management Plan in terms of a critique of the social relationships which cause and result from the environmental situation in Los Angeles.

The 1989 Air Quality Management Plan laid out a program to clean up the south coast air basins during the next two decades. Its more than 120 measures were equally universal and specific in their appeal to change local styles of production and consumption. Their expected repercussions would have equalled a redefinition of the basic tenets of the Fordist consumer city: the automobile culture and the suburban life-style. In its proposed form, however, the Air Quality Management Plan would have strengthened and not weakened the power of increasingly internationalized capital in the region. It was the most comprehensive attempt at establishing a clean and mean post-Fordist urban environment and – despite the almost insurmountable odds it faced down the road – the sharpest tool yet to define a mechanism for regional government in Southern California.

Yet, the clean air utopia totalized the urban experience into a single narrative under the ideological battle cry of a purified environment. In an area where the environment is absurdly fragmented into places with good or bad air, more or less pure water, 'dirty' and 'clean' industries, incinerators and frozen yogurt shops, the myth of a clean *every*-topia served as a giant smokescreen hiding divisive political, social and spatial contradictions. For the myth of 'clean air' implied the non-existence of these contradictions. Cleaning the air, in the eyes of the Watchdog, had to be viewed as first and foremost a public health issue and social equity issue and as a clear priority for decision-makers in Los Angeles. The Watchdog has been aiming at social change and political emancipation through environmental politics. *L.A.'s Lethal Air* begins where the Air Quality Management Plan of 1989 left off. It shows that the air is not the same for everyone in Los Angeles and that the pollution or the protection of natural resources (and of human communities) does not have the same price everywhere in the urban region. The study showed that the official plan overlooked both the social differences undergirding the general problem of air pollution and the differentials in damage done to individual communities in the Los Angeles air basin. The demand for clean air, therefore, was linked to the call for social justice and political democracy. When, for example, Los Angeles County intended to create a negative incentive for its 40 000 employees to carpool by introducing parking fees, although the collective agreement stated that employee parking was to be free, the Watchdog and other organizations showed that in the absence of a viable alternative in public transportation, the workers would, in fact, have to pay a fee to go to work. While this issue, which emerged from discussions on the Air Quality Management Plan's Regulation 15, put the Watchdog on the map of environmental politics in Los Angeles, the organization won its biggest victory in December of 1991 by forcing the AQMD to hold a special hearing on the effect of toxics in communities located close to major polluters. Another central site of struggle in which the Watchdog attached an emancipatory strategy to environmental concerns was its attempt – however unsuccessful – to subject the appointed board of the AQMD to more democratic representation and procedures.

Since the mid-1990s, the Labor/Community Strategy Center (L/CSC) has turned its attention away from the Air Quality Management Plan – which it saw increasingly out of the reach of democratic challenge due to the market orientation of the 1991–97 plans (see Keil and Desfor, 1996). Instead, this organization has become instrumental in organizing a Bus Riders' Union (BRU) in Los Angeles in an attempt to represent the interests of low-income customers of the Metropolitan Transportation Agency. While this struggle reconnects the L/CSC with its civil rights tradition, it also maintains the environmental aspects of public transportation as its mandate in fighting for the rights of the poor. Meanwhile, the environmental justice movement has had additional organizing successes. On important case in point has been the Communities for a Better Environment (CBE)/La Causa who have rallied around an agenda of social liberation and environmentalism. In a prominent case, CBE together with local communities and politicians, fought the pollution caused by a commercial construction waste facility in a poor residential neighborhood in Huntington Park in the southeast of Los Angeles (Bacon, 1994).

Each of the campaigns of the L/CSC bore the characteristics of those movements which Christopherson (1994: 423) sees as having 'the ability to transcend narrow community boundaries'. In fact, the multiracial, labor-oriented strategy of the L/CSC has constantly redefined the meaning of community 'from the bottom up' and through the eyes of the various working-class communities in Southern California. The core of each of the L/CSC's campaigns has been an anti-hegemonic appropriation of the political space of the urban area: from the shop floor at GM to the airshed in the Southland, from working-class residential communities to the transit routes in the communities of color, the L/CSC's politics have established

***Plate 11.3*** *Demonstration of Bus Riders Union, MTA Building 1996 (Roger Keil)*

new spatial meanings. Like the L/CSC, other community groups have participated in redefining their political space innovatively. In almost all such cases there is an aspect of territoriality and political control over space involved. A slew of initiatives to renaturalize and resocialize the Los Angeles River and to make it an axis for community development along its banks as well as a current research and action project of the Department of Urban Planning at the University of California, the Los Angeles Manufacturing Action Project (LAMAP) which seeks to organize workers along the industrial Alameda corridor in Los Angeles' industrial core, are cases in point.

These (and other) cases of applied insurgent civility have usually been left out of the analysis of social relationships in Los Angeles, particularly out of common interpretations of the 1992 uprising. I have argued here that what happened in those few days in April and May 1992 has to be seen against the attempt by many antiracist, labor, community, church and environmental groups to create an alternative Los Angeles. The riots of 1992 did not make these politics irrelevant, but highlighted their importance in the face of the breakdown of the official plans for the formation of the 'world city'.

## CONTINUITY AND CHANGE: IMMISERATION, WORLD CITY FORMATION AND THE SPARK OF VIOLENCE

A generation passed between the uprising of Watts 1965 and the rebellion of April 1992. In these 27 years, Los Angeles changed its face. A majority white city with small black and Latino minorities became an international melting pot, a world city with a nonwhite majority. One thing that did not change – or rather, did not improve – was the social situation of the African American poor in Los Angeles.

***Plate 11.4*** *Riot is the language of the unheard; mural in South Central Los Angeles (Roger Keil)*

Unemployment, gang violence, homelessness, drugs and the destruction of residential spaces have assumed catastrophic proportions in the traditional black south-central areas of the urban region. While community networks based on churches and schools have continually diminished in significance as social stabilizers, south-central Los Angeles has become a storage space for people of color unneeded by the larger economy of the world city (Hamilton, 1988).

The Watts uprising highlighted with a bang the crisis of the Fordist arrangement of Southern California. The black working class had been integrated into the Keynesian social contract only incompletely; the black population remained segregated at the margins of the American society. The burning bungalows in August of 1965 underscored this situation in no uncertain terms. Yet, whereas black impoverishment and cultural and racist exclusion continue to be a constant of misery in Los Angeles (Johnson and Oliver, 1993; Oliver, Johnson and Farrell, 1993; Scott and Brown, 1993), the situation has also changed dramatically: Watts and similar riots in the 1960s like those in Detroit or Newark were a reaction by African American inner-city residents against the repressive power of white America; in contrast, the rebellion of 1992 was the first full-scale explosion of a multinational metropolis, in which the black–white antagonism was only one – albeit an essential – moment.

The geography of racism in Los Angeles involves not just the drawing of borders around the residential neighborhoods of the people of color – at times enforced in police raids, neighborhood sieges, curfews and street closings – but also the deliberate distancing of the minority white middle-class population from the rest of the city. The white middle classes have increasingly left the central lowlands for the coasts and desert valleys where many have barricaded themselves in gated communities and cultural homogeneity. The acquittals of Simi Valley were pronounced from the milieu of white exurbia, the most visible built environment of racism. Rather than leaving the city behind by moving to the desert frontier, the white middle classes continue to impose their hegemony over the central city where many of them still work, study or consume entertainment. The skyscraper-dotted citadel of downtown Los Angeles was built up to its current scale only after the flight to the desert suburbs had already begun. The destruction and marginal-ization of inner-city residential neighborhoods, and the erection of bank towers and domiciles of the newly internationalized business services of downtown Los Angeles (and edge centres such as Century City), went hand in hand with the exurbanization of the region's white middle class.

The retreat of the white middle class was accompanied by the consolidation of poverty in the inner city. Deindustrialization heightened unemployment in the African American neighborhoods in South Central, particularly among an entire generation of black teenagers. Latino immigrants, on the other hand, tended to be included into the new low-wage industries of Southern California. A new type of working poor emerged in the world city. African Americans and Latinos are today concentrated in the south and east of the city. Their residential areas are subject to ceaseless attacks as a result of planning phantasies and speculative real estate activities. Only a few years before the rebellion of 1992, Cynthia Hamilton (1988) wrote that South Central was threatened to be extinguished by the historical process without leaving a trace, and that its land would be cleared and developed by a newer, whiter class of people. The already visible result of these dynamics has been the production of a 'Bantustan' on American territory. One project follows the next to prepare the ground of the ghetto and the barrio for a use other than that of being a home for poor people: waste incinerators, prisons, garment factories, university expansion, freeway construction and downtown extension. After the destruction of 1992, Rebuild LA continued this tradition.

Parts of the working classes of Los Angeles appear as the locally incarcerated surplus population of the global economy; others have become integrated into the new structure of precarious jobs and minimum wages. Left behind and concen-trated in the structural misery of the ghetto and in the barrio, both fragments of the urban proletariat have had an increasingly hard time surviving in the region. In South Central unemployment runs at about 50%; among those who find work, the fastest growing labor market segment has been in sales where wages average $4.75 an hour. The annual income of black high school graduates dropped by 44% between 1973 and 1986; the corresponding figure for Latinos is 35%. Compared to the rest of the city, twice as many families in South Central were below the poverty line in 1990; this figure is 30.3% higher than at the time of the Watts riots (Rutten, 1992a).

## WHAT KIND OF AN UPRISING?

The shock following the series of riots that made some American cities into a home front of the Vietnam War in the 1960s triggered a number of commissions of inquiry which tried to explain the racist foundations of American society and to find remedies for an explosive situation. The rebellion of 1992 differed from these historical examples in three ways. First, there were already entire libraries replete with analyses and models that could help explain what had happened; second, there was no shock because after the acquittal of the four white policemen in the Rodney King case, there was no need to search for immediate causes, nor was there reason for surprise; and third, the commissions poised to provide explanation were already in place and the effort to rebuild Los Angeles could be engaged in right away. After the brutalities committed against Rodney King in March 1991, a fact-finding commission under the chair of Warren Christopher had been founded. In their report, the Christopher Commission lambasted the racist practices of the Los Angeles Police Department. At the same time, Peter Ueberroth, former head of the Olympics in Los Angeles and baseball commissioner, a market-oriented Republican from Orange County, had just delivered his report on the restructuring of the California economy to California Governor Pete Wilson. Before the last fires in Los Angeles were put out, Ueberroth's public–private development agency, Rebuild LA was already cleaning up the debris.

Among the general explanations often given for the uprising are the restructuring of the US economy, institutionalized racism, Reaganist urban policies, austerity policies on all government levels, etc. We can add a few local peculiarities to this catalogue of contextual causalities. As demonstrated in the preceding pages, Los Angeles has been both a synonym for the historical development of capitalism and its maverick challenger. In this sense, the city has recently been at once the most vivid expression of the crisis of American Fordism, and also the experimental field of new urban and regional modes of regulation. An essential feature of these new developments has been the globalization of the city which has led Los Angeles astray from the trajectory of American urbanism. A new urban world has emerged. Conversely, one can argue that globalization has prompted a redefinition of the very concept of the 'American city'.

Although many commentators agree that the events of 1992 differed from those in 1965 in a variety of ways (Baldassare, 1994), most publications on the riots have operated with images of American cities etched into our collective mind during the post-World War II era. These are comfortable images because they suggest a simple understanding of the events: the ghettoization of African Americans, the suburbanization of the white middle class, racism and police brutality are the terms we carry in our tool bag from the previous round of urban uprisings in the 1960s.[3] These terms were ready to use and seemed to fit here and there in the analysis of the 1992 uprising, but they were ultimately apt to fog our view on the reality of contemporary Los Angeles. Literal black and white thinking is not sufficient for the interpretation of what happened in 1992 (see Figure 11.2).

Analyses of the events ranged from the conservative rejection of the violence in the streets to a glorification of the uprising, from the label of 'the first rainbow uprising' to its denunciation as social nihilism and Hobbesian war of all against all (Davis, 1992a, b; Gooding-Williams, 1993; Institute for Alternative Journalism, 1992; Jah and Shah'Keyah, 1995; Johnson and Oliver, 1993; Mayer, 1992; Ruddick and Keil, 1992). Although the event that immediately triggered the uprising was the verdict of a white jury acquitting white policemen who had brutalized a black man, the uprising was mostly seen as a multicultural affair. A multiethnic coalition of disenfranchised and poor people had blown off some steam by attacking the

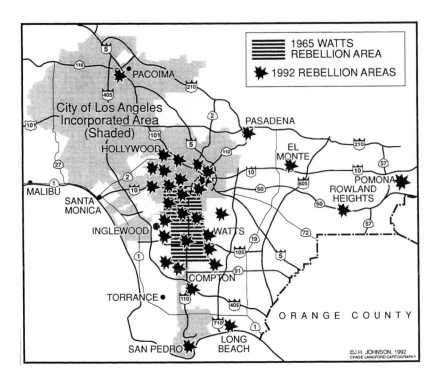

**Figure 11.2** *Comparison of Flash Point Locations in the 1965 Watts and 1992 Los Angeles Rebellion (Source: Johnson and Oliver, 1993: 9; courtesy of the authors)*

symbols and institutions of their oppression in the new Los Angeles. And they had done so in an area not as spatially restricted as Watts but in places as far apart as Pacoima in the north, Pomona in the east and San Pedro in the south of the urban region (Johnson and Oliver, 1993). Tim Rutten (1992a) detected a new kind of riot because of the event's geographic extension and the ethnic composition of the rioters. Cynthia Hamilton (1992) assumed that Los Angeles had joined the list of cities where IMF-triggered austerity riots had taken place earlier in the 1980s.

Mike Davis correctly points out that looking for singular essentialist modes of explanations for the events of 1992 would prove unsuccessful. For black youth, the uprising was a struggle for their civil rights; for the Korean merchants whose stores were looted and burnt, it was a pogrom; and for the city's poor, it was a protest against bad times (Davis, 1992b). While the riots of the 1960s had been ontologized as necessary and historically placeable events in the life of the Black Liberation Movement, the 1992 uprising does not find as comfortable a place in the history books.

Any attempt to streamline our understanding of 'the riots' into *one* singular explanation (such as the two-nations thesis of the Kerner Commission 25 years earlier) cannot succeed (Gooding-Williams, 1993). If this were tried, failure and ridicule would be imminent in the face of a tremendously diverse reality (and its diverging readings). Analytical unidimensionality appeals mostly to those in power: 'The system is intellectually limited; it can "think" only one thought at a time' (Omi and Winant, 1993: 101). Instead, the inherent fragmentation of counterhegemonic discourses and explanations can be turned into an asset in the face of a rigid and inflexible power structure which looks for simple explanations (and solutions) in a period of complexity by introducing a newly invigorated discourse of solidarity to the fragmentation. The explanations will remain multiple and contradictory. In keeping with this theme, I want to offer one such partial interpretation, which links the uprising to the specific conditions of world city formation in Los Angeles.

## WORLD CITY POLITICS

To a large degree, progressive politics in Los Angeles has been characterized by a careful dance around the confines of a post-cold war anticommunist climate and an explosive racialized environment. Radical activists have operated in communities which are often more conservative than the activists are themselves. When middle-class radicals took power in combination with tenant and gay rights movements in Santa Monica and West Hollywood, these were exceptions (see Chapter 10). Redbaiting and political repression in the wake of the cold war have not allowed for left-wing groups to operate openly. Consequently, progressive individuals, many of them members of revolutionary groups of all sorts, have submerged their radical agendas to radical populist programs of community action. The absence of party politics at the local level and the predominance of candidate-oriented political campaigns have made it difficult to establish broad progressive agendas. Individualized power brokerage around single policy issues prevails in Los Angeles. Perlman and Hopkins (1996); Hopkins (1995) have identified a large number of innovative community initiatives and up to 200 'innovative grassroots leaders'. While many of these organizations and individuals are tied into the campaigns of Democratic politicians at all levels, their main activity is grassroots mobilization around bread-and-butter issues. The progressive politics movement in Los Angeles has been largely nonideological and often anti-intellectual. While no comprehensive social or ecological program drives progressive politics openly in Los Angeles, politics is strongly characterized by 'catastrophic' policy issues such as drug use, violence, homelessness, the AIDS crisis, the economic collapse of the major industries and the aftermath of the natural and social upheavals of the 1990s.

Progressive politics operates at a numerical disadvantage, at least at the polls. Coalition building, then, is part and parcel of any progressive strategy. While in Los Angeles any reference to social class has been almost inaudible in official political parlance, progressive coalitions have tended to place it at center stage. When Los Angeles progressive activists speak of coalitions, the prefix 'labor/community' is usually implied. In the late 1970s, middle-class activists rushed to east-end communities to lend strategic support to antiplant closing struggles from inside and outside the factories (Donahoe, 1987; Haas, 1985). In the 1980s, community support for the struggle to keep the GM plant in Van Nuys open was considered crucial to the success of the threatened boycott strategy used by the workers (Mann, 1987). Organizing drives of garment workers and janitors in the 1980s and 1990s were built on a program of social unionism which afforded a central role to mostly immigrant inner-city communities. When labor organizers in the 1990s set out to mobilize hundreds of thousands of Los Angeles County manufacturing workers (mostly Latinos), they explicitly built part of their strategy on 'community assets' and existing political infrastructures in immigrant communities (LAMAP, 1995). The rhetoric of labor/community coalitions in Los Angeles usually implies the notion of a cooperation of local working-class activists and residents from communities of color.

In the absence of a metropolitan emancipatory strategy, progressive social activists in Los Angeles have restricted their coalition-building efforts to the mobilization of partial territories and political spaces. The agents in these spaces are not members of any middle segments of urban society, but rather are peripheralized by economic exploitation and racism. In Los Angeles, progressive politics has been the attempt by displaced industrial workers, impoverished and marginalized citizens (and noncitizens) and radical activists to fight the wave of Republicanism and globalization that threatens to wipe them from the landscape of their city.

Racialization and ghettoization in Los Angeles has been a threat to survival for many Angelenos. Los Angeles-style progressive politics has been concerned with basic needs, welfare, police brutality and the survival of children in an unbelievably adverse urban environment. Social struggles have centered around the fight against the dystopian city of *Blade Runner* which was constantly held up as the future alternative to an already bleak urban present. That the *Blade Runner* scenario has been championed as the dystopia of choice by both conservatives and progressives in Los Angeles makes breaking the cycle of doom that has enclosed progressive politics in that city even more difficult.

Let me relativize what I said about the metropolitan view and the apparent lack of middle-class-led progressive coalition-building in Los Angeles. It has not escaped my attention, of course, that this hypothesis runs counter to the existence, between 1973 and 1993, of the tremendous historical achievement of the Bradley electoral coalition of African American and Jewish voters (Sonenshein, 1993). Indeed, this longest and most liberal of all such coalitions in an American city had an enormous impact on progressive politics in Los Angeles. For many years, liberal and left-wing activists from all communities in Los Angeles would work under the umbrella of Bradley's political leadership. However, as the Bradley regime, through its world-class city project, moved closer to serving the coalition's 'silent partner' – international business – and as the Community Redevelopment Agency took over more and more of the negotiation between global capital influx and local concerns, the progressive character of Bradley's coalition withered.

The other qualification I want to make refers to the lack of utopian character in Los Angeles progressive politics. The exceptions, again, are the middle-class communities of Santa Monica and West Hollywood where coalitions of activists and residents from established and marginal middle-class groups have created some degree of symbolic liberation and utopian design linked to urban space- and place-making (Forest, 1995). In these relatively small urban enclaves in the Los Angeles metropolitan area, a specific brand of local progressive politics did not just claim local control over 'the urban'; they also aspired to hold a proactive mediating position between the global and the local. They became negotiators of globalization.

In *Postmodern Geographies*, Soja (1989: 219) speaks of a 'cacophonous silence' when describing the politics of restructuring, and he elaborates: 'For the most part, the restructuring of Los Angeles has proceeded with remarkably little resistance.' Soja's understanding of power and politics is, of course, strongly influenced by Foucault. He follows Foucault in arguing that the 'links between space, knowledge, power, and cultural politics must be seen as both oppressive and enabling, filled not only with authoritarian perils but also with possibilities for community, resistance, and emancipatory change' (Soja, 1996: 87). In the real world of urban (cultural) politics, however, Soja trivializes oppositional thinking and conjures up a tightly controlled hegemonic master space of 'an imposed territoriality of apartheids, ghettos, barrios, reservations, colonies, fortresses, metropoles, citadels, and other trappings that emanate from the center–periphery relation. In this sense, hegemonic power universalizes and *contains* difference in real and imagined spaces and places' (1996: 87). Despite the invocation of radical sub-jectivities, we are incarcerated in a seemingly unbreakable web of hegemony in Soja's political world.

In this section, I have taken a different view. The transition from Fordist to post-Fordist Los Angeles has been characterized by lively, at times violent struggles of social classes and collectives. In the face of economic and political power of the protagonists of restructuring on the side of global capital and the local state, the social and political organizations in the described spectrum have suffered many defeats. Yet, as the narrative of this chapter intended to show, new coalitions of workplace, community, identity and environmental movements in Los Angeles have forced more than negligible concessions. The practical inter-vention of newly assembled movement fragments in Los Angeles represents the latent civility of a multicultural society which has organized itself from the grassroots up and which has attempted – often successfully – to counteract the destructive tendencies of the 'project world city'.

The forced ethnicity of the world city has brought people from all over the globe into immediate urban proximity. In contrast to earlier periods of immigration, however, the classical integration mechanisms of the American melting pot have all but ceased to function properly as a release valve. As part of this dramatic socioeconomic and demographic restructuring, new modes of regulation have come into existence, in which immigrants and natives, the Korean middle class and the African American working class, Chinese bankers and Central American refugees are directly forced into sociospatial relationships with one another. These new proximities are the seams of the regulation of the world city as the typical locality of the globalized world economy. Some of these seams, most visibly the one between African Americans and Koreans, burst in April 1992 (see Figure 11.3).

The forced ethnicity of the world city is not an accidental product of market processes but to a large degree the consequence of local policies. In particular, Tom Bradley's attempt to create a world class city in Los Angeles stood out as a conscious political program in this context. In reality, Bradley's policies –

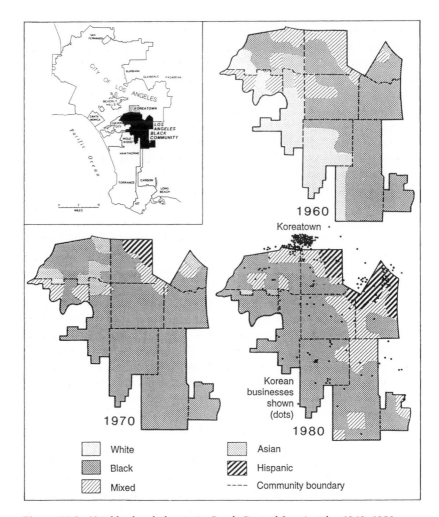

**Figure 11.3** *Neighborhood change in South Central Los Angeles 1960–1980 (Source: Johnson and Oliver, 1993: 13; courtesy of the authors)*

presumably in attempting to marry social integration with complete internationalization – undermined the social contract on which his power was founded. The city's riches were not redistributed in favor of the Latino and African American proletariat but flowed – via community redevelopment and similar mechanisms – into the coffers of the local real estate industry and of multinational corporations, making Los Angeles the second most important urban center after Tokyo on the Pacific Rim. Urban policies partitioned the city into investment zones and created planning regulations which helped funnel international capital into neighborhoods; they created a local (shadow) welfare state which offered special services to immigrants, and pursued urban development strategies which made certain ethnic groups, like the Koreans, spearheads of globalization in impoverished inner-city areas. The combination of general economic and political tendencies (particularly of deindustrialization and racism) and specifically local policies (world city formation) created the conditions which led to the explosion of 1992. The destructive effect of local policies such as community redevelopment combined with austerity policies of the Reagan and Bush administrations to form an amalgam of negative effects for poor neighborhoods. The 'Reagan revolution' had one of its major testing grounds in Southern California. Among the consequences of this period, which brought Third World living conditions to American cities and made infant mortality, hunger, unemployment, survival delinquency and inadequate medical services ubiquitous, was a racism which, being tolerated and sometimes politically legitimated, provided the discursive plane on which the globalization of the area proceeded.

Besides the struggles between the riotous masses and the many thousand troops which encircled South Central ever more tightly, the attacks against Korean stores were foregrounded in most accounts of the uprising. The sharpness of the conflict had its roots in the specific ways in which the lives of African Americans and Koreans have been affected by world city formation and by each other. Both ethnic communities have played entirely different roles in the political economy of Los Angeles. The former have been major losers in the process of globalized urbanization, and have been segregated and enclosed in the inner city; the latter are part of the Korean diaspora, who landed on the shores of Southern California and settled in the *cordon sanitaire* between wealthy white and poor black neighborhoods. While African Americans tend to be under- or unemployed, Koreans tend to own or rent stores in minority neighborhoods and have become epitomic redefiners of the 'American Dream'. The Koreans took the destruction of their property and the threat to their lives during the uprising as a blow to their newly gained economic and social self-confidence and to the viability of their highly indebted family enterprises (mortgaged with between $200 000 and $500 000 on the average; Rutten, 1992a: 52).

The 1992 uprising represented not the failure of a concept of multiculturality *per se*, but the failure of multiculturalism understood as hierarchization of ethnic groups under the hegemony of the world city economy. The riots of April 29, 1992 were the death knell for the world class city as proposed by the ruling elites of the urban region. Perhaps they represent the birth of an international city with a human face. In order for this to occur, however, it will be necessary to strengthen the popular or insurgent civil society of the poor, the marginalized and the oppressed.[4]

## AFTERMATH

> Every radical democratic politics should avoid the two extremes represented by the totalitarian myth of the Ideal City, and the positivist pragmatism of reformists without a project (Laclau and Mouffe, 1985: 190).

> The riot has been our voice, the only voice that you will listen to (Gang member in May 1992; quoted in Katz and Smith, 1992).

The aftermath of the uprising was characterized by a nervous flurry of attempts to put back together what never had been whole. Four kinds of initiatives stand out.

First, there were the official attempts by Ueberroth's Rebuild LA to continue the project world class city under a new program of market-oriented (rather than local corporatist as under Bradley) global capitalism. This initiative was countered, secondly, by voices from the same communities that had presented social alternatives even before the riot. Among these voices was the L/CSC which published, in 1992, a counterprogram with the title *Reconstructing Los Angeles from the Bottom Up* (L/CSC, 1992). Thirdly, 'peace feelers' among the city's gangs, whose existence predated the riots, now led a concerted effort on the side of the main protagonists – the Bloods and the Crips – to negotiate a truce. A programmatic statement called 'The Plan' circulated for a while during the summer of 1992. It contained a mixed agenda of classical urban planning recipes, neoliberal economics, education, urban design and neighborhood security (Walker, 1992; *The Economist*, May 23 1992 p. 57; Bloods and Crips, 1992). 'The Plan' was greeted with some (mostly sensationalist) interest by the public, but was mostly met with hostility. Los Angeles society had declared the gangsters as incommunicado and unfit to make proposals of this nature. This hard-nosed rejection of attempts by the criminalized and the marginalized to enter the mainstream fit well into the post-uprising mood in America: the inner cities were essentially given up as territories of reform and social change. Finally, new multicultural initiatives emerged from the devastation of Los Angeles. Among them has been the MultiCultural Collaborative, an umbrella organization for the coordination of interethnic conflict mediation. About a dozen community-based organizations and civil rights groups coalesced in 1992 to 'build a working coalition of individual, community, and institutional leaders that would commit to working collectively across racial lines to advance human relations programs and infrastructure in the context of social and economic justice' (quoted in Lehrer and Friedmann, 1997: 440).

## CHAPTER 12

# CONCLUSION: *UNE FIN DE SIÈCLE AMÉRICAIN(E)*

In the face of the centrifugal forces pulling Los Angeles apart, is there any way to put the city back together? . . . Los Angeles, in reality, is only governable by justice (Davis, 1991a).

Whether the rebellion of 1992 can be seen as a divide or as an interim stop in the history of world city formation in Los Angeles still remains to be seen. The constellation of social contradictions that led to the riots have not changed since the event. Interpretations of Los Angeles after 1992 need to pick up where the uprising left off. The preceding chapters have shown that there is no direct and predictable correlation between globalization and local politics. The incorporation of globalized streams of capital and of new flexibilized accumulation regimes – in the form of localized industrial districts – involves the conflictual emergence of a new mode of regulation. Guided by global (and culturally internationalized) laws of economic motion, this process is by no means entirely determined by global forces (i.e. global capital markets, transnational corporations, etc.). Much more, global tendencies are refracted in multiple ways locally on the economic, the social, the spatial, the cultural, the political and the ecological level.

In a mosaic made up of many 'politics of place' the future spatiality of Los Angeles is taking shape. The complexity of contradictions which has been borne out in Los Angeles cannot be brought under control with purely state-centered political or administrative reform (Schockman, 1996). Neither do shifts in political leadership – like that from the Bradley coalition to the Riordan administration – suffice in bringing about much needed fundamental change to how the city is run. Yet despite the necessary uncertainty over the future development of urbanization dynamics in Los Angeles, the analysis presented in this book allows a few careful conclusions.

The understanding of the current restructuring process which is turning Los Angeles into an entirely internationalized urban region presupposes some knowledge of local history, at least of the preceding, Fordist, period. Los Angeles became a Fordist city under the impact of local class struggles, local politics, specific economic developments and conceptual ideologies boosted by local place entrepreneurs and other place-defined influences. These local formation processes occurred in the context of the generalized development of Fordism in the United States during this century. 'Para-Fordist' structures, which had their roots in specific local milieus of Los Angeles, thus contributed to the decentralization of a mode of regulation which became national standard after 1945. The specific local formation of social and spatial conflicts, carried out in the political and social realms, which together can be called a 'local mode of regulation', created Fordist Los Angeles. Its historical geography is the ground on which the more recent restructuring of the region has been played out and experienced. The specific extant mix of industries, labor markets, governance and political institutions, consumption patterns, civic organizations and ecologies has shaped the way in which a new globalized and flexibilized urban complex has emerged.

Because of the complex nature of restructuring, our analysis must be open to competing views and approaches. But the history of recent restructuring in LA is by no means an arbitrary compendium of parallel experiences but a process well ordered and structured by the preconditions of local historical geography. The actors in this process have some space in which to make a difference. This makes predictions on the outcome of individual processes difficult. Purposeful agents modify the general lines of development, sometimes in such a decisive fashion that they fundamentally change the structures and extent of the local regime of accumulation and mode of regulation. The formation of the world city, therefore, is simultaneously a political process and a historic–geographic one. The individual and collective actors who make up the urban region's structured coherence form and act in such a way that the plane on which they position themselves towards each other and towards third parties starts to move, too.

On the most simple, and at the same time most abstract, level of understanding, the formation process is the product of new kinds of transnational (meaning deterritorialized) movements of capital in global space. Cities, places, social collectives, are, in this view, merely accidental products of decisions outside their reach, decisions which places have to submit to or react to. This view does not suffice, however, in order to grasp the specific social and spatial fabric of a certain internationalized city. Operations in the vacuous (and depopulated) abstract space of electronic capital accumulation have no access to (and no power over) the real contradictions in the sociospatial relationships of the world city. Both access and power would be necessary in order for them to play a role in regulation. If, for example, one talks about the flexibilization of the economy of a certain city or about the emergence of post-Fordist modes of regulation, one also needs to specify how this city's situation differs from comparable cities elsewhere. This seems the more necessary, the more the role of a given city in the globalized urban network depends on the specific tasks this city's economy performs in the international division of labor. In the case of Los Angeles, the internal structure of the world city is closely linked to Southern California's role in the global economy. The class struggles in the de-, re- or neoindustrialized sectors of the Southland's economy – old industries, craft industries, services and high tech – have been shown to be a major influence in shaping the local accumulation regime.

Space is produced socially. Global space does not entirely dominate local space. Place entrepreneurs (who have a more or less vested interest in the valorization of space), homeowners, neighborhood organizations, environmentalists, workers and others struggle with each other and with global interests (who tend to be represented by local agents), over the use of space. In the production of space under these circumstances, spatial images and narratives play an important role. These images help transmit and mediate discourses on the use of space between the global and the local level (as much as we can keep these apart). The real estate market in Los Angeles has historically been dependent on the design of utopian (or dystopian) and fantastic landscapes. The globalization of the real estate market occurs by imbricating externally produced images with local and traditional designs. Artists, politicians, intellectuals and real estate professionals play an important role in the production of such images. This production has become the everyday work of local states.

In order to position themselves effectively in opposition to the negative effects of current urban restructuring, local social actors need to be prepared to at least partly accept globalization as the terrain of local politics and social change. Denial and blindness to internationalization are two of the main reasons why local states, communities, place entrepreneurs and others feel railroaded by globalization. From this perspective, the process of internationalization is less a reordering of global–local relationships than a catalyst for the revolution of the structured coherence of each place. Class relations, spatial relations, racialized and ethnic relations, gender relations, identities and societal relationships with nature *locally* are the objects of global restructuring. Both challenges and opportunities spring from this situation. In no case can these new relationships be understood in a simple dichotomy of perpetrators and victims.

The formation of the world city, ultimately, is a social process. The example of Los Angeles points to two important, relatively independent, but connected processes of the societalization of a new accumulation regime. On one hand, there are multiple processes of self-regulation in the internationalized communities of the world city which lead to both an elite cosmopolitanization and a popular 'Thirdworldization' of the new social structure. Individual and collective patterns of consumption are changing in the process. On the other hand, between shadow state and local welfare state, a set of new 'official' modes of regulation of the internationalized social structure come into being. These new modes are critical for the formation of social regulation in the world city.

The structured coherence of an urban region is an unstable condition dependent on the region's technological base, its social infrastructure, the nature of the local labor markets, local politics and the role of the city in the global economy and in interurban competition, among other factors. The materiality of the structured coherence is subject to globally induced restructuring and to local class struggles in space. In any case, the production of a structured coherence is unthinkable without the actions of local purposeful actors who constitute specific urban class and spatial alliances. The formation of the world city does not eliminate these actors from decision making; it changes their position in, and perspectives on, their role in shaping the urban region. Since the structured coherence is precarious and contradictory by definition, the fissures of the next conflict are already built into any new mode of governance and regulation. With the help of local agents, global actors continuously undermine the basis of the currently most beneficial conditions for local capital accumulation. Urbanization, to paraphrase Henri Lefebvre, is a concrete contradiction. It can be assumed, therefore, that the emergence of a new urban mode of regulation will continue to be played out in the contradictory fields of action which are formed and reformed between local and global, hegemonic and insurgent actors.

Los Angeles defies everything most people commonly refer to as 'city'. It seems almost as if a new entity has emerged located between a nation and a city both in terms of size and function. To speak of Los Angeles as an urban unit in the political sense is hardly convincing. Only authoritarian phantasies would allow us to come up with a believable unified image of the urban region. We could imagine a sense of citizenship and identity which would encompass all 15 million people in Los Angeles inside the '60-mile-circle' drawn around City Hall. Yet that circle, which includes one of the strongest regional economies in the world, does not, in itself, constitute a political reality, neither in the territorial nor in the intentional sense. Political community and social territoriality have to be created in and beyond the economic.

Richard Weinstein has called Los Angeles 'the first American city' (Weinstein, 1996). He argues that Los Angeles is the fulfillment of the antiurban Jeffersonian dream. In a period in which urbanization appears as sub- or exurbanization, Los Angeles is, in the words of Lewis Mumford, the built proof of the collective effort to lead a private life. Extracted from an external nature deemed largely threatening and inimical, Los Angeles has nurtured a domesticated urban nature whose frontyards are the symbol of human domination of all other nature. The frontyard nature radiates groomed civility and democratic solidarity. The 'extended city', the urban form of these single-family monads of Fordist urbanization, 'is now characterized by a medium-density housing tissue of subdivisions laced with commercial strips, including small industrial spaces, and periodically marked by centers of varying size that consist of a shopping mall with a cineplex, a cluster of commercial buildings and a health care facility' (Weinstein, 1996: 29). As in digital landscapes, the urban region and its inhabitants are ordered in abstract topographies of matrices, lines and nodes. Nature is replaced by themeparks and historical consistency by adhocism. Instead of the temporal dimension of urban life, we now experience spatial passages (Weinstein, 1996: 29–35). Weinstein's argument concludes with an appeal to create, on the basis of this exurban form, a new mode of governance in a new kind of public space:

> [it] would take an opportunistic, pragmatic (convenient) shape, patched together from leftover spaces and negotiated contributions from private and public owners, compromised with messy edges, imperfect, surprising in idiosyncrasy, mixing solids and voids in ambiguous relation, but nevertheless possessing a public character through shared, connected space, coherent greenery tied to gardens, enhanced public circulation, public places to sit, and the penetration of these spaces into the body of private and institutionalized buildings, through courtyards and glass-covered passages (Weinstein, 1996: 41).

This diffuse space, where the middle classes celebrate the end of history, is seen as the space of a complex democratic society of postmodern differentiation.

Such accolades for the possibilities of the technoburbs at the doorstep of Los Angeles urban intellectuals seem to have replaced critical observation and distance.[1] In the light of the narrative presented in this book, I want to take issue with two aspects of Weinstein's view in particular. First, the underlying assumptions of a rather simplistic correspondence of urban form and social governance is not convincing. The form of Los Angeles contains multiple socialities and cannot be interpreted as growing out of any one – let alone Jeffersonian – dream. As we have seen, Los Angeles can be interpreted as a negotiated outcome of a tension between general tendencies of capitalist urbanization and specific social struggles, between utopian designs and real politics. The suburban ideal has been only one factor in this process (see also Hise, 1997). Second, the designation of Los Angeles as the 'first American city' is highly problematic. The genealogy of Los Angeles is as much global as it is American. In fact, we only recognize Los Angeles as 'an American city' now that it is entirely globalized. We know its Americanness from how it has reworked global trends in defined urban and social terms. While small-town Midwest mentalities were plausible as elements of an explanation for the contourless suburbanization of Los Angeles during the first half of the twentieth century, the suburban and exurban success stories only materialized entirely under the metropolitan hegemony of the Fordist industrial culture after World War II. The recourse to the rural substrate of the current phase of disurbanization, for which Los Angeles has become a stand-in, is totally impossible today, even though the appellation of rural–agricultural spaces is a pervasive element of neourbanist and edge city experiments in the extended city. This new space – i.e. the space that is Los Angeles – is sold to us as postindustrial, American and nonurban. In reality, it is hyperindustrialized, completely globalized and pervasively urbanized. We have reached the end of the American century of urbanization. Communitarian, middle-class political phantasies of general liberation will, therefore, not carry very far. As shown in this book, politics in world city Los Angeles is a more complex and complicated affair.

## THE CITY

At this point let me recall, on one hand, the monadic and anarchic Los Angeles of *Short Cuts* and *Pulp Fiction* and, on the other hand, the image of a structured hegemony of the world city as presented in the scholarly literature. They are both partial representations of contemporary Los Angeles. To both representations, though, a sense of political agency seems all but unimportant. In order to resurrect a sense of politics, we need to develop a working definition of the social in the city. Subject positions and identities in urban society cannot be determined by purely socioeconomic indicators (Lustiger-Thaler, 1992). The Los Angeles riots of 1992 made it clear that being poor was not the only reason to revolt. Complicated ethnic and cultural loyalties and identities overrode the purely economic explanation. While massive unemployment and dramatic poverty were fueling the rebellion, it was triggered by a human rights incident, the police beating of African American Rodney King and the subsequent acquittal of the officers involved. Where the battle lines were drawn had only partly to do with the socioeconomic situation in Los Angeles. Individual and collective identities are being formed along several lines, the most important ones certainly being class, gender and ethnicity. Yet, the creation of identity is a discursive process and not mere combination of objective cultural characteristics. Furthermore, identity does not yet explain social and political agency. Agency, again, has to be set in motion through discursive practice. It cannot be taken for granted. The urban is a special space where these discursive processes take place and shape. The city is, as Lustiger-Thaler says, 'prima facie a contested public arena adjudicating multiple spheres of agency' (1992: 192). And he considers the city 'as a dedifferentiating instance with the capacity to mediate its own cultural and political fragmentation' (1992: 193). The city appears to be an ideal space to deal with difference through subsuming it under the equalizing mechanisms of the urban. The conflict between specific, identity-based aspects of sociality and the more universal character of the urban is often played out between 'community' and 'city' as places and modes of operation of our social and political agency. While relying solely on the limited identity of community, more authentic politics seem possible, yet building a more united front against the ravages of globalization seems also more difficult; and particularist and right-wing populist movements claiming similar authenticity often reverse progress made in earlier periods of social struggles. This inherent contradiction of sublocal politics has prompted suggestions to 'go beyond the community and back to the city' (Christopherson, 1994: 422), to make connections between the specific issues of individual groups in the city and the well-being and freedom of the larger collective that defines the urban.

Such a restatement of the relationship between urbanization and agency needs to be seen as a programmatic position against the neoconservative celebration of pluralism and fragmentation (which is a thin veil in front of deregulation and privatization) and could be used to begin to analyze the reappropriation of political space in Los Angeles. The reappropriation of the political, then, from both the debilitating competitive fragmentation of social communities and the false universalizing of globalization, which creates centrally controlled private spaces and destroys public spaces, needs to happen through a reappropriation of civil society as a political space and through a redefinition of citizenship. The reappropriation of the political occurs through the reorganization of urban space and territory. The convulsive movement of capital in space, which has characterized globalization and triggered countless instances of displacement, has been countered more or less successfully by political movements which decidedly curtail the pace of development and reclaim liberated spaces in the global city. This project harkens back to Manuel Castells' *The City and the Grassroots*, and the notion of the 'alternative city':

> Cities and space are the unfinished products of historical debates and conflicts involving meaning, function and form. (. . .) [G]rassroots mobilization has been a crucial factor in the shaping of the city, as well as the decisive element in urban innovation against prevailing social interests. (. . .) Any theory of the city must be, at its starting point, a theory of social conflict (Castells, 1983: 318).

Discussions on regulation and governance have given us some useful tools to develop a more differentiated view of restructuring and globalization in their relationship to local politics. As Margit Mayer has argued, the current period is characterized, in part, by the increased significance of local modes of regulation. Simultaneously, urban social movements must address the 'powerful trends towards inequality, which the post-Fordist regime entails, and (. . .) attack its social forms of division and its political forms of exclusion in order to strengthen the democratic potential of the new forms of urban governance' (Mayer, 1995: 246). The outcomes of these efforts are undetermined. As it stands, many of the changes in urban governance today are more likely to benefit the hegemonic powers; others seem more neutral, and yet others seem beneficial to subaltern groups. The 'devolution' and 'deregulation' of state power into civil society and the marketplace have increased the self-regulation of both. Although new institutions of governance seem to be more open to influences from civil society, they are often designed to facilitate the smooth diversion of streams of global capital away from the traditional regulation by the state and democratic control.

Our sense of what local politics generally – and progressive local politics in world cities in particular – can achieve in this age of globalization, is improving. In this book, I have made the case for the recognition of the role of local politics in world city formation in Los Angeles and elsewhere. In this process, we are confronted with an important faculty of globalization, as Hermann Schwengel has observed:

> The rhetoric of globalization hides the fact that the actual event does not consist of a process of graduation of responsibility but of a rather wild and unregulated process of taking the world. Only those who have something to contribute to the civilization of competition of spatial orders and who do not just echo on each level what the respective interests dictate, will participate in the emergence of new rules of the game of spatial competition (Schwengel, 1995: 15; translation R.K.).

Just as globalization is not a gradual process, world cities are not comfortable places where politics can be conducted in the fashion of business as usual. Local politics needs to move into the muddy waters created by globalization and stem the movement towards the conservative maelstrom. In order to be successful in its endeavor, local politics must strive to change the pace of globalization and the space(s) of global urbanization. Local politics must be aware of the central contradiction that characterizes its position in the political sphere of the city. It needs to be defensive of life spaces, cultural traditions and local economies that are threatened by globalization. But it also needs to be offensively aggressive and innovative in developing discursive and communicative forms that are more responsive to the challenges of a multicultural, postmodern political environment. In terms of its praxis, it needs to be committedly practical and small-scale, rooted in the everyday business of local politics as well as theoretically sophisticated and unflagging in its defense of theoretical discourse and avant-garde cultures of communication. It needs to speak the dialect of the local, the jargon of the times and the idiom of the world.

# NOTES

## PREFACE

1. Perhaps Howard Nelson's *The Los Angeles Metropolis* (1983) has been the last attempt at writing an encyclopedia of Los Angeles.
2. In his foreword, Wagner wrote: 'My stay in Los Angeles was mainly dedicated to inspecting the city, whose expanse exceeds Berlin's by far. Only with the most efficient use of time was it possible to walk through all neighborhoods' (Wagner, 1935: vii).
3. One could count Soja's *Postmodern Geographies: the Reassertion of Space in Critical Social Theory* (1989) and his more recent *Thirdspace: Journeys to Los Angeles and Other Real-and-Imagined Places* (1996) as well as Scott's *Metropolis* (1988b) and *Technopolis* (1993a) among this group. But these highly important works have theoretical rather than empirical interest in Los Angeles, which sets them apart from the others mentioned. Of the recent edited works Scott and Soja (1996) and Dear, Schockman and Hise (1996) deserve special attention. Similarly, Fulton (1997) and Hise (1997) have added to our understanding of Los Angeles. There are, of course, numerous other monographs of lesser weight on Los Angeles and also a growing number of edited volumes which have added significantly to our understanding of Southern California. I will refer to these in the various chapters of this book.
4. The full list of interviews is attached to the bibliography at the end of the book. Most of these conversations were conducted in the late 1980s. They have only been used where they are of historical significance to the narratives in this book. I have recorded almost all of these on tape. I decided not to use any direct quotations from this material. In many cases, I have depersonalized references to interviewees in the text in order to keep their contribution anonymous.

## INTRODUCTION

1. For a discussion of this Southern Californian conundrum see Vidler (1997) and Ventura (1997).
2. Examples of this tendency are Fredric Jameson, 'Postmodernism, or the Cultural Logic of Late Capitalism' *New Left Review*, No. 146, (1984) pp. 53–92; and Philip Cooke, 'The Postmodern Condition and the City' *Comparative Urban and Community Research*, **2** (1989) pp. 62–80.
3. The other counties are Orange, San Bernardino, Riverside and Ventura.
4. This bank was swallowed by the Bank of America in 1991.
5. Although the MTA has no turnstiles for ticket control, it maintains a heavy security force presence on the trains and in the stations. Sporadic controls will fetch hefty fines if caught without a ticket.
6. It is interesting to note, perhaps, that just as Los Angeles once again rids itself of a rail-based modernization project, trains, subways and light rail transit are all the rage in Hollywood with movies as diverse as *White Men Can't Jump*, *Speed* and *Virtuosity* availing themselves of the aesthetic and dramatic possibilities of rail in the film industry's backlot.

# CHAPTER 1

1. 'LA School' refers to an informal grouping of scholars predominantly at UCLA and USC who worked in and on Los Angeles during the 1980s. A special issue of *Environment and Planning D: Society and Space*, **4**, 3, Fall 1986 presented the work of some of these scholars for the first time collectively. A more recent publication bringing together some of the same authors is Soja and Scott (1996). This group has been partly modelled on the Frankfurt School (named after the place of their activity) and partly after the Chicago School (named after the object of their research and action). The LA School's dilemma, which places them between the production of and the critique of the myth that Los Angeles has been as well as between academic and political practice, was described in Davis and Keil, 1992. See also Cenzatti (1993) for a brief history of the LA School.

2. This is an expanded version of an argument I made in Keil (1990) where I distinguished three such discursive lines. Six is a more or less arbitrary number which could easily be added to and certainly will as my research on Los Angeles progresses.

3. In this definition, I follow the suggestion of German urbanist Walter Prigge who opts for an urban rather than a local politics. He calls it 'the politics of the urban in the intermediary space of civil society' (1995: 185). And he continues: 'Urbanity has always been structured in polarities, contained oppositions, which were integrated by it (proletariat and bourgeoisie in former times). The current social oppositions and fragments confront urban politics with new problems' (Prigge 1995: 185). Sociospatial contradictions now need to be made public, need to be moderated, civilized, discussed, decentered. See Keil (1996) and forthcoming for an elaboration of this argument.

4. In California, the Citizens for a Better Environment, a statewide environmental organization with new roots in communities of color and immigrant neighborhoods, and with an emerging program of environmental justice has changed its name to Communities for a Better Environment, since 'citizens' is by definition exclusionary to exactly those constituents who suffer most from environmental racism.

5. In Los Angeles, much of the future debate will center on air pollution and the consequences of industrial pollution to residential communities.The current vocabulary of environmental justice has been developed with at least a glance at the inequalities in Los Angeles (Keil and Desfor, 1996).

# CHAPTER 2

1. This dynamic was perhaps never illustrated more bluntly than in the products that emerged from the Hollywood dream factory in the 1940s and 1950s. One excellent example is the 1951 movie *When Worlds Collide*, which shows how human civilization – in the movie equated throughout with contemporary Los Angeles – is saved from a planetary collision. A modern Noah's ark carries a group of blond and white Angelenos to an inhabitable planet somewhere in space and saves them from earthly extinction. All passengers of the ark – except for a taxi driver who is needed at the helm and a child – are scientists, engineers and technicians and reflect the ideal-typical sociography of traditional designs for Los Angeles' future – a future devoid of working classes and people of color.

2. Irrespective of which version of rhetoric dominated the field at any point in time, it was always a form of identity creation. This can be understood as the attempt of 'locally dependent actors' (Cox and Mair, 1988), to suspend conflicts inside the community in favor of some kind of solidarity inside the locality. This solidarity, then, became the basis for the competition with other places. In the history of Los Angeles, the arc of interurban competition spans the struggle over California primacy with San Diego and San Francisco to the current reach for the crown of the Pacific Rim. For recent as well

as for historic plans, 'the construction of a feeling of community' remains a key element of urban discourse in Los Angeles.

3.  Growth has always also been used as a biographical metaphor: growth as growing up. Dykstra wrote in 1941 that Los Angeles was still 'an adolescent city' (Dykstra, 1941: 1). In hindsight, the adolescence of Los Angeles was the period of the Fordist city. By the end of the 1980s, then, the city was considered grown up: 'Los Angeles comes of age', wrote Lockwood and Leinberger in a widely received article in *Atlantic Monthly* which became the blueprint for the hegemonic discourse. On April 4, 1988, *The Los Angeles Business Journal*, for example, wrote that Leinberger and Lockwood had defined the Los Angeles problem for all of us for the years to come. Ironically the recent declaration of completed growth occurred at a time when Los Angeles rather threatened to burst at the seams, and when the 'growth debate' determined the discourse in the region. Declaring Los Angeles having come of age meant, at the same time, the acknowledgement of the internationalization of the region, the competition of the city for the crown of the Pacific, maybe also the global financial economy and the development of a Third World sociology (Lockwood and Leinberger, 1988).

4.  The term 'place entrepreneur' is John Logan and Harvey Molotch's (1987).

5.  The Air Quality Management Plans and policy documents regarding the Los Angeles River establish a certain order in the societal relationships with nature. This order is part of either the regulation and reproduction of the hegemonic regime of accumulation or of a strategy to alter it in compliance with larger elite-driven change. The elite concepts for the city imply recipes both for the regulation of nature and for the regulation of people. These intersecting regulations are best described by the notion of *control*. Policing ecology and policing people are elements of maintaining the order of the day. Associated notions are efficiency, state power and the free reign of the market. Elite concepts typically are developed in the bureaucracies of the local state and in the environment departments of major corporations. They reflect the standard practices of administration, management and state control. The opening scene of Robert Altman's *Shortcuts* illustrates this aspect of environmental policy in Los Angeles. The helicopters spraying pesticides to rid the city of a ubiquitous medfly infestation also symbolize total control; the ubiquitousness of the ecological crisis is replaced by the ubiquitousness of the panacea of control, regulation and techno-fix.

# CHAPTER 3

1.  Let me maintain at the outset that the analytical separation of nature and society in the text must not be misread as a dichotomizing of the two concepts. For insightful recent discussions of this issue see Kipfer, Hartmann and Marino (1996).

2.  Kisch continues his diatribe against the fake nature of Southern California by pointing out that the mansions are pure kitsch and the parks are filled with pot-herbs; and that the 'nature' of Hollywood does not lend itself to be the backdrop of romantic love scenes.

3.  Adding 'working' here exposes a particular middle-class preconception which views the city from the standpoint of spaces of consumption. Work is uncharted territory whose reality remains a mystery to most urban observers of that class. This explains, perhaps, that Jacobs overlooks an important fact (and origin of civil society) in her portrait of Los Angeles: the world of work. In the late 1950s, Los Angeles was one of the major Fordist production places in the United States with mass factories unrivalled by most other urban areas. The working-class communities that sustained this complex are still a source of communitarian social organization today.

4.  Among other things, Banham stated categorically: 'Insofar as Los Angeles performs the functions of a great city, in terms of size, cosmopolitan style, creative energy, international influence, distinctive way of life and corporate personality . . . to the extent that Los Angeles has these qualities, then to that same extent all the most

admired theorists of the present century, from the Futurists and Le Corbusier to Jane Jacobs and Sibyl Moholny-Nagy, have been wrong. The belief that certain densities of population, and certain physical forms of structure are essential to the working of a great city, (. . .) must be to the same extent false' (Banham, 1971: 236).

5.  It is no surprise, then, to find the following passage in a recent book on managing European cities: 'The late twentieth century has seen a resurgence of critical accounts of urban life. The storyline of these accounts tends to emphasize the dangerous and threatening aspects of the city. Los Angeles, once the symbol of a new frontier in innovation in urban form and lifestyle, now instead seems to encapsulate these dangers, functioning as a kind of "aversion therapy" in our discussion of the urban' (Healey *et al.*, 1995: 3).

6.  Neera Chandhoke (1995: 37) has summarized this succinctly: 'Civil society is not always marked by civility. For Hegel, Marx and Gramsci, the domain, constituted as it is by the logic of the capitalist economy, is an unequally constructed space where social and economic practices functioning according to the principles of market evaluation constitute individuals hierarchically.'

7.  Egon Erwin Kisch wrote about real estate agents who advertised new subdivisions in the 1920s by luring passersby into an organized sales trip into the desert frontier of Southern California: 'Fever, intoxication, adventure, jungle, wilderness, hunt urge themselves upon us. . . . Where? In the well-paved, streetcar-filled roads of the civilized city Los Angeles, Cal.' (Kisch, 1948: 130).

8.  This is an intended parallel to Lefebvre's 'absolute space' (1991: 48). Jennifer Wolch reminds me, though, that 'the discussion of absolute versus relative nature is anthropocentric'. She also alerts me to the increasing liminality of territory where 'we find the spaces for renaturalization – where a wide variety of organisms can exist/adapt to human presence, and where people can experience some aspects of ecological process, risk the nonhuman, and reground (but not necessarily deromanticize) their ideas of nature' (personal communication). Being mindful of this important observation, I nevertheless decided to retain the Lefebvreian terminology for the sake of the argument I am trying to make.

9.  Thanks to David Browne for pointing out the existence of this website to me. Its address is: WWW.lalc.k12.ca.us/laep/smart/river/tour/index.html. Thanks also to the creator of the site, Kurt Ballash, Jefferson High School, LAUSD for giving me access to the material presented at the site. Web page consultant was Jeff Hill. Photos were by Grant Te Vault. It is copy written by Target Science 1995 and was last updated on Sept. 3, 1996. On May 29 it was awarded the Times Pick by the *LAT*.

# CHAPTER 4

1.  The term 'Frontstadt' denotes city at the front. It also reminds one, of course, of Los Angeles' role, throughout much of the last 100 years, as a true frontier town, at the edge of the continent, a place so far away from the rest of America that myth-building became almost instant.

2.  An important aside seems necessary at this point. Just as immigrants cannot be blamed for taking away jobs from Americans, restructuring processes have not been caused by globalization. These processes were underway independently of globalization. If anything, globalization has always been imbricated with local and national dynamics. This seems important to mention in order to avoid any racist and xenophobic arguments on these questions.

3.  The concept of subnational modes of regulation has now gained widespread currency. See Keil and Lieser (1992); *Economy and Society*, Special Issue, 1995.

4.  This result expressed the relative position of the diverse and divergent elements of the national New Deal Coalition whose struggle ended in the compromise of the Wagner–Steagall Act (Feldmann and Florida, 1988: 192).

5. Local housing authorities had already been given the mandate to build and administer public housing units in the legislation of 1937. In 1988, about 1.3 million units of public housing were occupied. This amounted to less than 1.5% of the total of 92 million housing units in the country (Marcuse and Hartman, 1988).

6. 'Had the region built a system prior to the war, the federal government could have more efficiently moved men and material throughout Southern California, now an area with several major defense-related industries' (Bottles, 1987: 226–227). In the wars against Korea and Vietnam, the USA encountered a much more efficient Fordist urban landscape in Los Angeles. Soja (1989: 222f.) has pointed out the fortified construction of the Los Angeles region. The specificity of this landscape of horror has its counterpart in the internal security city which characterizes both the Fordist and the post-Fordist city (Flusty, 1994).

7. The growth of Los Angeles can be understood in part as the suburbanization of the eastern cities, from whose density and squalor people migrated to Southern California precisely because the sunny suburbs of Los Angeles offered a real place to live the national antiurban ideology. 'The growth of Los Angeles has been strongly influenced by urban crises back East, and by a whole national ideology where the city is feared and hated. Los Angeles, as the 'good community' tried from the very start to define itself as a sort of counter-city, free from most urban diseases, from social conflicts and modern sins. The dialectics of urban evolution have changed this "perfect" settlement into a super-metropolis charged with all the defects and all the sins it was supposed to be guarded against' (Marchand, 1986: 69).

8. Mass production and crafts production traditions in automobile manufacturing emerged side by side in Southern California without combining their respective different strengths to form an integrated industrial district (Morales, 1986).

9. The history of the link between real estate speculation and railway construction, as well as the consequences of this alliance for the decentralized spatial structure of Los Angeles, have been documented elsewhere and need not be repeated here. For details see Fogelson (1967: 85–107); Gottlieb and Wolt (1976: 11–117); McWilliams (1979); Wagner (1935: 99–143).

10. In 1919, 141 000 automobiles were on the roads of Los Angeles County; in 1929 there were 777 000 (Wachs, 1984: 304). This increase outweighed population growth significantly. While the city had already the highest traffic density in the world, the worst was still to come. After the successful establishment of the Fordist nexus of production, consumption and the urban infrastructure, 3.4 million cars 'populated' the streets of Los Angeles County in 1961. In 1979, this number had grown to 5.2 million vehicles (Light, 1988).

11. I will not take up the battle which has been fought in the literature for at least 20 years over whether and to what degree there was a conspiracy of General Motors, Firestone and Standard Oil of California in order to destroy mass transit in Southern California. It suffices to say that, in fact, in 1949 these three companies were found guilty of criminal conspiracy to acquire, motorize and resell electric streetcar lines. The same companies had already replaced electric streetcars with GM buses in 45 American cities (Light, 1988: 66). Bottles (1987) makes consumer preference rather than the profit drive of the automobile multinationals the focus of his analysis of why Southern Californians deserted rail transit – once in exemplary shape in the region – in favor of the automobile. Making the assumption that everybody just wanted to drive rather than to ride transit, is, in itself, a rather unconvincing analysis, however. Whatever the final jury decision on the intent of the dismantling may bring, Angelenos, by the end of the 1940s, had been made compulsory consumers in an exploding regional, automobile-based economy.

12. It is noteworthy that this indicated a historical shift in the financing practice for infrastructure. Up until the 1930s, it was mostly automobile drivers who had paid for urban streets and highways. This became impossible with the Depression (Bottles, 1987: 232).

13. The Arroyo Seco Parkway (built 1938–40), renamed the Pasadena Freeway in 1954, was the first piece of the Los Angeles freeway system (Brodsly, 1981). Like New York in the

East, Los Angeles was anxious to create an automobile-oriented urban landscape which was to provide the foundation for the comprehensive automobilization of the years to come (Wachs, 1984; Foster, 1971).

14. 'Not another New York, but a new Los Angeles. Not a great homogenous mass with a pyramiding of population and squalor in a single center, but a federation of communities coordinated into a metropolis of sunlight and air', Fogelson quoted from a document of the Los Angeles City Planning Department from the 1920s (Fogelson, 1993: 163).

15. Progressivism had its share of influence in one respect, though: in contrast to other American cities, the nonpartisan electoral system in Los Angeles (and other Californian cities) prevented the emergence of political machines (and consequently eliminated the last bit of proletarianism in urban politics) (Carney, 1964).

16. A recall vote entails the withdrawal of the mandate, and usually the replacement, of an elected politician during his or her time in office. Next to the initiative and the referendum, it is the most important means of direct democracy in the California constitution (Crouch, Bollens and Scott, 1983).

17. See Gottlieb and Wolt (1977: Chapters 19 and 22); Parson (1985); Hines (1982).

## CHAPTER 5

1. Sonenshein also notes that among the original voters for Bradley a coalition of middle-class whites on the one hand, and Hispanic and black working classes on the other, were predominant (Sonenshein, 1988: 19).

2. By this I do not necessarily mean electoral support, but strong ties between his administration and relevant groups in civil society.

3. Wood's affiliation was with the County AFL-CIO – an amalgamation of the American Federation of Labor and the Congress of Industrial Organizations in which he held various leading positions over time.

4. *The Impossible Dream* is the title of Tom Bradley's biography (Payne and Ratzan, 1987).

5. This assessment is based on an interview with a Bradley aide in 1989.

6. A similar lawsuit on the level of county government also led to a redistricting in favor of Latino voters (Boyarsky, 1988c). Gloria Molina ran in the newly created district for county supervisor and was elected in 1991.

7. Even though the relative number of Jewish politicians in Los Angeles declined slightly during the 1980s, the importance of Los Angeles' Jewish community in national and international politics has grown substantially during recent decades. With 600 000 Jews, Los Angeles is the second-largest Jewish city in the world after New York. Important political decisions in the American Jewish community have been increasingly made on the west coast rather than on the east coast (Libman, 1989). Through the Democratic Party, a group of powerful west Los Angeles Jewish politicians – sometimes called the Berman–Waxman machine – have become very influential in national and international politics in the USA (Davis, 1987).

8. The west of the city is more potent than any other part not just for economic reasons but also in political and social terms. It is the place where the decision-making structure of the Democratic Party is located. Most political dignitaries and members of the highly important citizen commissions of the City Council live there (Harris and Roderick, 1988).

9. Conot (1986); Curran (1988a); Shapiro (1986).

10. Rob Glushon, a member of the environmental commission of the city, warned at the time against using the alleged elite base of environmental politics in Los Angeles to create class struggle, neighborhood discord and ethnic strife (Glushon, 1987).

11. This assessment and the analysis that follows was derived, in part, from interviews by Roger Keil with the personal deputies of the candidates Michelle Krotinger, Alisa Katz,

Gary Bozé and Mark Fabiani. The best and most gripping report on the affair that forced Yaroslavsky to resign can be found in Joan Didion's 'Letter from Los Angeles' in the April 24, 1989 issue of the *New Yorker* (Didion, 1989). See also Ron Curran's 'BAD Boys' in the *L.A. Weekly* (Curran, 1988b) and Roderick and Vollmer (1989).

12. 'Not Yet New York' was the name of an alliance of neighborhood organizations in the west of the city. During the second half of the 1980s, growth was not just a current issue in the city of Los Angeles but also a deciding factor in elections in many of the smaller communities in the suburbs. Political success in these communities came to be connected to taking a position critical of growth (cf. Boyarsky, 1988b).

13. A *Los Angeles Times* survey just after the 1989 election showed that Yaroslavsky would have earned around 27% of the vote had he stayed in the race. Since Bradley would probably have received fewer than half of the votes, Yaroslavsky would have forced him into a runoff election in which the Westside councilman would have had an excellent chance of succeeding. Holden (14%) and Ward (7%) would have clocked in far behind the frontrunners (Boyarsky, 1989b).

14. As shown to the world on a now infamous amateur video, King was beaten brutally by four officers of the Los Angeles Police Department (LAPD). The Police Commission and the mayor demanded the immediate suspension of Police Chief Daryl Gates. The City Council countered this demand, arguing that such a dismissal was an intrusion into its rights, and demanded a judicial decision that would clarify the power relationships between the mayor, the City Council and the commissions. In their first decision, the courts decided that the commissions were subordinate to the City Council (Murphy, 1991).

15. On one level, the fight between the commissions and the City Council is to be understood as a fight by council members against the mayor. The considerable influence that commission members obtain through their donations to Bradley is the main issue. Of the 244 commission members appointed by Bradley, 107 contributed $673 661 to various Bradley campaigns between 1983 and 1989 (Murphy, 1991).

# CHAPTER 6

1. Unless otherwise mentioned, internationalization and globalization are used interchangeably in this chapter. See Chapter 1 for a brief clarification of the terms.

2. This latter development is best expressed by the attempt of the Los Angeles Manufacturing Action Project (LAMAP) which attempts to analyze and organize Los Angeles County's industrial workforce of 660 000 men and women (LAMAP, 1995).

3. See Amin (1994) for a recent collection of papers on this subject; see also a recent issue of *Economy and Society* (Fall 1995).

4. While a definition of the service sector is highly contentious, this refers to those activities listed under US SIC Codes 70–89.

5. I acknowledge the support of Julie Aha, organizer of Local 399, Service Employees International Union, Los Angeles, in researching the building management industry and the work conditions of janitors in Los Angeles.

6. 'Textile production is one of the County's newest success stories, generating a fast growing, sophisticated production industry in the heart of some of the most depressed parts of the region. Much like entertainment, its expansion was driven by the need for increasingly high-quality, but smaller lot sizes of knitted, dyed and printed fabrics to supply local garment makers' (The New Vision Business Council, 1994: III-9).

7. Listing furniture here is a bit of a problem. While the industry stayed steady through the 1980s, it might now face close to total extinction in the wake of market pressures and new environmental regulations which are pushing many firms south of the border into Mexico. See Bloch and Keil, 1991 for further information on this sector. In 1986, the industry had 54 371 jobs in Southern California, 39 000 of which in Los Angeles County. In 1979 already 35% of the industry's workers were Mexican immigrants, a

figure which may well be higher today. In November of 1990, the furniture and fixtures industry (SIC 25) employed 35 700 people.

8. The researchers of LAMAP noted a similar problem with regards to the food industry where they 'learned that SIC classifications do not necessarily correspond to *coherent industrial segments* that contain companies who produce similar products and compete with one another' (1995: E-28).

9. This is probably a conservative estimate in a hard-to-pin-down sector characterized by volatile capital structures subdivided into ethnic fiefdoms and swiftly changing labor markets (mostly Latina) which go with the tide of the Immigration and Naturalization Service (INS)-controlled cross-border economy. In the late 1980s one could speak of 125 000 workers in this industry in Los Angeles County.

10. Sidney Vogel, a garment manufacturer from the first post-World War II generation of Jewish capitalists who came from New York to Los Angeles, explained in an interview why his industry offered itself as a place for immigrant capital and labor: the industry has a low capital intensity. Many former workers form companies since they think – due to their previous experiences in the work process – that they can do things better than their boss. Vogel, who at the time was also vice-president of the local Garment Manufacturers' Association, notes a high rate of new company starts primarily by Latino and Korean entrepreneurs. The flipside of this steady and fast capitalization process in the sweatshops is, however, a comparatively high failure rate: 50% of firms disappear soon from the landscape of garment shops. In a highly competitive environment, successful business demands more than technological expertise and knowledge of the work process; the constantly precarious calculation of piecework, and the competition between contractors forces many new businesses to give up after a short time (Interview Vogel).

11. I wish to thank Robin Bloch and Peter Olney, previously with Local 1010 of the International Union of Electronic, Electrical, Salaried, Machine & Furniture Workers, Huntington Park, California for many insightful discussions on the situation in the local furniture industry.

12. Scott continues here as follows: 'We may add to this litany of problems the crisis of local government in Southern California, where a disjointed and irrational mosaic of seven counties and close to 200 municipalities attempt to manage an urban region whose dense internal interdependencies extend far beyond the bounds of any single local and administrative unit.(. . .) It would seem, in short, that some form of regional government is long overdue, and any such rationalization would be beneficial for industrial growth because it would facilitate overall harmonization of urban development projects across the whole region' (Scott, 1993a: 254).

## CHAPTER 7

1. 'The 1965 reform transformed the immigration system with a few bold strokes. First, it abolished the old country-of-origins quotas, which allotted small quotas to southern and eastern Europe and still smaller – almost prohibitively small – quotas to Asia. Second, it established two principal criteria for admission to the United States: family ties to citizens or permanent residents or possession of scarce and needed skills. Third, it increased the total numbers of immigrants admitted to the United States' (Waldinger and Bozorgmehr, 1996b: 9).

2. Muller uses the concept of gateway cities in a way that is related to the notion of primary world cities as introduced by Friedmann (1986). Yet Muller points to the positive impact of immigration on the economy of these cities while he criticizes Friedmann for his 'mostly negative assertions about those cities' (Muller, 1993: 114).

3. Normally, Korean immigrants have been subject to social degradation in this process. Often, Korean middle-class people like academics put the money they receive from selling all their belongings in Korea into a small business in Los Angeles and live their

lives as petty entrepreneurs. Many others, however, fall even one rung below this stage. Most Korean immigrants, in fact, are not business owners at all. Much more often they work as warehouse hands or shop clerks in food stores, as service personnel in restaurants, as workers in garment factories, or as janitors in airports or hotels (Takaki, 1989b).

4. Vergara also mentions that this do-it-yourself program 'contrasts with the much smaller government efforts at subsidizing housing through churches and local community development organizations' (Vergara, 1997: 4).

5. Ethnic communities are striving for political recognition as defined and separate spaces. This has occurred in Koreatown and Filipinotown. Similarly, ethnic communities are attempting to hegemonize the political process in existing political structures. This was the case in the 'first Chinese suburb'– Monterey Park, east of Los Angeles – where a growing Chinese presence has changed the political structure of the city. Another aspect of the redefinition of the meaning of urban space in political terms is the symbolic journalistic designation of Los Angeles as the '24th ward of Tokyo' (Frantz and Collins, 1989).

6. In their analysis of migration, locality and civil society in the context of immigration policy in Los Angeles, Lehrer and Friedmann (1997: 442; my translation) reach a similar conclusion: 'Community-based organizations (CBOs) are important social institutions corresponding to the needs of ethnic groups with a palette of services (English courses, assistance with the filling out of forms, etc.) They represent not only the interests of new immigrants but also of established immigrants.'

7. In Southern California, Safeway-Markets, which were the fifth largest chain in the area, with 15.3% market share in 1984, the supply of products in the fruit and vegetable departments grew from 150 to 300 products between 1982 and 1987. Among these newly offered fruits and vegetables were 19 different kinds of melon, 20 kinds of squash and 11 varieties of mushrooms (Berkman, 1987).

8. Until recently, supermarket chains had subdivided their market shares mostly by social and geographic criteria. A *Los Angeles Times* survey in 1983/84 showed that Asians and whites used to shop primarily at Ralphs and Vons, African Americans at Boys and Ralphs, and Latinos at Lucky and Alpha Beta (*Los Angeles Times* Marketing Research, 1986: 34). Incidentally, the social geography of Los Angeles retailing is characterized by the paradox that majority poor Latino and African American customers of Boys markets were paying up to 7% more for products than (white) customers in comparable neighborhoods. The price of individual reproduction tends to be particularly high for both the very rich (in places like Beverly Hills) and the very poor (Calpirg, 1987). When markets have located in 'problem areas' (as Watts was considered after the 1965 rebellion), they have usually charged a super-rent through the prices of their commodities. The willingness of Boys, which had 54 stores in the mid-1980s, to move into areas that had been abandoned by companies like Vons, Lucky and Ralphs, rested on the company's certainty that they could cushion their risk in profits derived from being the most expensive chain of all.

9. The following information relies on an interview conducted by the author in the fall of 1987 with Chris Linski, a Tianguis supermarket manager in Montebello.

10. A strategy committee on the highest management level met once a month for 14 months and visited retail stores in various regions of the American South and Southwest as well as Mexico in order to get an impression of how competitors in other regions catered to the specific needs of Latinos. The American market researchers took home two findings in particular from their trips to Mexico: first, compared to the uniformity of American food culture, the eating habits of Mexicans had a stunning differentiation; second, in Mexico – compared to the USA sales practices differed widely. Through detailed research on consumption practices of different Latino immigrant communities in Texas, Florida and California, further knowledge was gained about the differentiation of customer demand. In Southern California, a differentiation due to three levels of acculturation was noted. The result was the development of a product series which

integrated the results of more tests on color design, style, food supply, recipes and food samples (Interview Linski).

11. Estimates of the total number of US immigrants from this region vary between 750 000 and 1.3 million.

12. In a typical minimall in the center of Los Angeles, Sanchez discovered among eight tenants a woman from the Philippines who ran a beauty parlor, a former banker from Saudi Arabia who had a butcher's shop, two Cambodian brothers who had a donut shop, a Vietnamese refugee who had a gift store, a Filipino from Hong Kong who rented out videos, and a young Latino who was the manager of a pizza restaurant (J. Sanchez, 1987a).

13. A loan officer of the city's economic development department confirmed in an interview with the author her fears that many minimalls would rapidly deteriorate physically and would have to be bulldozed. She also maintained, however, that this assumption would not keep the city from giving out loans to small businesses locating in minimalls. See also Snyder (1987) and Garcia (1987).

14. Writing a generation after Banham, I am compelled to add that the evocation of the street (and the car) as a life space has become a forced experience for those Angelenos who cannot afford to rent or buy a place to stay. At many places in the city, along parks and in front of coin-operated laundries, the cars of the homeless, heavily laden with a person's or a family's belongings, line the street or sit in parking lots.

## CHAPTER 8

1. For this chapter, the author interviewed about 20 individuals who represent the types of organizations described in this paragraph. For the full list of interviewees see the table of interviews.

2. Thus new forms for the marketing of urban space come into being. A Southern California producer of commercial Japanese language videos offered middle-class customers in Japan optical impressions of Los Angeles and its surroundings in order to recruit them for the sale of residential objects. In a strongly segmented marketplace, American real estate firms use this scheme to get transnational deals outside of the megasales of spectacular downtown objects (Jones, 1989a, b).

3. Among them were, for example, Dan Garcia, former head of the Los Angeles Planning Commission, Arthur K. Snyder, a former Eastside councilman, and Michael Gage, former deputy mayor to Tom Bradley.

4. Sometimes foreign investors hire local politicians for the representation of their interests in the national political arena. The Japanese corporation Fujitsu, for example, which had 400 employees in Anaheim, used the mayor of that city as a lobbyist in an expected trade dispute with Washington (*LAT*, May 24, 1989: IV, 5).

5. While the discourse on 'new sensitivity' was primarily directed at mediation between the interests of foreign investors and local communities affected by their investment (often communities of color and of working class), this tactic was also meant to iron out differences between the foreigners and their local American counterparts, the place entrepreneurs of Los Angeles. This was obviously the case when the Japanese company Marukin bought the Riviera Country Club, a traditional playground of the super-rich in Los Angeles. The investor was subsequently reported to have been very 'sensitive', an observation noted – with much delight and surprise – by employees and club members alike (*LAT*, February 8, 1990).

6. In a commercial video for potential Japanese middle-class investors, this ideological distortion is clearly illustrated. The video shows a 'a strange land where every woman is tall and blonde and every man is a polo player. The cities are as homogeneous as Japan's, without blacks or Latinos or even Japanese. Everyone moves magically about in a landscape that is devoid of freeways. We see only mute, beautiful wanderers, or white-robed technicians dreaming of cancer cures at UCLA' (Jones, 1989a). The video-

produced image of Los Angeles runs into conflict with other images of Southern California held by potential Japanese buyers. Both larger events, such as the Los Angeles riots of 1992, and single acts of violence, like the killing of two Japanese students in the March of 1994 in San Pedro, are widely publicized in Japan. They affect not only the perceptions people in Japan might have of Los Angeles but also the behavior and attitude of Japanese expatriates in the Southland towards the place where they live. The perceived – and real – increase in violence and crime, as well as the real-life demands of a multicultural society tend to have heightened the insular separation of the local Japanese community of about 40 000, despite the efforts of the largely upper-middle-class population towards integration via activities in schools and through philanthropy (Moffat, 1994).

7. On the development of residential areas since 1940, Marchand wrote: 'The global spatial structure of Los Angeles, as a system of concentric rings, sectors and axes radiating from the center and channelling the main activities, has remained surprisingly stable over these three decades' (Marchand, 1986: 215). Marchand's observation is remarkable, although talking about concentric rings in Los Angeles demands much imagination on the part of the observer. What is important about Marchand's findings, however, is that sociospatial structures have great stability in the confirmation of power structures and serve as a template on which future investment will be distributed in the urban territory.

8. Urban redevelopment and internationalization processes have destroyed huge numbers of affordable inner-city residential units in order to expand the world city citadel (Haas and Heskin, 1981). Existing social ecologies, like the African American areas in South Central, are changing their character due to Latin immigration. This Latinization of the traditional neighborhoods of the African American working class has not led to large ethnic conflict, as expected by some (Oliver and Johnson, 1984). Even in the rebellion of April 1992 there were few clashes between the Latin and African American populations of south Los Angeles. The attacks against Korean stores and businesses could *not* be explained precisely by the notion of 'ethnic succession', as developed by the Chicago School. Rather, what were decisive here were the different class interests (and their ideological overdeterminations) of Korean (and other) merchants and of the African American (and other) poverty populations in the communities of south Los Angeles. See also Mike Davis (1992c) for a dystopian reading of Los Angeles' urban 'ecologies of fear' which uses the Chicago School model as a starting point. Rather than assuming the stabilizing effect of socioecological processes, Davis stresses the continuation of social contradiction and conflict in these new ecologies.

9. 'Nowhere else can you find as much energy being pumped into a major downtown area, from both domestic and foreign interests' (Ortiz, 1987: S-32).

10. Acquest accordingly writes to its customers: 'The emerging role of Los Angeles as the largest foreign trade center in the nation is anticipated to have a major impact on future foreign investment in the region and the value of downtown real estate specifically. Historically, finance generally follows trade. Centuries ago the world financial capital was Venice, followed by Amsterdam, London and then New York. The future Pacific Rim trade will likely position Los Angeles as the financial capital of the world. These projections have been made by many of the leading bankers, economists and financial experts, worldwide' (Acquest, 1987: 31). The role of academics in backing up such observations and of artists and intellectuals in providing other forms of legitimacy for such claims has been subject of Davis (1990) and Davis and Keil (1992).

11. In their 1997 year end review, the always real estate friendly *Downtown News* jubilantly continued the Japan-bashing attitude of previous years and reported: 'Get Real, Estate: Need more proof that the Japanese are clean? Just look at the bath they continue to take in 1997. As rising-sun companies unloaded property purchased at the top of the market, a number of wily players appeared in Downtown' (*Downtown News*, December 29, 1997: 5). Among these players are global property heavyweights like Toronto's TrizecHahn.

## Chapter 9

1. I am grateful to Cynthia Hamilton who first made this process clear to me with special attention to the Los Angeles case in a personal communication.

2. After a 1995 management audit of the CRA by the office of the chief legislative analyst of the City Council, which had severely criticized the management of the CRA, Mayor Richard Riordan was quoted with the following comment: 'Together we hope to restore the CRA to its central mission – revitalizing the community and creating jobs' (Toni Page Birdsong, 'Audit Calls CRA Confused', *Downtown News*, February 20, 1995: 1, 11).

3. Each project area is a stand-alone project, which means that tax increments can be spent only in the area where they are generated. The largest projects are Bunker Hill ($2.5 billion), Hollywood ($922 million), and the CBD ($750 million). Each project area has a maximum tax increment ('cap'), some of which have been enforced by redevelopment foes such as former Los Angeles councilman Ernani Bernardi who in a series of court battles prevented CBD tax increments from rising above $750 million. The total maximum tax increment stood at $5.5 in 1995 (Los Angeles City Council, 1995: 63).

4. This information is based on an interview by the author with Jim Wood on October 26, 1987. Throughout his tenure as the chairman of the board, Jim Wood was the most important individual actor in the redevelopment of Los Angeles. The former crown prince and current head of the AFL-CIO of Los Angeles County, a political ally of former Mayor Tom Bradley and County District Attorney Ira Reiner, as well as an influential member of the California Democratic Party, Wood has been located in the center of the Southern California power structure. Many of his critics considered Wood the epitomic Macchiavellian character who brought the subjective note of cold-blooded calculation to the destructive urban redevelopment process. His political past in the circles of the anticommunist 'social democratic' wing of the American labor movement identified Wood as a natural enemy of the progressive and anticapitalist elements in the redevelopment discourse (Meyerson, 1990: 11). In the 1990s, however, Wood has shown practical solidarity with nonmainstream activities in the Los Angeles labor movement such as the Justice for Janitors campaign and LAMAP (see below in this chapter).

5. Mo Nishida, an activist in the struggle against redevelopment in Little Tokyo since 1972, speculated in 1984 that fewer than 100 of those living in these units were from the area originally and that local people would not get one of these subsidized apartments but only end up on the waiting list (Condas *et al.*, 1984: 90).

6. After the end of his term as project director in Little Tokyo, Cooke Sunoo took on the same position in the Hollywood project area – created in 1986 (see below). Hollywood, like Chinatown, is a good example for a selectively altered redevelopment policy in Los Angeles.

7. The historical facade of Little Tokyo became an important asset in creating a retail center within a culture created and maintained by the heritage industry (*LABJ*, May 15, 1989: 8).

8. I owe much of the information given in this section to Sharon Lowe, Chinatown lawyer and anti-redevelopment activist with whom I had a lengthy interview on May 17, 1988.

9. Hollywood boosters commonly emphasize the 'urban' character of the area, referring mostly to its density and street life, so absent in other parts of Los Angeles. In a recent commentary on development in the area, city councilwoman Jackie Goldberg, who has represented the area since Michael Woo stepped down to run against Richard Riordan in the 1993 mayoral race, confirmed this view by pointing out that 'new projects cannot look like they've been transplanted from a suburban mall' (quoted in Boxall and Gordon, 1997: B10). The myth of the 'urban' character of Hollywood is much older, though. German geographer Anton Wagner wrote in 1935: 'Here, one wants to create the Paris of the Far West. Evening traffic on Hollywood Boulevard attempts to mimic Parisian boulevard life. However, life on the Boulevard is extinct before midnight, and the seats in front of the cafes, where in Paris one can watch street life in a leisurely manner, are missing' (Wagner, 1935: 156, my translation).

10. Davis (1995b: 270) writes that the Hollywood Red Line was never meant to service existing transit demand: 'The project became simply an aphrodisiac attracting real estate investment to the city's three largest redevelopment projects – in the Downtown–Hollywood–North Hollywood corridor.'

11. The most famous incident during the construction of the Red Line subway extension into Hollywood was the opening up, on June 22, 1995, of the 'Hollywood Sinkhole', a 'monstrous cavity, seventy feet deep and half a block in diameter' which Mike Davis called 'the taunting symbol of the biggest transportation fiasco in modern American history' (Davis, 1995b).

12. The biennual interim report of the Hollywood project area, for example, listed three large commercial projects in 1988 that had a total private investment of $27.5 million including $220 000 for art.

13. For the transfer of air rights for approximately 180 million square feet in the construction of the Library Tower (now First Interstate Tower) such fees were estimated at $86 million while the total construction sum was $1 billion (Chorneau, 1988b).

14. On the complexity of this problem and on the difficulties of containment strategies in light of the increasing diversification of homeless populations see Ruddick (1996); Wolch and Dear (1993).

15. At the time, Hall was quoted as follows: 'I think it's necessary that the agency begin focusing much of its attention on the problems of Skid Row, homelessness, families in poverty and other urgent needs', quoted in Stewart (1990b: B8).

16. After her election in the newly created First Council District in 1987, Molina quickly made a name for herself as an opponent of dominant urban development policies. At the same time, she pursued a new kind of urban development policy in Central City West, just west of the Harbor Freeway downtown. This policy, which was largely to rely on private financing and implementation, was to work with public–private partnership and social policy through linkage deals with development. Molina's switch from the City Council to the County Board of Supervisors and the crisis in Los Angeles real estate prevented major tangible results of this policy from materializing.

17. The City Council's activity was triggered by a $1.5 million severance payment to the former administrative head of the CRA, John Tuite.

18. After the previous regulation, the City Council had delegated territorial political power in the project areas to the CRA. Because of dominant legal understanding, the City Council could only vote 'yes' or 'no' on CRA projects. Since such votes were often held very late into project development, substantial discussion and/or influence by elected representatives was almost impossible.

19. In January of 1990, Yaroslavsky welcomed the appointment of moderate critics of the CRA to its board, yet added that, as long as Jim Wood remained chairman, he remained 'skeptical about whether the tough decisions that need to be made are going to be made. I think the problem with the agency is with the chairman, and the person who is chairman of that board and has been for, what, a decade now, has to take responsibility for the agency' (quoted in Stewart, 1990b: B8).

20. His critics point out, however, that in his 20-year term of office in his west Los Angeles district, Yaroslavsky pursued a straight policy of growth himself. Often, he supported privately the same projects to which he objected publicly (Boyarsky, 1988a). This was a factor in his loss of credibility and support with some of the slow-growth neighborhood groups.

21. An alliance of Jobs with Peace, Housing LA and Legal Aid.

22. In 1984 and 1986, Jobs with Peace had gained some respectable results at the polls when their 'Childcare not Warfare' campaign and their attempts to curtail military production in Southern California were main aspects of their organizing drives.

23. Sponsoring organizations were Jobs With Peace, Coalition for Economic Survival, Housing Los Angeles, Los Angeles Homeless Healthcare Project, Neighborhood Action Committee, Solidarity, City-Line, Health Access Coalition, Little Tokyo Service Center, Concerned Citizens of South Central Los Angeles, and the Labor/Community Strategy Center.

24. At the same time, other initiatives strongly pushed a community economic development agenda. In November 1989, a conference of about 200 representatives of social and ethnic minorities met at Occidental College in Los Angeles to discuss development strategies for their impoverished neighborhoods. One suggestion made at this gathering was that investors be required to develop a parcel of land in south or east Los Angeles for each parcel they developed downtown, or alternatively, pay fees to a housing fund (Gaw, 1989).

25. In August 1989, during their Justice for Janitors campaign, Local 399 published a brochure with the title 'From the Basement to the Boardroom: Los Angeles Should Work for Everyone', which included the demand for better social conditions and job security for low-wage employees in CRA project areas. The brochure also reported a decision by the CRA board on May 31, 1989 to commit the CRA to paying janitors decent wages (Schimek, 1989).

26. This is a noteworthy change since just a couple of years earlier, Jim Wood, CRA chair and County AFL-CIO official, had discouraged janitors and unions like SEIU Local 399 from participating in the activities of the Campaign for Critical Needs, which was critical of the CRA. In fact, Jim Wood had come around in 1991 to attack the corporate critics of the CRA's changed policy for making millions of dollars while opposing paying health insurance to people who cleaned toilets (Clifford, 1991).

# Chapter 10

1. In 1850, Los Angeles was the first incorporated city in the county. By 1997, there were 88.

2. Thanks to Don Parson for his input on the preceding section.

3. These communities were selected from an original sample group of 25 cities in Los Angeles County. I believe that they typify distinguishable ways in which local states have dealt with globalization. The existence of 'reform governments' or 'progressive governments' in Santa Monica and West Hollywood were an additional criterion for their selection. In each city, several interviews with city officials, local politicians and activists were conducted between 1986 and 1991.

4. An estimated one-third of the 36 118 (1990) inhabitants of West Hollywood are gays and lesbians (Law, 1994: 12). By the end of the 1980s, the city had more than 100 businesses and institutions owned and run by homosexuals including two banks, interior architecture and furnishing firms, bars, boutiques and restaurants. Many gays and lesbians are residential property owners in the city. The result is a lively, economically and culturally successful community in West Hollywood (Moos, 1989). There was a gay subculture before incorporation. The County Sheriff's Department was considered to be less stringent than the neighboring Los Angeles Police Department in the control it wielded over the homosexual subculture. Incorporation, however, could be interpreted as a response to the lack of political autonomy felt by the homosexual community, which, until then, did not have local representation. In 1997, West Hollywood had a majority gay city council (Catania, 1997: 11).

5. Under the jurisdiction of Los Angeles County, the area of West Hollywood had a residential density uncommon in Southern California. The zoning plan allowed for a floor area ratio of four in many parts of the city, which made West Hollywood the most densely populated urban area west of the Mississippi. Residential high rises dominated the urban structure. In 1985, 88% of the population were renters, many of them elderly citizens (who represented 28% of the total population of the area) (Moos, 1989).

6. In a critique of Moos' (1989) discussion of incorporation in West Hollywood, Forest (1995: 139–140) points out that gays had expressed early support for incorporation. This was evident in articles in the gay press starting in 1983.

7. 'Generate knowledge and experience in the region, State, nation and world of the unique character of West Hollywood. Encourage trend-setting by the City's special business

groups (interior design, clothing design, restaurants and commercial entertainment, motion pictures/TV/recordings, etc.). Maintain the linkage/recognition connection between themes like "creativity", "California look", "The New Southern California", etc., and identification with West Hollywood' (City of West Hollywood, 1988: 106).

8. Information on the formation of the local state in West Hollywood was obtained in part through interviews with social activists and politicians who participated in the process – Kimberley Kyle, Larry Gross, Gilda Haas and Rebecca Logue. Notes and tapes of these interviews are in my possession and are available on request.

9. Kirby notes that the forces that coalesced in West Hollywood were not 'interchangeable components of a homogenous underclass' and that homosexuals are 'a cross-section of the broader population':

> [C]onsequently there exists there tension between men and women, between races and ethnic groups, between young and old, and between affluent and poor. (. . .) To expect all members of a minority defined in one sphere to automatically hold identical opinions on other spheres is, tragically, to miss the point about the fragmented nature of urban society and also the differing potential of new social movements (Kirby, 1993: 75–76).

10. There remains today a creative tension inside the founding groups of West Hollywood in terms of the direction of their city's policies. While in 1997 a majority gay City Council was elected, the Coalition for Economic Survival lost in influence (Catania, 1997: 11).

11. Despite the absence of a general 'progressive' discourse and despite concentration on the allocation processes for urban services in favor of the founding constituencies of the city, the municipality of West Hollywood has had an extraordinarily high social welfare budget which rests on a politically progressive philosophy. While the county spent only $350 000 in 1984 to care for the needy, the city spent $3.5 million in 1987 for food, housing, transportation, counselling, legal aid, health services, financial services, drug programs, education, information and consultation. Citizens using these services numbers 10 000–14 000. In 1988, the city's social services budget stood at $2.5 million. The California League of Cities estimated that West Hollywood spent more money per capita on social services than did any other American city (*The Post*, September 28, 1989: 7; Waldman, 1988: 542).

12. On the other hand, some nongay residents have voiced their concerns about the 'perceived unfairness in the amount of attention that gay and lesbian issues received, rather than a hostility to gay and lesbian people themselves. A typical comment in this regard was "There is too much emphasis put on the gay lifestyle. They are only part of the community and should not be representative of West Hollywood as a whole"' (Law, 1994: v).

13. Background knowledge for this chapter was obtained partly through interviews with city officials, activists and developers in Santa Monica and on the Westside. Details and references can be obtained from the author and from Keil (1993). Tapes or notes exist for all interviews.

14. SMRR's political opponents on the right polemically likened the success of the 'middle-class radicals' to the establishment of a 'Soviet Monica'. Rent control, liberal urban development policy and a critical attitude towards the 'Reagan revolution', however, hardly justify the label of a 'communist conspiracy.' On the other hand, the successes of liberal urban politicians in Santa Monica were interpreted as a signal for a decentralized national liberalization process, as a grassroots countermovement against the policies of the Reagan and Bush administrations (see Shearer, 1984). It was believed that the space provided by home rule could be a basis from which to democratize American society from the bottom up. The experiment of Santa Monica was regarded as part of the neopopulist or left-populist revolt which gathered steam in the 1980s, and whose representatives believed that US society could be changed through a network of local political institutions and of liberated local spaces (see the analyses of Boggs, 1983; Kann, 1983, 1986).

15. The election of 'no-growth'-oriented candidates in other communities in west Los Angeles during the 1980s attests to the fact that the middle classes of these areas

became politicized around the preservation of their life spaces and neighborhoods. The slow-growth initiative, Proposition U, in Los Angeles in 1986, as well as other no-growth policies, had their origins in the districts of Los Angeles councilmen Zev Yaroslavsky and Marvin Braude, situated just east of Santa Monica. In Los Angeles' Venice/Westchester district, Ruth Galanter, a slow-growth candidate, was able to win the council seat from incumbent and Bradley supporter Pat Russell in 1987. SMRR's success in Santa Monica might have even had some catalytic influence on these cases. None of the other cases was, however, based on the distinctive critical mixture of liberal and radical intellectuals and a tenant majority that formed the base of a comprehensive redefinition of the local political and planning process in Santa Monica.

16. The fact that such inclusively zoned projects ended up being either in the sparsely populated inner city or in poor neighborhoods, where little resistance to higher densities was to be expected, was not incongruent with the good intentions of the reformers. Rather, it was its logical outcome: sociospatial restructuring was not to be to the detriment of the privileges of local citizens. However, the housing element of municipal planning and social welfare reform can be considered the only field where local redistribution policies were seriously attempted (Kann, 1986: 178–181).

17. One measure in this context was a zoning plan element passed in 1984 which introduced a special office district in a formerly light industrial area. This policy recognized that due to high land prices in the city, land uses would shift from industrial to office. The rationale for the designation of the special zone was for the city to approach developers with the offer of a 'garden office district'. The city envisioned creating a low-density office landscape (with a floor area ratio of 2.0) outside of residential areas in order to react to the growing pressure on Santa Monica's office space market. After initial acceptance and frictionless implementation of the first projects following this plan, citizen resistance against the unquestioned permission of large-scale office projects began to rise, mostly due to environmental impact concerns. The consequence was conflict between the investors, who had put money into the area, and the surrounding communities who started to question the extent of development there. In this period, the newly created bureaucratic planning apparatus of the reform government, which had developed a specific planning outcome in difficult negotiations, incurred opposition from within the local population. Despite appeals on the side of the municipal government and SMRR for democratization of the planning process, these local communities felt they had not been able to participate effectively in redrawing the zoning plan and felt threatened by large-scale projects in their neighborhoods.

18. At least partly – as in the case of the large-scale office project 'Colorado Place' – the community accused left-liberal politicians of treason and of abandoning their slow-growth convictions.

19. Land uses like gas stations, gardening businesses and nurseries increasingly disappeared from the map of the city because they were unable to pay the rent. In some cases, the city had to step in to keep necessary services in the community. A survey in 1998 showed that Santa Monica was, next to Los Angeles, the most expensive city in which to do business in all of Southern California (*LAT*, January 25, 1998: B1).

20. While formal democratic control over the growth process grew under the policies of the reform government, the government was less successful in influencing the rift in the discourse on growth that spread along socioeconomic lines. Poorer residents, for example in the African American Pico neighborhood, were dependent on certain public services funded by local property and commercial taxes, while more prosperous citizens were able to withdraw into the sphere of private consumption: the former needed public parks and the latter had their own backyards. In this context, the political interests of individual groups became more parochial and antagonistic.

21. Rent Control Charter Amendment, Article XVIII. Rent Control.

22. A difficulty with this reasoning is that in a situation of rapid change in tenure, the sociological character of the winners in this process will be hard to predict or determine because there has been a trend to gentrification in Santa Monica. Although rent control has kept the price of housing from skyrocketing, with many apartments changing

hands, the city has become richer and whiter (Interview Curran). Informal allocation policies of landlords, who include renovation clauses into leases, thus allowing only wealthy tenants to take over a vacant apartment, have supported this trend (Wilkinson, 1989a). Ironically, this gap in the praxis of strict rent control is used by landlords in their argument against the regulation; they maintain that it has added up to an interventionist subsidy by the local state for its Yuppie clientele. In the political jargon of the landlord groups, rent control 'takes from the poor and gives to the Yuppies' (Glover, 1989).

23. This remains true in the 1990s although the oppositional Coalition for a Safe Santa Monica which won three seats on council in 1994 has made sweeping attack on SMRR's major policy cornerstones. In this election, SMRR held on to a 4–3 majority on the City Council.

24. On the tenth anniversary of rent control in April of 1989, Santa Monica City Hall became the scene of a bizarre confrontation: 'Inside a City Hall courtyard, Santa Monica politicians and tenant activists sipped punch and nibbled cake, crackers and Brie. Transients who crashed the festivities shared in the finger foods under colorful balloons. "Thank God for rent control", beamed Mayor Dennis Zane, an original promoter of the system. "This would be a completely different city if it weren't for rent control." Outside, landlords with a different viewpoint marched under an American flag, waved placards and chanted through bullhorns: "Rent control for the rich! Help the needy, not the greedy!" The landlords had backup. A World War II armored car circled City Hall, symbolically aiming its 20-millimeter turret gun at the building that many of the protesters were calling "the Kremlin"' (Wilkinson, 1989a: I, 1–24).

25. In August 1989, the city hired a consultant to represent the interests of the homeless against the state and federal governments (Hsu, 1989). In December 1991, the Santa Monica Task Force on Homelessness lauded the city for its efforts to address the problem locally, but concluded that it was up to the state and federal governments to provide solutions (City of Santa Monica, 1991).

26. Particularly for the homosexual subculture which had created a niche for itself in local civil society already under county rule, the dilemma of a peripheral existence remains. Castells wrote about the gay population of San Francisco even before the onset of the AIDS epidemic which exacerbated the gay community's victimization: 'Society was responding to the real threat posed by gay values to the fundamental institutions of our civilization, such as family life and sexual repression. And so, in turn, the gay territory could not remain a cultural, Utopian community; either walls had to be elevated around the free city or the entire political system had to be reformed. This dilemma was still facing gays at the time of our research' (Castells, 1983: 145).

27. This is particularly noteworthy in a climate of increased attacks on progressive experiments in California such as ongoing attempts to restrict local rent control by state laws (Cogan, 1995; Jennings, 1995).

28. Carson seems to have been less affected by the economic recession in Southern California during the early 1990s. It continued to draw new investment but also 'initiated a heightened proactive program aimed at aggressively attracting new business' (Stelpflug, 1994: 3).

29. Information taken from 'Carson, The History of a City', an undated brochure distributed by the city. The data is based on an actual count by the municipality and on the 1990 census.

30. A local councilwoman was quoted in 1994 as saying: 'I consider myself a community activist – not a politician. Having said that, I would point out that myself and the rest of the city council are very dedicated to improving the quality of life in the City of Carson. We want to make sure that we continue to work to unite the business community, as well as the residents of Carson. We have never had ethnic or religious polarization in our community – nor do we want it. Yes we are a very diverse city, but we view that as one of our strongest assets' (Mary Anne O'Neal quoted in Stelpflug, 1994: 13).

31. Following workers' demands, the City Council of South Gate finally did a feasibility study of the continuation of production in the local General Motors plant and sent a

petitioning delegation to Detroit. The plant was closed in 1982. In 1985, the city's CRA bought the old factory and GM's property in order to erect a shopping center in its stead. Although the city had to suffer losses of $350 000 in annual taxes from GM, the City Council praised the multinational corporation as late as 1985 for its flexibility in setting the price for the property (Donahoe, 1987: Chapter 4).

32. The foundation's most famous supporter over the years has been Bruce Springsteen who has donated thousands of dollars to its cause.

33. Mike Davis has correctly warned against an overestimation of the emerging political representation of Latinos in the hub cities. Latino power, he argues, often takes the form of petty bourgeois small entrepreneurs and landlords. In Huntington Park, for example, two conservative Latinos were elected in the early 1990s. Davis, in fact, sees the hub cities as an ideal test area for the Latino strategy of the Republican Party (Davis, 1991c).

34. Bell Garden's City Council used the tax income from the Bicycle Club to finance aggressive urban redevelopment projects which destroyed hundreds of housing units. The policies of the City Council, who had been elected by less than 2% of the local population in the heavily immigrant city, led to protests by the town's Latino population when a land-use plan introduced more projected destruction of housing for redevelopment (Davis, 1991c).

35. The poorer communities are subject to different kinds of blackmail than their wealthier counterparts. They often receive offers from investors to allow toxic industries and garbage incinerators to be located on city land. In the mid-1980s, the city of Bell withstood the tempting offer of a toxic waste processor which would have brought $4.5 million to the city's exchequer (*LAT*, May 20, 1989).

36. An alternative story of Compton (and the entire southeast) is offered by Los Angeles' tireless confidence booster, Joel Kotkin, who has argued that the Latinization of southeast Los Angeles has turned the area into a booming business district (Kotkin, 1995b).

37. Mike Davis has pointed out that the local police database listed 10 435 gang members in the community where in 1990 only 8558 15–25 year old males were residing. This results in a paradoxical more than 100% rate of gang membership among the city's youth.

38. This notoriety was confirmed in the sad sequence of events which led up to and followed the shooting death in Las Vegas of Tupac Shakur, the top-selling hiphop artist for Los Angeles' Death Row Records based in Compton. After the shooting in September of 1996, a gang war erupted on the streets of Compton and Lakewood; a possible suspect in Shakur's murder was a Compton resident. When, in March of 1997, Brooklyn rapper Notorious BIG a.k.a. Biggie Smalls was killed leaving the annual Soul Train Awards, a celebration of African American music, a connection was made to the so-called 'coast wars' between the rappers from New York and Los Angeles (Compton). Biggie Smalls' death did not fit the pattern of the 'Compton thang' but the connection was made: 'They knew who they were shooting at. Look at the shot pattern – tight shots, not like a regular West Coast drive-by where gang members are spraying bullets all over the place', a security worker told the press (Anson and Rappleye, 1997: 21).

# CHAPTER 11

1. As late as June 1990, the *LAT* reported that the Van Nuys plant was supposedly to be saved by turning it into a 'flex plant' which would allow for quick model changes (Bernstein, 1990: D3).

2. I have, in this section, concentrated on working-class communities of the inner city. For a brilliantly critical account of middle-class homeowner associations' politics in Los Angeles see Davis (1990, Chapter 3).

3. There was, of course, an interim round of riots of which the Black-Out Riots in New York City in 1977 and the recurring upheavals in Miami during the early 1980s are the

most well-known examples. It seems to me that these events, more than the Watts riots of 1965, might give us some clues for the analysis of the 1992 uprising.

4. On December 19, 1997, Richard Choi, a Korean-American journalist from south-central Los Angeles, was arrested in South Korea on charges of having violated a publishing law. His arrest 'sparked an unusual show of solidarity between Korean American and African American leaders in Los Angeles. Often at odds in recent years, sometimes violently, Korean American and African American leaders have united in calls for Choi's release' (Abrahamson, 1998).

# CHAPTER 12

1. There are still more pronounced beliefs in the coming of an altogether new civilization. Joel Garreau, who in his trademark *Edge City* (1991: 3) remarks that '[E]very single American city that is growing, is growing in the fashion of Los Angeles, with multiple urban cores', speaks of these new urban forms as 'new hearths of civilization' (1991: 3). Others, like Gordon and Richardson (1996) have presented data to argue that Los Angeles is even moving 'beyond polycentricity'. There are numerous problems with this kind of rhetoric. It undercuts the notion of a 'dialectical centrality' (Lefebvre, 1996: 101) more useful to understanding urbanization today than stressing dispersal and decentralization only; and it is politically problematic because the discourse of the vanishing centers contains the danger of the disappearance from the public mind of central populations. It is a rhetoric of eviction, denial and, potentially, racism.

# LIST OF ABBREVIATIONS

| | |
|---|---|
| *AAAG* | *Annals of the Association of American Geographers* |
| ACLU | American Civil Liberties Union |
| *AJS* | *American Journal of Sociology* |
| BRU | Bus Riders' Union |
| CBD | central business district |
| CBE | Communities for a Better Environment |
| CDD | Community Development Department |
| CED | Campaign for Economic Democracy |
| CES | Coalition for Economic Survival |
| CRA | Community Redevelopment Agency |
| EVO | East Valley Organization |
| FHA | Federal Housing Administration |
| FIRE | finance, insurance and real estate |
| FoLAR | Friends of the Los Angeles River |
| *IJURR* | *International Journal of Urban and Regional Research* |
| INS | Immigration and Naturalization Service |
| JACCC | Japanese American Cultural and Community Center |
| *LABJ* | *Los Angeles Business Journal* |
| *LAHE* | *Los Angeles Herald Examiner* |
| LAMAP | Los Angeles Manufacturing Action Project |
| *LAT* | *Los Angeles Times* |
| L/CSC | Labor/Community Strategy Center |
| LTPRO | Little Tokyo People's Rights Organization |
| LTRA | Little Tokyo Redevelopment Association |
| MOCA | Museum of Contemporary Art |
| MTA | Metropolitan Transit Authority |
| NIDL | new international division of labor |
| *NLR* | *New Left Review* |
| *NYT* | *New York Times* |
| PAC | Project Area Committee |
| PACE | Pacific Asian Consortium of Employment |
| *PS* | *Political Science* |
| SCAG | Southern California Association of Governments |
| SCAQMD | South Coast Air Quality Management District |
| SCOC | South Central Organizing Committee |
| SMRR | Santa Monicans for Renters' Rights |
| SRO | Single Occupancy Room Hotel |
| *UAQ* | *Urban Affairs Quarterly* |
| UNO | United Neighborhood Organization |
| USC | University of Southern California |
| VA | Veterans' Administration |

# LIST OF FIGURES

# LIST OF TABLES

# LIST OF PLATES

# ACKNOWLEDGEMENTS

In Los Angeles there are many people who helped me understand what the city was all about. Without my colleagues at work, interviewees and friends, I would have no stories to tell of Los Angeles. The students and professors of the planning program at UCLA (formerly GSAUP) where I was a visiting scholar twice during my research, were critical advisors. Bob Gottlieb invited me first. John Friedmann and Ed Soja adopted me as their Frankfurt student. The advice of Michael Storper, Allen Scott and Stephanie Pincetl was always appreciated. Michael Dear and Jennifer Wolch of the USC were generous with their support and time.

Mike Davis gave me the key to 'his' city. He has been my teacher and guide through the tunnels of Los Angeles' underground. His friendship showed me that I was on the right track. Sophie Spalding passed on Los Angeles survival skills from one Northern European immigrant to another. Gilda Haas, Kim Kyle, Rebecca Logue and Gary Phillips were always there to answer my questions. Eric Mann almost succeeded in keeping me in Los Angeles as a labor and community organizer. Peter Olney and Christina Perez have been exceptional friends.

Sue Ruddick shared many of my travels and travails through Los Angeles. My friend Robin Bloch introduced me to the cultural madness that is Los Angeles. He has been a constant measure and challenger of my work and imagination and helped me understand the western frontier of which Los Angeles is a part. Steven Flusty pushed that frontier out more. Marla Fisher opened the doors of perception for me between Melrose Avenue and Laguna Beach. Liette Gilbert provided a lifeline of information when I was not in Los Angeles.

In Frankfurt, Joachim Hirsch supervised my dissertation and critically accompanied my work. Margit Mayer has created the basis for much of what can be read on the preceding pages. Peter Lieser gave me my first city map of Los Angeles and provided the wheels. Walter Prigge's trust and support always gave me courage. Klaus Ronneberger helped me repatriate my ideas about world city formation.

In Toronto, I would like to thank Gene Desfor and Stefan Kipfer for their friendship and collaboration on recent work. Sean Markey and Anton Krawchenko helped a crazed untenured junior faculty to stay afloat in a sea of files and papers. Pat MacBain did much of my correspondence. Special thanks to Carina Hernandez, who put the manuscript in shape in the most pressured of times. Jennie Barron is the best editor I can imagine. She taught me English once more. Or is it once again? It should go without saying that the mistakes that remain are mine. Many thanks also to Jutta Schaaf who kept her calm in the hectic phase of revising the manuscript. Finally, I wish to express my gratitude to Ron Johnson and Paul Knox for their continuous support and patience and to the editors at Wiley.

This book started as a collaborative project with my friend Don Parson. Don, in the end, chose to concentrate his strength on another project he had already

262

agreed to. I have learned endlessly from Don who is a goldmine of knowledge about Los Angeles' history, politics and popular culture. Don is one of the last true unbent spirits. I owe him much.

Toronto,
August 1998

Roger Keil

# PERSONAL INTERVIEWS

Acosta, Lydia. *Neighborhood Action Council, East Los Angeles*. May 10, 1988.

Altamirano, Sal. *Deputy of Councilman Lindsay, City of Los Angeles*. May 5, 1988.

Bernardi, Ernani. *Councilman, City of Los Angeles*. November 11, 1987.

Bickhart, Jim. *Deputy of Councilwoman Ruth Galanter, City of Los Angeles*. December 12, 1989.

Blight, Reynold. *Economic Development Department, City of Los Angeles*. July 20, 1987.

Boyarsky, Bill. *LAT*. July 14, 1987.

Bozé, Gary. *Deputy of Mayor Tom Bradley, City of Los Angeles*. November 28, 1989.

Briggs, Mark E. *President, M B and A, Tustin, Orange County*. March 18, 1988.

Bryant, David. *Homeless Service Coordinating Unit, City of Los Angeles*. March 21, 1988.

Cole, Benjamin Mark. *LABJ*. July 27, 1987.

Cole, George. *Steelworkers Oldtimers, South Gate*. April 25, 1988.

Carrigan, Kevin. *Community Development Commission, County of Los Angeles*. May 6, 1988.

Conn, James P. *Mayor, City of Santa Monica*. October 7, 1987.

Crow, Ellis K. *Manager, Long Range Planning, City of Long Beach*. November 22, 1987.

Curran, Peggy. *Economic Development, City of Santa Monica*. October 23, 1987.

Dartis, Carla. *Principal Loan Officer, Economic Development Office, City of Los Angeles*. October 19, 1987.

Dear, Michael. *Professor of Geography, USC, Los Angeles*. October 14, 1987.

Diamant, Fred. *Garment manufacturer, Los Angeles*. August 6, 1987.

Dimmitt, Greg. *Enterprise Zones, City of Los Angeles*. March 16, 1988.

Donoghue, Sister Diane. *SCOC, Los Angeles*. September 17, 1987.

Doi, Kerry. *PACE*. October 28, 1987.

Dovalis, Linda. *Department of Housing, City of Maywood*. March 14, 1988.

Ely, Geoff. *Building Owners and Managers' Association, Los Angeles*. March 28, 1988.

Fabiani, Mark. *Chief Deputy, Mayor Tom Bradley, City of Los Angeles*. November 28, 1989.

Fixler, Phil. *Local Government Center, Santa Monica*. September 10, 1987.

Foundation, Larry. *Organizer, SCOC, Los Angeles*. November 16, 1987.

Gatling, Eva. *Public Information Department, City of Carson*. October 20, 1987.

Ginise, Richard. *Lehndorff Properties, Los Angeles*. May 17, 1988.

Grannis, David. *Central City West Association, Los Angeles*. February 29, 1988.

Gross, Larry. *Organizer, Coalition for Economic Survival, West Hollywood*. November 12, 1987.

Haas, Gilda. *Planning Deputy, Councilman Mike Woo, City of Los Angeles*. November 27, 1987.

Hamilton, Cynthia. *Organizer, Concerned Citizens of South Central Los Angeles*. November 13, 1987.

Hicks, Martha Brown. *Skid Row Development Corp., Los Angeles*. March 2, 1988.

Hill, Terence. *Ocean Park Community Center, Santa Monica*. March 22, 1988.

Holl, Edward. *Bateman, Eichler, Hill, Richards Inc., Los Angeles*. March 4, 1988.

Jackson, Bob. *Los Angeles Police Department*. April 21, 1988.

Johnston-Weston, Judith. *V.P. Central City Association, Los Angeles*. November 12, 1987.

Jones, Dennis R. *United Auto Workers/Job Training Partnership Act*. May 5, 1988.

Kann, Mark. *Professor, Political Science, USC, Los Angeles*. October 5, 1987.

Katz, Alisa. *Deputy of Councilman Zev Yaroslavsky, City of Los Angeles*. November 2, 1989.

King, Verne E. *Los Angeles Police Department, Community Resources against Street Hoodlums Unit*. April 14, 1988.

Krotinger, Michelle. *Deputy of Councilman Zev Yaroslavsky, City of Los Angeles*. October 13, 1987.

Kyle, Kimberly. *Housing activist, Los Angeles*. October 27, 1987.

Lake, Laura. *Not Yet New York. Los Angeles*. September 25, 1987.

Law, Maynard. *Cudahy Private Industry Council, Cudahy*. April 27, 1988.

Linski, Chris. *Manager, Tianguis Supermarket, Los Angeles*. September 8, 1987

Logue, Rebecca. *Deputy, Councilwoman Abbe Land, West Hollywood*. October 16, 1987.

Lovejoy, Tracy. *Central City East Association, Los Angeles*. March 9, 1988.

Lowe, Sharon. *Lawyer, Chinatown, Los Angeles*. May 17, 1988.

Mann, Eric. *Coordinator, Labor Community Coalition to Keep GM Van Nuys Open, Los Angeles*. July 29, 1987.

Marriott, Graham. *President, Acquest International, Los Angeles*. April 19, 1988

Moser, Peter. *German American Chamber of Commerce. Los Angeles*. March 14, 1988.

Natker, Andrew. *Vice President, Alexander Haagen Company*. May 13, 1988.

Negrete, Lou. *Organizer, UNO, Los Angeles*. November 13, 1987.

Nichols, Marge. *Research Director, United Way of Los Angeles*. November 24, 1987.

Nishida, Mo. *Activist, Little Tokyo Center, Los Angeles*. March 25, 1988.

Perry, Pilar M. *Director, Public Affairs, Watson Land Co., Carson*. November 4, 1987.

Pisano, Jane. *President, Los Angeles 2000, Los Angeles*. November 20, 1987.

Quan, R.K. *Officer, Los Angeles Police Department*. April 21, 1988.

Reyes, Adolfo. *Redevelopment Department, City of Carson*. April 27, 1988.

Riopelle, Lois. *Community Development Commission, County of Los Angeles*. March 7, 1988.

Robertson, Marjorie. *Research Director, Homeless Youth Research Project. Olive View Medical Hospital, Los Angeles*. July 16, 1987.

Sanada, Glen. *PACE, Los Angeles*. October 28, 1987.

Schneider, Paul. *President, Chamber of Commerce, Carson*. November 4, 1987.

Shrieves, Jerry. *President, Local 645, UAW, Van Nuys*. November 10, 1987.

Sladky, Charles. *Homeless Services Coordinating Unit, City of Los Angeles*. March 21, 1988.

Springer, Arnold. *Activist, Venice Town Council, Los Angeles*. May 5, 1989.

Steiner, W.W. *Manufacturers' Council, City of Industry*. March 10, 1988.

Stewart, Christopher L. *President, Central City Association, Los Angeles*. November 12, 1987.

Sunoo, Cooke. *Project Manager, Hollywood Redevelopment Area, CRA of Los Angeles*. May 3, 1988.

Swimmer, Milt. *J. H. Snyder Company, Los Angeles*. May 26, 1989.

Tademy, Desiree. *Organizer, Jobs with Peace, Los Angeles*. November 14, 1987.

Takahashi, Michi. *Local Areas Formation Commission, County of Los Angeles*. October 28, 1987.

Vilmur, Robert. *Homeless Projects Coordinator, City of Los Angeles*. April 28, 1988.

Vogel, Sydney. *Garment manufacturer, South El Monte*. September 2, 1987.

Watanabe, Bill. *Little Tokyo Service Center, Los Angeles*. March 15, 1988.

Webster, Kenyon. *City Planning Department, Santa Monica*. June 1, 1989.

Welsh, Bill. *President, Hollywood Chamber of Commerce*. February 29, 1988.

Williams, Jasper. *Coordinator, Central City Enterprise Zone. Economic Development Department, Los Angeles*. March 16, 1988.

Wolff, Goetz. *Economic Roundtable, County of Los Angeles*. March 2, 1988.

Woo, Mike. *Councilman, City of Los Angeles*. August 10, 1987.

Wood, James. *Chairman, CRA, City of Los Angeles*. October 26, 1987.

# BIBLIOGRAPHY

Abrahamson, Alan (1998) 'L.A. Journalist Freed from S. Korean Jail' *LAT*. January 8.

ACLU (American Civil Liberties Union of Southern California) (1992) *Civil Liberties in Crisis: Los Angeles during the Emergency*. Los Angeles.

Acquest International (1987) 'Los Angeles Real Estate Market Analysis' Los Angeles: Acquest.

Acuna, Rodolfo (1990) 'America Retreats on Labor Laws' *LAT*. July 16.

Adler, Sy (1986) 'The Dynamics of Transit Innovation in Los Angeles' *Environment and Planning D: Society and Space*. 4: 321–335.

Agenda '77 Committee (1977) 'An Agenda for Los Angeles: A Report to Mayor Tom Bradley' Los Angeles: City of Los Angeles.

Aglietta, Michel (1979) *A Theory of Capitalist Accumulation*. London: Verso.

Alexander, Donnell (1997) 'Christopher Wallace, a.k.a. Notorious B.I.G., 1972–1997' *LA Weekly*. March 14–21: 20.

Allen, James P. and Eugene Turner (1997) *The Ethnic Quilt: Population Diversity in Southern California*. Northridge, CA: The Center for Geographical Studies, California State University, Northridge.

Amin, Ash (ed.) (1994) *Post-Fordism. A Reader*. Oxford, UK and Cambridge, USA: Blackwell.

Amnesty International (1992) *Police Brutality in Los Angeles, California. U.S.A.* London: Amnesty International.

*Amusement Business Magazine* (1997) December.

Anson, Sam Gideon and Charles Rappleye (1997) 'B.I.G. D.O.A. Who wanted Biggie Smalls dead?' *LA Weekly*. March 14–21: 20–22.

Antonioni, Michelangelo (1970) *Zabriskie Point*. Bologna: Cappelli.

Bacon, David (1994) 'Concrete Jungle. The Fight against Toxic Waste and Environmental Racism in Southeast Los Angeles?' *L.A. Village View*. 9, 20, December 16–22: 32.

Baer, W.C. (1986) 'Housing in an Internationalizing Region: Housing Stock Dynamics in Southern California and the Dilemmas of Fair Share' *Environment and Planning D: Society and Space*. 4, 337–349.

Baker, Bob (1986) 'Burning Unity: Grass-Roots Organizations Merge Efforts to Fight Trash-to-Energy Incineration Plants in Southland' *LAT*. September 7: II, 1.

Baker, Houston A. (1993) 'Scene . . . Not Heard' *Reading Rodney King – Reading Urban Uprising*. Ed. Robert Gooding-Williams. New York and London: Routledge. 38–48.

Baldassare, Mark (Ed.) (1994) *The Los Angeles Riots: Lessons for the Urban Future*. Boulder. San Francisco and Oxford: Westview Press.

Banham, Reyner (1971) *Los Angeles: The Architecture of Four Ecologies*. Harmondsworth: Pelican.

Baudrillard, Jean (1983) *Simulations*. New York: Semiotext(e), Inc.

Baudrillard, Jean (1987) *Amerika*. Munich: Matthes and Seitz.

Beauregard, Robert A. (1991) 'Capital Restructuring and the New Built Environment of Global Cities: New York and Los Angeles' *IJURR*. **15**, 1: 90–105.

Berelowitz, Jo-Anne (1990) 'A New Jerusalem: Utopias, MOCA, and the Redevelopment of Downtown Los Angeles' *Strategies*. **3**: 202–226.

Berkman, Leslie (1987) 'Demand Grows for Designer Fruits, Vegetables' *LAT*. October 11: IV, 6.

Bernard, Richard M. and Bradley R. Rice (1983) *Sunbelt Cities: Politics and Growth since World War II*. Austin: University of Texas Press.

Bernstein, Harry (1990) 'Ray of Hope for Van Nuys UAW' *LAT*. June 19: D3.

Bigger, Richard and James D. Kitchen (1952) *How the Cities Grew*. Los Angeles: The Haynes Foundation.

Bloch, Robin (1987) 'Studies in the Development of the United States Aerospace Industry' Graduate School of Architecture and Urban Planning, UCLA.

Bloch, Robin (1989) 'Southern California's Furniture Industry in National and International Context' A Report for International Union of Electronic, Electrical, Salaried, Machine, and Furniture Workers, Local 1010. Huntington Park, California.

Bloch, Robin and Roger Keil (1991) 'Planning for a Fragrant Future: Air Pollution Control, Restructuring, and Popular Alternatives in Los Angeles' *Capitalism, Nature, Socialism*. **2**, 1, Issue 6: 44–65.

Bloods/Crips (1992) 'Human Welfare Proposal' manuscript, Los Angeles.

Bluestone, Michael and Bennett Harrison (1982) *The Deindustrialization of America*. New York: Basic Books.

Bodaken, Michael (1989) 'Legal Aid Foundation of Los Angeles' Testimony in Favor of Establishing a Community Redevelopment Commission' Ms. Los Angeles: Legal Aid.

Bodaken, Michael, Larry Gross and Anthony Thigpen (1989) 'If the Public Decided On Next $4.25 Billion, Would Choices Resemble CRA's?' *LAT*. June 18.

Boggs, Carl (1983) 'The New Populism and the Limits of Structural Reform' *Theory and Society*. 12: 365–373.

Bollens, John C. and G. Geyer (1973) *Yorty: Politics of a Constant Candidate*. Pacific Palisades CA: Palisades Publishers.

Bottles, Scott L. (1987) *Los Angeles and the Automobile: The Making of the Modern City*. Berkeley: University of California Press.

Boxall, Bettina and Larry Gordon (1997) 'Fade In on 2 Ambitious Projects' *LAT*. March 28: B1–10.

Boyarsky, Bill (1987a) 'Vote Mirrors an Angry Constituency' *LAT*. June 4: I, 1.

Boyarsky, Bill (1987b) 'Bradley: Is He Losing Old Touch?' *LAT*. July 1: I,1.

Boyarsky, Bill (1987c) 'Old Alliance Loses Ardor for Bradley' *LAT*. July 2: I, 1.

Boyarsky, Bill (1988a) 'The Two Sides of Zev Yaroslavsky' *LAT*. February 21, II, 1.

Boyarsky, Bill (1988b) 'Issue of Growth Dominates Key Local Elections' *LAT*. April 13: II, 1.

Boyarsky, Bill (1988c) 'U.S. Pressures Board of Supervisors to Remap for Latino Representation' *LAT*. June 7: II, 1.

Boyarsky, Bill (1989a) 'In the Ring or in Politics, Holden Loves a Fight' *LAT*. April 3: I, 1.

Boyarsky, Bill (1989b) 'Yaroslavsky Would Have Forced Runoff' *LAT*. April 16: I, 1.

Boyarsky, Bill (1989c) 'Art Snyder in the Sprint for Growth' *LAT*. December 15: B: 2.

Boyarsky, Bill (1997) 'Latino Middle Class Emerges as a Force' *LAT*. April 10: B1.

Boyarsky, Bill and Glenn F. Bunting (1989) '"Street Money" Paved Way for Bradley Victory' *LAT*. August 17: II, 1.

Boyarsky, Bill/Frederick M. Muir (1989) 'Bradley's Budget: $3.2 Billion and 514 More Officers' *LAT*. April 14: II, 1.

Bradley, Tom (n.d.) 'Los Angeles 2000' Presentation. Los Angeles: Office of the Mayor.

Bradley, Tom (1974) 'A Vision of a Humane Urban America' *Nation's Cities*. **12**, 11: 20.

Bradley, Tom (1979) 'Management Techniques and the Urban Crisis' *The Changing Structure of the City*. Ed. Gary A. Tobin. Beverly Hills: Sage. 133–137.

Bradley, Tom (1985) 'Reduction in Federal Aid to Cities: The Cure That Kills?' *Commonwealth*. **79**, 36: 294–297.

Bradley, Tom (1988) 'State of the City Address' Los Angeles: Office of the Mayor.

Bradley, Tom (1989) 'Los Angeles Looks to the Future' Keynote address, Japan-American Conference of Mayors and Chamber of Commerce Presidents, May 15. Los Angeles: Office of the Mayor.

Brodsly, David (1981) *L.A. Freeway: An Appreciative Essay*. Berkeley, Los Angeles, London: The University of California Press.

Brooks, Nancy Rivera (1987) 'Growth Still Fuels Southland's "Factory"' *LAT*. November 15: IV, 1.

Brooks, Nancy Rivera (1988) 'Beverly Hills vs. West Hollywood' *LAT*. May 30: IV, 1.

Browne, David and Roger Keil (1996) 'Planning Ecology in Los Angeles: The Los Angeles

River and Air Pollution Regulation'. Paper given at the Association of Collegiate Schools of Planning Annual Conference, Toronto, Ontario, July 26.

Browning, Rufus P., Dale Rogers Marshall and David H. Tabb (1984) *Protest is Not Enough: The Struggle of Blacks and Hispanics for Equality in Urban Politics*, Berkeley, Los Angeles, London: University of California Press.

Bullard, Robert (1993) 'Anatomy of Environmental Racism and the Environmental Justice Movement' *Confronting Environmental Racism: Voices from the Grassroots*. Ed. R. Bullard. Boston: South End Press: 7–13.

Bunting, Glenn F. (1988a) 'Bradley's Busy Social Life Pays Dividends in Politics' *LAT*. June 13: I, 1.

Bunting, Glenn F. (1988b) 'The Mayor Lends an Ear to Haves and Have-Nots' *LAT*. June 14: I, 1.

Bunting, Glenn F. (1988c) 'Bradley Sheds Consensus-Maker Role' *LAT*. June 15: I, 1.

Bunting, Glenn F. (1988d) 'Ex-Bradley Aides Cash in on Influence' *LAT*. June 12: I, 1.

*Business Week* (1987) 'For Sale: America' September 14: 52–62.

*Business Week* (1989) Title-story 'Rethinking Japan' August 7: 44–52.

Butler, Judith (1993) 'Endangered/Endangering: Schematic Racism and White Paranoia' *Reading Rodney King – Reading Urban Uprising*. Ed. Robert Gooding-Williams. New York and London: Routledge. 15–22.

Byron, Doris A. (1982), 'Downtown L.A.: High Price Boom Molds New Skyline' *LAT*. April 25: I, 1.

Cahn, Matthew Alan (1995) *Environmental Deceptions: The Tension between Liberalism and Environmental Policymaking in the United States*. Albany: State University of New York Press.

California Department of Commerce, Office of Economic Research (1987) 'Foreign Direct Investment in California' Sacramento.

California Public Interest Group (Calprig) (1987) 'News Release: Food Price Survey' Los Angeles, September 21.

Campbell, Murray (1992a) 'It Never Rains in California, it Pours' *The Globe and Mail*. November 30: B1.

Campbell, Murray (1992b) 'Resentment Lingers, Smoldering' *The Globe and Mail*. December 8: A1.

Campbell, Murray (1992c) 'Trying to Bridge the Great Divide' *The Globe and Mail*. December 9.

Carlson, Margaret (1989) 'How to Make Boring Beautiful: Or, Why California Has such Glitzy People and such Dull Polls' *Time*. April 24: 20.

Carney, Francis M. (1964) 'The Decentralized Politics of Los Angeles' *The Annals of the American Academy of Political and Social Science*. Issue 353: 107–121.

Castells, Manuel (1983) *The City and the Grassroots: A Cross-Cultural Theory of Urban Social Movements*. Berkeley and Los Angeles: University of California Press.

Castells, Manuel and Peter Hall (1994) *Technopoles of the World: The Makings of 21st Century Industrial Complexes*. London: Routledge.

Castells, Manuel and Jeffrey Henderson (1987) 'Techno-economic Restructuring, Socio-political Processes and Spatial Transformation: a Global Perspective' *Global Restructuring and Territorial Development*. Eds. Jeffrey Henderson and Manuel Castells. London: Sage. 1–17.

Castro, Tony (1985) 'How Politics Built Downtown' *LAHE*. March 10: A, 1.

Catania, Sara (1997) 'West Hollywood Goes Gay' *LA Weekly*. March 7–13: 11.

Central City Association of Los Angeles (1986) 'Activities Report' Los Angeles.

Cenzatti, Marco (1993) *Los Angeles and the L.A. School: Postmodernism and Urban Studies*. Los Angeles: Los Angeles Forum for Architecture and Urban Design.

Chandhoke, Neera (1995) *State and Civil Society: Explorations in Political Theory*. New Delhi, Thousand Oaks, London: Sage Publications.

Chase-Dunn, Christopher (1985) 'The System of World Cities, A.D. 800–1975' *Urbanization in the World Economy*. Ed. Michael Timberlake. New York: Academic Press. 269–292.

Chase-Dunn, Christopher (1989) *Global Formation: Structures of the World Economy*. Cambridge, Massachusetts: Basil Blackwell.

Chorneau, Tom (1987) 'Foreign Investors Think L.A.'s the Place' *LABJ*. September 28–October 4: 1.

Chorneau, Tom (1988a) 'Zev Still Prefers to Ride the Fence Than Make a Move in Mayoral Run' *LABJ*. February 29: 1.

Chorneau, Tom (1988b) 'CRA Expected to Double Air Rights Transfer Costs' *LABJ*. July 4: 7.

Chorneau, Tom (1988c) 'Growth Issues Take Center Stage as Los Angeles Considers Its Future' *LABJ*. January 18: 6.

Christensen, Terry and Larry Gerston (1987) 'West Hollywood: A City Is Born' *Cities*. 4, 4: 299–303.

Christopherson, Susan (1994) 'The Fortress City: Privatized Spaces, Consumer Citizenship' *Post-Fordism: A Reader*. Ed. Ash Amin. Oxford: Blackwell: 409–427.

Christopherson, Susan and Michael Storper (1986) 'The City as Studio; The World as Back Lot: The Impact of Vertical Disintegration on the Location of the Motion Picture Industry' *Environment and Planning D: Society and Space*. 4: 305–320.

Cisneros, Henry and Ryszard Kapuscinski (1988) 'American Dynamism & The New World Culture' *New Perspectives Quarterly*. Summer: 36–46.

Citron, Alan (1986) 'Coalition Won When It Went to the Renters' *LAT*. November 9: I, 1.

Citron, Alan (1987) 'New Leaf: Santa Monica Sheds Radical Image as Factions Learn to Compromise' *LAT*. September 27: W1.

Citron, Alan (1988) 'West Hollywood – Small Thinking Big' *LAT*. July 10: II, 1.

Citron, Alan (1989) 'Task Force Formed to Study Legalizing of Street Vendors' *LAT*. July 8: IV, 1.

City of Carson (n.d.) 'Carson: The History of a City' Carson, California.

City of Carson (1987) 'Future Unlimited' Carson, California.

City of Los Angeles (1994) 'Mayor Riordan Delivers Economic Vision for City' press release, Los Angeles: Office of the Mayor, September 30.

City of Los Angeles Blue Ribbon Committee for Affordable Housing (1988) 'Housing Los Angeles: Affordable Housing for the Future' Los Angeles.

City of Santa Monica (1991) 'The Santa Monica Task Force on Homelessness: A Call to Action' (unpublished report).

City of West Hollywood (1987) General Plan. (Draft) West Hollywood, CA.

City of West Hollywood (1988) General Plan. West Hollywood, CA.

*City* (1996), Special Issue: It all comes together in Los Angeles? 1/2.

Clark, David L. (1983) 'Improbable Los Angeles' *Sunbelt Cities: Politics and Growth Since World War II*. Eds. Richard M. Bernard and Bradley R. Rice. Austin: University of Texas Press. 268–308.

Clavel, Pierre (1986) *The Progressive City: Planning and Participation 1969–1984*. New Brunswick: Rutgers University Press.

Clayton, James L. (1967) 'The Impact of the Cold War on the Economies of California and Utah' *Pacific Historical Review*. **36**: 449–473.

Clayton, Janet (1987a) 'New Council District is Quilt of "Leftovers"' *LAT*. January 18: II, 1.

Clayton, Janet (1987b) 'Molina Victory May Give Council More of Tilt Toward Slow-Growth' *LAT*. February 5: II, 1.

Clayton, Janet (1989) 'Suddenly, Tom Bradley Looks Mortal, and L.A. Blacks Feel Orphaned' *LAT*. May 28: V, 5.

Cleland, Robert Glass and Osgood Hardy (1929) *March of Industry*. Los Angeles: Powell Publishing Company.

Clifford, Frank (1989) 'LA's Past May Be Part of Its Future' *LAT*. December 25: A1.

Clifford, Frank (1990) 'Bradley Adopting New Stance on Growth' *LAT*. January 7: B1.

Clifford, Frank (1991) 'CRA Seeks New Powers over Wages' *LAT*. March 28: B1.

Clifford, Frank and Jane Fritsch (1990) 'CRA Head Is Subject of Probe' *LAT*. June 19: B1.

Coburn, Judith (1994) 'Down by the (L.A.) River (Whose River is it anyway?) *Los Angeles Times Magazine*. November 20: 18–24, 48–54.

Cockburn, Alexander (1989) 'Crack-ups, Crackdowns and Mayor Bradley: Black Political Power in Its Moment of Crisis' *LAWeekly*. May 19–25: 10.

Cockburn, Alexander (1992) 'Bloods Money' *New Statesman*. March 15: 24–25.

Cogan, David (1995) 'Decontrol Freaks' *LA Village View*. May 5–11: 6.

Cohen, Robert B. (1981) 'The New International Division of Labor, Multinational Corporations and Urban Hierarchy' *Urbanization and Urban Planning in Capitalist Society*. Eds. Michael J. Dear and Allen J. Scott. London and New York: Methuen. 287–315.

Cole, Benjamin M. (1987) 'More Manufacturers Make Home in L.A.' *LABJ*. September 7–13.

Cole, Benjamin M. (1988) 'Reports Call L.A. America's First Third World City' *LABJ*. May 23: 16.

Cole, Rick (1989a) 'Glory Days: There Is no Place Like West Hollywood and no Time Like the Present' *West Hollywood Magazine*. **1**: 7–8.

Cole, Rick (1989b) 'Transformation' *West Hollywood Magazine*. **1**: 35–39.

Collins, Catherine (1989) 'Could Japanese Realty Holdings Hurt U.S.?' *LAT*. May 7: VIII, 3.

Colvin, Richard Lee and Gabe Fuentes (1989) 'Developers Borrow Politicians' Tactics to Campaign for Projects' *LAT*. April 26: II, 1.

Committee for Central City Planning (1972) *Central City Los Angeles 1972/1990 (Silverbook)*. Los Angeles: City of Los Angeles.

Condas, John, David Etezadi, Gary Eto, Ray Nakano and Bill Wong (1984) 'Redevelopment in Los Angeles' Little Tokyo,' Los Angeles: Graduate School of Architecture and Urban Planning, UCLA.

Conot, Robert (1986) 'When More Is Too Much: Putting Limits on Growth' *LAT*. October 5: V, 1.

Conot, Robert (1989) 'Saul Alinsky Lives: Populist Groups Go Back to Basics, Revive Poverty War' *LAT*. September 17: V, 3.

Core Laboratory Workshop, Master of Planning Program, School of Urban and Regional Planning, University of Southern California (1987) 'Low Wage Employment in Downtown Los Angeles' Los Angeles: USC.

Covert Action Information Bulletin (1993) 'Uprising and Repression in L.A.: An Interview with Mike Davis' *Reading Rodney King – Reading Urban Uprising*. Ed. Robert Gooding-Williams. New York and London: Routledge. 142–156.

Cox, Kevin R. and Andrew Mair (1988) 'Locality and Community in the Politics of Local Economic Development' *AAAG*. **78**, 2.

Crail, Thomas (1989) 'Frankly, Sweet Success' The West Hollywood *Chamber of Commerce Newsletter*. September: 1.

Crenshaw, Kimberlé and Gary Peller (1993) 'Reel Time/Real Justice' *Reading Rodney King – Reading Urban Uprising*. Ed. Robert Gooding-Williams. New York and London: Routledge. 56–72.

Crouch, Winston W., John C. Bollens and Stanley Scott (1981) *California Government and Politics* (7th edition). Englewood Cliffs, N.J.: Prentice-Hall.

Crouch, Winston W. and Beatrice Dinerman (1963) *Southern California Metropolis: A Study in Development of Government for a Metropolitan Area*. Berkeley and Los Angeles: University of California Press.

Curran, Ron (1988a) 'Putting Politics before Planning' *LAWeekly*. February 12–18: 8.

Curran, Ron (1988b) 'BAD Boys' *LAWeekly*. August 19–25: 8.

Curran, Ron (1989) 'Hot Air?' *LAWeekly*. April 14–20.

Davis, L.J. (1993) 'Is Riordan Tammany's blast from the past?' *The Sacramento Bee*. October 31.

Davis, Mike (n.d.) 'Sunshine and the Open Shop: The Urbanization of Los Angeles – 1880–1930,' unpublished ms, Los Angeles.

Davis, Mike (1986) *Prisoners of the American Dream*. London: Verso.

Davis, Mike (1987) 'Chinatown Part II? The Internationalization of Downtown Los Angeles' *NLR*. Issue 164: 65–86.

Davis, Mike (1990) *City of Quartz: Excavating the Future in Los Angeles*. London: Verso.

Davis, Mike (1991a) 'While the City Spins out of Control' *LAT*. June 2: M1.

Davis, Mike (1991b) 'The New Industrial Peonage' *Heritage*. Summer: 7–12.

Davis, Mike (1991c) 'Latinos Rise up in the Rust Belt' *LAT*. December 20: B7.

Davis, Mike (1992a) 'Burning All Illusions in LA' in *Institute for Alternative Journalism*: 96–100.

Davis, Mike (1992b) 'Realities of the Rebellion' *Against the Current*. **7**, 3, Issue 39: 14–18.

Davis, Mike (1992c), 'Beyond Blade Runner: Urban Control: The Ecology of Fear' Westfield, New Jersey: Open Pamphlet Series.

Davis, Mike (1994a) 'Cannibal City: Los Angeles and the Destruction of Nature' *Urban Revisions: Current Projects for the Public Realm*. Ed. Ferguson, Russel. Los Angeles: Museum of Contemporary Art: 38–57.

Davis, Mike (1994b) 'The Sky Falls on Compton'. *The Nation*. September 19.

Davis, Mike (1995a) 'Los Angeles after the Storm: The Dialectic of Ordinary Disaster' *Antipode*. **27**, 3: 221–241.

Davis, Mike (1995b) 'L.A.'s Transit Apartheid: Runaway Train Crushes Buses' *The Nation*. September 18: 270–274.

Davis, Mike (1996) 'How Eden Lost Its Garden: A Political History of the Los Angeles Landscape' *The City: Los Angeles and Urban Theory at the End of the Twentieth Century*. Eds. Allen Scott and Edward W. Soja. Los Angeles and London: University of California Press. 160–185.

Davis, Mike and Roger Keil (1992) 'Sonnenschein und Schwarze Dahlien: Die ideologische Konstruktion von Los Angeles' *Städtische Intellektuelle*. Ed. Walter Prigge. Frankfurt: Fischer: 267–297.

Day, Rebecca Lois (1985) 'Redevelopment in Chinatown: The Role of Immigration and Ethnic Conflicts' Master's Thesis, Graduate School of Architecture and Urban Planning, Los Angeles: UCLA.

Dear, Michael J. (1986) 'Postmodernism and Planning' *Environment and Planning D: Society and Space*. 4: 367–384.

Dear, Michael J. (1996a) 'In the City, Time Becomes Visible: Intentionality and Urbanism in Los Angeles, 1781-1991' *The City: Los Angeles and Urban Theory at the End of the Twentieth Century*. Eds. Allen J. Scott and Edward W. Soja. Berkeley, Los Angeles, and London: University of California Press. 76–105.

Dear, Michael J. (Ed.) (1996b) *Atlas of Southern California*. Los Angeles: Southern California Studies Center, University of Southern California.

Dear, Michael J., Schockman, Eric H. and Hise, Greg (Eds) (1996) *Rethinking Los Angeles*. Thousand Oaks, California: Sage Publications.

Dear, Michael J. and Jennifer Wolch (1987) *Landscapes of Despair: From Deinstitutionalization to Homelessness*. Princeton, N.J.: Princeton University Press.

Decker, Cathleen (1986) 'Tribute to Immigrants: Firm Presents Bradley Check for Monument' *LAT*. September 16.

Decker, Cathleen (1989) 'Black Leaders Rally Support for Bradley' *LAT*. May 24: II, 1.

Delgado, Hector L. (1987) 'The Unionization of Undocumented Workers in the Los Angeles Bedding Industry: A Case Study' Paper presented at the workshop 'The Changing Roles of Mexican Immigrants in the U.S. Economy: Sectoral Perspectives' Center for U.S.–Mexican Studies, UC San Diego, August 27.

DeMarco, Gordon (1988) *A Short History of Los Angeles*. San Francisco: Lexikos.

Desfor, Gene and Roger Keil (1997) 'Zivilgesellschaft, lokaler Staat und urbane Umweltpolitik in Los Angeles und Toronto' *Zivile Gesellschaft*. Eds Klaus M. Schmals and Hubert Heinelt. Opladen: Leske & Budrich. 291–323.

Deutsche, Rosalyn (1996) *Evictions. Art and Spatial Politics*. Cambridge, Mass. and London, England: The MIT Press.

De Wolfe, Evelyn (1987) 'Realtor Says Foreigners Buy for the Long Haul' *LAT*. June 28: VIII, 11.

Didion, Joan. (1979) *The White Album*. New York: The Noonday Press.

Didion, Joan (1989) 'Letter from Los Angeles' *The New Yorker*. April 24: 88–99.

Doi, Christopher, Tom Fujita, Lewis Kawahara, Brian Nuva and Karen Umemoto (1986) 'Little Tokyo Redevelopment: The North Side of 1st Street' Los Angeles: Asian American Studies 2000, UCLA.

Donahoe, Myrna Cherkoss (1987) *Workers' Response to Plant Closures: The Cases of Steel and Auto in Southeast Los Angeles, 1935–1986*. Ph.D. Dissertation, Department of History, UC Irvine.

Douglass, Mike and John Friedmann (1998) *Cities For Citizens*. Chichester, England: Wiley.

Downtown Strategic Plan Advisory Committee (1989a) 'Public Meeting Notice, September 28.' Los Angeles.

Downtown Strategic Plan Advisory Committee (1989b) 'Minutes, Meeting of the Full Committee, September 28.' Los Angeles.

Duffy, Robert E. (1989) 'An Assessment of the Environment for Japanese Real Estate Investment in California' *The Real Estate Magazine*. Issue 1: 12–13.

Dunne, John Gregory (1991) 'Law and Disorder in Los Angeles' *The New York Review*. October 10: 23–29; and October 24: 62–70.

Dykstra, Clarence A. (1941) 'The Future of Los Angeles' *Los Angeles. Preface to a Master Plan*. Eds George W. Robbins and L. Deming Tilton. Los Angeles: The Pacific Southwest Academy. 1–10.

Dymski, Gary A. and John M. Veitch (1992) 'Race and the Financial Dynamics of Urban Growth: L.A. as Fay Wray' *City of Angels*. Eds Gerry Riposa and Carolyn Dersch. Dubuque, Iowa: Kendall Hunt. 131–157.

Dymski, Gary A. and John M. Veitch (1996) 'Financing the Future in Los Angeles: From Depression to 21st Century' *Rethinking Los Angeles*. Eds Micheal J. Dear, Eric H. Schockman and Greg Hise. Thousand Oaks, California: Sage Publications. 35–55.

Engels, Frederick (1971) 'The Condition of the Working Class in England' (excerpts) in Karl Marx and Frederick Engels, *Ireland and the Irish Question*. London: Lawrence and Wishart: 47–53.

Faggen, Ivan (1989) 'Real Estate Is Best Place for Japanese Money' *LAT*. May 21: VIII, 3.

Feinbaum, Robert (1987) 'Counties Lose: Climate Right for Creating New Cities' *California Journal*. **18**, 10: 497–499.

Feldman, Paul (1989) 'Mayor's Fifth Term May Be One of Provocative Ideas' *LAT*. April 14: II, 1.

Ferraro, Cathleen (1988) 'Fragmentation, Competition Inhibit L.A.'s Union Growth' *California Apparel News*. February 12.

Finzsch, Norbert (1982) *Die Goldgräber Kaliforniens. Arbeitsbedingungen, Lebensstandard und politisches System um die Mitte des 19. Jahrhunderts*. Göttingen: Vandenhoeck und Ruprecht.

Fisher, Marla Jo (1998a) 'Disney Makes Stadium its Own' *The Orange County Register*. January 20: 1 and 8.

Fisher, Marla Jo (1998b) 'It's Constructionland' *The Orange County Register*. January 23: 1 and 8.

FitzSimmons, Margaret and Robert Gottlieb (1996) 'Bounding and Binding Metropolitan Space: The Ambiguous Politics of Nature in Los Angeles' *The City: Los Angeles and Urban Theory at the End of the Twentieth Century*. Eds Allen Scott and Edward W. Soja. Los Angeles and London: University of California Press. 186–224.

Flanigan, James (1987) 'Foreign Investment in U.S. Is Vital Sign of the Globalization of Industry' *LAT*. November 17: IV, 2.

Flanigan, James (1989a) 'Stability Draws Foreign Money to U.S. Markets' *LAT*. May 24: IV, 1.

Flanigan, James (1989b) 'Challenging the System' *LAT*. May 28: IV, 1.

Florida, Richard L. and Marshall M.A. Feldman (1988) 'Housing in U.S. Fordism: The Class Accord and Postwar Spatial Organization' *IJURR*. **12**: 187–209.

Flusty, Steven (1994) *Building Paranoia: The Proliferation of Interdictory Space and the Erosion of Spatial Justice*. West Hollywood: Los Angeles Forum for Architecture and Urban Design.

Fogelson, Robert M. (1993, orig. 1967) *The Fragmented Metropolis: Los Angeles, 1850–1930*. Cambridge, Mass.: Harvard University Press.

Forest, Benjamin (1995) 'West Hollywood as Symbol: The Significance of Place in the Construction of a Gay Identity' *Environment and Planning D: Society and Space*. **13**: 133–157.

Foster, Mark S. (1971) *The Decentralization of Los Angeles during the 1920s*. Ann Arbor, Michigan.

Frantz, Douglas and Collins, Catherine (1989) *Selling Out: How We Are Letting Japan Buy Our Land, Our Industries, Our Financial Institutions, and Our Future*. Chicago: Contemporary Books.

Fraser, Graham (1997) 'Left–Right Showdown in City of Angels' *The Globe and Mail*. April 8: A14.

Friedman, David (1995) 'Reforms That Can Save L.A. from Extinction' *LAT*. February 19: M1.

Friedman, Joel H. (1978) 'The Political Economy of Urban Renewal: Changes in Land Ownership in Bunker Hill, Los Angeles' Master's Thesis, Graduate School of Planning and Architecture, UCLA.

Friedmann, John (1986) 'The World City Hypothesis' *Development and Change*. **17**: 69–83.

Friedmann, John (1995) Where We Stand: A Decade of World City Research, *World Cities in a World System*. Eds. Paul L. Knox and Peter J. Taylor. Cambridge: Cambridge University Press. 21–47.

Friedmann, John and Robin Bloch (1989) 'American Exceptionalism in Regional Planning, 1933–2000' *IJURR*. **14**, 4.

Friedmann, John and Goetz Wolff (1982) 'World City Formation: An Agenda for Research and Action' *IJURR*. 6: 309–344.

Fritsch, Jane (1989) 'Council Members Attack "Misleading CRA Budget"' *LAT*. October 17: B1.

Fritsch, Jane and Gabe Fuentes (1989) 'Bradley Objects to Plan for Porter Ranch' *LAT*. December 3: B1.

Fritsch, Jane and Jill Stewart (1990) 'Wood's Reappointment as CRA Leader Opposed' *LAT*. April 3: B1.

Fuentes, Gabe (1990) 'Porter Ranch Plan Too Big, AQMD Says' *LAT*. January 25: B1.

Fulton, William (1994) 'Riordan Quietly Kills the CRA, Thereby Starting a Jobs-vs.-Revitalization Debate' *LAT*. April 24: M6.

Fulton, William (1997) *The Reluctant Metropolis*. Point Arena, California: Solano Press Books.

Furlong, Tom (1986) 'Foreigners Build New Base in U.S.' *LAT*. October 28: I, 1.

Furlong, Tom and Nancy Yoshihara (1987) 'The Japanese Landrush in America' *LAT*. February 1: IV, 1.

Gabriel, Stuart A. (1996) 'Remaking the Los Angeles Economy: Cyclical Fluctuations and Structural Evolution' *Rethinking Los Angeles*. Eds Michael J. Dear, Eric H. Schockman and Greg Hise. Thousand Oaks, California: Sage Publications. 25–33.

Garcia, Daniel P. (1987) 'City Planning Chief Favors More Controls' *LAT*. June 28: VIII, 11.

Garcia, Dan and Ray Remy (1990) 'Consolidate California Sprawl by Regional Responsible Government' *LAT*. March 25: M4.

Garreau, Joel (1991) *Edge City: Life on the New Frontier*. New York: Doubleday.

Gaw, Jonathan (1989) 'Linking City's Growth to Help for Poor Urged' *LAT*. November 19: B8.

Gee, Emma (Ed.) (1976) *Counterpoint. Perspectives on Asian America*. Los Angeles: Asian American Studies Center, UCLA.

Geiger, Robert K. and Jennifer R. Wolch (1986) 'A Shadow State? Voluntarism in Metropolitan Los Angeles' *Environment and Planning D: Society and Space*. 4: 351–366.

Gilderbloom, John I. and Richard P. Appelbaum (1988) *Rethinking Rental Housing*. Philadelphia: Temple University Press.

Glickman, Norman J. (1987) 'Cities and the International Division of Labor' *The Capitalist City: Global Restructuring and Community Politics*. Eds Michael Peter Smith and Joe R. Feagin. Oxford: Basil Blackwell. 67–86.

Glickman, Norman J. and Douglas P. Woodward (1989) *The New Competitors: How Foreign Investors Are Changing the U.S. Economy*. New York: Basic Books.

Glover, Kara (1989) 'Rent Control in Santa Monica: A Decade Later, Opposing Sides Still Argue S.M. Rent Control' *Daily Commerce*. May 8.

Glushon, Bob (1987) 'L.A.'s Poor and Minorities Also Have a Big Stake in Controlling City's Development' *LAT*. October 13.

Gooding-Williams, Robert (Ed.) (1993) *Reading Rodney King – Reading Urban Uprising*. New York and London: Routledge.

Gordon, Peter and Harry W. Richardson (1996) 'Beyond Polycentricity: The Dispersed Metropolis, Los Angeles, 1970–1990' *Journal of the American Planning Association*. **62**, 3: 289–295.

Gottlieb, Robert and Margaret FitzSimmons (1991) *Thirst for Growth: Water Agencies as Hidden Government in California*. Tucson and London: University of Arizona Press.

Gottlieb, Robert and Irene Wolt (1977) *Thinking Big: The Story of the Los Angeles Times*. Los Angeles: G.P. Putnam and Sons.

Gregory, Derek (1994) *Geographical Imaginations*. Cambridge, Mass.: Blackwell.

Grover, Ronald (1988) 'Why Sake Flows at Tom Bradley's Fund-Raisers' *Business Week*. July 11: 69.

Haas, Gilda (1985) *Plant Closures: Myths, Realities and Responses*. Boston: South End Press.

Haas, Gilda (1986) 'Hurray for West Hollywood!' *City Limits*. **11**, 8: 16–21.

Haas, Gilda and Allan David Heskin (1981) 'Community Struggles in L.A.' *IJURR*. **5**, 4: 546–564.

Haas, Gilda and Rebecca Morales (1986) 'Plant Closures and the Grassroots Responses to Economic Crisis in the U.S.' Graduate School of Architecture and Urban Planning, UCLA.

Haefele, Marc B. (1997) 'Rich Man, Poor Mayor' *LA Weekly*. March 7–13: 20–25.

Hahn, Harlan (1996) 'Los Angeles and the Future: Uprisings, Identity, and New Institutions' *Rethinking Los Angeles*. Eds Michael J. Dear, Eric H. Schockman and Greg Hise. Thousand Oaks: California. 77–95.

Hajer Maarten (1995) *The Politics of Environmental Discourse: Ecological Modernization and the Policy Process*. Oxford University Press.

Hall, Peter (1966) *The World Cities*. New York/Toronto: McGraw-Hill.

Hall, Peter and Ann Markusen (Eds) (1985) *Silicon Landscapes*. Boston: Allen & Unwin.

Hall, Peter *et al.* (1985) 'The American Computer Software Industry: Economic Development Prospects' *Silicon Landscapes*. Eds Peter Hall and Ann Markusen. Boston: Allen & Unwin. 49–64.

Hall, Stuart (1991) 'Brave New World' *Socialist Review*. **21**, 1: 57–64.

Hamilton, Cynthia (1988) 'The Making of an American Bantustan' *LAWeekly*. November 27.

Hamilton, Cynthia (1992) 'L.A.'s IMF Riot' Unpublished manuscript.

Harris, Scott (1987a) 'A Bitter Battle on Home Turf: Garment Plant is not Welcome' *LAT*. October 25: II, 1.

Harris, Scott (1987b) 'Community Crusaders: Three Groups Wage Hard-Nosed Struggle for Social Change' *LAT*. November 29: II, 1.

Harris, Scott (1988) 'Freeway Arch to Honor L.A. Immigrants' *LAT*. February 13: I, 1.

Harris, Scott (1989) 'Bradley Says Racism Stirs Foreign Investors' Critics' *LAT*. February 17: II, 18.

Harris, Scott and Kevin Roderick (1988) 'Westside Gets Big Share of City Commission Posts, Study Shows' *LAT*. March 23: II, 1.

Harvey, David (1982) *The Limits to Capital*. Oxford: Basil Blackwell.

Harvey, David (1985a) *The Urbanization of Capital*. Baltimore, Md: Johns Hopkins University Press.

Harvey, David (1985b) *Consciousness and the Urban Experience*. Baltimore, Md: Johns Hopkins University Press.

Harvey, David (1989a) *The Urban Experience*. Baltimore: The Johns Hopkins University Press.

Harvey, David (1989b) *The Condition of Postmodernity: An Enquiry into the Origins of Cultural Change*. Oxford: Basil Blackwell.

Harvey, David (1996) *Justice, Nature and the Geography of Difference*. Cambridge, US and Oxford, UK. Blackwell.

Hayden, Tom (1993) 'A Revolutionary Idea for L.A.: Put the People in Power' *LAT*. February 23.

Healey, Patsy, Stuart Cameron, Simon Davoudi, Stephan Graham and Ali Madani-Pour (1995). *Managing Cities: The New Urban Context*. Chichester: Wiley.

274

Henderson, Jeffrey and Manuel Castells (Eds) (1987) *Global Restructuring and Territorial Development*. London: Sage.

Heskin, Allan David (1983) *Tenants and the American Dream: Ideology and the Tenant Movement*. New York: Praeger Publishers.

Hicks, Jonathan (1989a) 'The Takeover of American Industry' *NYT*. May 28: 3, 1.

Hicks, Jonathan (1989b) 'Foreign Owners Are Shaking up the Competition' *NYT*. May 28: 3, 8.

Hines, Thomas S. (1982) 'Housing, Baseball and Creeping Socialism: The Battle of Chavez Ravine, Los Angeles, 1949–1959' *Journal of Urban History*. 8, 2: 123–143.

Hirsch, Joachim and Roland Roth (1986) *Das neue Gesicht des Kapitalismus. Vom Fordismus zum Post-Fordismus*. Hamburg: VSA.

Hirsch, Werner Zvi (Ed.) (1971) *Los Angeles: Viability and Prospects for Metropolitan Leadership*. New York: Praeger.

Hise, Greg (1997) *Magnetic Los Angeles – Planning the Twentieth Century Metropolis*. Baltimore and London: The Johns Hopkins University Press.

Hitz, Hansruedi, Roger Keil, Ute Lehrer, Klaus Ronneberger, Christian Schmid and Richard Wolff (Eds) (1995) *Capitales Fatales: Urbanisierung und Politik in den Finanzmetropolen Frankfurt und Zürich*. Zurich: Rotpunkt Verlag.

Hoch, Charles (1981) *City Limits: Municipal Boundary Formation and Class Segregation in Los Angeles Suburbs, 1940–1970*. Ph.D. Dissertation, Graduate School of Architecture and Urban Planning, UCLA.

Hoch, Charles (1984) 'City Limits: Municipal Boundary Formation and Class Segregation' *Marxism and the Metropolis*. (Eds) William K. Tabb and Larry Sawers. New York: Oxford University Press. 101–119.

Hoch, Charles (1985) 'Municipal Contracting in California: Privatizing with Class' *UAQ*. **20**: 303–323.

Hockney, David (1988) *A Retrospective*. Los Angeles: LACMA.

Holland, Max (1989) 'The Buying of America' *LAT*. May 28: Book Review, 4.

Hopkins, Elwood (1995) 'At the Cutting Edge: A Portrait of Innovative Grassroots Organizations in Los Angeles' *Critical Planning*. **2**: 39–59.

Horton, John (1995) *The Politics of Diversity: Immigration, Resistance and Change in Monterey Park, California*. Philadelphia: Temple University Press.

Housing Los Angeles (1988) 'We Want a Public Hearing . . .' Los Angeles: Housing Los Angeles.

Howard, Bob (1987a) 'West Hollywood Unfurls Splashy Marketing Campaign to Meet Competition from Westside' *LABJ*. September 23.

Howard, Bob (1987b) 'Local Ad Agencies Rise and Fall on Japanese Accounts' *LABJ*. July 13: 15.

Howard, Bob (1988) 'Change on the Horizon' *The Magazine*. March 21: 12–16.

Hoy, Anne (1988) 'Hockney's Photocollages' in David Hockney, *A Retrospective*. Los Angeles: LACMA. 55–66.

Hsu, Spencer S. (1989) 'Santa Monica May Hire Consultant to Lobby for Homeless' *LAT*. August 17: W1.

Hymer, Stephen (1979) *The Multinational Corporation: A Radical Approach*. Eds Robert B. Cohen *et al*. Cambridge: Cambridge University Press.

Industrial Areas Foundation Network of Southern California (n.d.) 'To Establish Justice' Los Angeles.

Institute for Alternative Journalism (Ed.) (1992) *Inside the L.A. Riots*. New York: IAJ.

Jacobs, Jane (1993, orig. 1961) *The Death and Life of Great American Cities*. New York: Vintage Books.

Jacoby, Russell (1989) 'L.A. Slips Into the Mud of the Mainstream' *LAT*. August 7: II: 5.

Jah, Yusuf and Sister Shah'Keyah (1995) *Uprising: Crips and Bloods Tell the Story of America's Youth in the Crossfire*. New York: Scribner.

Jeffe, Sherry Bebitch (1989) 'Bradley and the Reality of Perception' *LAT*. May 21: V, 1.

Jeffe, Sherry Bebitch (1997) 'L.A. Politics 2000' *LAT*. April 13: M1–6.

Jennings, Tom (1995) 'Rent Control Shutdown' *Los Angeles Reader*. May 5: 7.

Jerrils, Jack E. (1972) *The History of a City . . . Carson, California*. Carson: City of Carson.

Johnson, James H. Jr, and Melvin L. Oliver (1993) 'Retrospective Analysis of the Los Angeles Rebellion, 1992' *Policy Options for Southern California*. Ed. Allen J. Scott. Lewis Center for Regional Policy Studies. 7–31.

Jones, Helen L. and Robert F. Wilcox (1949) *Metropolitan Los Angeles: Its Governments*. Los Angeles: The Haynes Foundation.

Jones, Robert A. (1989a) 'A Sales Pitch Made to Order for Japanese' *LAT*. May 9: I, 3.

Jones, Robert A. (1989b) 'Sayonara to the Best of California' *LAT*. May 30: I, 3.

Kang, Connie (1995) 'LAPD Begins Campaign to Recruit Asians' *LAT*. May 11: B2.

Kann, Mark E. (1983) 'The New Populism and the New Marxism: A Response to Carl Boggs' *Theory and Society*. **12**, 3: 365–373.

Kann, Mark E. (1986) *Middle Class Radicalism in Santa Monica*. Philadelphia: Temple University Press.

Kapuscinski, Ryszard (1987) 'America as a Collage' *New Perspectives Quarterly* (Summer).

Katz, Cindi (1995) 'Major/Minor: Theory, Nature, and Politics' *Annals of the Association of American Geographers*. **85**, 1: 164–168.

Katz, Cindi and Neil Smith (1992) 'L.A. Intifada: Interview with Mike Davis' *Social Text*. **33**: 19–33.

Katznelson, Ira (1981) *City Trenches: Urban Politics and the Patterning of Class in the United States*. New York: Pantheon.

Kayden, Xandra (1991) 'Political Paralysis – Los Angeles City Fathers Wanted It This Way' *LAT*. May 12: M6.

Kayden, Xandra (1996) 'What the Mayor's Race Should Be All About' *LAT*. April 14: M3.

Keil, Roger (1987a) '"An Omen of Things to Come": Politische Grenzkämpfe und sozio-ökonomische Restrukturierung in Los Angeles' *Kommune*. **5**, 2: 39–42.

Keil, Roger (1987b) '"Keep GM Van Nuys Open": The Strike against the Empire – Perspektiven eines südkalifornischen Arbeitskampfes' *Kommune*. **5**, 6: 56–60.

Keil, Roger (1988) 'Regionalplanung von Unten: Der Kampf von GM Van Nuys. Ein Interview mit dem Aktivisten Eric Mann' *Kommune*. **6**, 5: 62–65.

Keil, Roger (1990) 'Urban Future Revisited: Politics and Restructuring in Los Angeles after Fordism' *Strategies*. **3**: 105–129.

Keil, Roger (1993) *Weltstadt-Stadt der Welt: Internationalisierung und lokale Politik in Los Angeles*. Münster: Westfälisches Dampfboot.

Keil, Roger (1995) 'The Environmental Problematic in World Cities' *World Cities in a World System*. Eds Paul Knox and Peter Taylor. Cambridge: Cambridge University Press. 280–297.

Keil, Roger (1996) 'World City Formation, Local Politics, and Sustainability' *Local Places in the Age of the Global City*. Eds Roger Keil, David V.J. Bell and Gerda R. Wekerle. Montreal, London, New York: Black Rose Books. 37–44.

Keil, Roger (1998) 'Greening the Polis or Policing Ecology? Local Environmental Politics and Urban Civil Society in Los Angeles' *Planning and The Rise of Civil Society*. Eds John Friedmann and Mike Douglass. London: Wiley. 91–105.

Keil, Roger (forthcoming) 'Globalization Makes States: Perspectives of Local Action in the Age of the World City' *Review of International Political Economy*. 514 (winter): 616–646.

Keil, Roger and Gene Desfor (1996) 'Making Local Environmental Policy in Los Angeles' *Cities*. **13**, 5: 303–313.

Keil, Roger and John Graham (1998) 'Reasserting Nature: Constructing Urban Environments after Fordism' *Nature at the Millenium*. Eds Bruce Willems-Braun and Noel Castree. London: Routledge.

Keil, Roger and Stefan Kipfer (1994) 'Weltwirtschaft/Wirtschaftswelten' *Stadt-Welt*. Eds Peter Noller, Walter Prigge and Klaus Ronneberger. Frankfurt and New York: Campus Verlag. 83–93.

Keil, Roger and Peter Lieser (1992) 'Global City – Local Politics', *Comparative Urban and Community Research*, 4: 39–69.

Kepler, Jean (1989) 'Los Angeles Pace Setters: West Hollywood and West L.A.' *ASU Travel Guide*, January–April: 10.

Kim, Elaine H. (1993) 'Home Is Where the *Han* Is: A Korean-American Perspective on the Los Angeles Upheavals' *Reading Rodney King – Reading Urban Uprising*. Ed. Robert Gooding-Williams. New York and London: Routledge. 215–235.

King, Anthony D. (Ed.) (1991a) *Culture, Globalization and the World-System*. Binghamton, New York: Department of Art and Art History, State University of New York.

King, Anthony D. (1991b) 'Spaces of Culture, Spaces of Knowledge' *Culture, Globalization and the World-System*. Binghamton, New York: Department of Art and Art History, State University of New York. 1–18.

Kipfer, Stefan, Franz Hartmann and Sara Marino (1996) 'Cities, Nature and Socialism: Towards an Urban Agenda for Action and Research' *Capitalism, Nature, Socialism: A Journal of Socialist Ecology*. **7**, 2, June: 5–19.

Kipfer, Stefan and Roger Keil (1995) 'Urbanisierung und Technologie in der Periode des Globalen Kapitalismus' *Capitales Fatales: Urbanisierung und Politik in den Finanzmetropolen Frankfurt und Zürich*. Eds Hansruedi Hitz, Roger Keil, Ute Lehrer, Klaus Ronneberger, Christian Schmid and Richard Wolff. Zurich: Rotpunkt Verlag. 61–87.

Kirby, Andrew (1993) *Power/Resistance: Local Politics and the Chaotic State*. Bloomington and Indianapolis: Indiana University Press.

Kisch, Egon Erwin (1948) *Paradies Amerika*. Berlin: Aufbau.

Knight, Christopher (1988a), 'From Agriculture to Aerospace: The Hard Sell. Chamber Publicity Shots a Tribute to Hucksterism' *LAHE*. February 28: E2.

Knight, Christopher (1988b) 'Composite Views: Themes and Motifs in Hockney's Art' in David Hockney, *A Retrospective*. Los Angeles: LACMA. 23–38.

Knight, Christopher (1990) 'Is L.A. a World-Class Art City?' *LAT*. April 8: Calendar, 7.

Knox, Paul (1993) *The Restless Urban Landscape*. Englewood Cliffs, New Jersey: Prentice Hall.

Knox, Paul and Peter Taylor (Eds) (1995) *World Cities in a World-System*. Cambridge: Cambridge University Press.

Kofman, Eleonore and Elizabeth Lebas (1996) 'Lost in Transposition – Time, Space and the City' introduction to Henri Lefebvre *Writings on Cities*. Eds Eleonore Kofman and Elizabeth Lebas. Oxford: Blackwell Publishers Ltd: 3–60.

Kotkin, Joel (1989) 'Foreigners Buying U.S. Dynamism' *LAT*. April 17: V2.

Kotkin, Joel (1995a) 'L.A.'s Latest Economic Force: Gays and Lesbians' *LAT*. February 26: M1.

Kotkin, Joel (1995b) 'Latinization of South Los Angeles' *LAT*. May 28: M1, 6.

Kotkin, Joel (1997) '"Unite" for Whose Sake?' *Los Angeles Downtown News*. **26**, 52, December 29.

Kotkin, Joel and Yoriko Kishimoto (1987) 'The Japanese Are Banking on Los Angeles' *LAT*. July 26.

Krieger, M.H. (1986) 'Ethnicity and the Frontier in Los Angeles' *Environment and Planning D: Society and Space*. **4**: 385–389.

Krim, Arthur (1992) 'Los Angeles and the Anti-tradition of the Suburban City' *Journal of Historical Geography*. **18**, 1: 121–138.

Kristof, Kathy M. (1987) 'Asian Banks & Thrifts: L.A. Is Worth a Thousand Ventures' *LABJ*. August 17: 15.

Kwong, Peter (1992) 'The First Multicultural Riots' *Inside the L.A. Riots*. Ed. Institute for Alternative Journalism. New York. 88–93.

LA 2000 (1986) 'Annual Report 1986' Los Angeles.

LA 2000 (1987) 'Annual Report 1987' Los Angeles.

LA 2000 (1988) 'Final Report' Los Angeles.

*LABJ* (1989) 'Japan–American Conference, LA89 Convention News' Special Issues, May 14–18.

Laclau, Ernesto and Chantal Mouffe (1985) *Hegemony and Socialist Strategy: Towards a Radical Democratic Politics*. London and New York.

Lafferty, Elaine (1987) 'Growth: The Cautious Approach is Politically Popular' *California Journal*. **18**, 10: 487–489.

Laganiere, Dennis (1989) 'Jim Wood: Architect of 21st Century Los Angeles' *The Real Estate Magazine*. **1**: 3–5.

Lake, Laura Bartels (1989) 'Incumbency Is the Culprit at L.A. City Hall' *LAT*. May 22: II, 5.

LAMAP (Los Angeles Manufacturing Action Project) (1995) 'Union Jobs for Community Renewal: A Feasibility Study,' Culver City, CA: LAMAP.

Lappin, Senja *et al.* (1985) 'A Feasibility Study of a Boycott of General Motors Products in Southern California' Graduate School of Management, UCLA.

Laslett, John H.M. (1996) 'Historical Perspectives: Immigration and the Rise of a Distinctive Urban Region, 1900–1970' *Ethnic Los Angeles*. Eds Roger Waldinger and Mehdi Bozorgmehr. New York: Russell Sage Foundation. 39–75.

*LAT* (1989a) 'Japanese Pass British to Become Largest Foreign Investors in U.S.' June 28, V, 5.

*LAT* (1989b) 'New Challenges for United Way' (Editorial) July 22, II, 8.

*LAT* (1989c) Metro Section Special on Bradley Crisis, July 30.

Lauria, Mickey (Ed.)(1997) *Reconstructing Urban Regime Theory: Regulating Urban Politics in a Global Economy*. Thousand Oaks: Sage Publications.

Law, Robin (1994) 'West Hollywood: Community Needs Assessment' West Hollywood: City of West Hollywood.

*LAWeekly* (1990) 'Monop-L.A.' March 2–8.

Lazarovici, Laureen (1990) 'Foreign Capital, Local Lockouts' *LAWeekly*. 26 January–1 February: 14.

L/CSC (Labor/Community Strategy Center) (1992) *Reconstructing Los Angeles from the Bottom Up*. Los Angeles: L/CSC.

L/CSC (1996) *A New Vision for Urban Transportation*. Los Angeles: Strategy Center Publications.

Lee, John H. (1989) 'Postscript: Snyder out of City Hall but Not Advocacy Business' *LAT*. December 14: B3.

Lefebvre, Henri (1972) *Die Revolution der Städte*. Munich: Athenäums Verlag.

Lefebvre, Henri (1975) *Die Stadt im marxistischen Denken*. Ravensburg: Otto Maier Verlag.

Lefebvre, Henri (1991) *The Production of Space*. Oxford: Basil Blackwell.

Lefebvre, Henri (1996) *Writings on Cities*. Oxford: Blackwell.

Lehrer, Ute (1995) 'Ethnicity and the (re)production of every day life' Los Angeles Department of Urban Planning, UCLA, manuscript.

Lehrer, Ute A. and John Friedmann (1997) 'Migration, Lokalität und Zivilgesellschaft: Immigrationspolitik in Los Angeles' *Zuwanderung und Stadtentwicklung. Leviathan Sonderheft 17*. Eds Hartmut Häußermann and Ingrid Oswald. Wiesbaden: Westdeutscher Verlag: 427–445.

Leinberger, Christopher B. (1988) 'Turning Sprawl into Urban Villages' *LAT*. April 30: II, 8.

Leinberger, Christopher B. (1989) 'The 25-Downtowns Solution' *LAT*. June 4: V, 5.

Leinberger, Christopher B. and Charles Lockwood (1986) 'How Business is Reshaping America' *The Atlantic Monthly*. **258**, 4: 43–52.

Lemann, Nicholas (1988) 'Growing Pains' *The Atlantic Monthly*. **260**: 57–62.

Lemon, T. James (1996) *Liberal Dreams and Nature's Limits*. Toronto, New York, Oxford: Oxford University Press.

Lewis, Michael (1989) 'How a Tokyo Earthquake Could Devastate Wall Street and the World Economy' *Manhattan, inc.* **6**, 6: 69–79.

Libman, Gary (1989) 'Los Angeles Jews Gain Clout as Power Shifts to the West' *LAT*. May 18, 1.

Lieser, Peter (1985), 'Stadt/Land/Fluss: Bilder zur Zukunft der Stadt' *Und hinter der Fassade*. Ed. Wolfgang Kabisch. Cologne: Edition Fricke im Rudolf Müller Verlag: 384–415.

Light, Ivan (1984) 'Immigrant and Ethnic Enterprise in North America' *Ethnic and Racial Studies*. **7**, 2: 195–216.

Light, Ivan (1988) 'Los Angeles' *The Metropolis Era*. Vol 2. Eds Mattei Dogan and John Kasarda. Beverly Hills: Sage. 56–96.

Light, Ivan and Edna Bonacich (1988) *Immigrant Entrepreneurs: Koreans in Los Angeles, 1965–1982*. Berkeley, Los Angeles, Oxford: University of California Press.

Lipietz, Alain (1982) 'Towards Global Fordism' *New Left Review*. Issue 132: 33–47.

Lipietz, Alain (1992a) 'A Regulationist Approach to the Future of Urban Ecology' *Capitalism, Nature, Socialism*. **3**, 3 (September): 101–110.

Lipietz, Alain (1992b) *Towards a New Economic Order: Postfordism, Ecology and Democracy*. New York: Oxford University Press.

Lipietz, Alain (1995) *Green Hopes: The Future of Political Ecology*. Cambridge: Polity Press.

Lipsitz, George (1986/7) 'Cruising around the Historical Bloc – Postmodernism and Popular Music in East Los Angeles' *Cultural Critique*. Issue 5: 157–177.

Little Tokyo Anti Eviction Task Force (1976) 'Redevelopment in Los Angeles' *Counterpoint. Perspectives on Asian America*. Ed. Emma Gee. Los Angeles: Asian American Studies Center, UCLA. 327–333.

Little Tokyo People's Rights Organization (1979) *Little Tokyo News*. May.

Lockwood, Charles and Christopher Leinberger (1988) 'Los Angeles Comes of Age' *The Atlantic Monthly*. **260**: 31–56.

Logan, John R. and Harvey L. Molotch (1987) *Urban Fortunes: The Political Economy of Place*. Berkeley: University of California Press.

Logan, John R. and Todd Swanstrom (1990) *Beyond the City Limits*. Philadelphia: Temple University Press.

*Los Angeles* (1969) 'The Intellectual Discovers City Hall' **14**, 27–28.

Los Angeles Area Chamber of Commerce (n.d.) '1980 Census Summary: Highlights of Population and Economic Characteristics of the Los Angeles Five-County Area' Los Angeles.

Los Angeles Area Chamber of Commerce (1985) 'Dimensions of a World-Class Market' Los Angeles.

Los Angeles Chamber of Commerce (n.d.) 'Marketplace of the World' Los Angeles.

Los Angeles City Council (1995) 'Final Report. Management Audit of the Community Redevelopment Agency (CRA)' Los Angeles: Office of the Chief Legislative Analyst.

Los Angeles County Department of Public Works (1995) *Los Angeles River Master Plan: Progress Report*. Alhambra, CA: LA County Department of Public Works.

Los Angeles County Department of Regional Planning, Research Section and Affiliate Census Data Center (1986) 'Los Angeles County Data Book' Los Angeles.

Los Angeles County Grand Jury (1988/89) 'An Interim Report on Community Redevelopment Agency: Los Angeles' County of Los Angeles.

Los Angeles Economic Roundtable (1986) 'The Los Angeles Job Machine' Los Angeles.

Los Angeles Goals Council (1969) 'Summary Report' Los Angeles: City of Los Angeles.

Los Angeles Times Marketing Research (n.d.) 'Los Angeles: The Market and the Media.' Los Angeles: *LAT*.

Los Angeles Times Marketing Research (1986) 'Ethnicity in Los Angeles: A Cultural Mosaique' Los Angeles: *LAT*.

Lotchin, Roger W. (1984) *The Martial Metropolis: U.S. Cities in War And Peace*. New York: Praeger.

Lozano, Carlos V. and Sheldon Ito (1987) 'In Three Years, Identity Shifts from "Gay Camelot" to "Creative City"' *LAT*. December 3: IX, 1.

Lustiger-Thaler, Henri (1992) 'New Social Movement Discourse: The Unsolved Democracy' *Organizing Dissent: Contemporary Social Movements in Theory and Practice*. Ed. William Carroll. Toronto: Garamond Press: 174–199.

McPhee, John (1989) *The Control of Nature*. New York: Farra, Strauss, Giroux.

McPhee, John (1994) *Assembling California*. New York: The Noonday Press.

McWilliams, Carey (1979, orig. 1946) *Southern California: An Island on the Land*. Santa Barbara and Salt Lake City: Peregrine Smith, Inc.

Mann, Eric (1987) *Taking on General Motors: A Case Study of the UAW Campaign to Keep GM Van Nuys Open*. Los Angeles: Center for Labor Research and Education, Institute of Industrial Relations, UCLA.

Mann, Eric (1989) 'New Coalitions for L.A.'s Future' *LAWeekly*. February 12–March 2.

Mann, Eric (1990) 'Environmentalism in the Corporate Climate' *Tikkun*. **5**, 2: 60–65.

Mann, Eric (1991) *L.A.'s Lethal Air: New Strategies for Policy, Organizing and Action*. Los Angeles: L/CSC.

Marchand, Bernard (1986) *The Emergence of Los Angeles*. London: Pion.

Marcuse, Peter and Chester Hartman (1988) 'Länderbericht USA' *Sozialer Wohnungsbau im internationalen Vergleich*. Eds Walter Prigge and Wilfried Kaib. Frankfurt: Vervuert. 231–271.

Martínez, Rubén (1991) 'Sidewalk Wars. Why L.A.'s Street Vendors Won't Be Swept Away' *LA Weekly*. December 6–12: 18–26.

Matsuoka, Jim (1971) 'Little Tokyo, Searching the Past and Analyzing the Future' *Roots: An Asian American Reader*. Eds Amy Tachiki, Eddie Wong, Franklin Odo and Buck Wong. Los Angeles: UCLA Asian American Studies Center. 322–334.

Mayer, Margit (1991) 'Politics in the Post-Fordist City' *Socialist Review*. **21**, 1: 105–124.

Mayer, Margit (1992) 'Aufstand in Los Angeles' *Prokla*. Issue 22: 323–331.

Mayer, Margit (1994) 'Post-Fordist City Politics' *Post-Fordism. A Reader*. (Ed.) Ash Amin. Oxford, UK and Cambridge, US: Blackwell. 316–337.

Mayer, Margit (1995) 'Urban Governance in the Post-Fordist City' *Managing Cities: The New Urban Context*. Eds Patsy Healey *et al*. Chichester: Wiley. 231–249.

Mayo, Charles (1964) 'The 1961 Mayoralty Election in Los Angeles: The Political Party in a Nonpartisan Election' *Western Political Quarterly*. **17**.

Mead, Walter Russel (1989) 'Japan-Bashing, an Ugly American Tradition' *LAT*. June 4: V, 2.

Merl, Jean (1995) 'The Mayor's Midterm Exam' *LATM*. June 11: 9–12; 30–32.

Merl, Jean and John Schwada (1995) 'Riordan Faces Tough Call on Chief' *Los Angeles County News*. June 11: B12, 14.

Merritt, Richard (1987) 'Mid-Wilshire Maintains Growth' *Western Real Estate News*. December 20: 22.

Meyer, Josh (1990) 'Golf Club Pros' *LAT*. February 8: J, 1.

Meyer, Larry L. (1981) *Los Angeles, 1781–1981*. Los Angeles: The California Historical Society.

Meyerson, Harold (1989) 'Tom Bradley Becomes His Opposition' *LAWeekly*. July 14–20.

Meyerson, Harold (1990) 'Jim Wood – Architect of the New L.A.' *LAWeekly*. March 2–8.

Meyerson, Harold (1992) 'LA Leaderless' *Inside the L.A. Riots*. Ed. Institute for Alternative Journalism. New York. 108–109.

Miller, Gary J. (1981) *Cities by Contract: The Politics of Municipal Incorporation*. Cambridge, Mass.: MIT Press.

Moffat, Susan (1994) 'No Longer Living on an Island' *LAT*. April 4: B1.

Mollenkopf, John (1978) 'The Postwar Politics of Urban Development'. in William K. Tabb and Larry Sawers (Eds), *Marxism and the Metropolis*. New York: Oxford University Press: 117–153.

Moody, George F. (1987) 'We All Benefit from the United Way's Efforts to Make Life Better in Our World-Class City' *LABJ*. November 30: 13.

Moore II, James E., Harry W. Richardson and Peter Gordon (1997) 'The MTA Makes a Right Turn: Will It Stay on Course?' *LAT*. December 28: M6.

Moos, Adam (1989) 'The Grassroots in Action: Gays and Seniors Capture the Local State in West Hollywood, California' *The Power of Geography: How Territory Shapes Social Life*. Eds Jennifer Wolch and Michael Dear. Boston: Unwin Hyman. 351–369.

Morales, Rebecca (1982) 'Unions and Undocumented Workers' *Southwest Economy and Society*. **6**, 1.

Morales, Rebecca (1983) 'Transitional Labor: Undocumented Workers in the Los Angeles Automobile Industry' Graduate School of Architecture and Urban Planning, UCLA.

Morales, Rebecca (1986) 'The Los Angeles Automobile Industry in Historical Perspective' *Environment and Planning D: Society and Space*. **4**: 289–303.

Morales, Rebecca (1992) 'Place and Auto Manufacture in the Post-Fordist Era' *The Car and the City: The Automobile, the Build Environment, and Daily Urban Life*. Eds Martin Wachs and Margaret Crawford. Ann Arbor: The University of Michigan Press. 204–221.

Morales, Rebecca and Goetz Wolff (1986) 'Los Angeles Labor Union Responses to the Growth in Immigrant Labor and Plant Closings' Graduate School of Architecture and Urban Planning, University of California, Los Angeles.

Moran, Julio (1989a) 'Santa Monica OKs Major Revisions to Rent Control' *LAT*. June 10: II, 1.

Moran, Julio (1989b) 'Landlords Reject Rent Plan, Call It a Sham' *LAT*. July 13: W1.

Moran, Julio (1989c) 'Santa Monica Puts Creativity in Conservation' *LAT*. July 30: W1.

Moran, Julio (1989d) 'Tenants Join Landlords in Rejecting Rent Compromise' *LAT*. August 3: W1.

Muller, Thomas (1993) *Immigrants and the American City*. New York and London: New York University Press.

Muller, Thomas and Thomas J. Espenshade (1985) *The Fourth Wave: California's Newest Immigrants*. Washington, DC: The Urban Institute Press.

Mulligan, Thomas S. (1995) 'Two Biggest U.S. Apparel Unions Will Join Forces' *LAT*. February 21: D1–6.

Murase, Ichiro Mike (1983) *Little Tokyo. One Hundred Years in Pictures*. Los Angeles: Visual Communications.

Murphy, Dean (1990) 'City Council May Curb Catering Trucks' *LAT*. January 4: J16.

Murphy, Dean (1991) 'City Charter Outmoded, Critics Say' *LAT*. May 16: A1.

Myers, David M. (1987) 'City Mini-Mall Legislation Creates Major Controversy' *LAT*. June 24: VIII, 11.

Nelson, Howard J. (1983) *The Los Angeles Metropolis*. Dubuque, Iowa: Kendall, Hunt.

Neutra, Richard J. (1941) 'Homes and Housing' *Los Angeles. Preface to a Master Plan*. Eds George W. Robbins and L. Deming Tilton. Los Angeles: The Pacific Southwest Academy. 189–201.

Newton, Edmund (1988) 'Isolated Slow-Growth Groups Find Strength in Unity' *LAT*. March 9: II, 1.

Newton, Edmund (1990) 'San Gabriel Valley Becomes the New Power Base of Latino Voters' *LAT*. January 21: B1.

Newton, Jim (1997) '3 Huge Projects Could Define 21st Century L.A.' *LAT*. December 14.

New Vision Business Council of Southern California, The (1994) 'The New Economy Project: Final Report' Los Angeles: The New Economy Project.

Ohmae, Kenichi (1990) 'Borderless Economy Calls for New Politics' *LAT*. March 26: B7.

Oliver, M.L. and J.H. Johnson (1984) 'Interethnic Conflict in an Urban Ghetto: The Case of Blacks and Latinos' *Research, Social Movements, Conflict and Change*. Ed. R.L. Ratcliff. New York: JAI.

Oliver, Melvin L., James H. Johnson Jr and Walter C. Farrell Jr (1993) 'Anatomy of a Rebellion: A Political–Economic Analysis' *Reading Rodney King – Reading Urban Uprising*. Ed. Robert Gooding-Williams. New York and London: Routledge. 117–141.

Olmos, David (1989) 'Fujitsu Enlists Anaheim Mayor to Fight Trade War Worries' *LAT*. May 24: IV, 5.

Olney, Peter (n.d.) 'The Struggle for Plant Closing Legislation in the U.S.: A Reflection on the Dilemma of U.S. Trade Unions' Manuscript.

Olney, Peter B. (1987a) 'A Targeting Proposal for Los Angeles County' Report for the Western States Region of the International Ladies Garment Workers Union. Los Angeles: IGLWU.

Olney, Peter B. (1987b) 'Rags, Riches and Immigrant Labor: Everything Under the Sun' *Forward Motion*. **65**: 20–24.

Olney, Peter and Roger Keil (1988) 'Needles and Pins: Schatten im Paradies' *Kommune*. 6, 3: 37–50.

Omi, Michael and Howard Winant (1993) 'The Los Angeles "Race Riot" and Contemporary U.S. Politics' *Reading Rodney King – Reading Urban Uprising*. Ed. Robert Gooding-Williams. New York and London: Routledge. 97–116.

Ong, Paul (1988) 'The Hispanization of Los Angeles's Poor' Graduate School of Architecture and Urban Planning, UCLA.

Ong, Paul (1989) 'The Widening Divide: Income Inequality and Poverty in Los Angeles' University of California, Los Angeles: Graduate School of Architecture and Urban Planning.

Ong, Paul and Rebecca Morales (1988) 'Mexican Labor in Los Angeles' Graduate School of Architecture and Urban Planning, UCLA.

Ortiz, Robert A. (1987) 'Downtown Los Angeles – the World's Most Exciting City' *Western Real Estate News*. December 20: 32.

Pacheco, Jesse and Michael Wilson (1986) 'The Team Concept at Work' Shop Floor Newsletter, Van Nuys, CA.

Palazzo, Anthony (1989) 'Busted for Vending' *LAWeekly*. August 4–10: 10.

Palermo, B.J. (1994) 'After the Bloom' *LAT*. October 30: 12–16.

Palm, Risa and Michael E. Hodgson (1992) *After a California Earthquake*. Chicago and London: The University of Chicago Press.

Parson, Donald (1982) 'The Development of Redevelopment: Public Housing and Urban Renewal in Los Angeles' *IJURR*. 6: 393–413.

Parson, Donald (1983) 'Los Angeles' "Headline-Happy Public Housing War"' *Southern California Quarterly*. 65: 251–285.

Parson, Donald (1985) *Urban Politics during the Cold War: Public Housing, Urban Renewal and Suburbanization in Los Angeles*. Ph.D. Dissertation, Graduate School of Architecture and Urban Planning, UCLA.

Parson, Donald (1991) 'Many Histories. Postmodern Politics in Los Angeles' *Science as Culture*. 2, part 3, no. 12: 411–425.

Parson, Donald (1993) '"This Modern Marvel": Bunker Hill, Chavez Ravine, and the Politics of Modernism in Los Angeles' *Southern California Quarterly*. 333–350.

Pasadena Research Institute (1982) 'Watson Industrial Center' *Industrial Development*. May and June.

Payne, Gregory J. and Scott Ratzan (1987) *Tom Bradley: The Impossible Dream*. Toronto and New York: Paperjacks.

Perlman, Janice E. and Elwood M. Hopkins (1996) 'Urban Leadership for the 21st Century: Scaling Up and Reaching Out from the Neighborhood Level' (unpublished final report of the Mega-Cities Project), New York City.

Peterson, Paul (1981) *City Limits*. Chicago: University of Chicago Press.

Phillips, Kevin (1989), 'California' *LAT*. November 19: M, 1.

Pine, Art (1989a) 'Nippophobia' Affects Making of Trade Policy' *LAT*. April 24: IV, 10.

Pine, Art (1989b) 'Motorola's Washington Lobbyists Keep Heat on Japanese Trade' *LAT*. May 27, IV, 1.

Pine, Art (1989c) 'Much of Trade Deficit May Be Made in the U.S.A.' *LAT*. August 9: IV, 1.

Pine, Art and Tom Redburn (1989) 'Shift of Priorities: U.S. Sounds an Economic Call to Arms' *LAT*. August 6: I, 1.

Piore, Michael and Charles Sabel (1984) *The Second Industrial Divide: Possibilities for Prosperity*. New York: Basic Books.

Porter, Douglas (1987) 'Slow Growth Gusto Hits L.A.' *Urban Land*. 46, 12: 30–31.

Portes, Alejandro and Saskia Sassen-Koob (1987) 'Making it Underground: Comparative Material on the Informal Sector in Western Market Economies' *AJS*. 93, 1: 30–61.

Prigge, Walter (1988) 'Mythos Metropole: Wallmann lesen' *Das NEUE FRANKFURT: Städtebau und Architektur im Modernisierungsprozess 1925–1988*. Eds Walter Prigge and Hans-Peter Schwarz. Frankfurt: Vervuert. 209–240.

Prigge, Walter (Ed.) (1992) *Städtische Intellektuelle: Urbane Milieus im 20. Jahrhundert*. Frankfurt: Fischer.

Prigge, Walter (1995) 'Urbi et orbi – zur Epistemologie des Städtischen' *Capitales Fatales: Urbanisierung und Politik in den Finanzmetropolen Frankfurt und Zürich*. Eds Hansruedi Hitz *et al*. Zurich: Rotpunktverlag. 176–187.

Pulido, Laura (1994) 'Restructuring and the Contraction and Expansion of Environmental Rights in the United States' *Environment and Planning A*. 26: 915–936.

Pulido, Laura (1996a) *Environmentalism and Economic Justice*. Tucson: The University of Arizona Press.

Pulido, Laura (1996b) 'Multiracial Organizing among Environmental Justice Activists in Los Angeles' *Rethinking Los Angeles*. Eds Michael J. Dear, H. Eric Schockman and Greg Hise. Thousand Oaks: Sage. 171–189.

Pyncheon, Thomas (1990) *Vineland*. Boston: Little Brown and Co.

*Real Estate Magazine* (1989) 'President's View' Interview with Kobayashi, *Shuwa Investments*, Issue 1, 8–11.

Rebuild LA (1997) *Rebuilding LA's Urban Communities: A Final Report from RLA*. Los Angeles: Milken Institute.

Redburn, Tom (1989) 'Difference between "Us" and "Them" Blurs in a Global Economy' *LAT*. August 8: IV, 1.

Redburn, Tom and Art Pine (1989) 'Clamor Increasing in U.S. for Trade War with Japan' *LAT*. August 10: I, 1.

Regalado, James A. (1991) 'Organized Labor and Los Angeles City Politics: An Assessment in the Bradley Years, 1973–1989' *UAQ*. **27**, 1: 87–108.

Reinhold, Robert (1989) 'Los Angeles Mayor, Once Challenged, Regains Winning Ways' *NYT*. January 29.

Reinhold, Robert (1992) 'After Riots, a Return to the Extremes That Pass for Normalcy' *NYT*. June 7.

Rieff, David (1993) *Los Angeles: Capital of the Third World*. New York: Simon and Schuster.

Riposa, Gerry and Carolyn Dersch (Eds) (1992) *City of Angels*. Dubuque, Iowa: Kendall Hunt.

Robbins George W. and L. Deming Tilton (1941) *Los Angeles. Preface to A Master Plan*. Los Angeles: The Pacific Southwest Academy.

Robertson, Roland (1991) 'Social Theory, Cultural Relativity and the Problem of Globality' *Culture, Globalization and the World-System*, Ed. Anthony D. King. Binghamton: Department of Art and History, State University of New York at Binghamton. 69–90.

Robinson, Cedric J. (1993) 'Race, Capitalism, and the Antidemocracy' *Rethinking Rodney King – Rethinking Urban Uprising*. Ed. Robert Gooding-Williams. New York and London: Routledge. 73–81.

Roderick, Kevin (1987) 'L.A. Splits down Ethnic Issues' *LAT*. June 21: I, 1.

Roderick, Kevin and Ted Vollmer (1989) 'Yaroslavsky Analysis: Bradley Too Popular' *LAT*. January 7: I, 1.

Rodríguez, Nestor P. and Joe R. Feagin (1986), 'Urban Specialization in the World-System – an Investigation of Historical Cases' *UAQ*. **22**, 2: 187–220.

Rose, Frederick (1989) 'The City of the Future Is a Troubling Prospect If It's to Be Los Angeles' *The Wall Street Journal*. June 12: 1.

Rosenstiel, Thomas B. (1989) 'Media, L.A.: A Cycle of Fascination' *LAT*. September 24: I, 31.

Ross, Robert and Kent Trachte (1983) 'Global Cities, Global Classes: The Peripheralization of Labor in New York City' *Review*. **6**, 3: 393–431.

Ruddick, Susan (1996) *Young and Homeless in Hollywood: Mapping Social Identities*. New York and London: Routledge.

Ruddick, Susan and Roger Keil (1992) 'Let it Bleed: Alltäglicher Rassismus und ein kurzer Frühling der Anarchie in Los Angeles' *Kommune*. **10**, 6: 9–13.

Russell, Ron (1988) 'W. Hollywood Coalition May Hold the Key to City Council Election' *LAT*. February 21: IX, 1.

Rutton, Tim (1992a) 'A New Kind of Riot' *The New York Review*. June 11: 52–53.

Rutton, Tim (1992b) 'Looking for Source of a City's Troubles' *LAT*. December 17.

Ryon, Ruth (1988) 'Village Concept an Urban First' *LAT*. October 1.

Sabagh, Georges and Mehdi Bozorgmehr, 'Population Change: Immigration and Ethnic Transformation,' in Roder Waldinger and Mehdi Bozorgmehr (Eds) *Ethnic Los Angeles*. New York: Russell Sage Foundation, 1996: 79–108.

St Vincent de Paul Church (1987) Information Sheet Maple Avenue Amendment (Flyer).

Saltzstein, Alan L. and Sonenshein, Raphael J. (1991) 'Los Angeles: Transformation of a Governing Coalition' *Big City Politics in Transition*. Eds H. V. Savitch and John C. Thomas. Thousand Oaks: Sage.

Saltzstein, Alan L., Raphe Sonenshein and Irving Ostrow (1986) 'Federal Grants and the City of Los Angeles: Implementing a More Centralized Local Political System' *Research in Urban Policy*. **2**, part A: 55–76.

Sambale, Jens (1994) 'Fluchtpunkt Los Angeles – zur Regulation gesellschaftlicher

Beziehungen über lokale Umweltpolitiken in einer globalen Region' Diploma Thesis, Political Science, Free University Berlin (unpubl.): 117 pages.

Sanchez, Jesus (1987a) 'Mini-Malls: Stores of Opportunity' *LAT*. September 20: IV, 1.

Sanchez, Jesus (1987b) 'Taco Trucks Put Aspiring Immigrants on Wheels' *LAT*. November 16: IV, 1.

Sanchez, Jesus (1989) 'Politics Also Undergird Skyscraper' *LAT*. April 17: I, 1.

Sanchez, Raymond L. (1987) 'Street Vendors Pay High Price for Unlicensed Trade in L.A.' *LAT*. October 26: II, 1.

Sandercock, Leonie (1998) *Towards Cosmopolis*. Chichester, UK: Wiley.

Sappell, Joel (1989) 'Access to Mayor's Office Becomes Path to Power' *LAT*. December 19: A1.

Sassen, Saskia (1991) *The Global City: New York, London, Tokyo*. Princeton: Princeton University Press.

Sassen, Saskia (1994) *Cities in a World Economy*. Thousand Oaks: Pineforge Press.

Sassen-Koob, Saskia (1984a) 'The New Labor Demand in Global Cities' *Cities in Transformation: Class, Capital and the State*. Ed. M.P. Smith. Beverly Hills, Calif.: Sage. 139–171.

Sassen-Koob, Saskia (1984b) 'A New Industrial Zone for World Capital: Southern California' Center for U.S.–Mexican Studies, University of California, San Diego.

Sassen-Koob, Saskia (1985) 'Capital Mobility and Labor Migration: Their Expression in Core Cities' *Urbanization in the World Economy*. Ed. Michael Timberlake. New York: Academic Press. 231–268.

Sassen-Koob, Saskia (1986) 'New York City: Economic Restructuring and Immigration' *Development and Change*. **17**: 85–119.

Sassen-Koob, Saskia (1987a) 'Growth and Informalization at the Core: A Preliminary Report on New York City' *The Capitalist City: Global Restructuring and Community Politics*. Eds Michael Peter Smith and Joe R. Feagin. Oxford: Basil Blackwell. 138–154.

Sassen-Koob, Saskia (1987b) 'Issues of Core and Periphery: Labour Migration and Global Restructuring' *Global Restructuring and Territoriality and the Los Angeles Police Department*. Eds Jeffrey Henderson and Manuel Castells. London: Sage Publications. 60–87.

SCAG (Southern California Association of Governments) (1987) 'The Port of Long Beach and its Impact on the Southern California Economy' Los Angeles: SCAG.

SCAG (1993) *Draft Regional Comprehensive Plan*. Los Angeles: SCAG.

SCAQMD (South Coast Air Quality Management District) (1989) *Air Quality Management Plan*. El Monte: SCAQMD.

SCAQMD (1991) *Air Quality Management Plan*. Diamond Bar: SCAQMD.

SCAQMD (1994) *Air Quality Management Plan*. Diamond Bar: SCAQMD.

SCAQMD (1997) *Air Quality Management Plan*. Diamond Bar: SCAQMD.

Schiesl, Martin J. (1984) 'Airplanes to Aerospace: Defense Spending and Economic Growth in the Los Angeles Region, 1945–1960' *The Martial Metropolis: U.S. Cities in War And Peace*. Ed. Roger W. Lotchin. New York: Praeger. 135–150.

Schimek, Paul (1989) 'From the Basement to the Boardroom: Los Angeles Should Work for Everyone' A Report for SEIU Local 399 Justice for Janitors Campaign, Los Angeles.

Schine, Eric (1988) 'Sanctions Fail to Cut Alien Jobs' *LAT*. May 2: I, 1.

Schneider, Iris (1987) 'Carrying Oranges to Angelenos' *LAT*. November 26: V-A, 1.

Schockman, Eric (1990) 'Nonpartisan City Elections Produce a Leaderless Ship' *LAT*. February: M5.

Schockman, H. Eric (1996) 'Is Los Angeles Governable? Revisiting the City Charter' *Rethinking Los Angeles*. Eds Michael J. Dear, Eric H. Schockman and Greg Hise. Thousand Oaks, California: Sage Publications. 57–75.

Schwada, John and Jean Merl (1995) 'L.A. to Get Infusion of Federal Funding' *LAT*. May 10: B1.

Schwengel, Hermann (1995) 'Wechselwind und Machtlücke' *Ästhetik & Kommunikation*. **24**, Issue 89:11–18.

*284*

Scoble, Harry M. (1967) 'Negro Politics in Los Angeles: The Quest for Power' Los Angeles: Institute of Government and Public Affairs, University of California: 1–40.

Scott, Allen J. (1983a) 'Industrial Organization and the Logic of Intra-Metropolitan Location, I: Theoretical Considerations' *Economic Geography*. **59**, 3: 233–255.

Scott, Allen J. (1983b) 'Industrial Organization and the Logic of Intra-Metropolitan Location, II: A Case Study of the Printed Circuits Industry in the Greater Los Angeles Region' *Economic Geography*. **59**, 4: 343–367.

Scott, Allen J. (1984a) 'Industrial Organization and the Logic of Intra-Metropolitan Location, III: A Case Study of the Women's Dress Industry in the Greater Los Angeles Region' *Economic Geography*. **60**, 1: 1–27.

Scott, Allen J. (1984b) 'Territorial Reproduction and Transformation in a Local Labor Market: The Animated Film Workers of Los Angeles' *Environment and Planning D: Society and Space*. **2**: 277–307.

Scott, Allen J. (1988a) 'Flexible Production Systems and Regional Development: The Rise of New Industrial Spaces in North America and Western Europe' *IJURR*. **12**, 2: 171–185.

Scott, Allen J. (1988b) *Metropolis: From the Division of Labor to Urban Form*. Berkeley and Los Angeles: University of California Press.

Scott, Allen J. (1993a) *Technopolis: High Technology Industry and Regional Development in Southern California*. Berkeley, Los Angeles and Oxford: University of California Press.

Scott, Allen J. (Ed.) (1993b) 'Policy Options for Southern California' Working Paper No. 4, Los Angeles: The Lewis Center for Regional Policy Studies, UCLA.

Scott, Allen J. (1996) 'High-technology Industrial Development in the San Fernando Valley and Ventura County: Observations on Economic Growth and the Evolution of Urban Form' *The City: Los Angeles and Urban Theory at the End of the Twentieth Century*. Eds Allen J. Scott and Edward W. Soja. Berkeley, Los Angeles and London: University of California Press. 276–310.

Scott, Allen J. and Richard E. Brown (1993) 'South-Central Los Angeles: Anatomy of an Urban Crisis' (Working Paper No. 6) Los Angeles: The Lewis Center for Regional Policy Studies, UCLA.

Scott, Allen J. and Edward W. Soja (1986) 'Editorial: L.A., Capital of the Late 20th Century' *Environment and Planning D: Society and Space*. **4**, 3: 249–254.

Scott, Allen J. and Edward W. Soja (Eds) (1996) *The City: Los Angeles and Urban Theory at the End of the Twentieth Century*. Berkeley, Los Angeles and London: University of California Press.

Scott, Allen J. and Michael Storper (Eds) (1986) *Production, Work and Territory: The Geographical Autonomy of Industrial Capitalism*. Boston: Allen and Unwin.

Scott, Austin (1982) 'Powerful Decision-Makers: Little-Known L.A. Agency Sculpts a New Downtown' *LAT*. April 26, I, 1.

Sears, Cecil E. (1987) 'Japanese Real Estate Investment in the United States' *Urban Land*. **46**, 2: 6–11.

Security Pacific Corporation (1984) 'The Sixty Mile Circle: The Economy of the Greater L.A. Area' Los Angeles.

Security Pacific Corporation (1987) 'The Sixty Mile Circle: The Economy of the Greater L.A. Area' Los Angeles.

Shapiro, Dan (1986) 'Give Citizens a Role in L.A.'s Growth: Excluded as They Are, They Naturally Become Obstructionist' *LAT*. September 7: V, 5.

Shearer, Derek (1984) 'Citizen Participation in Local Government: The Case of Santa Monica, California' *IJURR*. **4**: 573–586.

Shearer, Derek (1987) 'Not Yet "Blade Runner"' *LAT*. June 5: II, 5.

Shearer, Derek (1988) 'Slow Growth: The Irresistible Force in Los Angeles' *LAHE*. February 14: F1.

Shiver, Jube (1989) 'Topic Turns to Minorities at U.S.–Japanese Talks' *LAT*. May 17: IV, 2.

Shogan, Robert (1989) 'Making U.S. No.1 Again by Remedying Ills at Home' *LAT*. August 7: I, 1.

Sibilsky, Steve (1987a) 'Just What Is USC Up to Downtown' *Downtown News*. November 23: 1.

Sibilsky, Steve (1987b) 'What about the Housing Lost on Bunker Hill?' *Downtown News*. November 16.

Simon, Richard (1998) 'Day of Reckoning of MTA on whether to Delay Rail Lines' *LAT*, January 14, A1.

Smith, Michael Peter and Joe R. Feagin (Eds) (1987) *The Capitalist City: Global Restructuring and Community Politics*. Oxford: Basil Blackwell.

Snyder, Arthur K. (1987) 'Shop Centers Held Victims of "Political Fad"' *LAT*. June 28: VIII, 11.

Soja, Edward W. (1989) *Postmodern Geographies: The Reassertion of Space in Critical Social Theory*. London: Verso.

Soja, Edward W. (1992) 'Inside Exopolis: Scenes from Orange County' in Sorkin, Michael (Ed.) *Variations on a Theme Park: The New American City and the End of Public Space*. New York: The Noonday Press. 94–122.

Soja, Edward W. (1996) *Thirdspace: Journeys to Los Angeles and other Real-and-imagined Places*. Cambridge, US and Oxford, UK: Blackwell.

Soja, Edward W., Allan D. Heskin and Marco Cenzatti (1985) 'Los Angeles through the Kaleidoscope of Urban Restructuring' Graduate School of Architecture and Urban Planning, UCLA.

Soja, Edward W., Rebecca Morales and Goetz Wolff (1983) 'Urban Restructuring: An Analysis of Social and Spatial Change in Los Angeles' *Economic Geography*. **59**, 2: 195–230.

Soja, Edward W. and Allen J. Scott (1996) 'Introduction to Los Angeles: City and Region' *The City: Los Angeles and Urban Theory at the End of the Twentieth Century*. Eds Allen J. Scott and Edward W. Soja. Berkeley, Los Angeles and London: University of California Press. 1–21.

Sokolovsky, Joan (1985) 'Logic, Space, and Time: The Boundaries of the Capitalist World-Economy' *Urbanization in the World Economy*. Ed. Michael Timberlake. New York: Academic Press. 41–52.

Sonenshein, Raphael J. (1985) 'Bradley's People: Biracial Coalition Politics in Los Angeles' Paper for the 1985 Annual Meeting of the American Political Science Association, New Orleans, August 29–September 1.

Sonenshein, Raphael J. (1986) 'Biracial Coalition Politics in Los Angeles' *PS*. 19: 582–590.

Sonenshein, Raphael J. (1988) 'The Dynamics of Biracial Coalitions: Crossover Politics in Los Angeles' Paper for the Roundtable on Big City Politics at the 1988 Annual Meeting of the Western Political Science Association, San Francisco, March 9–11.

Sonenshein, Raphael, J. (1989) 'The Los Angeles Brand of Biracial Coalition Politics' *LAT*. April 16: V, 1.

Sonenshein, Raphael J. (1993) *Politics in Black and White: Race and Power in Los Angeles*. Princeton: Princeton University Press.

*South Coast Business* (1986) 'Carson: A City With A Future Unlimited.'

Squier, Gary (1988) 'The State of Housing in Los Angeles' Lecture, Homeless Symposium Graduate School of Architecture and Urban Planning, UCLA, May 16.

Starr, Kevin (1985) *Inventing the Dream: California through the Progressive Era*. New York: Oxford University Press.

Starr, Kevin (1988) 'Epilogue' *Los Angeles 2000: A City for the Future (Final Report of the Los Angeles 2000 Committee)* Ed. Los Angeles 2000 Committee. Los Angeles: LA 2000 Committee.

Stelpflug, Steven (1994) 'City of Carson Attributes Continued Success To Key Business-Friendly Policies; Community Reaps Rewards' *Long Beach Business Journal*, special supplement 'Focus on Carson'. October: 3–5.

Stephens, Philip (1986) 'California's Economy: Uneasy Realities Behind a Post-Industrial Dream' *Financial Times*. October 15.

Stewart, Jill (1988) 'Advocates of Poor Assail Plan to Revamp Downtown' *LAT*. November 28: I, 1.

Stewart, Jill (1989) '"Teflon Mayor" Bradley: The Blame Doesn't Stick' *LAT*. April 8: I, 1.

Stewart, Jill (1990a) 'Housing Effort Gets an Activist' *LAT*. January 12: B3.

Stewart, Jill (1990b) 'Mayor Picks 2 for Redevelopment Board' *LAT*. January 13: B1.

Stewart, Jill (1991) 'Council Presses Reforms of Redevelopment Agency' *LAT*. February 6: A1.

Stewart, Jill (1992) 'Our Perot' *LA Weekly*. December 10: 19–27.

Stone, Clarence N. (1982) 'Social Stratification, Non-Decision-Making and the Study of Community Power' *American Politics Quarterly*. **10**, 3: 275–302.

Stone, Clarence N. and Heywood T. Sanders (1987) *The Politics of Urban Development*. Lawrence: University of Kansas Press.

Storper, Michael and Allen J. Scott (1986) 'Production, Work, Territory: Contemporary Realities and Theoretical Tasks' *Production, Work and Territory: The Geographical Autonomy of Industrial Capitalism*. Eds Allen J. Scott and Michael Storper. Boston: Allen and Unwin. 3–15.

Storper, Michael and Allen J. Scott (1989) 'The Geographical Foundations and Social Regulation of Flexible Production Complexes' *The Power of Geography: How Territory Shapes Social Life*. Eds Jennifer Wolch and Michael Dear. Boston: Unwin Hyman.

Storper, Michael and Richard Walker (1989) *The Capitalist Imperative: Territory, Technology and Industrial Growth*. New York and Oxford: Basil Blackwell.

*Strategies: A Journal of Theory, Culture and Politics* (1990) 3: Special Issue: In the City, Strategies.

Sudjic, Dejan (1992) The 100 Mile City, San Diego, London and New York: Harcourt Brace.

Tabb, William K. and Larry Sawers (Eds) (1984, orig. 1978) *Marxism and the Metropolis*. New York: Oxford University Press.

Tachiki, Amy, Eddie Wong, Franklin Odo and Buck Wong (1971) *Roots: An Asian American Reader*. Los Angeles: UCLA Asian American Studies Center.

Takaki, Ronald (1989a) *Strangers from a Different Shore: A History of Asian Americans*. Boston: Little, Brown and Company.

Takaki, Ronald (1989b) 'Asian Newcomers Who "Get Ahead So Fast" May Be Far Behind Where They Started' *LAT*. August 20: V, 5.

Thrift, Nigel (1987) 'The Fixers: the Urban Geography of International Commercial Capital' *Global Restructuring and Territorial Development*. Eds Jeffrey Henderson and Manuel Castells. London: Sage Publications. 203–233.

Tianguis (n.d.) 'Informacion' Los Angeles.

Timberlake, Michael (Ed.) (1985) *Urbanization in the World Economy*. New York: Academic Press.

Timberlake, Michael (1987) 'World System Theory and the Study of Comparative Urbanization' *The Capitalist City: Global Restructuring and Community Politics*. Eds Michael Peter Smith and Joe R. Feagin. Oxford: Basil Blackwell. 37–65.

Tobar, Hector (1989a) 'L.A. Opens Day-Laborer Hiring Site to All Comers' *LAT*. October 27: A28.

Tobar, Hector (1989b) 'Hope of Jobs Surmounts Illegals' Fears' *LAT*. October 28: B1.

Torres-Gil, Fernando (n.d.) 'Ethnic Diversity and Its Implications for Southern California' Los Angeles: United Way of Los Angeles, Community Issues Council.

Turner, Janet L. (1987) 'Foreign Direct Investment in California' Sacramento: State of California Department of Commerce, Office of Economic Research.

Turpin, Dick (1986) 'Selling of Los Angeles: No Shortage of Buyers' *LAT*. September 21: VIII, 1.

Turpin, Dick (1988) 'Foreigners See L.A. Center as "Mark of Leader"' *LAT*. March 13: VIII, 1.

Unger, Henry (1988) 'Asian Banks in U.S. Bow to Tradition' *LAHE*. May 22: D5.

United Way of Los Angeles (1986) 'Ethnic Diversity in United Way: Serving Our Global City' Los Angeles: Planning and Resource Development Division.

United Way of Los Angeles (1987) 'State of the County' Los Angeles: Planning and Resource Development Division.

United Way of Los Angeles, Asian Pacific Research and Development Council (1987) Pacific Rim Profiles. Los Angeles: United Way.

University of Southern California/Pacific Asian Consortium on Employment (1980) 'New Asia Corridor Project' University of Southern California, School of Urban and Regional Planning.

*Update* (1987) 1, 2, Building Service Division, Service Employees International Union.

US Immigration and Naturalization Service (1990) *Statistical Yearbook of the Immigration and Naturalization Service, 1989*. Washington: US Government Printing Office.

Valle, Victor and Rodolfo D. Torres (1994) 'Latinos in a "Post-industrial" Disorder: Politics in a Changing City' *Socialist Review*. **23**, 4: 1–28.

Ventura, Michael (1997) 'The Urban Landscape . . . and in Its People' *LAT*. October 5.

Vergara, Camilo José (1997) '"They saw a very great future here": L.A. Latino Metropolis' Lecture, Perspectives on Los Angeles: Images, Narratives, History, The Getty Research Center, Santa Monica, CA, April 8.

Vidler, Anthony (1997) 'L.A.'s Only Constant Is Change in Its Architecture' *LAT*. October 5.

Viehe, Fred W. (1981) 'Black Gold Suburbs: The Influence of the Extractive Industry on the Suburbanization of Los Angeles, 1890–1930' *Journal of Urban History*. **8**, 1: 3–26.

Vollmer, Ted (1988) 'Bradley Proposes $2 Billion Fund for Homeless Housing' *LAT*. January 8.

Wachs, Martin (1984) 'Autos, Transit, and the Sprawl of Los Angeles: The 1920's' *Journal of the American Planning Association*. **50**, 3: 297–310.

Wagner, Anton (1935) *Los Angeles: Werden, Leben und Gestalt der Zweimillionenstadt in Südkalifornien*. Leipzig: Bibliographisches Institut.

Waldinger, Roger (1996) 'Ethnicity and Opportunity in the Plural City' *Ethnic Los Angeles*. Eds Roger Waldinger and Mehdi Bozorgmehr. New York: Russell Sage Foundation. 445–470.

Waldinger, Roger and Mehdi Bozorgmehr (Eds) (1996a) *Ethnic Los Angeles*. New York: Russell Sage Foundation.

Waldinger, Roger and Mehdi Bozorgmehr (1996b) 'The Making of a Multicultural Metropolis' *Ethnic Los Angeles*. Eds Roger Waldinger and Mehdi Bozorgmehr. New York: Russell Sage Foundation. 3–38.

Waldman, Tom (1988) 'West Hollywood – Creative City; Diverse Constituencies' *California Journal*. **19**, 12: 541f.

Walker, Richard A. (1977) *The Suburban Solution: Urban Geography and Urban Reform in the Capitalist Development of the United States*. Ph.D. Dissertation, Johns Hopkins University, Baltimore.

Walker, Richard A. (1981) 'A Theory of Suburbanization: Capitalism and the Construction of Urban Space in the United States' *Urbanization and Urban Planning in Capitalist Society*. Eds Michael J. Dear and Allen J. Scott. London and New York: Methuen. 383–429.

Walker, Martin (1992) *The Guardian* May 30/31, p. 9.

Walsh, Joan (1985) 'Union Threatens GM Boycott' *These Times*. November 27–December 10.

Warner, Sam Bass (1972) *The Urban Wilderness: A History of the American City*. New York: Harper and Row.

Watanabe, Teresa (1989) 'Piercing Japan "Myths"' *LAT*. November 27: D1.

Watson Land Company (n.d.) 'Watson Land Company' Carson, California.

Watts, Jerry G. (1993) 'Reflections on the Rodney King Verdict and the Paradoxes of the Black Response' *Reading Rodney King – Reading Urban Uprising*. Ed. Robert Gooding-Williams. New York and London: Routledge. 236–248.

Weinstein, Henry (1987) 'Minimum Wage in State Goes to $4.25' *LAT*. December 12: I, 1.

Weinstein, Henry (1988) 'Janitors Stage Vigil as Part of National Protest' *LAT*. March 31: II, 1.

Weinstein, Richard S. (1996) 'The First American City' *The City: Los Angeles and Urban Theory at the End of the Twentieth Century*. Eds Allen J. Scott and Edward W. Soja. Berkeley, Los Angeles and London: University of California Press. 22–46.

Wells Fargo Bank (1986) 'California: A Business and Economic Appraisal' San Francisco: Wells Fargo Bank Economics Division.

West Hollywood Marketing Corporation (1988) '"The Creative City": Promoting West Hollywood' (Internal Report).

Wiley, Peter and Robert Gottlieb (1982) *Empires in the Sun: The Rise of the New American West*. New York: Putnam.

Wilkinson, Tracy (1989a) 'Santa Monica: A House Divided by Rent Control' *LAT*. April 29: I, 1.

288

Wilkinson, Tracy (1989b) 'Public Discontent Spurs New Wave of Development Bans' *LAT*. May 21: W1.

Wilkinson, Tracy (1989c) 'Santa Monica Finds Transients Are Here to Stay' *LAT*. June 11: W1.

Wilkinson, Tracy (1989d) 'Bridging the Chasm' *LAT*. June 15: W1.

Wilkinson, Tracy (1989e) 'Councilman's Idea to House the Homeless' *LAT*. June 25: W1.

Wilkinson, Tracy (1991) 'L.A.'s Turn as Urban Laboratory' *LAT*. December 11.

Will, George (1987) '"Slow Growth" Is the Liberalism of the Privileged' *LAT*. August 30.

Williams, Rhonda M. (1993) 'Accumulation as Evisceration: Urban Rebellion and the New Growth Dynamics' *Reading Rodney King – Reading Urban Uprising*. Ed. Robert Gooding-Williams. New York and London: Routledge: 82–96.

Wilson, Kenneth L. and W. Allen Martin (1982) 'Ethnic Enclaves: A Comparison of the Cuban and Black Economies in Miami' *AJS*. **88**, 1: 135–160.

Wolch, Jennifer R. (1989) 'The Shadow State: Transformations in the Voluntary Sector' *The Power of Geography: How Territory Shapes Social Life*. Eds Jennifer Wolch and Michael Dear. Boston: Unwin Hyman. 197–221.

Wolch, Jennifer R. (1996) 'From Global to Local: The Rise of Homelessness in Los Angeles during the 1980s' *The City: Los Angeles and Urban Theory at the End of the Twentieth Century*. Eds Allen J. Scott and Edward W. Soja. Berkeley, Los Angeles and London: University of California Press. 390–425.

Wolch, Jennifer R. and Michael Dear (Eds) (1989) *The Power of Geography: How Territory Shapes Social Life*. Boston: Unwin Hyman.

Wolch, Jennifer R. and Robert K. Geiger (1986) 'Urban Restructuring and the Not-for-Profit Sector' *Economic Geography*. **62**: 3–18.

Wolch, Jennifer and Michael Dear (1993) *Malign Neglect: Homelessness in an American City*. San Francisco: Jossey-Bass.

Wolf, Steven (1989) 'A Bird's-Eye View of City North Plan' *Downtown News*. December 11: 1.

Wolff, Goetz (1991) 'Los Angeles Labor Market Report: Job Growth in Los Angeles County Industries: Service and Goods Production Sectors, 1979–1990' Resources for Employment and Economic Development, Los Angeles.

Woody, Bette (1982) *Managing Crisis Cities: The New Black Leadership and the Politics of Resource Allocation*. Westport, Conn.

Yancey, William L., Eugene P. Ericksen and Richard N. Juliani (1976) 'Emergent Ethnicity: A Review and Reformulation' *American Sociological Review*. **41**, 3 (June): 391–403.

Yaroslavsky, Zev (1990) 'Reforms Failed the Test of Faults and Consequences' *LAT*. February 4: M5.

Yoshihara, Nancy (1989), 'California Style Strikes Gold in Japan' *LAT*. September 24: IV, 1.

Zasada, Marc Porter (1987) 'An Endpoint to Renaissance?' *Downtown News*. October 19: 1.

Zasada, Marc Porter (1988) 'The "L.A. Problem" Defined for Us All' *Downtown News*. April 18: 1.

Zasada, Marc Porter (1989a) 'First Street Plaza Will Fit in with the Civic Center' *Downtown News*. May 15: 8.

Zasada, Marc Porter (1989b) 'Visionary Search for 100,000 New Residents in Central City' *Downtown News*. October 9: 1.

Zwahlen, Cynthia (1988) 'Gourmet Grocers and Markets Feast on Profits from the Rich and Hungry' *LABJ*. March 28.

# INDEX

*Index compiled by Geoffrey C. Jones*